Cinema's Sinister
Psychiatrists

Cinema's Sinister Psychiatrists

From Caligari to Hannibal

SHARON PACKER, M.D.

McFarland & Company, Inc., Publishers
Jefferson, North Carolina, and London

LIBRARY OF CONGRESS CATALOGUING-IN-PUBLICATION DATA

Packer, Sharon.
Cinema's sinister psychiatrists : from Caligari to Hannibal /
Sharon Packer.
p.   cm.
Includes filmography.
Includes bibliographical references and index.

ISBN 978-0-7864-6390-9
softcover : acid free paper ∞

1. Mental health personnel in motion pictures.   2. Psychiatry in
motion pictures.   3. Psychoanalysis in motion pictures.   I. Title.
PN1995.9M462P33 2012   791.43'6165 — dc23   2012030298

BRITISH LIBRARY CATALOGUING DATA ARE AVAILABLE

On the cover: Anthony Hopkins as Dr. Hannibal Lecter
in *The Silence of the Lambs* (1991) (Orion/Photofest);
background images © 2012 Shutterstock

Manufactured in the United States of America

McFarland & Company, Inc., Publishers
Box 611, Jefferson, North Carolina 28640
www.mcfarlandpub.com

In memory of my father,
Max Packer

Acknowledgments

My first thanks go to my husband, George Chaim Higham, who deserves 100 pages of acknowledgments rather than just one. My next acknowledgments go to my long-deceased father, Max Packer, who insisted that I see *Cabinet of Caligari* when it was first released in 1962 because it was based on the "most important movie ever made."

I want to extend special thanks to Dr. Goldfinger and Jill Gruber, of the American Psychiatric Association's Institute of Psychiatric Services, for taking a chance on what must have sounded like an eccentric proposal, and for realizing that the original workshop was distinct from anti-psychiatry approaches that invalidate the concept of mental disease, or that dismiss the utility of all treatment for psychological distress, simply because some treatments of the past were insufficient or inappropriate.

I wish I could name the many attendees at these APA/IPS workshops who added their insights and made the material richer, but, unfortunately, I can't. I can extend thanks to psychiatrist Maj. Steven Pflantz and his thought-provoking APA seminars on film.

Special thanks to Phil Miller, Ph.D., M.L.S., who headed Hebrew Union College's library for decades and hosted the Yiddish film festival that introduced me to *Where Is My Child?* Thanks to Sharon Pucker Rivo of the National Center for Jewish Film at Brandeis University for her help in locating this hard-to-find film. My thanks to Kim's Video, from the old days on St. Marks, to Film Forum and Elliot Kanbar of the Quad Cinema. Extra thanks to the Anthology Film Archives programming and library, and for hosting an influential seminar on Fritz Lang with Professor Tom Gunning and other scholars. I thank Holli Schwartz for alerting me to *Mr. Frost*, and Tom Graney of *Hollywood Outsider*, who has more fast film facts on hand than imdb.com. Special thanks to Christine Quigley, a McFarland author and blogger at *Quigley's Cabinet*, for blogging about "*Caligari's Cabinet*" and my film book.

Fuat Ulus, M.D.'s enthusiasm about film and psychiatry has been an inspiration, as has an online forum, "The Academy of Film and Psychiatry," hosted by Fred Miller, M.D., Ph.D, as well as the New York Academy of Medicine's staff, librarians, and members of the Committee on Psychiatry, who focus on the depiction of mental patients in movies (a very different matter from the subject of sinister psychiatrists in cinema but an equally interesting issue). Thanks to Dr. Arnold Winston and Dr. Michael Serby of Beth Israel Hospital and Albert Einstein College of Medicine, and to Dean Spiegel and Albert Einstein's library staff for expressing their support for my book projects.

Heated discussions about sinister cinema psychiatrists that pre-dated *Caligari* took place at Cornell's History of Psychiatry seminars, headed by Dr. George Makari, which made me realize what a tinderbox this topic can be. Former students from the New School's media studies department added their ideas to the mix. Plus, the listening ears of the psychiatry staff at the Brooklyn VA Hospital, and especially Dr. Wayne Ayers and Dr. Bennett Cohen, who scheduled Grand Rounds on "Mad Bad Military Mind MDs," helped shape the chapter that resulted.

In conclusion, I express special appreciation to Jim Carlson for rescuing not one but two laptops from extinction, and for "saving the lives" of the chapters ahead.

Table of Contents

Preface

They say that a picture is worth a thousand words. So a few dozen photos should say many, many thousand times as much. There's a good chance you've already thumbed through this book and seen the first few photos. If so, you may already have some ideas about how it came to be.

Perhaps you noticed shots of the top-hatted Dr. Caligari, from silent cinema. His image is iconic. Dr. Caligari looks a little chunky under his cloak and does not appear to be anywhere near as menacing as in the film that bears his name.

There is a good reason that so many photos of Dr. Caligari appear in this book. His name received top billing in workshops on which this book is based. Actually, three workshops that inspired this book, one in Chicago, the next in New York, and the third in Boston. They were conducted at the Institute of Psychiatric Services, one of two annual conferences hosted by the American Psychiatric Association, an organization to which I belong.

Why do I belong to the American Psychiatric Association? Because I am a psychiatrist (psychiatric physician) who spends most of my time treating patients. (Supervising psychiatry residents on behalf of NYC's Beth Israel Medical Center and Albert Einstein College of Medicine consumes far less time than hands-on patient care; writing and researching books about psychiatry and cinema is a treat reserved for off-hours.)

Maybe it seems strange to think that the APA would host workshops on "Sinister Psychiatrists in Cinema" but it didn't seem strange to most (but not all) of the people who crowded into the auditorium, leaving many attendees standing in the back, with some spilling outside into the corridors. No one protested any of these presentations, even though many protestors attend these conferences, including Scientologists and anti-psychiatry activists who rent booths or carry placards that criticize psychiatric theories and treatments.

Quite the contrary. The psychiatrists in attendance seemed to be interested not only in their images on screen, but in ways that imperfect presentations from the past could be used to improve practices in the present and future. Residency training directors and medical school faculty seemed especially intrigued by the idea of using films to teach trainees. That is not surprising, since seminars about psychiatry and film tend to be popular at APA functions.

It goes without saying that film fans have reason to watch movies about sinister psychiatrists, and this book is written with media people in mind as well. Cinema fans or movie people are typically less concerned with the political implications of such films —

1

although film critics have much to say on this subject. Those involved in production are more focused on the artistry or the cinematography, or the costumes, sets or acting, or the dramatic devices that push the plot, or with the ways that music impacts mindsets, and so on. Several of those people had interesting insights to offer, based on their own areas of expertise. Having taught college classes on "Dream and Film" and "Movies and Madness" for the media department, I tailored my presentation (and this book) with that audience as much in mind as the mental health crowd.

However, one well-known, white-haired psychiatrist who attended the last workshop in Boston had his own approach (or at least he was confident enough to express it). After we concluded the workshop, just before the audience left and the porters pushed the crowd from the room, this doctor asked a very salient question, one that I am still contemplating today. It was the kind of single-sentence question that takes years upon years of psychiatric (or perhaps psychoanalytic) practice to perfect. It was not the kind of cut-and-dried question that we tend to ask in clinical practice today in our era of fast–Pharma psychiatry.

He simply asked: "Why did you *not* choose to run a workshop about the idealized cinema psychiatrists of the 'Golden Age'?" In the late 1950s and early '60s there was a brief interlude when "perfect" psychiatrists were shown on screen. That era is discussed in detail in the Gabbards' classic *Psychiatry and the Cinema, 2nd Edition* (1999). That question made me think for a moment, as I recalled how much I adored so many of those films, which screened when I was still a child.

But the fact of the matter is that, as an adult, and as a practicing psychiatrist, I feel cheated by those films. They depicted doctors as miracle workers who cured catatonia as easily as Moses parted the Red Sea. It is now easy to look back and see how much I was influenced by those films, and how much those idealized mind doctors made me believe that I, too, could affect cures, provided that I acquired the proper credentials and all the requisite education.

Today we realize that many of the conditions that were instantly cured in '50s–era films are far more complex, and that some of those conditions do not necessarily exist in ordinary life. Some films that revolve around "repressed memories" or "family romances" look good on screen and make for a good story, but may concern problems that are more biologically-based.

Time has proven that those "Golden Age" films about psychiatrists were closer to fairy tales than to true clinical practice. They were intriguing in their own era, but many lost their staying power because they presented propaganda and fantasy rather than fact — even though many of them were well-made and so will endure on those merits.

Unfortunately, many people have taken those "Golden Era" movies seriously and still expect instant relief from almost anything via "the couch cure" or from "talking things through." Anyone who claims that Big Pharma has launched a wave of unrealistic expectations about mood meds has not seen enough of the old movies to understand the influence media wielded in the late '50s and early '60s. I myself was not aware of the power of those films until I viewed them again while writing two of my previous books on film (*Dreams in Myth, Medicine and Movies* [2002], and *Movies and the Modern Psyche* [2007] and while teaching college media studies courses on "Madness in Movies" and "Dream in Film" throughout the 1990s.

It was another book entirely that pushed me to study cinema about sinister psychiatrists.

That book was Kracauer's *From Caligari to Hitler* first written in 1947 and reprinted many times over. The title was too intriguing to pass up when I first spotted the book at Kim's Video store on St. Mark's Place in the East Village of New York City. Kim's left St. Mark's Place some years ago and donated its amazing collection of classic videos to a library in Europe. But Kim's never disappears from memories of film fans who trekked up the stairs of the unassuming store to find buried film treasures and books about them. In much the same way, Kracauer's book never completely disappears from the consciousness of anyone who reads it.

From Caligari to Hitler has been kicked around a lot over the years. Parts of the book have been redacted, and enthusiasts have edited the book over time, adding their own insights. But the ideas it generated in its readers have remained grown, and those who appreciate Kracauer's ideas can overlook some flaws found in his scholarship. Besides, Kracauer anchors the history of sinister psychiatrists in cinema in Europe, where film began, and does not restrict himself to American-made movies, as some of our more esteemed sources do.

Kracauer's *From Caligari to Hitler* is the kind of book that can lead its readers in many directions. For Kracauer, the primary point of his book was his endpoint — namely, Hitler. He aimed to show how Weimar films predicted the rise of the most evil ruler and the most evil reich the world has yet witnessed. (Even though there are some close competitors to Hitler around the world, those despots lack the technological know-how of 20th century Nazi-era Germany.)

For me the endpoint has changed, even if some of the trajectory remains the same. Although I remained intrigued by his theories about the sinister and charlatan asylum director named Dr. Caligari, I became more interested in the theme of sinister psychiatrists in cinema in general, for their own sake and for what those films reveal about society's anxieties, and about our changing attitudes toward psychiatry.

In homage to Kracauer's contribution, I named my workshops "From Caligari to Hannibal the Cannibal" and retained that title for the introduction of this book.

Introduction:
From Caligari to Hannibal the Cannibal

Once upon a time, cinema psychiatrists enjoyed a "Golden Age." During that "Golden Age" screen psychiatrists were always good. They were brilliant and benevolent, omniscient and omnipotent, caring and compassionate. Some resembled the oracles of old. They could peer into the past and foretell the future. They could change fate through their psychoanalytic skills, which were far more effective on screen than scientific experiments showed them to be. Sometimes they used hypnotic trance. Rarely, they resorted to shock therapy to work their wonders.

That Golden Age did not last long. In fact, it lasted for only a few fleeting years. The Golden Age arrived in 1957, the year after the centennial of Freud's birth. By then, America was infatuated with all things Freudian (although Freud's native Austria did not show such admiration). By 1963 the Golden Age was starting to show signs of tarnish. It soon faded to grey and disappeared, like a dissolving screen shot.

Some people revere that long-gone time. They lament its passing and long for the return of those all-good and all-knowing screen shrinks, the ones who cured distress and disease with ease. It didn't matter that some of the mental diseases they treated did not exist off screen. It was irrelevant that cinema psychopathology sometimes inspired real-life epidemics of otherwise rare psychiatric ills (such as multiple personality disorder, which premiered in *The Three Faces of Eve* [1957], and gained more fame after the spurious made-for-TV movies *Sybil* [1976]).[1]

Psychiatric success stories appealed to the public at that time, whether accurate or not. This was the "triumphalist" age, when history told unsullied success stories that were very different from the mud-raking exposés favored by today's journalists, some retired medical editors and revisionist historians.[2] Not surprisingly, those stories on screen also appealed to psychiatrists, who enjoy good press and positive feedback as much as anyone else. The Fifties, and even the early Sixties, were very good years for positive portrayals of doctors of the body and of the mind. Oddly enough, scattered literary critiques of psychiatric treatment began to pop up at that time,[3] but readers are not the same lot as viewers, so cinematic portrayals remained unsullied—for a while.

A broader look at medical history sheds light on why cinematic spectators of the later fifties applauded the positive and believed the best about doctors and medical researchers. In 1954, Dr. Jonas Salk discovered the polio vaccine. Salk offered hope for this dreaded childhood disease that killed or crippled children. Polio left youngsters languishing in iron lungs for years on end. Other youthful polio victims limped for the rest of their lives — should they even attain adulthood. Dr. Salk was a secular saint. A few years later, Dr. Sabin improved the vaccine, and further reaffirmed belief in medical miracles. Comic books were written about these physician-researchers who saved entire societies in one fell swoop, just like the comics' superheroes.[4]

Why shouldn't psychiatry bask in the glow of those spectacular successes, especially now that Thorazine (phenothiazine), the first effective anti-schizophrenia medication, had arrived? Thorazine was already available in France and was released in the U.S. in 1954. It held the promise of freeing psychotics from their delusions and maybe even unlocking the doors of asylums that held them captive. This was prime time to return to the past and revel in the glories of "modern" 20th century psychiatry — whether or not those "glories" were really so glorious.

Like fairy tales, the stories of Golden Age screen psychiatrists were more romanticized than realistic. Two of the most beloved Golden Age films — *Fear Strikes Out* (1957) and *The Three Faces of Eve* (1957) — were based on the lives of real people who endured symptoms similar to those on screen but who never achieved the Lourdes-like cures portrayed in the movies. The films highlighted their temporary successes rather than their repeated relapses or their downward spirals over time. But a good story is still a good story, and the movies are made to entertain, not to educate. In commercial film, dramatic appeal trumps fact.

The same people who sentimentalize the Golden Age of screen psychiatrists typically curse the films that came later, the ones that show less than stellar portraits of mind doctors. But idealized doctors proved to be the exception rather than the rule. So if we want to understand society's reaction to psychiatry, we need to examine the most common media representations (or misrepresentations) rather than the comparatively rare idyllic portrayals. Those perfect practitioners of the Golden Age enjoyed six years in the limelight — but our sinister psychiatrists and their progenitors prevailed for over 106 years. That's quite a difference.

Why did sinister psychiatrists persist far longer than perfect psychiatrists (and psychoanalysts), and why did they multiply and mutate into so many different forms? They even spawned their own subgenre of cinema. We must ask why sinister psychiatrists, took center stage, not just from the mid-sixties onward, but since the start of cinema, which coincided with the birth of psychoanalysis near the end of the 19th century.

Hypnotists, some of them doctors but most of them not, appeared in silent shorts almost immediately, even before the 20th century. Evil experimenters quickly followed, playing upon the legacy left by famous 19th century literary figures, such as Dr. Moreau, Dr. Frankenstein, and Dr. Jekyll.

Answering these questions is much more intriguing than mourning the passing of perfect screen shrinks, and probably more important, too, given the numerical differences in their representation. The so-called "Golden Age" boasts only twenty-five films, according to Gabbard and Gabbard's authoritative *Psychiatry and the Cinema, 2nd Edition* (1999). It is nearly impossible to count the number of sinister cinema psychiatrists that have appeared on film, video, and even in video games (such as *Arkham Asylum*, based on the *Batman* comics). The majority of the most demeaning representations go straight to video and are never included in formal film counts.

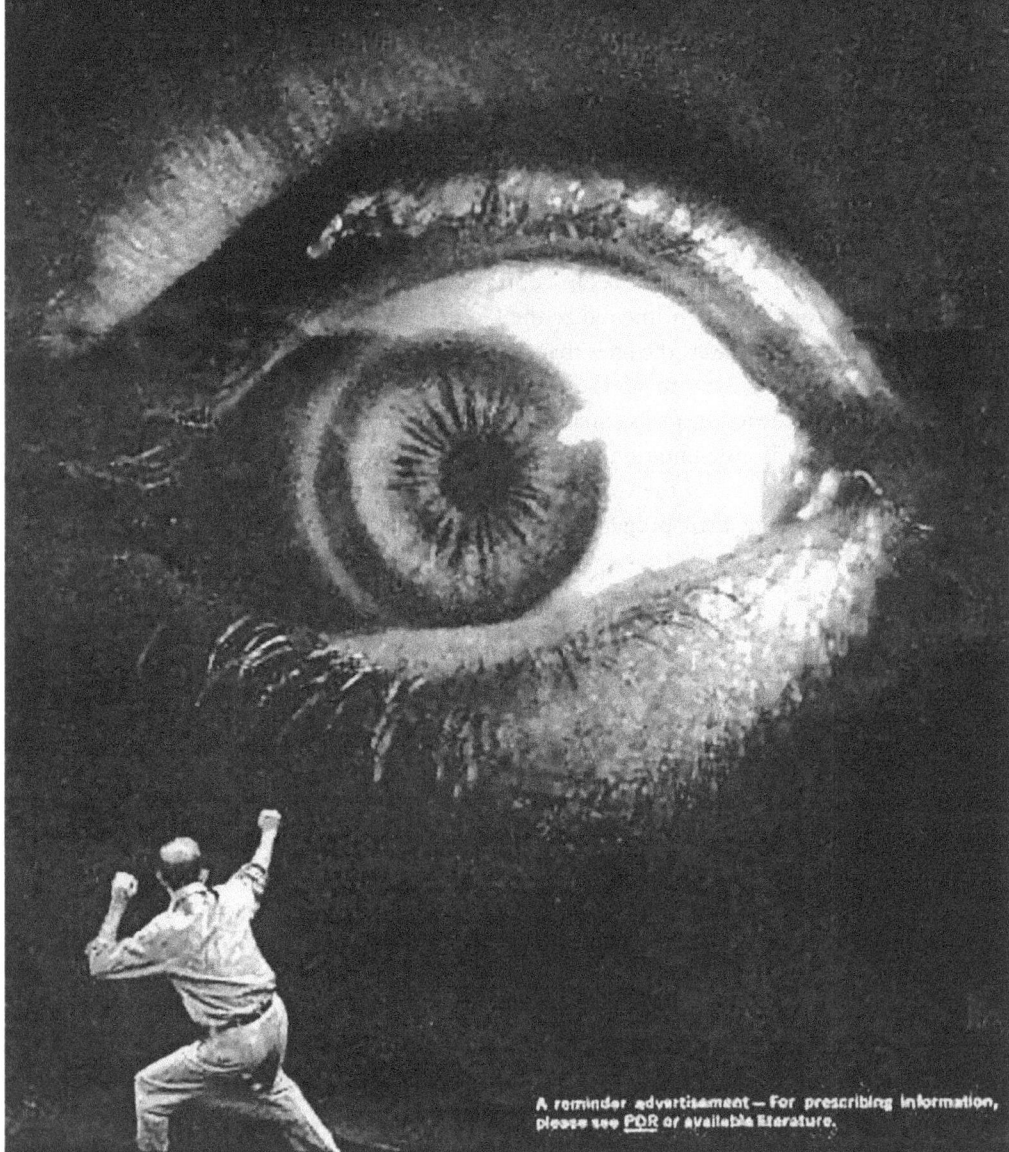

There seems to be something Darwinian about the survival of sinister celluloid psychiatrists. They must serve a greater purpose than is apparent on the surface, for how else would they have survived at a time when half the American public seeks some form of psychotherapy at some point in their lives, and thereby seems to endorse the value of psychiatric treatment?

For one thing, these diabolical doctors make for more interesting dramatic devices than the idealized mind doctor. There are many more varieties of mad and bad movie MDs, but "good screen psychiatrists" only need to be caring and competent (even though they have many treatment techniques to choose from). (This reflects Tolstoy's observation that "all happy families are alike, but each unhappy family is different in its own way.")

Most likely, these mean-minded doctors exploit innate fears about mind control that continue to plague the public, even though laws were enacted to regulate unilateral medical decision-making, or stop the use of unapproved or unsafe medications and limit involuntary incarceration. Of course, we know that these protective measures are not failsafe, and people and prescription medications can fall through the cracks, regardless of safeguards.

Perhaps these bad movie MDs even tell some truths about imperfections in the profession. Some of the most enduring cinema psychiatrists function as metaphors for social, political or even theological issues that are more meaningful than medicine alone.

There is a reason that producers continue to create such films. If there were no demand, there would be no market. There is a reason — or many reasons — that audiences are willing to pay more and more money to view these commercial releases when they have so many other themes to choose from. Even if these films are presented as pure fiction (and most are, with some important exceptions), they must be capable of making us "suspend disbelief" for an hour or two, and convince us that bad or mad movie MDs really exist somewhere, somehow.

We know for a fact that some sinister celluloid shrinks and some screen asylums are not pure imagination. Some films called attention to shortcomings in the system, prompting improvements in health care and closer regulation of hospital admission standards. Others instigated unwarranted fear, and even prompted anti–ECT legislation, even though ECT (electroconvulsive therapy) can be lifesaving under certain circumstances and can be safer than most medications for persons with certain medical conditions.

There are many varieties of sinister cinema psychiatrists. Besides the psychiatrists themselves, we must concern ourselves with the cultural and political climates — as well as the contemporary clinical trends — that exist backstage, pulling the strings, so to speak. Those trends are just as important as the screen shrinks and asylums that take center stage.

There has been no shortage of sinister psychiatrists on the silver screen. Mad or bad psychiatrists (and neuroscientists) have been a staple of cinema since its inception. Evil hypnotists, seductive psychoanalysts, and MD murder machines abound. Movie mind doctors have been responsible for deceptive drugging, simulated psychosis, involuntary incarceration, even insulin coma. Then there are the more standard melodramatic love-murder triangles and criminal collaborations.

Opposite: **1962 advertisement for the anti-psychotic medication Thorazine (phenothiazine), from SKF Labs. Thorazine revolutionized treatment of schizophrenia when it arrived in the U.S. in 1954.**

Some movie MDs use futuristic devices to effect their evil, devices that actually appeared in medical settings some half-century later. *Batman* films and serials (and comics) include a surprising number of sinister psychiatrists among their villains, and have an amazing ability to anticipate advances in "invasive techniques" in neuropsychiatry.

"Asylum thrillers" and "shock schlock" are so plentiful that each spawned their own film genres. I propose that prison psychiatrist films be made a subgenre of the already popular prison genre — especially given the popularity of Hannibal the Cannibal films in the last few decades.

Not all of these movies are exploitative. Some of the finest films ever made feature diabolical mind doctors. Moreover, this theme is not a Hollywood invention. Some of the best sinister screen psychiatrists pre-date Hollywood's ascendance to prominence in the worldwide film scene. The most memorable screen shrinks got their start on the European silent screen. *The Cabinet of Dr. Caligari*, from 1919, is a prime example. The very best of these mad medico movies embed important messages — as well as images — and comment on contemporary clinical controversies. Others use mind MDs as metaphors for wide-reaching social and political concerns. Specifically, the despotic Dr. Caligari, who commanded his

Dr. Caligari (Werner Krauss), in top hat, stands next to his somnambulist, Cesare (Conrad Veidt), whom he turns into a murderer via hypnosis in *The Cabinet of Dr. Caligari* (1919).

surrogate, Cesare, to kill, was compared to Hitler by a very influential author. Dr. Caligari's name appears in the title of Kracauer's much-reprinted (and much-refuted) book *From Caligari to Hitler* (1947).

Dr. Caligari was compared to many other important characters as well — namely, Freud, Charcot, Janet, and the fictional hypnotist Svengali, who lived on in film and theater even if he never lived in real life. More recently, the character of Dr. Caligari was linked to the despised European military psychiatrists who sent shell shocked soldiers back to the front during World War I.[5]

Fritz Lang's *Doctor Mabuse* film followed on the heels of *Dr. Caligari* in 1922. Dr. Mabuse was always more popular in Europe than in America (for reasons that will be discussed later). *Mabuse* was reworked many times over before meeting his demise in Fritz Lang's final 1960 version. (A remake of *Testament of Dr. Mabuse* appeared in 1962.)

Even after Lang died, Dr. Mabuse reappeared in remakes and spin-offs. He continues to inspire various German musicians and songwriters. Mabuse even earned a mention by the esteemed American writer David Foster Wallace. Sadly, Wallace's literary career was interrupted by psychiatric hospitalizations and shock therapy, before ending entirely through suicide.

Hannibal the Cannibal (Dr. Lecter) currently holds the record for repeat American films about sinister psychiatrists. To date, the character has appeared in only half as many movies as Dr. Mabuse, but his end is nowhere in sight. Hannibal the Cannibal — aka Dr. Hannibal Lecter — is currently Hollywood's best recognized movie villain. He even surpassed Freddy, the child-molesting janitor from *Nightmare on Elm Street* (1984), which also spawned many sequels.

One of the tasks of this book is to explore the reasons this screen psychiatrist should enjoy this "honor" (or suffer such ignominy). Clearly, some of that fame derives from sheer cinematic skill and the acting artistry of Anthony Hopkins, but some of Dr. Lecter's popularity may involve his ability to dispel (yes, *dispel*) fear among potential consumers of psychiatric care. For just about any practicing psychiatrist — of any persuasion — seems to be as mild-mannered as Clark Kent when compared to Hannibal the Cannibal.

Hannibal Lecter's capers are so outrageous that they have a curious effect: they make us disbelieve that mind doctors could commit such diabolical deeds. (However, Hannibal does cast harsh shadows on the field of forensic psychiatry, which took some beatings after the infamous "Hostess Twinkie" insanity defense used in the 1979 Harvey Milk trial.)

Many critics claim that films about sinister psychiatrists discourage people who need treatment from seeking it, or that they leave people who do get psychiatric care feeling stigmatized or ostracized. I beg to differ. However, I must admit that I do not have any better statistics to back up my contentions than the detractors do. But I can point to the fact that "evil scientists" have populated literature, theater, film, and occasionally even opera at least since the 19th century. Yet virtually no one refuses to try the latest scientific inventions produced by these potentially "evil scientists."

Those fictional stories about evil scientists allow for the open expression of fears about unforeseeable and upsetting changes that came in the wake of scientific inventions. Similarly, films about sinister psychiatrists also act as conduits for anxiety (and much more). Such films provide potential patients with opportunities for dress rehearsals of their fears about relinquishing control to a mind doctor who might "read their minds" or manipulate their psyches. Thus, the "stage fright" of the first visit is sometimes less overwhelming.

I make this claim based on my clinical experience as a psychiatrist rather than on any difficult-to-collect numerical data. Quite commonly, I hear a first-time patient say, "This office isn't like anything I expected." When I ask what they expected, they typically tell me about a movie, one that shows small, shabby rooms with cracked grey walls and maybe even an iron gate. We talk about the films that prompted such ideas, and they tell me how they prepared themselves for the worst before they mustered their courage to show up for their appointment.

Consider this: almost 50 percent of Americans are diagnosed with a mental illness[6] at some point in their lives. About 25 percent of the population currently takes prescription psychotropic medications. More than one out of ten Americans over the age of ten is currently on an antidepressant (as of an APA bulletin based on a CDC report from October 2011). Antidepressants are the most commonly prescribed medications in America (according to CDC statistics from 2007).[7] Given these numbers, we can see why such a large proportion of the public has concerns about psychiatrists.

Importantly, many concerns revolve around treatments or settings used in the past that are rarely, if ever, employed in the present day. But the general public is often not aware that insane asylums or men in white coats are relics of long-gone eras, and that even locked wards are used only in extreme circumstances. Most people don't realize how hard it is to gain admission to a psychiatric ward in a general hospital or in a specialty hospital now that managed care is in place and strict criteria must be met before accepting prospective patients.

Because of the process of "cultural sedimentation"—and the fact that it generally takes twenty years for information known to specialists to seep into public awareness and become common knowledge—there is a long lag in the dissemination of *accurate* information about psychiatrists and psychiatric institutions. That holds true even in our era of instant Internet information. Or perhaps I should say this is *especially* true in our era of Internet information, since so much online medical information contains misinformation that must be corrected.

This book explains why this seemingly unsavory topic of sinister psychiatrists appeals to so many members of the public. It explores why such themes

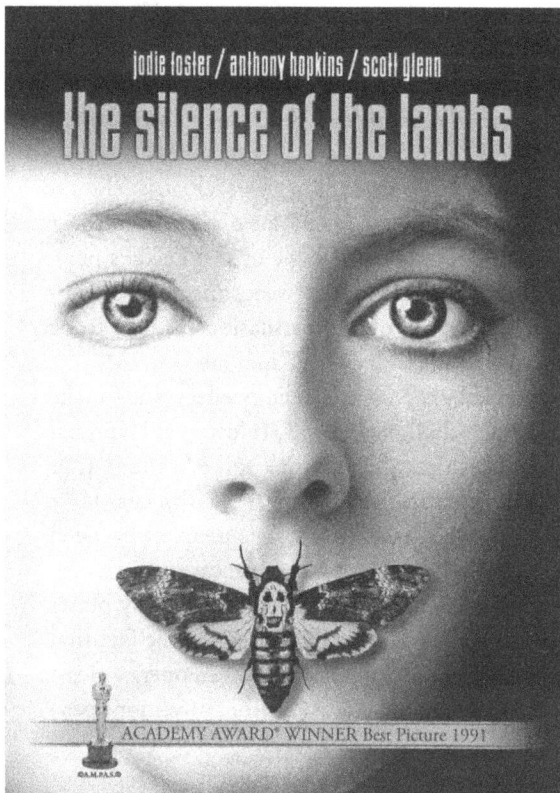

Poster for Jonathan Demme's *The Silence of the Lambs* (1991), starring Jodie Foster as the FBI's Special Agent Starling, Anthony Hopkins as Dr. Hannibal Lecter and Scott Glenn as Agent Crawford.

are especially compelling in certain political and social climates, and how these general themes change to meet changing needs.

Admittedly, such films often anger the psychiatric "establishment" and the watchdogs of the profession's reputation. They are particularly off-putting to psychiatrists-in-training, who typically prefer to see idealized projections of their future selves rather than magnifications of their flaws. Yet these films also assuage some psychiatrists (who may be dedicated film fans themselves), for films about sinister psychiatrists can reassure practitioners that they are nowhere near as bad as the diabolical doctors seen on screen.

Most importantly, the chapters that follow identify trends in the depiction of sinister psychiatrists. They look at type and place of treatment, and the type of treater (with respect to gender, race, nationality, ethnicity, and education). They compare men to women, doctors to nurses, talk therapists to biological psychiatrists, office-based care to sanitariums, asylums, prisons and poorhouses. They compare the past to the present, and explain why so many present-day films about sinister psychiatrists and asylums are set in the past when institutionalization and involuntary admission was far more prevalent than it is today. Alternatively, films are sometimes set in abandoned asylums (haunted or not), which remind us that most asylums were, in fact, abandoned when treatment techniques (as well as financial incentives) changed.

We will see how shortened hospital stays (courtesy of managed care restrictions and, to a lesser extent, public health law protections) have led to a surge of period films set during eras when involuntary incarceration and indefinite hospital stays were closer to reality than they are now. *Shutter Island* (2010) is one such film. The '50s–style fedoras of the lead characters shout out "period piece" even to those of us who don't know that most "funny farms" (like the one seen in the first scene on *Shutter Island*) belong to the distant past.[8]

Two years earlier there was *Changeling* (2008), which starts in 1929 and continues through the early thirties. *Changeling* stars Angelina Jolie sporting silver-fox flapper furs and a classic 1920s cloche. Her wardrobe reminds us that this film is set in another era, after the suffragettes gave way to the flappers that made the Roaring Twenties roar. Both *Shutter Island* and *Changeling* concern themselves with involuntary incarceration of people who do not seem to need such intense treatment. Each of these examples ends in very different ways, and one of them, *Changeling*, is almost a docudrama because it has such a strong moral to tell and such a clear connection to historical facts.

Today, professionals worry more about the revolving door of mental hospitals than about people "locked away" behind gated doors. We are concerned about patients released from psychiatric facilities before their symptoms cease. In recent years we have witnessed senseless murders committed by persons with long histories of schizophrenic symptoms. News reports tell of parents who pleaded with emergency room staff or begged administrators to admit their adult children to mental wards, only to see them turned away or discharged too soon. And then such people go on to commit unspeakable acts, as happened in the case of a chronically disturbed young man named Andrew Goldstein.[9]

Goldstein pushed a young blonde woman from a New York City subway platform. This event horrified New Yorkers, who were shocked and saddened that this young Midwestern tourist lost her life. Goldstein's complicated clinical and legal situation made headlines nationwide and was detailed in literally dozens of *New York Times* articles over the course of years. His behavior inspired Kendra's Law, which opened the door to "outpatient commitment" to psychiatric treatment in a clinic rather than in a locked hospital.[10,11]

In June 2011, newspapers told the shocking story of an idealistic young woman who worked alone as a counselor in an unsupervised and unlocked "adult home."[12] She died at the hands of a psychotic resident who refused to take his antipsychotic medications. He was clearly ill and hearing voices, but was "not ill enough" to qualify for commitment in one of the few remaining state hospitals that offer long-term care for chronically-ill persons.

Several weeks later, the press told an equally sad story of an unsung young male shelter worker who died under similar circumstances. But Jose Rouldon's death did not receive as much media attention at the time as that of Stephanie Moulton in June of that same year.[13]

These dangerous people described on the nightly news make up only a tiny minority of those who suffer from serious mental illness. But these tragic events make front page news when they do occur. They remain etched in our memories, largely because of the extreme harm that results, and also because of the extreme remorse that follows in the wake of seemingly preventable tragedies. Clearly, there are two sides to the story, and stories like these make it seem that contemporary psychiatrists, psychiatric hospitals or public health systems are not doing enough to restrain dangerous patients, as opposed to doing too much, as is typically the case in "sinister psychiatrist cinema."

In this review of sinister cinema psychiatrists, we will see how cinematic portrayals of forensic psychiatrists and prison-based treatments have increased in recent decades. At the same time that such films proliferated came public outcry and news exposés about the shortage of prison psychiatrists for those mentally ill inmates who genuinely need and want treatment. We also hear about the penal system's shortcomings when it comes to separating people with bone fide psychiatric or substance abuse problems from unrepentant sociopaths who would not benefit from psychiatric treatments.

Prison films are their own genre; asylum thrillers also spawned their own genre. Each has its devotees. Asylum films pre-dated prison movies and police procedurals, although some film historians erroneously conclude that asylum films splintered off of prison films and so should be considered to be a subgenre of prison movies. (Asylum films are also distantly related to hotel films.) Rather than arguing about whether prisons or asylums deserve top billing, it is more productive to identify a newer and separate subgenre of prison psychiatry cinema. This subgenre includes the remarkably popular Hannibal serials, but it hardly stops or starts with Hannibal. Movies featuring Arkham Asylum for the Criminally Insane, inspired by the *Batman* comics, are also excellent examples of prison psychiatry films. Such entries reflect recent concerns, even though Arkham Asylum began much earlier.

The chapters that follow will emphasize the cultural issues that color portrayals of "clinical" conditions and dictate our reactions to different treatments and treaters. I will discuss shifts in clinical psychiatric care, and show how the "miracle cures" of one decade can turn into the next generation's demon when initial optimism and idealization is tempered by new discoveries and reports of side effects. I will reveal how clinical psychiatric themes can serve as smokescreens for political polemics. And we will encounter mind doctors used as metaphors for broader political or philosophical positions.

Rather than condemning filmmakers for producing feature films about sinister psychiatrists, I argue that cinema's most memorable characters recollect the prominence and prestige that American psychiatry enjoyed for a good part of the 20th century and through the early 21st century. As they say, "No one ever kicks a dead dog." If psychiatric assessments and treatments were not deemed to be powerful, then there would be no need to condemn them, either on screen or in court.

But times have changed. Professional authority has been challenged by "consumers" who consult Internet-based information sites and web-based chat rooms, or hear direct-to-consumer pharmaceutical advertising. Health insurance regulations, easier access to non-medical mental health training, and the ever-present voice of insurance companies, HMOs and managed care also challenge the traditional medical hierarchy. We can expect even more challenges. For instance, pharmacists are attempting to abandon their time-honored "behind-the-counter" approach and are now counseling patients about medications. According to the *New York Times*, this pilot project is intended to increase pharmacies' income and presumably offer an advantage over cheaper mail-away pharmacies preferred by pinching pharmacy benefits managers.[14]

Many would argue that chinks in the medical armor appeared a few decades earlier when malpractice claims spiked. Attorneys with law degrees began countering doctors with years of medical training, and legislators usurped regulatory responsibilities that were once left to medical societies and closed-door hospital committees. While such disputes are bad for the accused MD, they are very good for film. Movies that add this medico-legal angle promise both courtroom and medical drama, along with personal tales of tragedy or triumph, driving the plot and promising a gripping, multi-faceted movie.

In this book I sometimes take an oppositional stance. Specifically, I review films that refute the often-cited claim that talk therapists are portrayed in a more favorable light than biological psychiatrists or "shock docs" who administer ECT (electroshock or electroconvulsive therapy). I also explore why (mostly female) psych nurses have been depicted as more diabolical than female physicians, who were rare in America until twenty years ago.

This book will note shifts in the education and gender of non-medically-trained psychotherapists and mental health counselors, whose numbers have multiplied over the last two decades, and explore how those shifts manifested themselves in film. We will see why medically-trained psychiatrists and psychiatric nurses remain center-stage in reel life (even if that is not necessarily so in real life). But we will also see examples of evil orderlies (*The Jacket*, 2005; *Sucker Punch*, 2011) or heartless adult home directors (*Spider*, 2002), who remind audiences that "there is no way out" for the chronically mentally ill.

I will show how some of the finest films include both "good" and "bad" doctors, more often as a dramatic driving device than as clinical commentary. Hitchcock's *Spellbound* (1945) and Frankenheimer's original *Manchurian Candidate* (1962) fall into this category. Some films include two sinister psychiatrists, one bad and one worse. The Hannibal films used this technique to great effect, and a Hannibal wannabe, *Gothika* (2003), takes a similar track.

Chapters include a discussion of "Mad Military Mind Docs," starting with *Cabinet of Dr. Caligari* (1919) and continuing on to the Scorsese film about *Shutter Island* (2010). The book will examine the political as well as clinical implications of *Manchurian Candidate* (both versions), *The Jacket* (2005), various Vietnam-related films, and movies about Nazi psychiatrists. We will see how these films use psychiatrists as dramatic driving devices and metaphors for power, murder, and genocide. I also consider how such films comment on contemporary realities at the same time that they mirror past horrors from the Nazi era and the Great War (World War I).

For instance, a military psychiatrist and Muslim militant turned into a serial killer at Fort Hood, and an otherwise sedate neuroscientist proved to be an Al Qaeda operative, both in the same year. This chapter also examines two important books that discuss despotic or deranged doctors and their relationships to cinema: Kaes' *Shell Shock Cinema* (2009), which links *Caligari* to World War I, and Kracauer's higher profile classic *From Caligari to Hitler* (1947), which claims that German-made films about sinister psychiatrists foreshadow the Nazi victory in Germany.

The next chapter, on Hypnosis, returns to the earliest days of cinema, when the hypnotic dream screen invited comparisons to stage hypnotists and clinical hypnosis alike. Hypnosis was an important treatment technique in the late 19th century, when both film and psychoanalysis were invented within one year of one another. Artists came to watch Dr. Charcot's "performances" as he studied hysterics and hypnotism in Paris. We can compare clinical hypnosis to the "hypnotic eye" of the "dream screen" (which is an apt expression for "film"). We will see how easily one can regress back in time, and view the "hypnotic eye" as the "evil eye," thereby turning the "hypnotic eye" of psychiatry into a signifier for sinister psychiatrists.

Primitive and silent cinema offer a wide range of evil hypnotists: Svengali, Caligari, and Mabuse, for starters. Hypnosis and "somnambulists" were popular subjects of 19th and early 20th century Symbolist art, which predated the invention of moving pictures and disappeared after World War I. Evil hypnotic themes surged again in the 1950s when mass media advanced, and when televisions made their way into most American homes, with advertisers "hypnotizing" the public into purchasing their products. But this later batch of evil hypnotists were less likely to be doctors and more likely to be showmen or con men. In fact, by the mid-to-late 1950s, idealized psychiatrists often hypnotize their ailing patients with great success (on screen, at least).

From there, I turn to the "dream doctors" who proliferated after Freud published his landmark book *Interpretation of Dreams* in 1900. Dream doctors, both good and bad, found their way onto the silver screen. Some of their techniques were nightmarish, although other dream analysts were idealized on screen. *Film noir* from the 1940s and early '50s made the best use of these dream themes, although even early cinema emphasized the power of dreams without necessarily condemning the budding psychoanalysts who interpreted them.

I compare films about deceptive dream analysis—*Nightmare Alley* (1947), *In Dreams* (1999), *Shutter Island* (2010)—to scenes of "good" dream analysis—*Spellbound* (1945), *The Three Faces of Eve* (1957). I shower praise on Hitchcock's *Spellbound* (1945). This underappreciated film combines both good and bad psychiatrists, to amp up the dramatic impact. (Hitchcock admitted that he was more concerned with producing a good film than with chronicling real life treatment techniques.)

Chapter 4, turns to "Spirit Possession and Supernatural Psychiatrists," a topic that shares some similarities with dream themes, since dreams were historically linked to the occult. This chapter recounts psychiatry's distant connections to "soul doctors," shamans, spiritualists, conjurers and occultism, and shows how those broken links live on in film. I reference the séance scenes in the first *Dr. Mabuse* movie in 1922, and explain why séances appealed to spectators mourning the millions who recently died during World War I or succumbed to the devastating flu epidemics that followed the world war.

Gothika (2003), *House on Haunted Hill* (1999), and *In Dreams* (1999) find their way into this curious chapter. I also review Stefan Andriopoulous' alternative approach to this topic, as described in his book, *Possessed* (2008),[15] and explore why he sees spirit possession as a political and power metaphor for early 20th century society. I counter his arguments by showing how spiritualism connects psychiatry to its skirmishes with exorcists, shamans, folk healers, and sorcerers in the past, and so is directly relevant on a surface level, and need not be seen as a metaphor only.

After that, the book moves to more contemporary concerns, albeit ones that appeared on screen decades ago. "Sex, Seduction, and the Couch Cure" revolves around steamy scenes of sexual exploitation from *film noir* and later 20th century films. I examine the sexual symbolism behind the "couch cure" and explain why seduction scenes by psychoanalysts recur.

Over time, we find that sinister screen psychiatrists employ more imaginative ways to upend vulnerable patients — and to keep increasingly jaded audiences entertained. Transvestism, sex surrogates, murder and mayhem find their way into psychiatrists' offices, as we see with *Dressed to Kill* (1980), *Cat People* (1942), and *I, the Jury* (1982), plus the *Hannibal* series. After Norman Bates' scene in *Psycho* (1960) inured moviegoers to unsettling psychiatric scenes and to slasher themes, anything else seemed tame.

There is so much to say about female film psychiatrists that an entire chapter is devoted to "The Not-So-Gentle Gender." In it I review the polarized depictions of female psychiatrists, who can be romantic objects, seducers, seducees, *femmes fatales*, or just plain suckers in films such as *Spellbound* (1945), *House of Games* (1987), *I, the Jury* (1982), *Sucker Punch* (2011), and some *Batman* films and games.

The next several chapters revolve around specific treatment techniques, and the ways movie makers make them more intriguing and off-putting. Chapters including "Shock Schlock," "Diabolical Drugging," "Unethical Experimentation," and "Lobotomy and the Like" zero in on these controversial approaches. We see how filmmakers often embed facts in fiction, either to make a political point or to help audiences "suspend disbelief," or simply to capitalize on contemporary concerns and engage audiences. A separate chapter, "In Control or in Cahoots," shows how psychiatrists can be depicted as kingpins of grander criminal operations, and how they are also painted as pawns, patsies, and pushovers for people with greater political power or economic clout.

The last chapter, "Madhouse Movies," is an uneasy fit in a book about "sinister psychiatrists in cinema." Even though the madhouse movies (also known as "asylum thrillers") usually — but not always — require the participation of a psychiatrist, the fact of the matter is that it is the institution rather than the professionals that is demonized. Not infrequently, lesser players, such as orderlies or nurses, are the prime movers in these films. They show their darker sides and enforce their evil with or without the consent of the (typically overwhelmed or occasionally overdosed) supervising psychiatrist.

The Jacket (2005) is a prime example of this ilk, as is the more recent and more comic book–like *Sucker Punch* (2011). An entire book about "Madhouse Movies" could be written, and perhaps should be written, especially since "madhouses" have almost faded away, but memories of those institutions live on in the imagination and in movie theaters.

A curious "madhouse movie" is *Shutter Island* (2010). This film is worth reviewing before proceeding further, since it includes many of the themes mentioned above, which will be detailed in the chapters that follow.

If we are looking for a single movie that references several earlier films about sinister psychiatrists and weaves them together seamlessly, we can turn to Martin Scorsese's *Shutter Island* (2010). *Shutter Island* prepares us for films we will discuss in the chapters ahead, even though the movie itself is best described as a palimpsest of films from the past, with layers upon layers superimposed upon one another to create a seamless whole. We will try to lift those layers, which weave a story as compelling as those told by Scheherazade herself.

There is one caveat to consider about *Shutter Island*: this is a film about a "pseudo-sinister psychiatrist" rather than an out-and-out sinister psychiatrist....

Like *The Cabinet of Doctor Caligari*, which was made in 1919 and which debuted in 1920, *Shutter Island* also capitalizes on the blurry line between sanity and insanity, and between dream and delusion. It uses this theme as a framing device. *Shutter Island* presents us with a protagonist who, for all intents and purposes, appears to be a reliable narrator. The protagonist, played by Leonardo DiCaprio, is a U.S. Marshall, after all, on an official mission, and so commands our respect. Yet he turns out to be unreliable because he suffers from delusions, intermittent intoxication, hallucinatory flashbacks, and an over-arching identity crisis that leaves him unsure of exactly who he is or where he is or why.

In *Caligari*, two men sit on a bench outside the asylum, conversing with one another, as they introduce us to the story of a conniving carnival showman who turns out to be a sinister asylum psychiatrist. The story that they tell engrosses us. But, as the film ends, and as it returns to the framing device, the narrators reveal themselves to be inmates of the very same asylum they have been critiquing. They instantly lose their credibility with this "reveal." We are left wondering if their tale could be true or if it was a figment of their imaginations.

Shutter Island's director, Scorsese, uses this technique to add to the adventure, whereas director Robert Weine reportedly added this framing device to *Caligari* as an afterthought, supposedly to soften the film making it more ambiguous and thus more appealing to broader audiences. (Scholars still debate the accuracy of the reports about the conflicts between *Caligari*'s screenwriters and the film's director, but that is another matter.)

Scorsese's 2010 film was based on a best-selling 2003 book by author Dennis Lehane. To be fair, it was not the filmmaker alone who introduced allusions to so many fine films of the past. Lehane himself said he intended his novel to be an homage to Gothic settings, B movies, and pulp. He described the novel as a hybrid of the writings of the Brontë sisters and the original *Invasion of the Body Snatchers* (1956).

When viewing the film, we see remnants of *The Cabinet of Dr. Caligari* (1919; and its unofficial remake, 1962), *The Manchurian Candidate* (1962), *One Flew Over the Cuckoo's Nest* (1975), the *House on Haunted Hill* remake (1999), *Gothika* (2003), the many *Mabuse* movies (1922–1960), *Silence of the Lambs* (1991) and other Hannibal films, *Spellbound* (1945), *The Jacket* (2005), and *The Sixth Sense* (1999), as well as *Invasion of the Body Snatchers* (1956), which the author mentioned directly. The inventive viewer can also find a bit of the *Arkham Asylum* (2009) videogame, which is named for the fictional city in H.P. Lovecraft's very gothic writings. Of course, the craggy cliffs that surround the asylum remind us of Heathcliff's last leap into the wild beyond in Emily Brontë's *Wuthering Heights* (1847), just as the novel's author intended.

The narrator and main character, Teddy Daniels, is a U.S. Marshal, expertly played by Leonardo DiCaprio. The film is set in 1954. DiCaprio's wide-brimmed fedora and baggy trousers mark the movie as a period piece, just as Angelina Jolie's silver fox fur, close-fitting cloche, and red, red lipstick remind us that the events chronicled in *Changeling* occurred in the late twenties and early thirties, and (theoretically) bear no relationship to events of the present day.

Early in the film we learn that Marshal Daniels was recently widowed. His wife allegedly died in a fire, set by a fire bug that supposedly lives on the secluded Shutter Island. The Shutter island houses the Ashecliffe Hospital for the Criminally Insane. As the film opens, Daniels and his partner arrive on the island by ferry boat. The ferry reminds us of Charon's ferry that carries human cargo on their one-way journey over the River Styx to an eternal life in hell. Shutter Island may just as well be Devil's Island, it is so secluded. It also houses prisoners, only these prisoners were sent for treatment because they were declared criminally insane.

The two marshals are sent to investigate the disappearance of one particular patient: a multiple murderess named Rachel Solando. Rachel may have left the isolated island, even though she was housed in a locked cell and kept under

Standing against the German Expressionist set of Robert Weine's *The Cabinet of Dr. Caligari* (1919), Cesare (Conrad Veidt) carries Jane (Lil Dagover) to safety after she faints from fright.

constant supervision. This is a mystery that warrants federal investigation. Finding Rachel is the MacGuffin that drives the plot.

Initially, we experience the marshals' anxiety as they exit the ferry and step onto the island, approaching a warehouse for people too sick and unsafe for mainland society. Soon we see remnants of an old-fashioned "funny farm" where patients rake leaves and tend an overgrown garden. Our fears are set aside — temporarily. We are reminded of *King of Hearts* (1966), the Laingian-influenced anti-psychiatry classic from the mid-sixties in which patients dance and play and bear the names of flowers and live more enviable lives than the so-called sane people on the outside.

Then we meet Sir Ben Kingsley, who plays the chief psychiatrist, Dr. Cawley. Kingsley won a Best Actor Academy Award for his portrayal of Gandhi in *Gandhi* (1982), and was nominated for an Academy Award as Best Supporting Actor for his role as the Jewish arch-gangster Meyer Lansky in *Bugsy* (1991). Here Kingsley looks sinister, with his hairless head, halting speech and piercing stare. As Dr. Cawley, he exudes that "creepy, crawly" feeling that Freud describes in his essay on "The Uncanny." Dr. Cawley could definitely be sinister — and maybe even a distant relative of the Jewish crime boss Meyer Lansky. But Dr. Cawley is a doctor, and he clearly went on to study psychiatry after medical school, as many Jewish-American doctors did in 1954.

After having seen so many Hannibal the Cannibal films over the past few decades, we are fully prepared to meet a sinister psychiatrist who practices unconventional medicine on an island (and in a prison, to boot). We already know, from the remake of *House on Haunted Hill* (1999), that atrocities happen in psychiatric hospitals, acts that differ little from the heinous experiments that Nazi doctors conducted on Jews. Besides, who doesn't know about the malevolent Dr. Moreau and his island (even if we do not necessarily know that *Island of Lost Souls* [1932] refers to Moreau's island)? Moreau was not a psychiatrist; he was simply a mad scientist who tried to twist the minds of animals and confuse the evolutionary process that separated humans from beasts. Curiously, the director of the latest remake of *The Island of Dr. Moreau* (1996) was none other than John Frankenheimer, who created the original *Manchurian Candidate* in 1962.

Every step of the way on *Shutter Island* we are confronted by memories of earlier films starring sinister psychiatrists. Upon learning that the film is set in 1954, the same year that saw the first effective anti-psychotic tranquilizer — Thorazine (chlorpromazine) — used in the U.S., we reflexively expect to find half-baked experiments being conducted upon prisoner-patients. And by now we know that prisoners have been fodder for illicit experiments, from Tuskegee, Alabama, to the more recently disclosed STD (sexually-transmitted disease) studies conducted in Guatemala. Like Leonardo DiCaprio, we doubt the sincerity of Ben Kingsley's Dr. Cawley and grow concerned that he is so evasive.

It is important to know that *Shutter Island* is set in 1954. That dates it to the very start of the Thorazine era (and the heyday of the lobotomobile). Thorazine produced major changes in seriously psychotic patients who had been institutionalized and unable to function on their own. It was the first medication of its kind. Thanks to Thorazine, many people who seemed destined to live out their lives in asylums were suddenly able to return home. True, Thorazine also caused a "Thorazine shuffle" and induced a "pseudo–Parkinson syndrome" that made over-medicated patients look like zombies, but it worked better than anything else available at the time.

There was a downside to the Thorazine era. Excessive optimism led to a prematurely positive view of its long-term benefits. Thorazine led to a massive de-institutionalization movement, which in turn led to widespread closing of "asylums," sanitariums, state hospitals and custodial "funny farms." People with schizophrenia, the most severe mental illness, no longer suffered from intense hallucinations, but they were still ill-equipped to live alone.

Outside a protective environment, many drifted into homelessness in the urban areas. Without supervision, more than a few succumbed to serious substance abuse. On the streets, they were forced to interface with hard-core criminals and sometimes resorted to criminal acts themselves. The repercussions continue to this day. Even the illustrious psychiatrist who orchestrated the "emptying of the asylums" after the advent of Thorazine eventually conceded defeat and declared that decision to be the worst he made during his otherwise celebrated career.

There is an advantage to setting *Shutter Island* in 1954 instead of situating it in the present. To maintain credibility in our era of shortened hospital stays and managed care, movie makers must postdate a film about a state hospital and turn it into a period piece. Today, few people who need psychiatric treatment face the prospect of indefinite hospital stays. (However, those rare persons who successfully plead insanity in court may spend more time in mental institutions than they would have served in prison had they been sentenced for their crimes.)

Very few state hospitals remain open today, and even those that survive often come equipped with revolving doors. Neither our private insurance system nor our government-funded programs are willing to pay for lengthy hospital stays that stretch on for months or years. Select forensic facilities do warehouse dangerously psychotic people indefinitely, but there is reason to believe that even some of those patients are released prematurely.

In order to instill the necessary sense of fear, a film such as *Shutter Island* has to be set in the past. We could not "suspend disbelief" if it were set in the present day. It is also reassuring to watch a movie that chronicles events from the past that no longer happen today. If that film is frightening at the time of viewing, there is an even greater sense of relief when it ends.

Even though the action in *Shutter Island* is backdated, we feel DiCaprio's fears in the present tense. We perceive the tension that he projects. We side with DiCaprio when he hears Austrian waltz music wafting through a cavernous consulting room. Then we hear Max Von Sydow's distinctly Germanic accent (or is that an Austrian accent, we ask ourselves). Von Sydow plays a psychiatrist with a nearly unpronounceable name.

DiCaprio suspects that Von Sydow is a Nazi and implies that he, like other Nazis, could be conducting unethical experiments. The American version of *The Debt* (2011) had not yet been released when *Shutter Island* opened, so the story of the Nazi eye surgeon who blinded children while changing their eye colors had not been told on screen. But enough people have heard of characters like the "Butcher of Buchenwald" or the "Surgeon of Treblinka" or Dr. Mengele, and so we second DiCaprio's suspicions and do not dismiss his insinuations outright.

It's true that dangerous Nazi doctors escaped capture in post-war Europe and found refuge in South American jungles. Some 10,000 Nazi war criminals clandestinely entered the U.S. through the Displaced Persons Act. As shown in traveling exhibits at the U.S. Holocaust Memorial Museum (Washington, D.C.) and the Museum of Jewish Heritage (New York City), several Nazi doctors and scientists continued illustrious careers openly after the war. So it isn't so far-fetched to think that one or two of them sequestered themselves on secluded North American islands, like Shutter Island, to escape detection. That's what Teddy Daniels thinks, and that's what we wonder as well.

DiCaprio starts to experience flashbacks to his wartime experiences, when he and other soldiers liberated Dachau and saw skin-and-bone bodies of concentration camp inmates, some dead some nearly dead. We have been primed to think that these flashbacks are typical of PTSD (post-traumatic stress disorder) suffered by soldiers returning from Iraq or by Vietnam vets who lobbied for recognition of their persistent mental distress. We do not think of these flashbacks as delusions or hallucinations produced by a deluded or deranged mind — at least not yet.

PTSD and its flashbacks get so much press these days that we don't bother to weigh in on the possibility that Teddy is experiencing "alcoholic hallucinosis," which causes visions when some alcohol-dependent persons stop drinking. Yet we learned that Teddy Daniels had been a heavy drinker. So we should not be shocked if he shows signs of alcohol-induced brain disease.

The jury is still out, the pathology report is not back, and the tension is still on. We have reason to concur with DiCaprio, and we have just as much reason to question DiCaprio's assumptions about von Sydow's psychiatrist. Yes, he could be a Nazi doctor who left Europe, weaseled his way into the U.S., and now conducts illicit studies on island inhabitants, as Dr. Moreau did on the imaginary island invented by H.G. Wells.

In reality, Nazi doctors used human prisoners for dubious and dangerous studies, operating without anesthesia and without regard for human life, because they considered Jewish and gypsy prisoners to be sub-human. The *House on Haunted Hill* remake (1999) taught us that (as did academic texts, newspaper articles and TV specials about escaped war criminals). The Hannibal prequel *Hannibal Rising* (2007) links Hannibal's later cannibalistic behavior to Nazi-era atrocities inflicted on his beloved sister. If we are versed in history—or if we watched *The Boys from Brazil* (1978)—we know that many Nazis, Eichmann included, made their way to South and Central America, where they survived in hiding for decades.

Alternatively, there is good reason to believe that Von Sydow is exactly who he says he is. Some Jewish psychiatrists who escaped the Nazis by emigrating to the U.S. before and after the second World War also had Austrian accents. Even the founder of psychoanalysis, Sigmund Freud, was an Austrian-born Jew who was forced to immigrate to England. For all we know, Von Sydow's character might have studied with Freud while in Europe. Then again, he could be a Nazi doctor. Perhaps he was one of the psychiatrists who sent mental patients to their doom, to suffocate in gas chambers later used to kill Jews. Scorsese keeps us guessing and second-guessing.

We start to realize that we really don't know who is who. The same could be said for *Spellbound* (1945), one of Hitchcock's most under-rated masterpieces. *Spellbound* also revolves around a psychiatrist who has lost his memory and his identity. He may be exactly the man he says he is—or he may be an imposter. Like *Spellbound*, *Shutter Island* does not uncloak the master criminal until the very end. But since we know that *Spellbound*'s retiring head psychiatrist (played by Leo G. Carroll) pulls a gun and points it at Dr. Peterson (Ingrid Bergman) as the film comes to a close, we expect to see the same behavior from Von Sydow—sooner or later.

In the meantime, DiCaprio's character busies himself with investigating the disappearance of Rachel Solando, just as we busy ourselves with finding clues to other films and books that interject themselves into *Shutter Island*. We learn about "the Lighthouse," the place where the most incorrigible criminals are subjected to end-of-the-line treatments like lobotomy. Even that suggestion is not so far-fetched, considering how casually lobotomies were performed in the fifties, when Dr. Freeman drove his lobotomobile around to advertise the new technique. Here, we see shades of *One Flew Over the Cuckoo's Nest* (1975), where Nurse Ratched orchestrates psychosurgery when she wants to tame an intemperate Jack Nicholson. *Gothika* (2003), also comes to mind because of its forensic psychiatric setting and the confusion between life and death, ghosts and living beings.

The Jacket (2005), with Adrian Brody playing a wounded soldier who lives in a time warp, offers further associations. Brody is unfairly charged with killing a police officer, but he is acquitted for reasons of insanity once his combat-related head injury and subsequent amnesia become known. He is committed to a mental institution, where he is injected with experimental drugs. Then he is shoved into a straitjacket, body bag, and morgue-like cell. We think of Kris Kristofferson playing the part of a disheveled psychiatrist who looks like he himself injects drugs and then leaves his patients' care to the caprices of sadistic orderlies.

Throughout the time that DiCaprio searches for the missing Rachel Solando, he sees fleeting images of his dead wife, wearing the same flowered dress. Sometimes she looks water-logged. Sometimes, he sees her crumbling into dust like a burnt log, seemingly confirming DiCaprio's story about her death in a fire.

As the film progresses, we see a little girl appearing and disappearing and asking why she was not rescued. We do not know the identity of this child until the film's end. What we do know is that Rachel Solando was sent to Shutter Island because she drowned her little children. She reminds us of Andrea Yates and Yates' many trials (2002–2006), and the forensic psychiatric debates generated by her horrific acts. Yates was a psychotic woman who lived in a trailer with her husband. He objected to her seeking psychiatric treatment. She home-schooled her children and drowned all five when she came to believe they were possessed by the Devil.

Much more happens on screen (and even more happens in the mind of the viewer who has seen previous films about sinister psychiatrists). In the end we learn that DiCaprio's character was not sent to Shutter Island to investigate the whereabouts of a missing person or an absent patient. We learn it was DiCaprio's wife who murdered the children — not Rachel Solando — and that it was DiCaprio who shot his delusional wife when he discovered his drowned children. And it is DiCaprio (like Andrea Yates' husband) who holds himself accountable for not getting her psychiatric help when she first showed signs of psychosis.

Like Adrian Brody in *The Jacket*, DiCaprio's character is acquitted of murder in the first degree. He is deemed insane because of his wartime experiences, his long history of hallucinations, and his presumptive PTSD (which was not called PTSD at that time). He was sent to Shutter Island, not as an investigator but as a patient. His compassionate psychiatrists have made him believe that he is charged with solving these strange occurrences on Shutter Island, in hopes he will regain his memory of the crime. It turns out that Rachel Solando, the supposed murderess, is not a patient. Rather, she is a staff psychiatrist pretending to be a patient. DiCaprio's good-natured partner is not a U.S. Marshal; he, too, is a psychiatrist. An elaborate ruse has been conducted by well-meaning medical staff hoping to break through Teddy Daniels' psychological defenses and end his dissociation to bring him back to reality.

We come away from this film uncertain whether we have seen a great new mystery by Scorsese (one that rivals Hitchcock's *Rope* [1948], but for different reasons) or schlock that plays upon sensationalized child murder cases of the 21st century. One thing is certain: we received a crash course on "sinister psychiatrists in cinema." With that, we can begin this book in earnest.

1

Mad Military Mind Docs

When a psychotic army psychiatrist opened fire on his base on November 5, 2009, it seemed like an isolated incident. Thirteen lives were lost. Thirty more were wounded, including the shooter himself. In the end, the psychiatrist — who was also an army officer — would be permanently paralyzed by bullets fired by men and women who tried to stop his one-man attack.

It is shocking enough to hear of a soldier going berserk after being isolated in the deserts of Iraq. But Major Hasan was a medical doctor, a commissioned officer, and a psychiatric specialist. He was not an ordinary recruit. He was stationed in Texas, and was not surrounded by miles of mirage-inducing sand or subjected to endless nights of mortar fire.

As a psychiatrist, Major Hasan was expected to treat distraught soldiers and prevent them from harming themselves or anyone else (who was not an officially-designated enemy). Yet he proved to be more dangerous — and presumably more deranged — than his patients.

Because he was known as a Muslim militant, and because he yelled "Allahu Akbar" just before firing, most people focused on his religious convictions and ignored his professional status. When viewed through the lens of religious extremism, his acts followed a twisted logic that makes sense to religious extremists and no one else.

The fact that he was trained as a psychiatrist who treated mental disorders faded from memory, forgotten by bystanders. Yet this fact was painfully obvious to fellow physicians and other mental health professionals. Most wondered why his medical team failed to foresee the deadly scene that came to pass at Fort Hood. In retrospect, the warning signs were everywhere.

Yet psychologists and psychiatric nurses from his clinic were among the first to fall victim. A civilian physician's assistant who tried to stop Hasan died in the process. Shot dead on the spot, those health professionals did not have the chance to self-reflect or second guess. It is still unclear what Major Hasan thinks of his acts, as he sits in his wheelchair, unable to walk because of his wounds yet able to contemplate the possible death sentence that lies ahead.

Less than a year had passed when a Harvard-educated neuroscience researcher shot six colleagues, killing three of the six victims. This mass-murdering neuroscientist was also a wife and mother. She was not a military MD who wore army fatigues. Nor was she a Muslim militant, like the army major mentioned above. She lived a seemingly normal life in Massachusetts. Then she and her family moved to a small college town in Alabama, far from the maddening crowds of urban colleges.

Dr. Amy Bishop earned her Ph.D in neuroscience. She married a loving man and bore four children. She corrected their homework and collaborated with her husband. She ran her lab and lectured in college classes. On paper she sounded like a so-called supermom and a potential role model for women in science. After her murder spree it was revealed that she had shot her brother and may have been responsible for mailing a pipe bomb to her senior professor.

What possessed her? Can a contagion infect those who research the intricacies of the brain and try to reach beyond the reasonable limits of human knowledge? One can only wonder.

In February 2010 another female neuroscience Ph.D stood trial for terrorism and attempted murder. Dr. Siddiqui was American-educated but Pakistani-born. She, too, had led a quiet life in Massachusetts at an earlier point in time and at a different stage of her life. She studied at MIT and Brandeis (a Jewish-sponsored institution that is open to persons of all religious persuasions). She did computer-based research in neuroscience and was far removed from patient care.

Dr. Siddiqui was the mother of three children. She was the daughter of a doctor. She was once the wife of a doctor — until she divorced the doctor and remarried an alleged Al Qaeda operative. There was a time when she could have eased into the select circles of Boston's educated elite. She could have cavorted with professors, educators and world-class computer geeks.

But Dr. Siddiqui also acquired credentials as a political militant along with the MIT Ph.D that supposedly taught her the techniques of chemical and biological warfare. Soon after she disappeared she was placed near the top of the FBI's most wanted listed. When apprehended in Afghanistan she grabbed an attack rifle and fired shots at American interrogators. Found in her possession were documents detailing bombing plans and locations of American landmarks. Even if there was doubt about her complicity with Al Qaeda, there was no denying that she attempted to assassinate federal agents. The events unraveled like scenes in a movie.

Dr. Siddiqui was returned Stateside, where she stood charges and disrupted the court. To bystanders she seemed to be paving the way for an insanity plea, as some celebrated pajama-clad Mafioso did in the recent past. But Dr. Siddiqui never claimed that she was insane, for she believed in her cause and was convinced of the correctness of her actions and affiliations.

Dr. Siddiqui was tried and convicted in a New York courtroom on February 9, 2010. Dr. Siddiqui might have made more waves had her mission succeeded and had her efforts not been aborted — and had Dr. Amy Bishop not arrived on the scene three days later. For Dr. Bishop stole the show when she shot and killed her colleagues on February 12, 2010.

The raving and raging Dr. Siddiqui was shoved aside by a more "successful" killer, one who was also a neuroscientist. Amy Bishop, mother of four, had a growing kill count rather than just fleeting ideas and affiliations with Al Qaeda operatives. Dr. Bishop was her own woman. She acted alone — not once, not twice, but probably thrice or maybe even more.

The world had gone awry. Who would imagine that mothers — and doctorate level neuroscientists at that — would compete for "kill counts"? Who would think that psychiatrists or psychologists or neuroscientists could collaborate with political conspiracies?

Hmmm. Maybe someone who saw *The Manchurian Candidate* in 1962 would imagine exactly that. *The Manchurian Candidate* was pulled from movie theaters a year after its release. Many believed that the film inspired the Kennedy killing. It was rereleased two and a half decades later — to equal aplomb. Anyone who saw the first *Candidate*, with Angela Lansbury playing the stop-at-nothing mother, would not have been fazed by Bishop or Siddiqui. (Actually, anyone who read newspaper accounts of a terrorist conspiracy among British physicians a few years earlier might have been waiting for an American counterpart to appear on this continent.) For many of us, watching (and re-watching) *The Manchurian Candidate* is even more compelling because it shows us how much life imitates art, or how much art anticipates life.

Candidate is a story about a murderous mom, a self-serving step-father, and a loveless (and unlovable) soldier-son who interact with political operatives, loyal army platoon mates, and diabolical mind doctors that live in Manchuria rather than Afghanistan or Pakistan. *Candidate* could be classified as a buddy film, a family melodrama, a romantic tragedy, an action-adventure, a social problem film, a mystery, thriller, conspiracy or spy film — because it is all of these and more. It is only parenthetically a commentary on psychiatry — but what a commentary it is!

Candidate does much more than demonstrate the evils of hypnosis, and behavioral conditioning and brainwashing (and brain implants in the remake), when wielded by the wrong hands. It also includes a surprisingly sympathetic shot of an African-American consulting army psychiatrist who is the polar opposite of so many military MDs from the movies. Played by Joe Adams, this psychiatrist listens to the distressed soldiers without dismissing them. He hears their worst fears expressed through their dreams and then recommends reassignment to "less stressful" and "less sensitive" desk jobs. Unlike European World War I psychiatrists, he does not send shell shocked soldiers back to the front or even hint at Kaufmannization or electric shock.

Adams' character does exactly what an early sixties-era psychiatrist should — except that he never expresses his own chagrin, much less anger, over his own marginalized position in American society and in American organized medicine. He is an exemplary American MD who makes the Manchurian mind docs look even more evil by contrast.

Joe Adams' character sends a political message to the American public in the spirit of the "social problem" films of the late fifties and early sixties. Those who saw the movie in 1962 knew that the Civil Rights Movement was percolating but had not yet boiled over. Military buffs probably knew that the army was integrated in the midst of the Korean War. Few were aware that the AMA excluded Black physicians from AMA membership until 1968. Oddly enough, the positive message about African-American doctors and soldiers is countered by racist stereotyping of the Asian soldiers and psychologists who operate out of the Pavlov Institute.

Were it not for a few salient facts, *The Manchurian Candidate* could theoretically be added to the long list of American films about the "Yellow Menace." Such movies include characters like the infamous Dr. Fu Manchu and Dr. No (from the James Bond film of the same name that was also released in 1962). But the facts are the facts. There are reasons behind these bad representation of Asians — or, I should say, of Asian Communists specifically — who were linked to the Russian-based U.S.S.R. (now called FSU).

John Frankenheimer's film (which was adapted from Richard Condon's book by the same name) opens with the caption "KOREA 1952." This recollects real-life events: the capture and brainwashing of American military men during the Korean War. That was the McCarthy era, when paranoia about a Communist takeover peaked. The public reaction to those events, and to the parade of press reports that followed, was almost as important as the event itself. These words remind audiences of times when Communists imprisoned Americans and subjected them to sleep deprivation, "re-education," and "brainwashing" before broadcasting their anti–American "confessions" on live TV the following year.

To the astonishment of American audiences who witnessed this spectacle, supposedly patriotic American servicemen publicly denounced their country and praised Communism instead. When it came time for the release of the remaining POWs, 21 POWs decided to stay in Communist-controlled North Korea. Actual occurrences like this one (and related events that preceded it) lent credibility to Joe McCarthy's concerns. This also fortified the claims of American academians and experimental psychologists, who were far more statistically-inclined and data-driven than the psychoanalysts who controlled psychiatry departments of medical schools in the 1950s and 1960s. Those professors and researchers insisted that behavioral conditioning was more effective in changing behavior and belief systems than long, drawn-out Freudian treatment techniques, which were very much in vogue at the time.

Prominent journalists had already written about related events in the early 1950s before the war ended. In 1951, Harold Martin, an editor at the *Saturday Evening Post*, published an account of the capture and indoctrination of eighteen Marines by Chinese authorities. He titled his essay "They Tried to Make Our Marines Love Stalin." (It is no surprise to see a Stalin poster in the brainwashing scene of *The Manchurian Candidate*.) Another journalist, Edward Hunter, coined the word "brainwashing" to describe the manipulation and "programming" of the minds of American soldiers when he wrote an article for the *Miami Daily News* in 1950.[1]

No matter how impressive those articles or publications were, nothing made as great an impact on the public as those broadcast confessions, especially since they came at a time when televisions were "invading" American homes and would become fixtures in most living rooms by 1954. Just in case anyone had forgotten those earlier articles and news shows, psychiatrist Robert Jay Lifton's book about *Thought Reform and the Psychology of Totalism: A Study of "Brainwashing" in China* (1961) arrived at a most propitious time.

In 1961, a year before the first release of *The Manchurian Candidate*, Lifton's book about brainwashing in China was published by W.W. Norton. A year after *Candidate* premiered, in 1963, the popular hardcover became a mass market paperback. Even though Lifton avoids a "totalizing" approach in his study of "totalism" and "brainwashing," this psychology book gained a following and was reprinted several times. Such a high-profile publication probably increased the critics' appreciation of *The Manchurian Candidate*, as they could read much more into the movie than the public, who were not too impressed by the film the first go-round.

Having this background information at hand helps us appreciate the depth of this film. After the caption "KOREA 1952," the first scene of *The Manchurian Candidate* introduces us to Captain Bennett Marco (Frank Sinatra) and Sergeant Raymond Shaw (Laurence Harvey). (Marco had not yet been promoted to Major at this point in the narrative.) The younger Shaw is the son of an incredibly evil mother (Angela Lansbury) and the stepson of an aspiring, self-serving and slimy senator and vice-presidential candidate-to-be (James Gregory).

Shaw has just returned home from Korea. He is about to receive the Congressional Medal of Honor for an act of heroism that he can't remember performing. On the podium, Shaw's commanding officer, Major Marco (Sinatra), describes Shaw's heroism: Shaw saved the lives of platoon mates after their capture by Manchurians (read North Koreans). The nine surviving members of his patrol parrot Marco's words. The President secures Shaw's pin to his lapel. This publicly-staged event was orchestrated by Shaw's publicity-seeking stepfather. Shaw and his mother and stepfather exchange hostile quips, foreshadowing future developments.

The scene shifts to Major Marco (Sinatra), who has been reassigned to a cushy post in Army Intelligence in Washington, D.C., partly because he suffers from recurring nightmares and panic attacks, as do many people with PTSD (post-traumatic stress disorder). These dream scenes (described below) are among the most famous in all film and are highlights of *Candidate*.

In the dream, Marco and his men sit together at a ladies' auxiliary meeting. Then the scene shifts. The camera pans the room 360 degrees. Soon enough, we see the "brainwashing" scene in Manchuria. Since we know that Marco is asleep, we the audience assume that the slow motion, disjointed sequences are "cinematic shorthand" for dreams. Then we realize that these juxtapositions simply act like dreams and tell truths that are hidden from the conscious mind.

The camera returns to the garden meeting, where an aging white woman speaks to twenty club members about "Fun with Hydrangeas." The soldiers look on from the sidelines as she speaks. Then the camera shifts to an Asian-featured doctor who stands in the same spot where the garden lady spoke. Captive American soldiers now sit behind posters of Stalin and Mao, while twenty Communist soldiers sit in the same section that was occupied by the club ladies.

The doctor announces that he will demonstrate the powers of hypnotism. He points to the American soldiers and states, "I have conditioned them — or brainwashed them, which I understand

John Frankenheimer's *The Manchurian Candidate* (1962) shows Sergeant Raymond Shaw (Laurence Harvey) strangling his platoon mate, Private Ed Mavpole (Richard La Pore), with a scarf in compliance with hypnotic commands issued by an unseen Manchurian psychologist.

is the new American word. They believe that they are waiting out a storm in the lobby of a small hotel in New Jersey where a meeting of the ladies' garden club is in progress."

Sinatra's dream scene shifts back to the garden, where Shaw (Harvey) simulates a game of solitaire. Shaw goes through the hand motions of dealing cards — even though he holds no cards in his hands. The evil Asian doctor asks Shaw if he has ever killed anyone. Shaw replies that he has not. The doctor disagrees and tells Shaw that he will demonstrate his ability to kill on command. He instructs Shaw to choose the platoon member whom he dislikes the least. Shaw initially chooses Captain Marco (Sinatra) but the doctor declines, stating, "That won't do, Raymond. We need the Captain to get you your medal." So Raymond names a second choice, Ed Mavole (Richard La Pore). Obediently, Raymond strangles Mavole with a scarf. Captain Marco (Sinatra) yawns, and the platoon members sit by, motionless and bored. In the dream, Mavole dies.

At this point, Major Marco awakens with a jolt, clearly upset by this nightmare. Distressed by these recurring dreams and unable to stop them, Marco consults an army psychiatrist, who happens to be African-American (even though there were — and still are — disproportionally few African-American psychiatrists in America). *Candidate* appeared before the Civil Rights Act of 1964, so a Black cinematic psychiatrist sends a message: he represents an alternative "establishment," even if he wears an army officer's uniform and salutes. We wonder if Joe Adams' psychiatrist is distinct from white European psychiatrists mocked by *Caligari*. He may be kinder than most military MDs, or he may be bitter, or his race may be immaterial.

Marco tells the "good" American doctor about his dream and explains that Shaw was honored for saving the lives of all but two of the men in the platoon. The two men whom Shaw was unable to save are presumed missing in action. One MIA was Mavole, the man who was murdered in the dream. After recounting the dream's details, Marco repeats a phase that will be pivotal to the plot. He says, "Raymond Shaw is the kindest, bravest, warmest, most wonderful human being I've ever known in my life." Major Marco is reassigned to a less stressful post.

When another platoon member has strikingly similar dreams about his wartime experiences, the plot thickens. This time around the dreamer is Black, and the dream characters are Black, but the story line is exactly the same. When Corporal Al Melvin (James Edwards) dreams of the garden party, he dreams of a garden club of equally boring Black ladies, dressed in their Sunday best, in the style of African-American churchwomen of that era.

Corporal Melvin's dream shows Sinatra stating that his first duty upon return will be to recommend Raymond Shaw for the Congressional Medal of Honor. Like Captain Marco, Corporal Melvin also sees Shaw kill. When he sees blood splatter on Stalin's portrait, Melvin awakens, screaming. He inadvertently wakes his wife, who hears him repeat the same line as Sinatra: "Raymond Shaw is the kindest, bravest, warmest, most wonderful human being I've ever known in my life."

Corporal Melvin is just as upset by these dreams as Major Marco, but he drafts a letter about the dreams to Shaw instead of consulting a psychiatrist. When Shaw reads the letter he shifts into playing solitaire, just as he did in the dream. To contemporary psychiatrists these recurring nightmares are typical of the disturbing dreams and disrupted sleep of "post-traumatic stress disorder" described by Vietnam vets, and now by Gulf War servicemen and servicewomen. Fortunately, *The Manchurian Candidate* was made before this diagnosis appeared in the DSM (Diagnostic and Statistical Manual), and so the clinical diagnosis does not distract from the story. We simply see the events unfold as they happened. Fortunately for Frank Sinatra's character, he starts to suspect that something is amiss. So he heads for New York, where he calls on Shaw.

When Sinatra arrives, Shaw is busy with Chinese agents in his Manhattan apartment. A furious fight erupts between Sinatra and Shaw's Chinese employee. Shaw then reveals to Sinatra that he has the same recurring dream that Corporal Melvin described in his letter.

From then on the plot become more complicated. Now that Sinatra and the audience have seen the truth through the dream scenes, they will learn that their wartime experiences were engineered through the evil Russian Pavlov Institute, which specializes in the kind of behavioral conditioning that won Pavlov a Nobel Prize in physiology in 1904. The Pavlov Institute reprogrammed the entire platoon into believing that Shaw was a hero, when he was really a killer who murders at the Communists' command. Moreover, Shaw can be commanded to kill again on cue. He is pre-programmed to enter a "twilight state" of hyper-suggestibility whenever he sees the Red Queen playing card. The Red Queen reminds us of the Red Queen's irrationality in *Alice in Wonderland* and also alludes to Shaw's "Red" mother.

As the film concludes, we learn that it is not the Communists per se who commit the ultimate evil. Rather, it is Shaw's own mother (Angela Lansbury). She is a secret Communist operative and a very real "Red Queen." She and her Commie cronies are plotting to kill the presidential candidate so her husband, the vice-presidential nominee, can become president. He will then hand the country over to the Communists. In the end, even the evil mother, who is a committed Communist, is horrified to learn that the Communists chose her only son to commit the murder that allows the Communist takeover.

In the meantime, Marco has been struggling to unravel the mystery about Shaw. He wants to test out his theories, and to rid Shaw of his irresistible urge that overtakes him when he sees the Red Queen in the cards. Sadly, the "cards have already been dealt," so to speak, and Shaw's tragic fate is sealed. An unspeakable event occurs before Marco can intervene: Shaw enters an "altered state," engineered by his evil mother. Entranced by the Red Queen card, he kills his fiancée and her father at his mother's command. He destroys the love of his life in an instant. She was the only person worth living for. He has lost his reason to forge on.

The grand finale occurs at the political convention, which is set in Madison Square Garden. Shaw stands on a balcony, now painfully aware that he is programmed to kill. He aims his rifle at the stage, according to plan, but realizes that he cannot rid himself of Communist or parental control. Unable to accept his complicity in the killings, and still shattered by his unwitting murder of his fiancée and her father, Shaw the sharpshooter shoots mother and stepfather as they stand on the stage. Then he turns the gun on himself. (This final scene is an homage to Hitchcock, who used a similar closing in *The Man Who Knew Too Much* [1956].)

The enduring appeal of *The Manchurian Candidate* is manifold. Many think that it was a wonderful way to show off Sinatra's talents as an actor as well as a singer. Aside from this commercial consideration, *Candidate* provides sophisticated political commentary about McCarthyism, and then-current concerns with brainwashing and America's involvement in the Korean War. It also touches on the social roles of African-Americans in proto–Civil Rights society. It comments on the evolving role of women in post–Eisenhower sixties' society. It forecasts evils that may befall society should women become more empowered, and should they owe allegiance to something or someone other than their families.

Alternatively, *Candidate* can be read as a proto-feminist message that is in the same spirit as Betty Friedan's *Feminine Mystique*, which would be published by W. W. Norton a year later, in 1963. The film implies that an un-empowered woman whose sense of self depends upon her husband's position and her son's accomplishments — rather than on her own achievements — can easily be controlled by a herd mentality and even turned into the ultimate traitor.

Above all, *Candidate* details a distorted and destructive oedipal relationship between an unassuming son and a narcissistic mother who will stop at nothing so that she can achieve her goal and bask in the glow of her husband's glory. Like many mother-son relationships portrayed in sixties-era film, literature and even psychiatric theories, this relationship shows that overly-involved mothers are more likely to poison their sons than protect them.

Candidate is also a Cinderella story with the genders reversed — where the evil stepparent is the stepfather and the hapless victim is the son. Long after it ceased to speak to contemporary social concerns, and long after the glory days of its all-star cast, the plot still resonates as classic a fairy tale story. *Candidate* invokes the most acrimonious Freudian-style "family romance" imaginable. But this is not a Disney cartoon. Here the evil stepfather colludes with his wife and other Communists. Together they send her son to his doom. But their plot backfires and unexpectedly dooms the stepfather, his wife, and the soldier-son.

The dream scenes in *The Manchurian Candidate* are among the most memorable ever seen on screen and can compete admirably with Dalí's dream scenes in *Spellbound*. One can argue that the dream theme in *Manchurian Candidate* is not about dreams at all, and that dreams merely propel the drama, revealing the plots and subplots. That would mean that the dream scenes should be read as dramatic devices and nothing but.

However, the director's use of dreams is deliberate. For dreams denote a double or alternative reality. That doubling, in turn, points to duplicity and double-dealing. The dream subplots make themselves manifest at night rather than during the day, and so they mirror the dual reality of human experience. The film also comments on the American concept of dreams and the American belief that "free associations" with dreams can override Communist brainwashing control and potentially lead to a "free world," with "free associations" for all.[2]

One could write an entire treatise on the oedipal relationships in this film. One could write a complete book chapter about the dream scenes in *Candidate* (as I did in *Dreams in Myth, Medicine and Movies*, Praeger, 2002). But, since our subject here is "sinister cinema psychiatrists" we will focus on those figures in the first (and best) version of *Candidate*.

But first I must add this caveat once again: *The Manchurian Candidate* is far, far, far more than a commentary on the competition between the two very different types of psychiatric treatment that available at the time, each of which had strong supporters and detractors. Yes it incorporates psychiatric commentary, and very successfully, but "psychological warfare" between warring psychological theories is just one of its many leitmotifs. It is true that psychoanalytic dream analysis is pitted against scientifically-proven behaviorism, just as Communism and democracy are pitted against one another. But it would be a mistake to imply that the war between opposing psychiatric theories carried the same gravity as opposing political theories that threatened to set off another world war — especially when we recall the gravity of the Cuban Missile Crisis that surfaced in October 1962, at the very same time that *The Manchurian Candidate* appeared.

Candidate is especially interesting for our study of sinister psychiatrists because it contradicts the common belief (among psychiatrists) that "talk therapists" or non-physicians are portrayed more benignly than biological psychiatrists. Clearly that is not the case in the original *Candidate* (although it is true for the remake). Rather, the film reinforces our contention that control and coercion is the most evil act committed by reel (or real) psychiatrists. It doesn't matter whether that control comes from physical restraints, mind control, or involuntary admission to an asylum, or if it reflects more generic "mind control," as occurs in *The Manchurian Candidate*.

When *The Manchurian Candidate* contrasts hypnosis with other psychiatric approaches, such as dream analysis and behavioral (Pavlovian) conditioning, it also plays upon the increased awareness of Freudianism and Freudian-style dream analysis that followed the celebration of the centennial of Freud's birth in 1956, a few years before the film opened in the Autumn of 1962. *Candidate* premiered at the tail end of the "Golden Years," when analytically-oriented psychiatrists and psychoanalysts were still idealized in cinema — even when they occasionally used hypnosis to facilitate "free associations" (rather than to implant false memories).

Still, the psychiatric "star of the show" is the Manchurian doctor who "brainwashes" the captive soldiers and makes them believe that they are attending a ladies' garden party. The fact that the Manchurian doctor works at the Pavlov Institute sends a strong political message. As he speaks, he stands before a larger-than-life poster of Stalin, as if to say that he "stands for" Stalin. Like Stalin, Pavlov was Russian. The Russian physiologist won a Nobel Prize for his studies of dogs' salivation, and later added new dimensions to existing psychological theories. Pavlov's experiments also added a scientific rigor that Freud's psychoanalytic techniques lacked.

The overt political message of *The Manchurian Candidate* is apparent, even though the commentary on psychological schools is more complicated than it seems on the surface. Some points are beyond dispute. Because behaviorism was invented by a Russian scientist, it represents Communist control and psychological brainwashing. Behaviorism was the polar opposite of the "free choice" of the "free world" and the democratic way of life advocated by Americans. When the Manchurian psychologist employs efficacious Pavlovian techniques, the film may also be saying (perhaps unwittingly) that Freudian approaches are outdated and have been displaced by more scientifically-conceived theories (that arrived by way of Russia).

There is a glitch here. By the sixties, most mainstream American academians also advocated behaviorism and viewed it as the most scientific school of psychology. Psychoanalysis was too unscientific a subject matter to be taught in college psychology classes (even though psychoanalysts dominated medical school psychiatry departments). It was well-known (thanks to McCarthy's inquisitions and thanks to listening carefully to lectures) that many of those academians were left-leaning. Some were accused of being fellow travelers, if not outright Communists and socialists, perhaps even distant cousins of the Manchurians seen on screen.

No matter, because the war between the behaviorists and the psychoanalysts became outdated long ago and were supplanted by war between rival psychodynamic schools and neuropsychiatrists, who believe that biology controls behavior and have studies to show it. Even more recently a faint battle cry against the psychopharmacologists was uttered by aspiring politicos and influential medical editors. It remains to be seen whether this will lead to a full-force war or whether the warning shots heard in the distance will eventually fade away.

The remake of *The Manchurian Candidate* in 2005 reminds us of shifts in psychiatric theories and treatment. The tide began to turn in 1977 when Dr. Melvin Sabshin, the medical director of the APA (American Psychiatric Association), declared that "a vigorous effort to re-medicalize psychiatry should be strongly supported." That sentiment was echoed by the APA's president, Dr. Jack Weinberg. The publication of the third edition of DSM-III in 1980 set the stage for the sea change of the mid-eighties. This turning away from theories of "mind" was in full force by 1990, and the nineties were declared to be "the Decade of the Brain." Nodding to the paradigm shift, and adding some sci-fi spirit to the mix, the second *Candidate* substitutes brain implants for behavioral conditioning. It also shifts the setting from Manchuria to the Mideast.

Unfortunately, it also substitutes global corporate enterprise for governmental control, and political theory for Communist threats that were so meaningful in the mid-fifties. Those Communist threats mimicked McCarthy-era paranoia and parodied his Hollywood witch hunts, but played to the public's anti–Communist sentiments at the same time. In making this switch, the remake loses its political poignancy. The film ends up looking like a by-product of the same commercial motivations that it criticizes.

John Frankenheimer, director of the first *Candidate*, was not involved in the remake. However, Frankenheimer had a hand in another intriguing remake. He directed *The Island of Dr. Moreau* (1996). *Moreau* spoofs scientists' ill-intended tampering with brains and behavior.

The director chosen for (or who chose) the *Candidate* remake was Jonathan Demme. Demme came with his own illustrious credentials. Among his many accomplishments was *Silence of the Lambs* (1991), the Hannibal the Cannibal film that spurred the most recent sinister psychiatrist craze. It is interesting to compare the sci-fi brain tampering in the *Candidate* remake to the medically-correct but utterly improbable kitchen table frontal lobotomy performed on Ray Liotta. Perhaps this directorial choice was intended to focus extra attention on the neuropsychiatric scenes, or even to continue the tradition of sinister psychiatrists in cinema.

The *Mancurian Candidate* remake retains dream sequences, but it omits hypnosis, brainwashing, and behavioral conditioning scenes, and so it loses the pervasive paranoid flavor and the basic political context. Instead, it capitalizes on the original's cache and on the box office draw of African-American actor Denzel Washington. The remake pushes the original's race-related subplot into prominence when it substitutes Washington for Sinatra and casts him in the lead role as Major Marco. This ploy draws attention to the fact that Washington gained film fame by playing the slain Civil Rights leader and radical Black activist Malcolm X in *Malcolm X* (1992). Some might say that Denzel Washington's heroic role as the lead military officer anticipated the election of America's first Black president — just as the original *Candidate* inadvertently anticipated the assassination of JFK. Coincidences may be just coincidences, but the filmmaker may have felt a pulse that was already present. The political significance of the remake ends there.

The subtlety of the original spoke louder than the direct message of the second. In the first *Candidate* the African-American soldier's dream about a garden party populated by Black women makes the dream scene convincing because Sinatra's Major Marco dreams an identical dream about white women in the same garden. The original also grants Blacks psychological autonomy when it shows that they dream of themselves as being Black and do not dream of being white.

The first *Candidate* portrays two African-American actors in non-traditional roles. In doing so, it challenged stereotypes of Black actors and Black people in general. Chronicling the camaraderie between soldiers of different complexions proved that this platoon is worlds away from World War II and its segregated troops. This choice suggests that racial harmony and equality are just around the corner, and directly dispels the concerns of some skeptics about the abilities of Blacks and whites to co-exist successfully in integrated military units.

Adding an African-American psychiatrist who is also an army officer is a first for film, for very few Black professionals had been featured in film and even fewer were represented as physicians, much less as psychiatrists. In that same year Sidney Poitier starred as the psychiatrist-in-chief in Stanley Kramer's *Pressure Point* (1962). More importantly, Washington played a "tough love" kind of psychiatrist in *Antwone Fisher* (2002) just a few years before the *Manchurian Candidate* remake. That poignant film (or tearjerker, if you will) is still one of the few movies that features an African-American psychiatrist, and it is based on a pastiche of real life characters to boot.

By highlighting racial factors in this film, the director calls attention to racial issues in society. When the remake makes racial issues central rather than peripheral, it obscures the real event that the original recollects: the televised confessions of American military captives from the Korean War. That brainwashing event made McCarthy's paranoid accusations credible. McCarthy's paranoid accusations, in turn, colored the fifties. What's more, McCarthy had a profound impact on the entertainment industry when numerous screenwriters and other film industry workers were blacklisted, with some being singled out to stand trial as the "McCarthy Ten."[3]

The brainwashing scene of the first *Candidate* was completely believable to sixties spectators, since college psychology classes taught about behavioral conditioning (or Pavlovian conditioning or Skinnerian conditioning), and many GIs attended college on the GI Bill. But the psychosurgery scene in the 2005 remake is less believable. It smacks of futuristic sci-fi, but not in the prophetic Philip K. Dick or Michael Crichton way. Psychosurgery does not parallel Russian-discovered Pavlovian conditioning. Pavlovian conditioning was a threat to Americans because of its Russian-ness, not necessarily because of its effectiveness. The Pavlov Institute of the first film directly addresses the perceived Communist threat of the Cold War.

The second film deserves some credit for attempting to update the movie by referencing neuroscience. But it doesn't deserve too much credit. Furthermore, at the time that the second *Candidate* was made, "invasive techniques" such as VNS (vagal nerve stimulation) or DBS (deep brain stimulation) or even TCMS (transcranial magnetic stimulation) were still experimental (and the experiments were showing that they are not yet especially effective at treating psychiatric symptoms, although DBS shows some promise for Parkinson's Disease).

The film fails for several reasons. Sci-fi strives to make spectators suspend disbelief, and so it relies upon a kernel of truth that merges fiction with fact. Sci-fi also functions as a conduit for debate about controversial treatments or strategies. These techniques are not useful enough to provoke debate about their use or misuse. Instead, the remake of *The Manchurian Candidate* mixes social critique with neuroscience that is not completely credible. It sends a muddled message — rather than a mixed message. A muddled message is the same as no message.

Thus, the remake abandons its political POV, and it was the political point of view that made the original *Manchurian Candidate* so memorable. The remake loses steam as a psychological thriller and reminds us of a rip-off of *Total Recall* (1990), which was based on Philip K. Dick's amphetamine-induced paranoid tale of a "brain bolus" that imparts false memories.

In *Total Recall* an attempt is made to implant an intra-nasal brain bolus into a government agent (Arnold Schwarzenegger). Schwarzenegger later became governor of California. Later still, he lost a reelection and has since returned to making movies. Schwarzenegger's character expects to enjoy false vacation memories of a trip to Mars, courtesy of a bolus that ablates his real memories. But a glitch occurs and changes the course of action.

The *Candidate* remake evokes memories of a sci-fi film whose star was elected to real-life political office. That is as close to political intrigue as the remade *Candidate* delivers. This coincidence makes us all the more disappointed that the later *Candidate* fails to offer any *real* links between sinister psychiatrists and political conspirators, as the first did.

Oddly enough, recent *Batman* comics from March 2010 add important commentaries about "invasive psychiatric treatment techniques" and TCMS (trans-cutaneous magnetic stimulation). Batman worries that "Big Pharma" will react badly to this new generation of "brain gadgets" and will retaliate when it looses market share.

In the meantime, we cannot conclude this section without paying homage to *The Cabinet of Dr. Caligari* (1919), the granddaddy of them all (in more ways than one). *Caligari* also comments on mad military MDs, even if it does so in a much more subtle and indirect manner.

This famous film about an evil psychiatrist appeared in the Weimar era, which immediately preceded the Nazis' rise to power. It is considered to be the ultimate example of German Expressionism. German Expressionism was a short-lived but immediately identifiable art form that was condemned as "degenerate" by the Nazis when they took power in 1933. Yet German Expressionism went on to live an everlasting life, thanks to *Caligari* and a few other surviving examples of this genre, and thanks to German Expressionism's influence on *film noir*.

It was a coincidence that a film about a sinister psychiatrist also turned out to be an epoch-making work of art, and a survivor of a world that would soon be destroyed or outlawed by the Nazis. Because of this coincidence, neither *Caligari* the film, nor Dr. Caligari the sinister psychiatrist and evil imposter, can be forgotten.

The Cabinet of Dr. Caligari (1919) owes some of its endurance to Siegfried Kracauer's book *From Caligari to Hitler* (1947). Kracauer argued (not completely convincingly but completely intriguingly) that Caligari and related cinematic characters foreshadowed Hitler's hypnotic-like hold over the German people and the German people's potential to respond to such a despotic dictator. More recent Holocaust historians have disputed the claim that the German people were mesmerized by the Nazis — but film historians still pay tribute to Kracauer in each and every book that is written about German Expressionism when they refute his ideas.

Even if we overlook Kracauer's role in reviving interest in Robert Weine's *Caligari*, we cannot overlook *The Cabinet of Dr. Caligari*'s cinematic accomplishments. One glance at this film assures us that *Caligari* the film deserves the recognition it has received. This silent classic is often erroneously assumed to be the first great film ever made, or the foremost example of German Expressionism, or the earliest horror film, or the first depiction of an evil psychiatrist.[4] None of those assumptions are true, but that does not detract from Caligari's stature. Other great films were made before Weine created *Caligari*. There were evil cinematic psychiatrists prior to 1919. Evil hypnotists of all persuasions were particularly plentiful in cinema's first two decades. Several excellent examples of German Expressionism exist (even though the Weimar era was short-lived). The horror genre was well-entrenched prior to *Caligari*. The subjects of sleep, dream, hypnotism, and psychosis were embedded in cinema before 1919.[5]

What did *Caligari* do? For one thing, the film introduced military metaphors in several different ways. *Caligari* plays upon the out-of-kilter angles of German Expressionism. Such distorted perspectives simulate the distorted experiences of a mad person (or at least they dramatize what we believe psychotics perceive when they are in the throes of psychosis). In German Expressionism, the actor, the scenery, the costumes, and the acting (the mise-en-scène) are accorded equal weight, and so they become indistinguishable from one another. Similarly, in a state of psychosis the individual feels that he has lost control of his environment and is no longer master of his surroundings. He is held captive by the circumstances that surround him.

There was a purpose to imposing this sense of psychosis on spectators: to remind them of the insanity of war in general and of the insanity of the Great War in particular. In the Great War, young soldiers were used as cannon fodder. They were sent to their deaths for no reason. Those who survived endured the deafening sounds of cannons and mortar fire and incessant shelling. They lay in trenches for years at a time, sometimes lying alongside decaying corpses. The motivations of the German Expressionists who simulated psychosis in their art were very different from the goals of the French Surrealists. The Surrealists admired the chaos of the dream state and sought to give the unconscious as much weight as waking consciousness. The German Expressionists disdained this chaos and lack of control — which is rather consistent with stereotypes about the German mindset and the need for order and structure.

Caligari's visuals are unforgettable, even if its convoluted story line is confusing. Its crooked streets, unsettling angles, and mismatched roofs were inspired by the art of Edvard Munch and Alfred Kubin, and by Max Reinhardt's theater. This imagery entered contemporary set design and children's books. Dr. Seuss books and Seuss's kaleidoscopic *5,000 Fingers of Dr. T* (1953) borrow from *Caligari*, as does Tim Burton's black comedy *Beetlejuice* (1988), which Burton made before he saw the silent film in its entirety.[vi]

Caligari was written by Carl Mayer and Hans Janowitz. Both writers had unique personal experiences that were woven into this cinematic masterpiece. The narrative is recounted by two gentlemen who sit on a bench, talking in a garden. Caligari is supposed to be the asylum director, but he turns out to be a fraud. He had been a carnival hypnotist and ends up as an insane asylum inmate himself. As hypnotist, he takes complete control of his somnambulist Cesare (played by Conrad Veidt, who went on to play the Nazi commander in *Casablanca* and related roles, even though he was a fervent anti–Nazi in real life). We must wait until the film's end to learn of Caligari the carnival performer's complex origins.

Early on we know that Caligari keeps the somnambulistic Cesare in a coffin when Cesare is not assisting Caligari in his sideshow performances of trance states. Caligari secretly commands Cesare to kill. He starts with a city clerk who humiliated Caligari when he applied for a permit to perform. The second victim of the somnambulist is the storyteller's friend, Alain.

Caligari cajoles Cesare into taking the life of the heroine, Jane. Cesare tries to stab Jane with a knife, but he cannot carry out Caligari's command because he has fallen in love with her. After Jane faints from fear when she sees the knife, Cesare swings her limp body over his shoulder, hoping to save her from Caligari's evil plans. But Cesare collapses and drops Jane, and then drops dead himself. Jane escapes as Cesare lies lifeless in the field. Then the truth is discovered.

By now, Jane's male companion Francis has grown suspicious of Caligari, and has secretly followed him and tracked him down to a nearby insane asylum. There he learns that Caligari is more than a carnival performer — Caligari is also the hypnotist who heads the asylum. Francis learns that Cesare was admitted to Dr. Caligari's asylum, where he was conscripted for Caligari's evil experiments. As the film ends, the asylum's staff realize that Caligari is psychotic and must be stopped. Caligari is straight-jacketed by his staff and stuffed into a cell.

When the story concludes, the film returns to its original framing device, where Francis the storyteller sits alongside another man in the garden. Spectators now learn that Francis — who portrayed himself as the story's hero — is also an asylum inmate. This revelation makes us wonder if this story really took place in real life or if was confined to Francis's imagination.

As imaginative as Caligari's plot is, it reflects a certain reality. One of the screenplay's authors, Janowitz, had good reason to portray the psychiatrist-hypnotist as the embodiment of evil. He received a dishonorable discharge from the military on psychiatric grounds. He subsequently blamed psychiatrists for disrupting his dreams, for cooperating with the war machine, and for turning unwitting soldiers into killing machines.

Carl Mayer, his collaborator, had other reasons to be bitter. Mayer's father had been a gambler who boasted about his grandiose gaming schemes, much as someone who suffers from bipolar disorder might. Mayer's father never received the help he needed (which wasn't available at that time, anyway). He lost his life to suicide instead, and Mayer lost a father. Mayer took charge of his younger siblings, and led an unusual and itinerant life from that point on, until he and Janowitz teamed up in Berlin.

To add to his angst, Mayer was walking through a Munich park one day when he saw a child disappear into the bushes. The next day he read that a little girl was murdered by a madman who was seen in that region. Wondering if she was the child he saw the day before, he mined his imagination and presumably unearthed memories of his father's tragic death, and then added details to flesh out Janowitz's core idea.

Kaes' 2009 book *Shell Shock Cinema*,[7] written by a professor of German and film studies, pushes the connection between *Caligari* and Janowitz's attitude-changing encounter with a military psychiatrist even further. Kaes argues that Dr. Caligari recollects not just Janowitz's personal experiences with an individual psychiatrist, but that the mad bad doctor represents the entire psychiatric profession. As Kaes points out, psychiatrists were among the most despised professionals of that era, since military psychiatrists forced shell shocked soldiers to return to the front during World War I and subjected them to painful treatments if they refused. The Great War had only recently ended when *Caligari* premiered, and such angry associations were part of the cultural currency. This link is not obvious to later generations.

From a film historian's point of view, this reinterpretation is important because it pushes the connection between *Caligari* and war back to the Great War (World War I), and disconnects *Caligari* from the Second World War (World War II) and from Hitler (a connection made by Siegfried Kracauer). Professor Kaes sees *Caligari* as a backward-looking film about the damage already done by World War I rather than as a forward-looking film that prophesizes the rise of the Third Reich.

This argument is convincing, and it is also intriguing when we consider some facets of the history of psychiatry. It is true that military psychiatrists had little sympathy for soldiers who fled the front. Doctors dismissed physical pain that had no verifiable source. They treated shell shock with a variant of Pavlovian conditioning, administering electric shocks to the soldiers as a form of "adversive conditioning" that was intended to discourage bad behavior. This approach shares similarities with the less extreme "rap on the knuckles" delivered by old-time schoolmasters who tried to enforce behavior codes.

Rather than offering the "rest and recreation" (R&R) that became standard during World War II, these mind doctors made medical treatment intentionally unpleasant so as to motivate enlistees to return to their posts. This technique was not always effective, and there were reports of suicides among soldiers who were subjected to such treatments. In less severe circumstances, these real-life sinister military docs simply made soldiers avoid psychiatric and medical care.

At least one man who encountered these doctors turned his experience into a century-shaping film. That man was Janowitz. However, we must credit Janowitz' talents, and not just his scarred psyche, for creating *Caligari*. It is ironic that Caligari's character was conceived by a man who was declared insane by a military psychiatrist, too insane to serve on the front at a time when deeply, deeply disturbed soldiers were deployed. Janowitz turned his grudge against war psychiatrists into a screenplay and work of art that endured far longer than his dismissive doctor.

Curiously, the strongest advocate of shocking soldiers was a psychiatrist who had as many sides to him as Caligari. Wagner-Jauregg conceived of this "treatment." He also pioneered "fever therapy" that relieved the "general paresis of the insane" of syphilis. His efforts helped persons suffering from advanced neurosyphilis. Neurosyphilis was endemic in 19th century Europe and put more people into mental asylums in that era than any other ailment. Penicillin's discovery was a long way's away, and arsenicals and mercury were incompletely effective. Fever therapy was the best treatment available.

It would be enough to contrast Wagner-Jauregg's cruel treatment of shell shocked soldiers with his amazing advances in the treatment of neurosyphilis. However, if we examine the details of "fever therapy" or "malarial therapy," the specifics start to sound less kind, even if the methods were ultimately effective. Syphilitics were intentionally infected with malaria, which causes shivering, chills and fevers that spike up to 105 degrees every three or four days.

The discovery of quinine, which cures some forms of malaria, made this painful treatment possible. When the treatment was completed, patients received quinine to stop the shakes and shivers produced by the malaria parasite. The malaria was cured, along with neurosyphilis. Clearly, this was not a pleasant treatment, but neurosyphilis was anything but pleasant, even if it did facilitate a large body of literature and philosophy in the late 19th century.

Around the same time, Freud was recommending psychoanalysis for the treatment of "shell shock." Freudian ideas about unconscious motivations exculpated shell shocked soldiers, who were deemed to be malingers at best, and cowards or even traitors at worst. It did not matter that administering psychoanalysis on the battlefield was impractical, to say the least. What mattered is that Freudian theories about the causes and cures of shell shock sounded so much more humane than Wagner-Jauregg's electric shocks. The fact that proximity to the front lines and direct exposure to "nerve gas" did not predict the risk of shell shock further fortified Freud's contentions that shell shock was largely psychologically-driven rather than physiological.

It is doubtful that many soldiers underwent psychoanalysis, either in the trenches or back home. No matter. There was no push to produce "evidence" to document the effectiveness of psychoanalysis. It is doubtful that anyone worried about whether or not analysis was effective. What mattered most is the fact that analysts did not push the poor soldiers back to the front, where they faced death or dismemberment. What mattered is that psychoanalysis was less painful than shocks — and that analysts showed sympathy for the soldiers' suffering.

Freud's reputation grew as a result of this debate with Wagner-Jauregg, who was the reigning authority in neuropsychiatry. Freud's so-called "Jewish science" won more adherents — for a surprisingly long time. After the Nazis took power, and several years before war was declared in Europe in 1939, Wagner-Jauregg applied for membership in the Nazi Party. He was rejected because his wife had been born Jewish. In contrast, Freud and his followers faced exile, if not death. Jewish doctors and psychoanalysis were expelled by the Reich, and Freud's books were burned. Freud's reputation was eventually sullied, but for very different reasons. Yet his spirit survived.

The Cabinet of Dr. Caligari will always be connected to the Second World War and to the rise of the Third Reich and Hitler's hypnotic power over the German people. Now we can see that *Caligari* owes just as much, if not more, to the First World War. But the madness captured by German Expressionism knows no bounds. The jagged lines and disjointed imagery and wacky perspective of the sets remind us of a world out of kilter, no matter which war is waged. The power of *Dr. Caligari* remains with us, as a reminder of sinister psychiatrists, sideshow charlatans, and murder machines, and so much more.

2

Hypnosis: Helping Hand or Evil Eye

Anyone who doubts the significance of hypnosis in either early silent cinema or in Weimar era–film from the 1920s should consult Siegfried Kracauer's book *From Caligari to Hitler* (1947). Kracauer's approach lays the groundwork for this chapter about hypnotists and sinister psychiatrists, but it is not the sole source of this study. As thought-provoking as Kracauer's work is, later generations of film scholars have redacted some of his central ideas.

In this chapter I turn back time and consider films that were made a decade or more before the Weimar era began in Germany in 1920. I also cross continents to see what was occurring in American film. I mention radio, which became commercialized in 1919 (the same year as *Caligari*), started to spread in the 1920s, and became wildly popular in the 1930s.

Since Kracauer's landmark *From Caligari to Hitler* serves as a springboard for this book, it is only fair that I address Kracauer's much-discussed and often-dismissed ideas. At the end of the chapter, I will explain why hypnotists make such good cinematic subjects, whether or not they are evil and whether or not they are psychiatrists.

Siegfried Kracauer — and his scholarship — would be interesting in their own right, even if he did had not published *From Caligari to Hitler* in 1947. Kracauer was a polymath who studied architecture in his native Germany, where he was born in 1889. He later earned a doctorate in engineering. He interfaced with important German intellectuals of his era, including Theodor Adorno, Walter Benjamin, and Ernest Bloch, and later became loosely connected with the Frankfurt School. Early on, Kracauer traveled in the same circles as renowned German-Jewish thinkers Martin Buber, Franz Rosenzweig, and Leo Lowenthal, partly because of his own interests and partly because of his brother's professional connections to Jewish theology.

Although he was formally educated in math and science, Kracauer published news articles from a fairly young age. By 1922 — when the first *Mabuse* movie premiered — Kracauer had become the leading film and literary editor of Frankfurt's best-known newspaper. He remained in that position until 1933, when Hitler became Chancellor of Germany and when the Nazis staged their book burning.

Kracauer's collected essays in *The Detective Novel* (1925) cemented his qualifications to comment on culture, current events, and the arts. *The Detective Novel* focused on everyday life in modern society. He went on to write about circuses, photography, films, advertising, tourism, city layout, and dance, all the while adding elements acquired from his multi-faceted education. His observations appeared in book form in *The Mass Ornament* in 1927, the very same year that talkies appeared. When we encounter elaborate descriptions of Dr. Caligari's carnival in *From Caligari to Hitler*, we see evidence of Kracauer's interest in and familiarity with circuses and carnival lights.

In 1930, Kracauer's *The Salaried Masses* examined the lifestyle and culture of the new class of white-collar employees who embraced Nazi ideology early on. This book shows the seeds of Kracauer's growing interest in the societal changes that catapulted Hitler to power. Unlike his more financially-minded colleagues, Kracauer does not dwell on the economic undercurrents that aided the rise of the Third Reich. Rather, Kracauer zeroes in on mass entertainment and movies and how they molded German mindsets. This approach prepares us for his overarching thesis in *From Caligari to Hitler*.

When Kracauer left his German homeland in 1933, he moved to Paris. In 1941, in the year the Nazi gas chambers began operating, he immigrated to the U.S., where he wrote his best-known (but not his last) work. Once in New York, Kracauer worked at the Museum of Modern Art (MOMA) and was commissioned to research "Propaganda and the Nazi War Film." This essay is appended to *From Caligari to Hitler: A Psychological History of the German Film* (1947). This book links the birth of Nazism to films from the Weimar Republic.

Initially, it seems that he conceived of this thesis after the war ended, as the enormity of the Holocaust became known through the Nuremberg Trials and other sources. One is tempted to see his study as his personal attempt to make sense of the maelstrom that drove him into exile and killed millions of his fellow Jews. But it is obvious that his earlier scholarship laid the groundwork for the electrifying ideas expressed in *From Caligari to Hitler*.

Kracauer focuses on the carnival hypnotist and charlatan psychiatrist Caligari, but he notes that Dr. Caligari was but one of several despotic characters of Weimar-era German film. Dr. Caligari hypnotizes his confederate Cesare and directs him to murder on command. In Kracauer's eyes, this recurring theme reflected the Germanic affinity for hypnotic dictators who mesmerize the masses and then mobilize them to participate in the worst atrocities of history. He claims that Dr. Caligari predicts Hitler's hypnotic appeal for the German populace, and implies that Germans were primed to comply with Hitler's genocidal policies. More recent scholarship confirms that the "masses" were not mesmerized nor compelled to support Hitler or the Nazis.

In spite of its glitches, many were fascinated by Kracauer's theory over the years, enough to ensure that the book remained in print for over sixty-five years to date. Later scholars proved that evil hypnotist themes are but a small fraction of Germanic themes from that era. Some, such as Elsaesser, use statistics to discredit Kracauer's arguments.[1] Still, Kracauer's book laid the foundations of modern film criticism. It also propels readers to rethink his thesis, view the films that he cites as evidence, and draw their own conclusions.

Kracauer's 1947 book about Caligari and Hitler gained more steam because it appeared at an especially sensitive time in history. The first edition was published shortly after World War II ended in 1945, and just after the Nuremberg Trials for judges, doctors and other Nazis were held between 1945 and 1946. As the world at large became aware of the extent of the Nazi horror, intellectuals in general and the Jewish community in particular struggled to understand how a cultured country like Germany had transformed itself into a murder machine.

Other important debates were taking place when *From Caligari to Hitler* surfaced in 1947. Those who survived the concentrations camps, or hid in forest hideaways or adopted secret identities during the war eagerly awaited visas that allowed them to enter the U.S. (legally). Visas became available when Congress passed the Displaced Persons Act of 1948.

Other survivors were hell bent on entering the still unborn state of Israel. Some were caught up in the 1947–1948 Civil War in Mandatory Palestine. Intriguingly, *From Caligari to Hitler* appeared shortly before the U.N. granted Israel statehood in 1948, when heated debates about establishing an official Jewish homeland in the aftermath of the Holocaust were in full swing. Diplomatic encounters between American president Harry Truman and Chaim Weizmann, future president of the State of Israel, were already underway in 1947.

Equally important, refugee Jewish psychoanalysts were appearing on American shores around the time that Kracauer's book appeared. Some analysts had arrived before the war, and some entered the U.S. via South and Central America. Hollywood's first psychoanalytic institute was established only one year earlier, in 1946, and presumably had extra reason for interest in Kracauer's innovative ideas about psychology and cinema. The psychoanalytic community became informed of *From Caligari to Hitler* when a favorable review appeared in a 1948 issue of the *Psychoanalytic Review* (1948. 35: 212–213).

The Cabinet of Dr. Caligari was already an important film, even before Caligari's name appeared in the title of this book. In 1947 it was still considered to be the finest film ever made. "Caligarisme" had become an expression unto itself, having been coined to promote German Expressionism to Frenchmen in the aftermath of World War I, when Frenchmen wanted nothing to do with anything German and would have rejected a title such as "German Expressionism." When *From Caligari to Hitler* arrived, the world was preoccupied with World War II and its aftermath.

The publication of Kracauer's English edition of *From Caligari to Hitler* renewed awareness of this silent classic and relic of the Weimar years. The concept of a sinister — and charlatan — psychiatrist and asylum director was etched into the public consciousness. Dr. Caligari and sinister psychiatrists became synonymous, and part of popular parlance. A year earlier, *Bedlam* (1946), with Boris Karloff, reminded moviegoers of the horrors of the mental asylums. A year later, *The Snake Pit* (1948), with Olivia de Havilland, reinforced the idea that mental institutions were almost as backward as they were two centuries earlier, when *Bedlam* was set. Albert Deutsch's hard-hitting book about *The Shame of the States* (1948) compared the inmates of contemporary American mental hospitals to survivors of concentration camps.

The mental health reform movement would soon be underway in America. Psychoanalysis was gaining steam on American soil in the late 1940s thanks to the influx of European Jewish émigré analysts, and thanks to America's admiration for continental education and their infatuation with those who lived on the same soil as Freud. Depicting asylum directors and psychiatrist-hypnotists as malicious murderers and subversive charlatans actually helped, rather than hurt, the cause of talk therapy and analytically-oriented treatment. For 1947 was the year when American psychiatry shifted gears and changed directions. As of 1947, more psychiatrists practiced in office settings than in institutions. This shift was unprecedented.

It was in the interest of office-based psychiatrists to encourage hostile portraits of their asylum-based predecessors and competitors. From our 21st century perspective, a film such as *The Cabinet of Dr. Caligari* belongs to the long list of anti-psychiatry diatribes seen on screen. But from the perspective of the psychiatric new guard of 1947, a film like this one supported the efforts of social reformers who took recent films such as *The Snake Pit* (1948) to heart.

Kracauer focused on German films between 1918 and 1933, although hypnotists starred on the silent screen well before the Weimar era. As I will explain at the end of the chapter, evil hypnotists held a special appeal for audiences of "primitive" cinema. As early as 1897, Méliès produced *The Hypnotist at Work* (*Le Magnetiseur*), shortly after the first moving pictures appeared. In the film, a young woman is put into a trance and disrobed.

Méliès was perfectly suited to showcase this subject, for the grand master of movies began his career as a magician. At a time when other luminaries of early film — Edison included — expected movies to become educational tools, Méliès took a different approach. Méliès realized that themes that worked well as carnival acts or sideshow stunts–as hypnosis did — were ideal subjects for cinema, which he viewed as a form of entertainment (and a magical one at that). In 1909, Méliès released another short, *The Hypnotist's Revenge*.

Other filmmakers followed suit. In the very same year, 1909, Pathé studios produced *The Hypnotic Wife* (1909) in France. In this film a wife casts a hypnotic spell on her husband. It seems that the French (and not just the Germans) were skilled at incorporating hypnosis themes early on. Although these French achievements partly contradict Kracauer's sweeping thesis about German audiences and their proclivities for movie mesmerism and social control, it makes perfect sense that the French would show such a fondness for hypnosis, given their history. For France had hosted fundamental experiments on hypnosis. The psychologist Pierre Janet (who trained and practiced as both a philosopher and a physician), the neurologist Jean-Martin Charcot and the proto-psychiatrist Hippolyte Bernheim were all French. When Freud wanted to study hypnosis (before he conceived of the concept of "psychoanalysis") he went to France. He even named his first-born son "Jean-Martin" in honor of Jean-Martin Charcot.

Charcot's dramatic lectures attracted artists and scientists alike. Symbolist artists sat in the lecterns alongside medical students and full-fledged physicians. Before World War I, French and French-speaking Belgian Symbolist painters featured "somnambulists" who glided around in dreamlike trances, their eyes half-closed as if peering into a dreamlike world that is inaccessible yet also perceptible. Occult symbols often appear in these enigmatic paintings.

The French were not the only ones to exploit hypnotic themes in film at this time. In 1909, the American filmmaker D.W. Griffith produced *The Criminal Hypnotist* (1909). Griffith was revered for his moviemaking skills but would be reviled for his racist beliefs. Curiously, 1909 was the year when Edison spoofed Edgar Allan Poe's story about the "lunatics taking over the asylum"; he titled that film *Lunatics in Power*.

The list goes on. In 1910, Lux made *Hypnotism*, a film about a girl who completes a robbery while under the influence of a (non-medical) hypnotist. The same year, Max Linder made a nine-minute film, *Max Hypnotisé* (*Max Hypnotized*), in France. In it, two servants hypnotize their master and order him to commit murder. This last film sounds like an obscure example, but it had stature in its era because it was created by Max Linder. Linder predated Charles Chaplin, Buster Keaton, and Harold Lloyd. Linder was as important a figure in early comedy as the three men mentioned above, even though he is little appreciated today. He helped create the classic style of silent slapstick comedy via his top-hatted dandy character named "Max."

By 1912, Max Linder was the world's highest-paid film star and had already begun directing. When the Great War erupted, Max was called up to fight; but he never fully recovered from his wartime experiences, including exposure to nerve gas. His life ended on a most unfunny note: he and his wife returned to France, made a suicide pact, and overdosed in 1925.

In the preceding years, other moving pictures about hypnotic crimes appeared in France and the U.S. Éclair's *Convicted by Hypnotism* (1912) focuses on a family murder, where a wife is hypnotized by her husband but accidentally kills her father. Around 1914, Warner's *The Hypnotic Violinist* ran a full 45 minutes and spanned three reels. This film revolves around a doctor's wife who is controlled by psychic powers — but this film is *not* about an evil doctor. Further "primitive" films about hypnosis were made in the first two decades of cinema.

Curse of the Hindoo Pearl (1912), *Curse of the Crimson Idol* (1914) and *Curse of the Scarabee Ruby* (1914) were parodied by Woody Allen in 2001 in *Curse of the Jade Scorpion* (2001). In Allen's 2001 film a stage hypnotist sends two dissimilar people into trance. He unites unlikely partners and convinces them to marry — until they learn that their magnetic attraction for one another in the face of personal repulsion had been a hoax orchestrated by the hypnotist.

Many silent films about hypnotists were made, although their titles do not necessarily mention the word "hypnosis." The word "doctor" or "psychoanalyst" or "psychiatrist" is also noticeably absent from most early movies about hypnosis — and for good reason. Most early films about hypnosis focus on family matters rather than medical ones. They suggest that families can entrance their relatives, take control of them, and force them to commit unconscionable acts. These films foreshadow psychological thrillers like *Gaslight* (1944). A decade later, hypnotist-psychiatrists take center stage and overshadow diabolical family members of early cinema. As we have seen, evil hypnotists on screen need not be psychiatrists.

However, a study about sinister cinema psychiatrists runs the risk of suggesting that the preponderance of evil film hypnotists are either psychiatrists, psychoanalysts or psychologists. That is simply not true. If anything, sinister psychiatrist-hypnotists are underrepresented when compared to generic hypnotists. Just because Dr. Caligari and Dr. Mabuse are so well-known does not mean that psychiatrists or psychoanalysts have exclusive rights on this dubious honor.

Curiously, one of the most important hypnotists in literary, theater, and film history has no medical or psychological training — but he is considered a "signifier" for the founder of psychoanalysis, Dr. Sigmund Freud. That hypnotist is named "Svengali," a man whose name still reverberates to this day. His subject is named "Trilby," and George du Maurier's 1894 novel *Trilby* is named for her. Trilby's name has faded from memory, but Svengali's legacy lives on. It's worth detouring for a moment, to understand the significance of Svengali and Trilby.

Along with cinema, which was invented in 1895, George Du Maurier's 1894 *Trilby* novel put the hypnotic eye in the public eye. *Trilby* made it to the stage, before resurfacing in several silent cinematic interpretations that predate *The Cabinet of Dr. Caligari*'s evil psychiatrist-hypnotist. The evil hypnotist "Svengali" usurps Trilby's will. Since then, Svengali's name came to denote "a persuasive person with evil intent." When we speak of someone with "Svengali-like powers," we recollect Du Maurier's hypnotist, who was neither psychiatrist nor physician.

Du Maurier's Svengali invokes another stereotype. We are told that Svengali is an "Oriental Israelite Hebrew Jew." That description is strikingly reminiscent of Freud, especially when we recall that Du Maurier's novel appeared just after Freud published his landmark paper on hypnosis. To make matters more interesting, Freud was categorized as an "Osjude" (Oriental Jew) because his family originated in Moravia (Bohemia) before moving westward to Austria.[2, 3]

Several early filmmakers brought Svengali's character to life on screen. Maurice Tourneur, father of the fabled horror film master Jacques Tourneur, was one of them. His film *Trilby* (1915) deserves mention, even if it did not earn many accolades. A successful screen adaptation of *Svengali* did not arrive until 1931, around the same time that Universal Pictures brought a string of 19th century movie monsters (and more contemporary monsters) to the silver screen. The 1931 version of Du Maurier's novel starred John Barrymore. That role catapulted Barrymore to fame. It also dispensed with the title *Trilby* to zoom in on the master hypnotist himself and cement an association between the words "evil" and "hypnotist."

Around the same time, another memorable movie about a hypnotist appeared. *Chandu the Magician* (1932) was followed by *The Return of Chandu* (1934). The *Chandu* films were adapted from a popular radio serial about a semi-mystical superhero, and later became movie serials. *Chandu* loosely follows in the footsteps of *The Shadow* and predates *Mandrake the Magician* (1934).

In the first *Chandu* horror meister Bela Lugosi plays the arch-villain Roxor, but then he plays Chandu in the Roxor-less *Return of Chandu*. Chandu is Causasian, but he wears an Oriental-style turban as he gazes into his crystal ball, creates illusions and makes doppleganger-like doubles of himself. Most importantly of all, Chandu fights evil and fends off the evil Roxor, the would-be world conqueror who tries to capture a scientist who possesses a ray gun that can destroy the world. As his costume implies, Chandu learned his powers from an Indian yogi. His feats parallel the super-powered skills of comic book heroes that emerged in the later 1930s.

Following the example set by Kracauer in his study of national psychology and cinema, I must point out that in the American-made *Chandu* films the protagonist stops the world destroyer, Roxor. Chandu uses "Orientalist" techniques that are as powerful as Caligari's or Mabuse's skills in hypnosis. In the German-made films that Kracauer alludes to the opposite occurs: the mass murderer succeeds, while his victims succumb, and no one stops anything.

This leads us into a discussion of *The Cabinet of Dr. Caligari*, which remains the most famous film about an evil hypnotist and evil psychiatrist. *Caligari* appeared in the early Weimar era, before the Nazis' rise to power. Kracauer argued that Caligari and related cinematic characters foreshadowed Hitler's hypnotic-like hold over the German people, and, conversely, that the German people were susceptible to hypnosis and authoritarian control. Today we don't accept Kracauer's thesis at face value. Nor do we agree that the German people were unwittingly "hypnotized" by Hitler, just like the suggestible masses in Weimar

In the first pre–Code *Chandu the Magician* (1932), the turbaned Bela Lugosi (far left) plays psychotic villain Roxor, who kidnaps a scientist, in an attempt to achieve world domination. To his right are Nadji (Irene Ware) and the "good" hypnotist Chandu (Edmund Lowe).

cinema. Most people who have visited Germany, and noted the impeccable attention to detail and exacting schedule of their mass transit, are likely to agree that Germans value obsessive traits.

Even if we overlook Kracauer's role in reviving interest in Robert Weine's *Caligari*, we cannot overlook *Caligari*'s cinematic accomplishments. One glance at this film assures us that *Caligari* deserves the recognition it has received. In fact, just a glance at film stills may suffice. Since the camera does not move along with the actors, the film stills capture the disjointed German Expressionist aesthetic just as much as the moving images.

This silent classic is often erroneously assumed to be the first great film ever made, or the foremost example of German Expressionism, or the earliest horror film, or the first depiction of an evil psychiatrist, or the best example of an evil hypnotist. None of that is true. What is true is that Dr. Caligari hypnotizes his somnambulist Cesare, whom he keeps in a coffin-like "cabinet," and commands him to kill, presumably without conscience. But Cesare falls in love with the young woman whom he is told to murder. He suffers a heart attack and dies rather than kill her.

Jane escapes from the grasp of Dr. Caligari and from his surrogate, Cesare, but her companion, Francis, has grown suspicious of Caligari and secretly follows him, tracking him down to a nearby insane asylum. Francis learns that Caligari is much more than a carnival performer. Caligari is also the hypnotist who heads the asylum. Caligari has followed the path of a long-dead mountebank named Caligari, who hypnotized subjects into committing murder. While in charge of the asylum, Dr. Caligari conscripted one of the patients, Cesare, and chose him as a subject for his evil experiments and as his surrogate to commit murder.

At the end, two important events occur. The asylum staff realize that Caligari is psychotic and must be stopped. So they capture him, stuff him into a straitjacket, and herd him into a cell. But then, when the story ends and the film returns to its framing device, we encounter Francis, the storyteller and supposed companion of Jane, and the presumptive hero who traced Caligari's roots and revealed him as an imposter. This time, Francis still sits besides another man in the garden, but we learn that the same Francis who painted himself as the story's hero is also an asylum inmate. This makes us wonder if this story ever took place in reality.

There is much debate about the framing device for this story, and there

Poster for *The Thousand Eyes of Dr. Mabuse* (1960), Fritz Lang's last Mabuse movie.

are heated discussions about the authorship of this framing device and the attitudes of the screenwriters towards its inclusion. Scholars have devoted their careers to tracking down these details. But no one denies that *Caligari* influenced other Weimar era films, which amplified the hypnosis theme. In fact, an entire book was written about *Caligari's Children* (1980).[4]

Caligari was completed in 1919, but it premiered in 1920 in Europe (and in 1922 in America). Soon after, Fritz Lang started his Dr. Mabuse series with *Dr. Mabuse, der Spieler* (*The Gambler*) (1922). Lang based his Mabuse series on popular novels by Norbert Jacques. Dr. Mabuse is clearly distinct from Dr. Caligari, although both are evil hypnotists and psychiatrists. In Lang's film, Dr. Mabuse stands at a podium and proudly announces that he is a psychoanalyst (and so implies that he is distinct from asylum superintendents like Dr. Caligari). Dr. Mabuse can cast hypnotic spells as deep as a sorcerer's sleep, and can control the wills of other humans.

Dr. Mabuse has many more "skills." He possesses a hypnotic-like charm that commands others to kill (both themselves and others). His gaze alone is enough to move men to suicide. He orchestrates schemes that are executed with impeccable *Mission Impossible*–like timing.

Dr. Mabuse begins as a hypnotist, but he hardly stops at hypnosis. He wears many masks, and he transforms into four different psychiatrists and into eleven other characters in all.

A year after the first Mabuse film, an unrelated film about hypnosis debuted in Austria: *The Lost Soul, or the Dangers of Hypnosis* (1923). This aptly-titled movie never gained the acclaim of *Caligari* or *Mabuse*, but it fortified Kracauer's theory about evil Germanic hypnotists.

Lang's Mabuse movies transitioned into talkies and were dubbed into English when they played for English-speaking audiences in the U.S. The series continued through 1970, when other directors made spin-offs of the Mabuse theme. But the Mabuse movies gained little traction among American audiences, which were not accustomed to such long films, and had little interest in allusions to specific German economic conditions in the Mabuse movies.

Still, the last days of Lang's Mabuse series touched a nerve among some film fans and anti-psychiatry activists. Lang's last Mabuse movie (made in 1960) added to the counter-culture's antagonistic attitude toward psychiatry, and intensified opposition to insane asylums and state control of the mentally ill. Mabuse movies (not all of which were made by Lang) turned mind-controlling doctors and other demagogues into objects of suspicion during the 1960s and strengthened theories coined by the likes of the French philosopher Michel Foucault during those same years. Those who were interested in R.D. Laing, the Scottish-born anti-psychiatrist who disliked the term "anti-psychiatry"[5] but nevertheless openly opposed what he deemed to be authoritarian control by psychiatrists, could find support for their suspicions in the Mabuse movies

When the New York Film Festival at Lincoln Center screened the 1922 *Doktor Mabuse* movie in 1973, a new (and more skeptical) generation was exposed to the Fritz Lang legacy. The film was praised by critics, and Mabuse seemed headed for a rebirth. Young Americans had seen protests and police riots at the 1968 Democratic Convention in Chicago, and watched the trial of the Chicago Seven, and chanced upon any number of other student uprisings of the 1960s. Comparisons between American authoritarianism and Nazi Germany were familiar to them. Viewing the original *Doktor Mabuse* movie made more sense at that point in time, but apparently did not make enough sense to generate large-scale or enduring appreciation of Fritz Lang.

Still, for film aficionados, Lang's *Doktor Mabuse* films are almost as famous as Weine's *Caligari*, not only because of their artistic and cinematic merit, but also because Mabuse, much like Caligari, became inseparable from Nazi era events that haunt us to this day. The fact that both films feature an evil psychiatrist and hypnotist may be the least important reason why these two cinematic characters retain such important holds on film history.

Even Lang's life story is intertwined with World War II intrigue (although some details of that intrigue may be as fictionalized as his film plots). The Viennese-born Lang claimed that Goebbels asked him to head the German film industry after *The Testament of Dr. Mabuse* premiered in 1933. Lang declined this offer, which was later accepted by Leni Riefenstahl. Lang's biography becomes more entangled from that time forward. The story he told of his escape from Berlin is as dramatic as the escapades he chronicles in his espionage films.

According to Lang, but not according to evidence found after the fact, Lang boarded a Paris-bound train in the middle of the night after this encounter with Goebbels (just as his *Ministry of Fear* characters might have done). Because his mother (Pauline Schlesinger)

Poster for *Die 1000 Augen des Dr. Mabuse* (1960), Fritz Lang's last Mabuse movie, a low budget, West German horror film made after he left Hollywood to return to his native Europe.

was born Jewish but converted to Catholicism when Fritz was ten, Lang felt endangered by Nazi policy on "Jewish blood." So he left his fortune, his art collection, and his wife behind when he headed to Paris, where he had studied art after World War I. His wife and former collaborator divorced him after he left. She remained in Berlin, where she became a Nazi filmmaker.

After Lang arrived in America he continued his long and illustrious cinematic career, with some caveats. His directorial style was not welcomed by American actors, who were put off by the excesses that their European counterparts had tolerated. For instance, it was said that Lang fired a gun in the studio to induce authentic expressions of fear on his actors' faces. He also set fire to an actress' skirt to ensure that she would scream in true terror. Still, his grounding in Weimar-era German Expressionism added flair to the *film noir* style that evolved in America.

Film noir, which borrowed from German Expressionism, remains remarkably popular today, more than half a century later. Lang's last Mabuse movie contributed to the counterculture's questioning of psychiatric and political authority, and so deserves a prominent place in the history of psychiatry and anti-psychiatry. Those anti-psychiatry sentiments are undergoing yet another mutation at this very moment, thanks in part to Senator Grassley's indefatigable efforts to untangle the links between Big Pharma payoffs, academic psychopharmacology researchers, and practicing psychiatrists. Dr. Marcia Angell's more recent 2011 two-part critique of psychopharmacology in the *New York Review of Books* added more fuel to the fire, and will be discussed in detail in the chapter on "Unethical Experimentation."

Yet it was Lang' s second Mabuse movie, *The Testament of Dr. Mabuse* (1933), that remains most important to world history. *Testament* expresses Nazi ideology through the mouth of a madman and thereby equates Hitler and Nazism with madness. Lang's film was soon banned by the Reich, who recognized that the madman-spokesperson made a mockery of Hitler. Creepy references to shower scenes and poisonous gases are eerily similar to actual events that came to pass in 1941 when the Germans herded Jews and gypsies into gas chambers that had been built for mentally and physically handicapped persons whose lives were deemed to be "not worth living." Such assessments were made by German psychiatrists. After clergymen protested the gassing of mental patients, the gas chambers were repurposed and used for Jews and gypsies.

Kracauer thought that Lang's evil hypnotist-psychiatrist Mabuse mirrored Hitler's hypnotic control over the German masses, just as Dr. Caligari did. Kracauer wrote from a psychological/sociological point of view and argued that movies open windows into the minds of the masses that pay money to patronize movie houses. However, we know that *The Testament of Dr. Mabuse* (1933) was made in the same year that Hitler assumed power and became Chancellor of Germany. We also know that Nazi leaders such as Goebbels watched the film *before* the Nazis built death camps and gas chambers, and might have been indirectly influenced by the media. On the other hand, scholars note that English translations of the original German dialogue are inexact or perhaps embellished, and may have been altered to reflect our expectations of that era. After viewing this unsettling film, we are left to wonder if Kracauer was completely correct, partly correct, or if this film (and a few other movies and literary works) ignited deadly ideas that were already simmering in evil Nazi minds.

The Mabuse films deserve a category of their own, even if they were underappreciated in America. The sinister hypnosis scenes in Mabuse movies are but one aspect of an entire armamentarium of evil. In the decades that follow the most compelling Mabuse film from 1933, we find several films about psychiatry, psychoanalysis, and hypnotism, and we find even more movies about evil hypnotists that bear no connection to the medical or mental health world.

Our closest American comparison to Dr. Mabuse is Dr. Hannibal Lecter. Dr. Lecter has starred in five films to date, as compared to the dozen Mabuse movies and spin-offs and remakes. But Hannibal's cinematic career is not yet complete. Although Hannibal earns most of his filmic fame from his cannibalism (and his combined cooking and surgical skills), Hannibal is also adept at hypnotism. Harris, author of the books that inspired the Hannibal films, is equally adept at dreaming up gut-wrenching examples of Hannibal's use of medical hypnotism.

Harris' books detail Hannibal's use (and misuse) of hypnotism, but hints alone remain in the currently available film versions of the books. In *Hannibal* we meet Mason Verger, the pedophile who underwent court-ordered treatment with Dr. Lecter. The film tells us that Lecter drugged Mason before ordering him to cut off his face and feed his flesh to the dogs. The book attributes this gruesome scene to a combination of hypnosis and hallucinogenic drugs. I will flesh out this disturbing episode in the chapter on "Diabolical Drugging." For now, though, it's worth mentioning that Hannibal's use of hypnotism *in this particular instance* is morally ambiguous, in that he uses his skills on a deserving victim instead of an innocent bystander. Dr. Mabuse shows none of Dr. Lecter's discretion and victimizes anyone available.

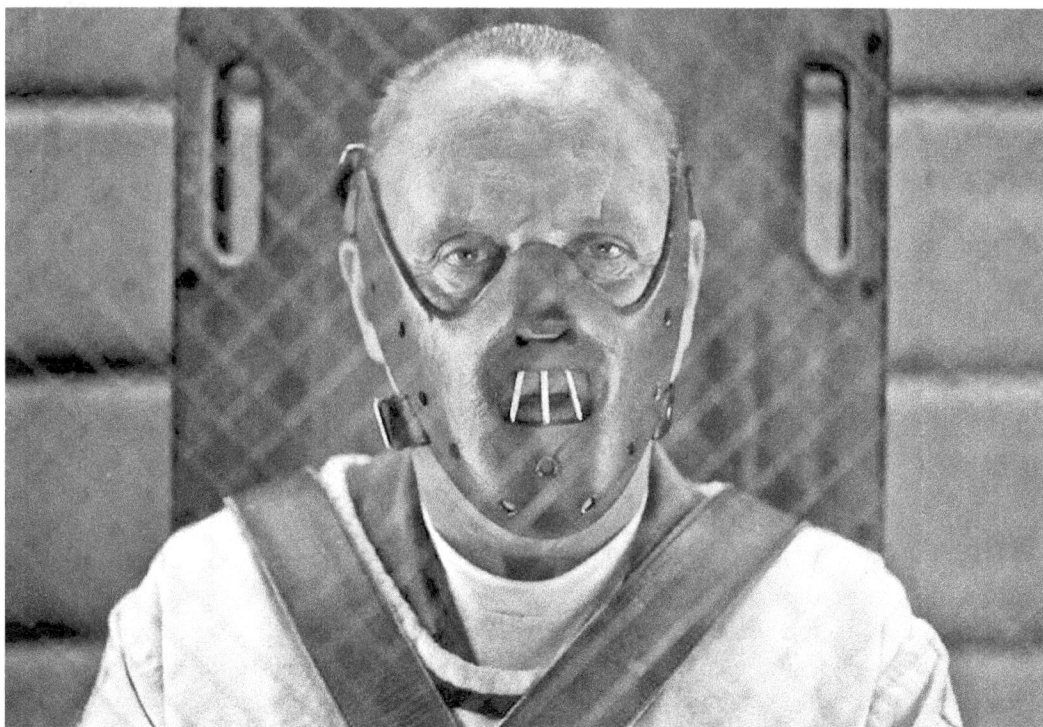

In the Academy Award–winning *The Silence of the Lambs* (1991) the cannibalistic Dr. Hannibal Lecter (Anthony Hopkins) is so dangerous that his face and teeth are muzzled.

It is important to note that many of the most memorable post–World War II psychiatrist-hypnotists are *not* evil. When we discuss *The Manchurian Candidate* (1962), we see that the evil hypnotist-psychologist is a Communist with links to Manchuria, Soviet Russia, and North Korea. His political connections are more significant in the film than his clinical techniques. In the aftermath of Kracauer's book *From Caligari to Hitler*, we see a discernable shift in the depiction of sinister psychiatrist-hypnotists in cinema. Considering how clearly Kracauer linked hypnotism with Nazism in his 1947 book, which was well-received at the time, it would have been politically improper — and probably economically devastating — to portray ordinary psychiatrists or psychoanalysts as evil (Nazi-like) hypnotists in the decade or two that followed.

Even before Kracauer's book appeared in 1947 we find a positive portrayal of hypnosis conducted by a psychoanalyst in a Hitchcock film. In *Spellbound* (1945) psychoanalyst Dr. Peterson (Ingrid Bergman) uses hypnosis, dream analysis, maybe some "insight," and some of the still popular concept of "women's intuition" to solve a murder mystery. In doing so, she exculpates an innocent man who just happens to be handsome and a potential romantic partner.

Two years later one of the most damning depictions of "psychologists" appears on screen in the *noir* classic *Nightmare Alley* (1947). Oddly enough, this gripping carnival film bypasses antiquated hypnotic themes and focuses on dream analysis and old-fashioned con games.

Another two years pass, and in 1949 we encounter a rather different and double-edged film about hypnosis. That film is *Whirlpool* (1949). *Whirlpool* pits a charlatan-hypnotist who works in a hotel against a psychiatrist-hypnotist. The psychiatrist-hypnotist is not sinister; he is merely stupid. Perhaps he is simply blinded by love, like Ingrid Bergman's Dr. Peterson, who abandoned her hospital post to pursue a handsome young doctor (Gregory Peck) in *Spellbound*.

If *Whirlpool* reminds us of *Spellbound*, that should not be surprising, because *Whirlpool* and *Spellbound* were written by the same screenwriter: blacklisted author Ben Hecht. Hecht used the name of "Barstow" in the McCarthy era when he and other left-leaning writers were hounded by government inquests and forced to go underground. Hecht and others of similar political persuasions either couldn't get any work at all or were compelled to work clandestinely, toiling under assumed names and accepting a fraction of their usual fees.

Like his screen characters, Hecht lived a double life that was riddled with deceit and fear of betrayal. Even though *Whirlpool* and *Spellbound* were made by different directors, both films concern themselves with double-dealing doctors, deceptive hypnotists, and supposed healers who kill competitors as readily as they cure patients. In each film a psychiatrist shows unwavering love for the would-be victim. This bond propels their quest for truth and drives the plot.

Although it can be classified as a *film noir*, *Whirlpool* (1949) is also an excellent example of the melodramas or "woman's pictures" that soared in popularity around World War II, when most men were away at war and women went to movies. These genre films were marketed to sad and lonely women, and were so super-sentimental that they were also called "weepies." In Otto Preminger's *Whirlpool*, Gene Tierney plays a beautiful woman who is married to a prominent psychoanalyst, Dr. Sutton (Richard Conte). Unbeknownst to her well-credentialed husband, Ann Sutton (Gene Tierney) is a kleptomaniac. The action starts when she is caught stealing jewelry from an exclusive department store.

A stranger (Jose Ferrer) witnesses her deed and speaks up for her, presumably in her defense. He persuades the store owners not to prosecute, assuring them that he knows that she is married to a wealthy and respected psychiatrist who can pay her store credit. The audience knows that the observant stranger is a hypnotist and an astrologer who caters to high society and operates out of a hotel office. This stranger claims to cure people who suffer from the same psychological maladies that the psychiatrist-husband treats under more respectable and socially-sanctioned circumstances.

The charlatan-hypnotist (Ferrer) assures Sutton (Tierney) that he can cure her compulsion to steal. Fearing that her husband will learn about her hidden secret and that his career will be jeopardized if her kleptomania and criminal acts become public, Tierney accepts the stranger's seemingly gracious offer. She agrees to meet him at his hotel for hypnosis sessions. Hotel staff take note of her visits to the suite of the handsome hypnotist and presume that the two are conducting a clandestine affair behind her husband's back.

However, the hypnotist is smarter than the hotel staff, and he is much smarter than Ann Sutton. He almost outsmarts the psychoanalyst-hypnotist husband, but not quite. The audience is smarter than everyone thanks to the "omniscient narration" that tells spectators more than the other characters know. It turns out that the hotel hypnotist plans to murder his mistress, who threatened to turn him in to the police as a thief.

There is another missing piece that is important to the plot. The hotel hypnotist knows that his mistress was treated by Tierney's psychiatrist-husband and suspects that she disclosed his misdeeds to the doctor. The hotel hypnotist also knows that the psychiatrist-hypnotist records his patients' sessions, and so he probably has proof of the hypnotist's crimes.

The hypnotist also knows that he needs an alibi if he wants to murder his mistress. Conveniently, he plans to hypnotize Gene Tierney and command her to steal her husband's recordings so that he can destroy the proof of his crimes. He uses hypnotic suggestions that she will not remember once she reenters the waking state, and instructs her to go to his mistress's home on the very night that he plans to murder the mistress himself. That will turn Gene Tierney into the prime murder suspect, especially since she has been seen entering the hypnotist's hotel room repeatedly during a supposed affair. The hypnotist expects the police to conclude that the psychiatrist's wife murdered his other mistress out of jealousy.

The action isn't over yet, for the hotel hypnotist must make his own alibi air-tight. So the hotel hypnotist feigns abdominal pain on the same day of the planned murder. He is admitted to a hospital and scheduled for an emergency appendectomy. The hospital staff visit his room regularly and record their observations in their charts, and unwittingly provide written proof of his whereabouts on the night of the murder. After all, who would suspect that a post-operative patient could leave his bed, much less leave the hospital, to commit a murder, especially since his nurses sign his record each shift, and especially since he is supposedly in so much pain after the procedure?

The hotel hypnotist has taken all of this into account. He hypnotizes himself to the point that he feels no pain. He then crawls out of the hospital window, drives to his mistress's home and murders her moments before the psychiatrist's wife arrives. He has stuffed pillows in his hospital bed to make it seem that he is sleeping soundly. No one is the wiser, except for the spectators, who have seen every step of the crime. Oddly enough, the psychiatrist-husband is convinced of his wife's innocence, no matter what. Yet the psychiatrist's wife is unsure if she committed the murder, for she saw a dead body lying in front of her just as she awakened.

The psychiatrist is suddenly suspicious, for reasons that are unclear. (After all, he never suspected his wife's kleptomania, and he never suspected that she sought treatment from a charlatan.) So he uses his hypnosis skills on his wife, sends her into a trance, and unearths buried memories of her encounters with the charlatan-hypnotist. At the same time, he learns where she hid his records while she was in her previous trance. Together they stake out his office and wait for the sham-hypnotist to return to retrieve the incriminating records. His hunch proves correct.

In the end, good wins out over evil, and the hypnotist is caught while trying to retrieve the records. He is shot dead on the spot. The kleptomaniac wife is cleared of murder charges, and the psychiatrist-husband reclaims his wife, his career, and his professional credibility. (His murdered patient, however, does not reclaim her life.) This twisted plot, as incredible as it is, turns into a compelling murder-mystery with twists and turns that recollect both *Spellbound* and Ben Hecht's double life.

Whirlpool (1949) shares features with *Spellbound* (1945), but it stands apart from *Nightmare Alley* (1947) in several important ways. Both films concern themselves with showmen-hypnotists and psychiatrist-hypnotists, but *Whirlpool* calls attention to the differences rather than the similarities. It casts the medical hypnotist as the hero and the showman-charlatan as the villain. Yet all is not black and white. Although the psychiatrist eventually comes out ahead in *Whirlpool*, his professional credibility is not unimpeachable. In the same way, even though Bergman's Dr. Peterson solves the murder-mystery, her professional integrity is sullied in *Spellbound* because she shirks her hospital duties in her quest to exculpate Gregory Peck.

On a related note, we know that the *Whirlpool* psychiatrist-hypnotist can be conned as easily as his wife (or, should I say, by his deceptive wife). And so we realize that he is not particularly perceptive, even though he has many impressive academic credentials. How could he have lived with this woman for years without once suspecting that she leads a double life and suffers from serious psychopathology? True, he is a good husband and a good hypnotist, and he was correctly convinced of her innocence after she was framed for murder. But he is a failed and flawed man, and an unimpressive psychoanalyst, in spite of the certificates on the wall.

We marvel at the skills of the hotel hypnotist, who is not only a superb strategist but who also hypnotized himself after surgery. We cannot avoid smirking at the psychoanalyst's shortcomings. If he is blind to his wife's illness, how much does he miss in his patients who spend so much less time with him? The mixed message about psychoanalyst-hypnotists in *Whirlpool* is not so hard-hitting as the direct condemnation in *Nightmare Alley* or *Spellbound*. But the message is unsettling just the same and is readily grasped by spectators.

Exactly one decade after *Nightmare Alley*'s debut (1947), a very different film about psychiatric hypnosis appeared — *The Three Faces of Eve* (1957). *The Three Faces of Eve* became the "poster film" for the Golden Age of psychiatry, when mind doctors were as idealized as medieval saints, Hindu holy men, and other religious miracle workers and healers. The psychiatrists in *The Three Faces of Eve* are all good, and their techniques, which include (but are not limited to) hypnosis, are also all good. However, the protagonist and the patient,

Eve, is not all good. She is either Eve White or Eve Black, before her personality is blended by her psychiatric treatments, and she decides to leave her husband and start a new life.

The Three Faces of Eve has none of the subtleties of Hitchcock's *Spellbound*, which showcases his signature plot twists and highlights his ability to paint character portraits in many different hues. Hitchcock's psychiatrists — and his other characters — are colored by a palette that spans the rainbow — even though the film itself is black and white. Yet *Spellbound*, with all its delicious subtleties, is relatively unknown, while the much more accessible and straightforward *Three Faces of Eve* still has strong name recognition more than fifty years after its premiere.

The Three Faces of Eve is best understood in context with other films of its era, instead of merely citing it as proof of the filmmaker's blanket support for psychiatrist-conducted hypnosis. In the short time between 1957 and 1963, cinema psychiatrists were portrayed sympathetically and idealistically. They were saviors who cured patients effortlessly. Even electroshock therapy received kudos in those years, as we will see with *Fear Strikes Out* (1957) in an upcoming chapter on "Shock Schlock."

During the interval known as "the Golden Age of Psychiatry," however, showmen-hypnotists who are not psychiatrists or psychoanalysts are portrayed badly, perhaps worse than Dr. Mabuse (if that is possible), and surely worse than the gangly Dr. Caligari. Even the murderous hotel hypnotist in *Whirlpool* pales in comparison to the wielder of *The Hypnotic Eye* (1960).

On the surface, *The Hypnotic Eye* (1960) is a sensationalistic and sadistic film. Yet it is a film with a message. That message does not dilute the impact of the movie's many gory and gruesome scenes. The message says little to nothing about psychiatric or medical hypnotism per se; *The Hypnotic Eye* comments on consumerism and the advertising industry's hold on '50s era women, who had undergone a tremendous transformation as a group since the Rosie the Riveter "war effort" days. Many women had become housewives after the war. They stayed home during the day and were able to watch TV, which recently arrived in most American homes by 1954.

Even though *The Hypnotic Eye* seems misogynistic because of the many mutilated women scenes, it can also be seen as a proto-feminist film because it condemns the transformation of post-war women from producers (like Rosie) into consumers. It fires a warning shot at those who do not heed its warnings. A few years later, Betty Friedan would publish similar messages, sans the sensationalism, in *The Feminine Mystique* (1963), which spearheaded the women's movement.

The Hypnotic Eye predates *The Feminine Mystique*, but it postdates Vance Packard's much-discussed book about *The Hidden Persuaders* (1957) and references that book. The pre-credits sequence parodies an often-aired television shampoo commercial and shows an unfortunate woman "washing" her hair in the flames of a gas stove. Other scenes comment on the belief that buyers are magically transformed by consumer goods. Here the cosmetics sold through "hypnotic" television commercials turn into tools for scarification and self-mutilation. We also find references to the "willful women" of late forties post-war films, especially since the detective's girlfriend suspects the culprit before he does but still needs his help to survive.

In *The Hypnotic Eye* a series of women become victims of self-inflicted harm that occur while they seem to be in a hypnotic trance. One woman puts her face in a fan, emerging

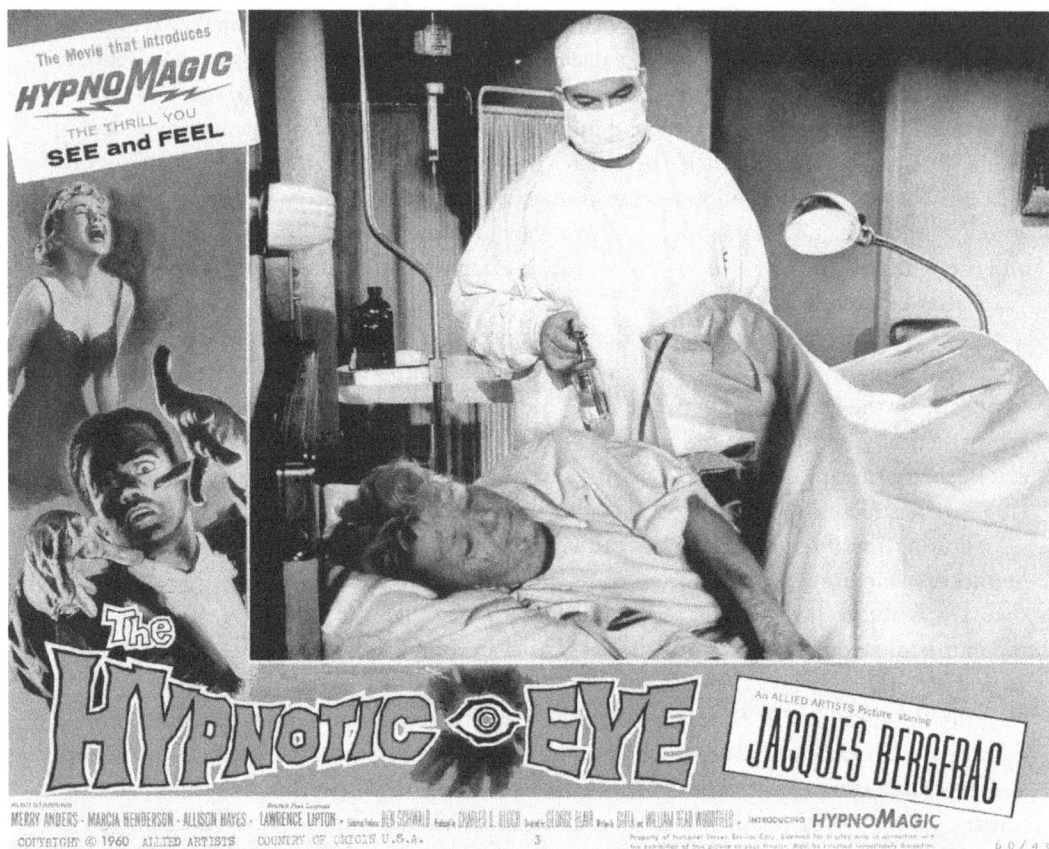

This lobby card for *The Hypnotic Eye* (1962) shows a masked and gowned doctor standing behind a reclining woman who disfigured herself beyond recognition because of hypnotic commands.

blind and scarred. Another washes her face in acid. And so on and so forth. These hypnotized women on screen are quite different from today's self-injurious women with "borderline personality disorders" or "eating disorders," or women who seek out cosmetic surgery because they have socially-conditioned "body dysmorphic disorders." Or are they all that different? A second viewing of this movie makes us think twice about today's relationship with "yesteryear."

There is no doubt that several victims suffer serious damage. The question about how such accidents occur remains open. A detective interviews each woman. Each one denies any motive, and each denies any encounters with hypnotists, even when asked. Yet the detective finds souvenirs from a stage hypnosis act in the bags of two of the victims and begins to suspect that something is amiss.

Working with his girlfriend, he traces the tragedies to a stage hypnotist named Desmond. To test their theories, his girlfriend has herself hypnotized. She barely escapes being scalded in her bath — which she herself made extra hot while in a trance. Luckily, her boyfriend appears at the last minute and saves her from the fate endured by the other women they interviewed.

Like the detective, Desmond works with a beautiful female partner. At the end, the detective and the girlfriend pry the truth from the hypnotist's helper. Just before she jumps to her death, she rips off a rubber mask to reveal her hideously scarred face that has been hidden beneath the mask. It is she who has goaded her husband into hypnotizing beautiful women who visit their act. It is he who plants hypnotic suggestions that tell them how to destroy their beauty and themselves.

The Hypnotic Eye is classified as a horror film, even though it revolves around important intellectual ideology. That is hardly uncommon. Horror films often have more to say than meets the eye, and this movie is an excellent example of the philosophical stream of horror films.

Another movie about hypnosis came on the heels of *The Hypnotic Eye* a mere two years later — *The Manchurian Candidate* (1962). That film is in a class of its own, and is difficult to out-class. *The Manchurian Candidate* remains the best film on hypnosis, brainwashing, and mind control that has ever been made. Many say that it is one of the best films of *any* kind ever made. The remake of the original, however, does not earn that praise.

The original *Manchurian Candidate* first screened in 1962 in the same year that the field of "clinical psychology" was officially approved. Clinical psychologists could now conduct therapy, perform hypnosis, and do many functions that were previously reserved for medically-trained psychiatrists. Until 1962, American psychologists conducted psychological testing or performed research or advised the industry, but they did not offer direct "clinical care" or treatment for patients. (Practice policies in the U.S. are not necessarily the same as policies elsewhere.)

It is unclear if that particular coincidence was particularly important to this film. It *is* clear that several other significant chronological correspondences can be identified, with respect to the Cold War, Korean Communist brainwashing, and even the integration of the American military in 1952. Suffice it to say that *The Manchurian Candidate* compares dream analysis to hypnosis, brainwashing and behavioral conditioning. Most significantly, behavioral conditioning is also known as Pavlovian conditioning, in recognition of the Russian physiologist Pavlov, who won the Nobel Prize in 1904 for his studies of conditioned salivation reflexes in dogs.

It cannot be stressed enough that behaviorism — or behavioral conditioning — was invented by Russians, even though it was later amplified by American scientists such as Skinner and Watson. Behaviorism was preferred by the Soviets in particular, for several reasons. First of all, they took pride in the Nobel Prize–winning studies of their Russian compatriot, Pavlov. Plus, the Communists were unconcerned with non-material concepts such as the "unconscious." They took their cues from Karl Marx, who espoused economic determinism, imputed personal problems to external economic forces, and deflected focus away from personal psychology, which Americans appreciated.

The Soviet Communists also valued the collective rather than the individual. Psychoanalytic ideas in particular, and psychology in general, revolve around the individual rather than the group. In short, the Soviet Russians — and other Communist-influenced cultures — had every reason to support Pavlov, and just as many reasons to avoid the "free associations" or emphasis on individualization preferred by psychologists from the Western World. Even though Freud first forged his ideas about depth psychology and psychoanalysis in Austria, it was in the Americas (both North and South) that his theories made their greatest mark, at least for a while.

In the 1960s — and in some places as early as the 1920s — many university-based American academians refused to include psychoanalysis in their college psychology classes because they found those theories to be too unscientific to deserve a place in the curriculum. (Psychoanalysis shifted to philosophy courses.) Psychologists advocated behaviorism instead, which was based on experimental evidence rather than on armchair hypotheses. During the time when *The Manchurian Candidate* was made, the behaviorists warred with the psychoanalysts as fervently as the psychoanalysts war with the neuropsychiatrists or psychopharmacologists today. The battle between the behaviorists and the analysts is just one of many dualities in this film.

The Manchurian Candidate owes its intensity to its plot, its many layers of allusions, its dualities, and its all-star cast (that includes Frank Sinatra and Angela Lansbury, among others). *Candidate* was well-timed — too well-timed, it turned out. *The Manchurian Candidate* is also connected, chronologically at least, to the JFK assassination in 1963. Legend says that it was pulled from theaters for fear that it inspired the Kennedy killing — which occurred on November 22, 1963, more than a year after the film's initial release in October of 1962. Rumors said that the 1963 assassination of civil rights activist Medgar Evers also played into the decision to take the film out of circulation. Its connection to the torrid political events of the early Civil Rights era, and to the start of a string of political assassinations in America, only added to its allure. *Candidate* went out of sight but was never out of mind.

Its star, Frank Sinatra, never lost faith in the value of the film and pushed to make it available once again. *Candidate* was officially re-released in 1988, over a quarter of a century later. By then, the political and cultural climate had shifted dramatically, and the film's symbolism was not as transparent to the average spectator as it might have been in 1962. Just the same, *Candidate* was very well-received the second time around, and was eagerly anticipated by audiences, especially since it had achieved cult status during its long imposed absence.

This complicated film was discussed in detail in the previous chapter, "Mad Military Mind MDs," and will be referenced in the next chapter, "Sweet and Sour Dreams." The chapter on "Lobotomies and the Like," will cover the remake of *The Manchurian Candidate*. The remake pales in comparison to the original, and omits the riveting brainwashing scenes that carried such political connotations. Instead, it updates the action by substituting brain implants for the hypnosis scenes of the 1962 version. It destroys the irreplaceable historical points of the first *Candidate* in its attempt to be current.

In short, in the original *Manchurian Candidate*, captive soldiers are hypnotized by an Asian man who speaks with an accent and sports the uniform of the "Manchurian" Communists. He identifies himself as a doctor — but he is not a physician. Rather, he is a psychologist of a very specific persuasion. He is no Freudian wannabe. He is a behaviorist, through and through. The Manchurian psychologist stands in front of larger-than-life portraits of Mao and Stalin. This tells us that he "stands for" the pillars of Communism. By implication, he denounces the values of the "free world," which include the "free associations" used in both dream analysis and psychoanalysis.

All members of the captured platoon are hypnotized, including Frank Sinatra, who leads the unit as Captain Marco. But it is Raymond Shaw (Laurence Harvey) who enters the deepest trance, and is taught to kill on command, as planned. When told to kill the platoon mate whom he dislikes the least, Shaw first chooses Captain Marco (Sinatra), but he is redirected by his Manchurian mentor, who tells him that "he needs the captain to give him his medal." So Shaw strangles another soldier with a scarf. His fellow soldiers sit by and watch, yawning throughout the horrifying performance, unaware that they are also in a trance.

The message of the movie is not that hypnosis per se is evil — even though evil hypnotists like Dr. Caligari were compared to Nazis in the not-too-distant past. Rather, hypnosis is evil when used as a Communist tool and employed to suppress the Free World and free will. It is evil when it interferes with free speech and other pillars of American culture, and when it promotes the platform of the Red Shirts (Communists) or the Brown Shirts (Nazis). Because the sinister psychologist in this film is an "other" — he is Manchurian rather than American, and he is a Communist rather than an advocate of democracy — the anti-psychiatry stance is softened.

However, since so many academians in the 1960s taught behaviorism in their college classes, the message is that the teachings of those college professors should also be suspect. The film implies American universities could contain Communist influences and might foment left-leaning sentiments — as indeed happened at Berkeley, with its Free Speech movement, and elsewhere. The shadow cast by Senator McCarthy is still visible in *The Manchurian Candidate.*

To conclude this chapter, let's turn back to the beginning to see why hypnosis became a favorite subject of early film, and why hypnosis, like dreams, is indelibly linked to the silver screen. To quote the much-quoted Marshall McLuhan, "The medium is the message." If the medium is hypnotic, then movie themes about hypnosis are apropos. The message and the medium augment one another and act synergistically so that the whole is greater than the sum of the parts. A medium that mirrors the message makes a stronger point. Hypnosis was well-suited to silent cinema, where actions speak louder than words, and where "psychic acoustics" and emotive acting and recognizable symbols substitute for dialogue (and sometimes even substitute for intertitles that explain the action or announce time changes).

To better appreciate the link between hypnosis and film, let's begin with a hackneyed expression: "Movies are mesmerizing." Or at least they *should* be if they expect to hold the audience's attention. Following this line of reasoning, one might say that mesmerism — a psychiatric practice that predated hypnosis by about a century — should also appear on screen. But mesmerism never gained a foothold in film, partly because it lost credibility long before movies appeared, and did not have the strength to make moviegoers "suspend disbelief" and lose themselves in the fiction of the film.

Even more importantly, mesmerism lacked the visual intrigue of hypnosis. And cinema needs more than mere subject matter to make it an art form and an entertainment venue that will attract audiences. Let's get back to the basics: cinema needs a good story with interesting imagery. Those are the building blocks for film. The story must be told without words and should not need dialogue to be understood. A story that employs easily identifiable signs and symbols, as well as gestures and movements that speak for themselves, especially in the pre-sound era (before 1927), is essential to silent cinema and useful for talkies as well.

That's where hypnotism comes in. Hypnotists wave a magic wand. Somnambulists walk stiffly, with closed eyes. Each says a thousand words without emitting a sound. Hypnosis is also versatile: it can be used for the betterment of humankind, or it can be exploited for evil. Ambiguity adds tension, and tension holds attention. And spectators must pay attention if they expect to be drawn into the story and captivated by the plot.

Hypnotism also had a proven track record: it was a fairground attraction, and an accoutrement to sideshows and other cheap entertainment venues. Short silent films got their start in penny arcades. They premiered in the lowbrow forums where hypnosis had an established audience. Adding a sinister psychiatrist to the mix was an obvious progression, considering that psychoanalysis was as modern an invention as the movies. Adding deceptive family members who hypnotize relatives into committing crimes was also a useful way of expressing doubt about the established social order. At a time when mass migration to America was taking place, movies that questioned the trustworthiness of family ties would be welcomed.

Hypnosis had an historical advantage. With its blinking eye or waving wand or glimmering lights, hypnosis evokes memories of sorcerers of old. In other words, hypnosis is magical and connected to the occult. Even if "modern" 20th century men and women no longer believed in magic (and even that claim is questionable), they still recalled times and places when people believed in magic, and more and more were taking such studies seriously.

Fascination with "primitive" societies was strong at the time that cinema and psychoanalysis were invented, thanks in large part to Frazer's *Study of Magic and Religion.* In 1890, Sir James Frazer published the first two volumes of *The Golden Bough: A Study of Magic and Religion* (1890). A total of twelve volumes of *The Golden Bough* appeared between 1907 and 1915. Freud himself quoted Frazer's pioneering studies. Even if Enlightenment era scientists and physicians loathed to mix magic and medicine, audiences nevertheless appreciated those atavistic themes and turned to them during times of transition, when stress peaks. And the century's end was definitely a stressful time.

Hypnosis had the advantage of being rooted in real medicine (even though it was co-opted by quacks and had been borrowed from non-medical sources). It was used by surgeons (and swamis) long before it was adopted by late 19th century neurologists and psychiatrists. Around the same time that Mesmer was practicing "animal magnetism," a Scottish surgeon named James Braid (1795–1860) substituted hypnosis for anesthesia. That occurred in 1843, at a time when anesthesia was a dangerous undertaking, and when many surgical patients literally "bit the bullet" after downing a bottle of alcohol.[6]

In Calcutta, on the other side of the world, the British doctor James Esdaile (1808–1859) also used hypnosis for medical purposes. When he was stationed in India — which was part of the British Empire — he learned Hindu trance techniques. He then incorporated those spiritually-based procedures into his otherwise Western medical practice. It is unclear if the association between hypnotism and trance and the "exotic East" can be traced to Dr. Esdaile, but it is clear that this connection never fully faded away. But all the better for film! For how else would we have had *Chandu the Magician* (1932) and Chandu's many manifestations in movies, radio, and serials?

When Jean-Martin Charcot or Hippolyte Bernheim or Sigmund Freud and Josef Breuer studied hypnotism, they were not aping Eastern traditions, as American New Age aficionados did in the more recent past. Rather, they studied techniques that had already proved successful at altering specific psychological states, such as hysterical movements or hysterical amnesia. For two decades before film was born, medical journals were filled with reports about hypnosis as a cure for hysteria. Fiery debates about the proper use of hypnosis, and how it functioned, took place in lecture halls, medical texts and treatment rooms.

Charcot's lectures on hysteria attracted local artists who were intrigued by the dramatic gestures of hysterics and were similarly impressed by the trance induced by hypnosis. When Freud (and Breuer) made even stronger claims about the value of hypnosis, and wrote that hypnotic trance reveals the inner workings of the unconscious, spectators were intrigued. But they were also scared by the power held by the psychoanalyst-hypnotist.

It is no wonder that the evil Svengali, a non-medical hypnotist, appeared a year after Freud and Breuer published their papers on hypnotism. In retrospect, it is no surprise that a sinister psychiatrist, carnival showman, and skilled hypnotist were combined into one person, and that a character named Dr. Caligari made his way to the silent screen two decades later. By then, there was even more to fear from psychiatrists, asylum superintendents, and the newly-minted field of psychoanalysis, which claimed to see into the unconscious *without* a crystal ball.

3

Sweet (and Sour) Dreams

Like hypnosis, dreams are connected to the occult. They always have been and they always will be. Dream interpretation is a throwback to earlier eras when dreams were attributed to divine (or demonic) sources.

Paradoxically, dream analysis also became a signifier of modernity because of its connection to 20th century psychoanalysis, which Freud invented as the 19th century ended, and which was deemed to be "modern," at least when compared to 19th century approaches and "pre-scientific" approaches. Freud touted psychoanalysis as a "modern science." He made a point of mentioning that his "scientific approach" to dreams was distinct from superstitious approaches of the past. (At this point, it's irrelevant that many of his ideas turned about to be inaccurate, and that some of his theories are closer to the superstition that he mocked than to the science that he admired. What's important is how his ideas were viewed at the time that they were first presented.)

Consequently, dream analysis links present-day, 21st-century, laboratory-based sleep science with superstitions of old. They are connected with a dotted line, but not with a direct line. This dotted line connects to history, and history cannot be erased, and so the link is indelible. Freudian psychoanalysis lies somewhere on the continuum between superstition and science, but it hovers closer to the occult than to theories that have been proven according to the standards of "evidence-based medicine."

In contrast, Jungian dream analysis is situated firmly in the occult. But Jung would not have objected to such an association, because this preacher's son borrowed so freely from religious and occult ideas, and he wrote admiringly about religion.[1]

Dreams held great interest for Freud and his followers — as did hypnosis. Thanks to Freud's century-shaping book *The Interpretation of Dreams* (1900), dream analysis turned into one of psychoanalysis's earliest tools. It arguably remains the most popular and most accessible. Dreams proved to be an easy way to excavate the unconscious, and also turned into cherished tools of artists, writers, poets, moviemakers and even dancers.

Hypnosis, on the other hand, was once Freud's preferred treatment for hysteria. (It was Breuer's and Charcot's and Hippolyte Bernheim's darling, as well.) That is not the same as saying that hypnotic trance was always successful as a treatment, even if it was touted as a success. Then Freud discovered the "talking cure," as psychoanalysis was called. But that discovery did not make hypnosis obsolete, for hypnosis still had its charms.

Hypnosis was also anchored in history. Its utility and its versatility ensured that hypnotherapy would never fully fade away. For sure, it never disappeared from the silver screen, although its popularity waxed and waned, and it often came to reflect political currents rather than clinical techniques (as we see with *Manchurian Candidate*).

Freud specifically derided Egyptian dream books, which were readily available when he wrote his all-important text on *The Interpretation of Dreams* (1900). Yet he collected Egyptian antiquities. He delighted in them, and decorated his treatment room with these archaeological curiosities. He called himself "the archaeologist of the mind."

Like hypnosis, dream scenes hold special significance for cinema. The silver screen recreates a "dream scene." Movies are dreamlike, with their morphing imagery and sometimes disjointed jump-cut scenes. Films have been described as "mind movies." Films are viewed in a darkened room, which is reminiscent of a bedchamber, where draperies substitute for eyelids that reveal or conceal the secrets of the night.

Dream themes were perfectly suited for cinema in much the same way that hypnosis scenes seemed to be made for movies, which are meant to be "mesmerizing." There is a long, long list of amazing dream sequences in cinema. Filmmakers and screenwriters and special effects artists alike realized that dream scenes can push the plot or reveal hidden subplots or uncover secret aspects of the characters' personalities. Dreams can flesh out unexpressed memories or substitute for flashbacks that make characters more multi-dimensional. Dreams can reveal their motivations — at the same time that they add visual interest to this predominately visual medium. Dream scenes also showcase the latest and greatest special effects and cinematographic skills (or, much more recently, computer tricks).

Like cinema itself, so-called "scientific" dream interpretation became a cornerstone of 20th century culture. The very earliest filmmakers, such as Méliès, used dream themes as early as 1898. In that year Méliès made *The Astronomer's Dream* (1898), which was the first of his many dream-themed shorts. These new "moving pictures" mirrored the fluid, morphing movements of dreams, and thus produced their own brand of "movie magic." This movie magic complimented the sleight-of-hand magic that Méliès used at his Robert Houdin Theater before he made his mark in filmmaking.

Like film itself, especially of the silent variety, dreams are primarily comprised of visual images. Disjointed narratives link dream images together to make for confusing but sometimes coherent stories. Those narratives are rarely as clear as the intertitles of silent cinema, but they are perceived by the dreamer nonetheless.

Occasionally, sound or other sensory perceptions occur during dream states, but visual imagery is primary during REM (rapid eye movement) sleep dreams. Non-REM sleep that occurs early in the morning, in a different stage of sleep, favors verbal narratives over the visual imagery that hallmarks REM sleep. Non-REM dreams are induced by many popular Prozac-type antidepressants, as well as dopamine-stimulating meds and a myriad of other medications as well. They produce dreams that are less personalized and more stylized. Those dreams are often frightening.

Importantly, classical Freudian dream analysis relies upon the "free associations" of the dreamer. This emphasis on individual freedom contrasts with hypnosis, which is controlling and which co-opts free will. Hypnosis is authoritarian by its very nature because it requires a hypnotist and a "subject" (or somnambulist). Thanks to this twist, dream interpretation does not depend upon the whims of the analyst, although sometimes the dreams themselves are influenced by objects in the waiting room, and patients are well-known to adjust their reports to meet the expectations of analysts they admire.

"The Eye Becomes 'I'" (pastel on black paper), by Sharon Packer, MD, shows the unconscious influence of Hitchcock's *Vertigo* (1958), *The Thousand Eyes of Dr. Mabuse* (1960), and *Spellbound* (1945).

It has been said that Freud's impressive collection of antiquities and primitive art helped his patients dream more dramatic dreams. A brief trip to the Freud Museum in North London can convince anyone that Freud's waiting room and analytic area were far-removed from the neutral stance demanded by American analysts who aped the "traditions" of Freudian analysis. It is documented that the dreams of analysands adapt themselves to the style of their analysis; consequently, Jungian analysands are much more likely to dream about mythical themes, whereas Freudian patients tend to experience "Freudian" dreams about sexuality and family conflicts and other Freudian-style topics.

But by and large, Freudian dream interpretation (and Jungian and Rankian) are democratic processes, and are much more democratic than the "couch cure" that seats the analyst on a chair, looking down on the patient, who in turn lies recumbent on a couch, unable to face his or her analyst. If control is lost during dream analysis, that control is lost to the "unconscious" or to the physiological forces of sleep states — in theory, that is.

The neutral analyst does not have direct control of the analysands during dream analysis, but the fact of the matter is that analysands reveal personal secrets during the dream interpretation process. Whoever hears those secret thoughts, wishes and memories holds a powerful position, and can manipulate the dreamer and use this information to extort the dreamer or influence the dreamer. Filmmakers have used this dynamic to create captivating plots and add interesting visual imagery. I will discuss *Nightmare Alley* (1947) and *Inception* (2010) soon to see how well such themes hold up over time, even though these films are separated by more than sixty years.

If someone chooses to believe that demons or deities influence their dreams or interjects ideas as they sleep, that, too, is their prerogative, even though psychoanalysts and scientists alike dismiss such ideas (unless they are Jungian-influenced, perhaps). But beliefs in supernatural influences on sleep and dreams have had such long and colorful histories that it is difficult to put them to rest completely. Many people are reluctant to part with such ideas, and enough people patronize fortune tellers and storefront psychics to keep these shady establishments in business (unless they are closed by the authorities for defrauding clients or robbing them outright).

Moviemakers in particular have been reluctant to dismiss such supernatural ideas, partly because these themes make for interesting cinematic scenes, with compelling characters, dramatic themes, and paranoid undertones that propel the plot. Besides, popular demand for such out-of-date but imaginative ideas persists. Many arcane ideas about demons and deities and dreams have been adapted to stage and cinema, and many have met with great success, even in the so-called scientific or modern era.

While occult themes do not appeal to everyone, the success of films such as *The Exorcist* (1973), *The Omen* (1976, 2006) and *Rosemary's Baby* (1968) proves that well-made genre films can become blockbusters. Some of those films entered the annals of "most important" or "best-remembered" movies, with some attracting the screen's top stars.

A recent and well-received film expanded on these odd ideas about dreams. *Inception* (2010) was directed by Christopher Nolan, of "Batman" fame (*Batman Begins* [2005], *The Dark Knight* [2008], *The Dark Knight Rises* [2012]). Leonardo DiCaprio stars in this dark dreamscape. That same year DiCaprio also played a mentally disturbed U.S. marshal in *Shutter Island* (2010).

Inception revolves around a "dream-hacking" crew that enters dreams. They conduct corporate espionage by extracting unconscious ideas even before these ideas become known to the dreamer or thinker. The crew accepts contracts from unscrupulous politicians and profit-minded entrepreneurs who want to outwit their competition. In the year 2010, when the film opened, this diabolical company does not have a psychiatrist on staff or as a consultant. These once-innovative ideas about dreams have become common knowledge and are part of popular parlance, and so do not require professional expertise. It is the technology rather than the dream theory that makes the difference in the 21st century.

Over half a century ago a less technologically-savvy cinema psychologist did something similar, but she did it on a much smaller scale and in a very different setting. The name of that therapist harkens back to ancient Babylonia and pre–Biblical times. Babylonian myths told of night demons and she-demonesses that haunt sleepers and paralyze dreamers. According to this ancient lore, these "lillot" go so far as to copulate with unsuspecting men as they sleep. That causes them to emit semen and create unborn and soulless infants that inhabit a spiritual netherworld. Their offspring go by the name of "Nefilim," which literally means "fallen ones."

The female of this species became known to Latin speakers as a "succubus." The reigning "sleep succubus" of the Ancient Near East went by the name of "Lilith." The ancient Hebrews appropriated beliefs about sleep succubae from their new Assyro-Babylonian neighbors after their arrival in the Promised Land. Some Hebrew Biblical books make passing references to these "lillot."

Hollywood, in turn, appropriated the Biblical term and made good use of a bad situation. Our film stars an evil "consulting psychologist" named Lilith Ritter. Ms. Ritter (who is not a doctor) behaves in the very same way that her name indicates. *Nightmare Alley* opens on a small-town carnival inhabited by small-time carnies who are dwarfed by the big-city dwellers in Chicago. This 1947 *film noir* reminds us of Dr. Caligari's carnival. Conveniently, *Nightmare Alley* premiered the very same year as Kracauer's much-discussed book *From Caligari to Hitler* (1947). Those who had forgotten about (or who had never known) the classic *The Cabinet of Dr. Caligari* (1919) could read Kracauer's book (or reviews of the book) to stimulate their interest in the subject of sinister psychiatrists. Even more conveniently, Kracauer devotes considerable attention to carnivals and lighting effects in film as he draws upon his architectural background and his early writings in *The Mass Ornament* (1927).

Those automatic associations, in turn, prepare spectators for the injustices that are about to occur, and the setting in which they occur. We have been primed to believe that a professional psychologist and a practicing dream analyst could indeed be a perpetrator who preys upon unsuspecting, sleeping patients. For that is exactly what Miss Lilith does: she secretly extorts her "clients" after revealing their secrets to her "carnie" accomplice.

Nightmare Alley also captures real-life anxieties of post-war America. It conveys the massive sense of dislocation experienced after World War II, when America's population shifted into bigger cities, which, in turn, spread into sub-urban areas (suburbs). Many left family farms and small towns, hoping to find better opportunities in these expanding urban and suburban areas. *Nightmare Alley*'s plot revolves around a sinister psychologist and her easily conned carnie accomplice, but it is a cautionary tale about the evils of the big city, and the dangers that await those who heed the words of city slickers and ignore the warnings of the simpler folks back home.

Recall that GIs had only recently returned from the war when *Nightmare Alley* debuted. Some ex-servicemen reunited with wives that they hardly recognized, either because their women had changed during the war or because they barely knew their young brides in the first place. Many men had entered into hasty marriages with "war brides" before being shipped overseas. These men encountered newly-empowered women who had worked at "Rosie the Riveter"–type jobs while the men were away. Some wives had been promoted to supervisory roles that would have been off-limits to women when more men were around. Some women made strides in white-collar workplaces. So men had reason to fear these unfamiliar females who evolved over time.

Today that small-town, carnival setting of *Nightmare Alley* seems out-of-date, but the characters in *Nightmare Alley* have a timeless quality. The fact that the scene shifts to the Magnificent Mile in the big city of Chicago intensifies Tyrone Power's sense of dislocation and his feeling of being out of his league when he teams up with Lilith, an educated "consulting psychologist." This unsettling sense of disconnection adds to the impact of the film. It also reminds us that some individuals possess diabolical traits, no matter how much time passes or how much the settings shift. It is useful to use Chicago, the so-called "Second City," as the exemplar of the "big city." Because Chicago is in the Midwest, it signifies "anywhere" or "everywhere" and does not carry any specific associations that New York or L.A. does (except, perhaps, an association with Al Capone, the notorious gangster who was based in Chicago).

Nightmare Alley casts a shadow over psychologists and dream analysts, and shows them as scheming, conniving charlatans, close in spirit to Dr. Caligari of the German Expressionist era (which directly influenced the *film noir* genre overall), and remote from Europe's educated elite. Like many films of its time, *Nightmare Alley* blurs the boundaries between psychiatrists, psychoanalysts, "consulting psychologists" and clinical psychologists. (It is noteworthy that "clinical psychologists" had not yet been "invented" and were not yet licensed to treat patients.) The term "consulting psychologist" is confusing by today's standards and is never used anymore. This choice makes us wonder if the term "consulting psychologist" was intended to contrast with medically-trained psychoanalysts who were proliferating in the post-war years and were gaining more professional prestige in 1947.

All in all, *Nightmare Alley* (1947) is one of the darkest tales ever shown on screen. It succeeds because *Nightmare Alley* is remarkably well-made, with consummate acting that is suited to its over-the-top theme. Visually, it offers deep shadows that contrast with eye-catching carnival lights and panning shots of Chicago's lit-up lakefront, where Miss Lilith Ritter maintains a Michigan Avenue office. These sharp photographic contrasts affirm the distinctions between light and dark, good and bad, and even between heaven and hell. This cinematography reinforces the film's focus on "absolute evil," and reminds us that evil is diametrically different from sweetness and innocence and light.

By casting the handsome Tyrone Power as the hapless carnie turned small-time crook, and by contradicting his typecasting as a swashbuckler-type or romantic lead, the film turns this tragic tale into a cautionary one that is relevant to "everyman." The director initially objected to this casting choice because it was so "out of character" for Power. Fortunately, he ultimately conceded.

Power's portrayal works well. His matinee idol looks and perfect features distinguish him from the usual "character actors" with misshapen faces and drooping jowls. Such "char-

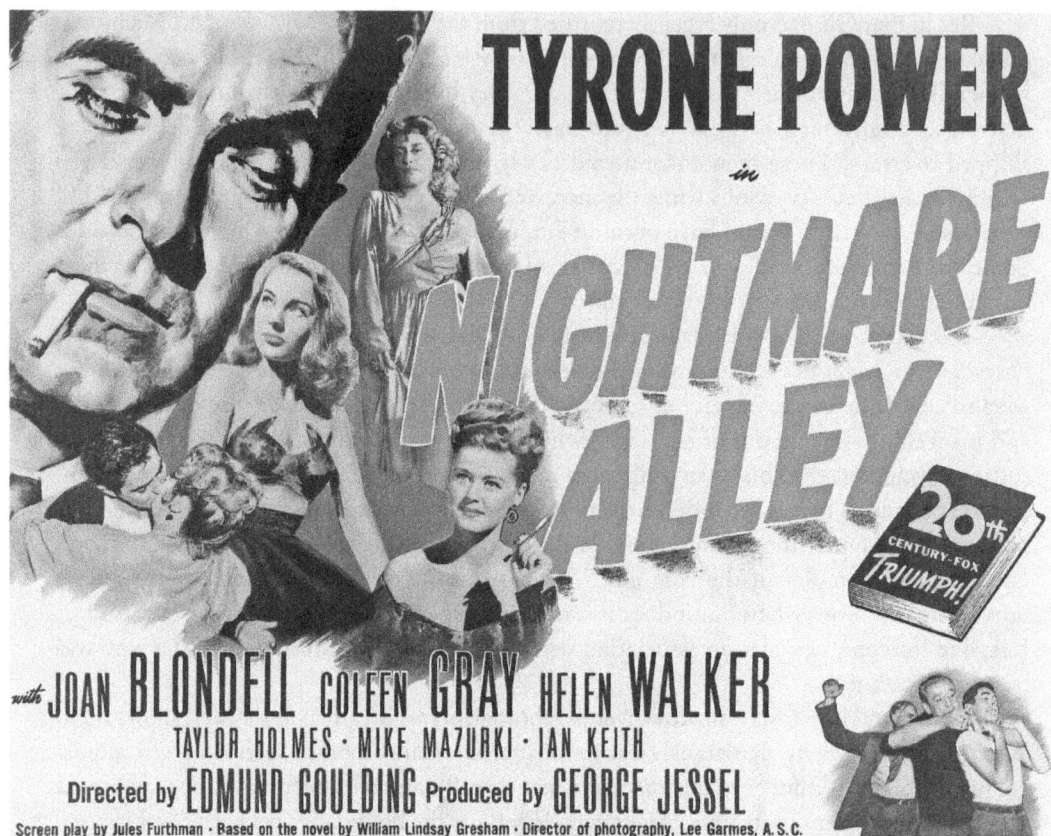

This poster for *Nightmare Alley* (1947) spotlights small-time carnie Stan (Tyrone Power), who falls for the big city scams of "consulting psychologist" Lilith (Helen Walker), far right, while his "other women," Mademoiselle Zeena (Joan Blondell) and Molly (Coleen Gray), literally stand between them.

acter actors" typically play thugs or lowlifes in *film noir*, and so are instantly identifiable by looks alone. Edward G. Robinson, with his bulldog face and bulky build, is a classic "character actor" of that era. Tyrone Power is a "pretty boy" who was far removed from such stereotypes. Yet Power reminds viewers that anyone, at any time, can be a con man. Even handsome men, like Power's hapless Stan, can behave in ugly ways.

This film tackles the blurry boundaries between the occult origins of dream interpretation and supposedly more scientifically sophisticated and ethics-bound psychological treatment. It is a morality tale as much as it is a commentary on clinical techniques. It revolves around the *film noir* convention of the *femme fatale*, to imply that women can be more dangerous than men (even more dangerous than the male soldiers who fired shots at American GIs). The Mary-like innocence of women has surely been lost after the Second World War.

Nightmare Alley arrived about ten years before the short-lived "Golden Age" of cinema psychiatry began in the early 1950s. But ten years is a long time in filmland, and it has proved to be a very long time in the rapidly changing post-war American social landscape. *Nightmare Alley* is a contemporary of both *Bedlam* (1946) and *The Snake Pit* (1948), two memorable films about the horrific conditions in "insane asylums," both in the past and in the present. *Nightmare Alley*'s deceptive dream "doctor," with her lavish office off Chicago's lakefront, reminds us that evil is everywhere, and that even the "classiest" office-based practices can be just as dangerous as the horrors of *Bedlam*, where inmates arm themselves with hoes and shovels to ward off other inmates.

Nightmare Alley appeared around the same time as *Whirlpool* (1949), which anticipates the idealized psychiatrists of *The Three Faces of Eve* (1957), and which I detailed in the last chapter. *Nightmare Alley*, in contrast, turned backwards and connects its "consulting psychologist" to the vilified charlatan psychiatrist of *The Cabinet of Dr. Caligari* (1919).

Nightmare Alley can be compared to (and contrasted with) Hitchcock's *Spellbound* (1945), which preceded it by two years. *Spellbound* is unique in that it shows how dream interpretation heals the amnesiac psychiatrist (Gregory Peck) and solves a murder mystery at the same time. *Spellbound*'s dream-deciphering psychoanalyst (Bergman) functions as a detective.

In *Spellbound*, a new asylum director (Gregory Peck) arrives, only to learn that the man he believes himself to be has been murdered. He has lost his memory, so he cannot recall details of his last contact with the missing man. Naturally, Peck's character, which identifies himself as "Dr. Edwardes," is suspected of murdering the missing doctor whose name he assumed. Another analyst at the sanitarium — the sexually repressed Dr. Peterson (Ingrid Bergman) — believes in his innocence. (Bergman had recently played the romantic lead in *Casablanca*, so she is credible as a proto-romantic in *Spellbound*.) Dr. Peterson is ready to risk her professional position in order to clear Dr. Edwardes of criminal charges. She abandons her hospital post.

Bergman's shy and retiring sanitarium psychiatrist cures the handsome young doctor (Gregory Peck) — but not until the groundwork for a romance between the two has been established. Bergman's Dr. Peterson restores Dr. Edwardes' memories by using hypnosis, dream analysis, and other "state-of-the-art" (for 1945) treatment tools.

Even though they presumably work wonders with their patients, the private lives of the psychiatrists in this film are not shown in a positive light. The itinerant head of the hospital (Gregory Peck) has lost his memory and his identity — even though he is entrusted with helping patients recover *their* memories and establish *their* identities. Plus, he is suspected of murdering the man whose identity he has adopted, but he cannot exonerate himself because he cannot remember who he is or what happened. Ingrid Bergman's Dr. Peterson is chided for her sexual repression, and contrasted with the histrionic women she treats in the sanitarium. Worse yet, the retiring hospital head (Leo G. Carroll) literally points a gun at Bergman after she confronts him with clues that she uncovered when analyzing Peck's dreams and deciphering their symbols.

Spellbound does not discredit the techniques used by mid-forties psychoanalysts or psychiatrists. The film shows no concern with the occult connotations of either dream theories or hypnosis. The title, *Spellbound*, is the closest the movie comes to admitting that hypnosis was once linked to sorcerers and spells. However, a decade later Leo G. Carroll would star in a TV comedy called *Topper* (1953–55), which revolved around a stodgy man who communicates with ghosts. But Carroll's later career as a spymaster in *North by Northwest* (1959) or television's *The Man from U.N.C.L.E.* (1964–68) overshadows that odd role.

If anything, *Spellbound* is a tribute to Surrealism and to Andre Breton's unique approach to the unconscious. Breton had been a medical student before he was waylaid by World War I, when he went to work with brain-injured patients and became interested in "neuropsychiatry." He never returned to his formal medical studies, but he admired Freud's ideas about dreams and the unconscious. He developed Surrealist literary techniques to tap into the dreamlike unconscious, and put it on par with the conscious waking state. Visual artists followed the lead of the poet Breton; Salvador Dalí remains the best-known of these Surrealist artists.

With evocative dream scenes illustrated by Surrealist master Salvador Dalí, the film pays homage to artistic interpretations of Freudian dream analysis that preceded the ascent of cinema. Those who have seen another dreamlike Dalí painting, "The Persistence of Memory," can connect imagery in the painting to the dream sequences in *Spellbound*. The melted, misshapen clocks in "Persistence of Memory" surface in Gregory Peck's dreams, connecting his dreams to the profound memory loss that drives the plot, and reminding us that "memories persist," even in dreams.

Dalí's dream sequence is so spellbinding that many viewers forget the details of the plot or the names of the actors. Instead, they exit the theater with the eidetic memory (recurring visual image) of eye-covered stage curtains, people who turn into rabbits, and a mélange of melting wheels. Few viewers realize that the dream scenes last a mere two-and-a-half minutes. Hollywood legend says that Dalí created a half-hour dream sequence that was cut to comply with obscenity laws.

If we did not know *Caligari*'s history, and if we did not know that Hitchcock once worked in Germany and studied German Expressionism, we might be tempted to say that *Spellbound* reflects postwar ambivalence about accepting or rejecting more modern methods

Dalí's dream scene in Hitchcock's *Spellbound* (1945) shows the significance of eye imagery.

of psychoanalysis and mental cures. Two years later, psychiatric practice would shift away from asylums and sanitariums, and most psychiatrists would occupy offices rather than institutions.[2] (Importantly, a shift in the opposite direction was cemented by 2002.)[3]

We might be tempted to say that *Spellbound*'s stately Green Manors and its imposter psychiatrists comment on the Jewish refugee psychoanalysts recruited to the stately Menninger Clinic. Those out-of-place European émigrés seemed like imposters to Midwesterners, who wondered how they suddenly replaced "home-grown" doctors.[4] Maybe that is true. Or maybe Hitchcock was simply a master of suspense and knew how to play upon ambivalence and double meanings, whatever the subject, and was an expert at forcing us to forge our own associations.

Spellbound concerns itself with the tarnished character of the head doctor, Dr. Murchison, and with the struggles that ensue when new replaces old and youth challenges age. In true Hitchcockian fashion, *Spellbound* proves that moral evil exists, even among those who have mastered the intricacies of the mind and can cure psychosis or hysteria. Plot wise, *Spellbound* is on a continuum with *Caligari* (1919) and its evil imposter doctor who runs an asylum and commits murder (albeit by proxy).

In the end, *Spellbound* offers a satisfying resolution: we learn that the aging head honcho has indeed murdered his younger rival, who was set to replace him. He set up an even younger (and better-looking) contender as the most likely culprit. When he points a gun at Bergman, and she turns and walks away, we suspect that she is stupid. Then, in the final scene (which largely takes place in our own imaginations), he turns the gun on himself and fires a single shot. The resolution is complete. We are left with a love story—a boy-meets-girl story—that is set in an asylum, and the asylum itself is run by a madman, just as Edgar Allan Poe predicted.

Nightmare Alley, on the other hand, offers no such redemption in the end. The evil psychologist does not meet her maker. She does not own up to her evil deeds, as Leo G. Carroll does in *Spellbound* when he aims his gun at his temple (and we imagine him pulling the trigger). Tyrone Power's real-life nightmares in *Nightmare Alley* turn out to be far worse than the worst sleep dreams described by Miss Lilith's subjects.

Nightmare Alley fascinates us for many reasons. It is one of the rare films that revolve around exploitative dream analysis conducted by a health care professional. Furthermore, this evil exploitation is conducted by a female "Consulting Psychologist" (as the shingle says on her office door). Female psychiatrists (or psychologists) are much more likely to be depicted badly on screen than their male colleagues, but they are far more likely to succumb to the amorous interest of their patients. This therapist and dream analyst always holds the upper hand, and there is never a hint of romantic interest between her and Tyrone Power.

The suave and sophisticated Miss Lilith preys upon her unsuspecting analysands as they sleep and dream. She also exploits the two-bit carnie (Tyrone Power), who has his own dreams and who aspires to something better than a secondary role in a third-rate traveling carnival show. The action starts after she convinces Stan (Tyrone) to team up with her and sell the secrets of his carnival act. Stan needs little convincing. He does not even need on-screen seducing. The complicated plot bears repeating here.

At the carnival, Power plays the stooge for his "clairvoyant" Tarot card–reading partner Zeena (Joan Blondell). Later in the film he will play the stooge for the evil psychologist Miss Lilith. But Stan started with a checkered past. He became a stand-in for the carnival act after he accidentally fed wood alcohol to Zeena's pathetic alcoholic husband, who begged for a drink. Zeena has no time (and perhaps no inclination) to mourn. Left without a sideshow partner, Zeena quickly trains Stan to act as her stooge and to transmit cues that makes her appear "clairvoyant" to the crowd.

Soon enough, Stan leaves the low-class carnival, hoping to revive the high-class night-club act that Zeena had perfected with her husband when he was alive. At the nightclub, Power wears a tie and tuxedo. The handsome Power appears to be worlds removed from the crass carnie scene that taught him his tricks. Then he meets the sociopathic shrink who teaches him even more tricks and leads to his undoing. Miss Lilith will confirm the ominous prediction made in the past, during Zeena's Tarot card reading about Stan's future.

The plot from this point on is fairly straightforward. Its twists and turns make sense. The psychologist Miss Lilith cons the con. She convinces Stan to reveal the secrets of his carnie act and goads him to abandon the carnival so that he can work with her. Stan complies and leaves his carnie partner in the lurch. This inconsiderate act will come back to haunt him later, when he needs help the most.

Miss Lilith Ritter, the consulting psychologist, inhabits a world that is dramatically different from the carnival. She treats well-heeled patients with dream analysis in a suite on Chicago's Magnificent Mile. She entrances her clients, listens to them recount their dreams, reveal their dark secrets, and confide their secret yearnings. She records their dreams on 78-rpm LPs as they speak.

She then transmits the details of the dreams to Tyrone Power, who plays a "mentalist" in nightclubs. Power uses this confidential information in his mentalist scenes, and shows an uncanny gift for intuiting the secrets of the nightclub guests — but only if they are also Miss Lilith's patients. After witnessing his remarkable "insight," nightclub patrons offer to pay for private séances with Stan. These séances, of course, are faked.

The crossover between séances and psychoanalysis, and between mentalists and mental health, reminds viewers that twentieth-century psychoanalysts who delve into dreams are little better (and maybe a lot worse) than nineteenth-century spiritualists who staged séances, faked rappings and passed off double-exposed trick photography as "spirit photography." One is as bad as the other, and one is on the same continuum as the other.

In the end, Miss Lilith betrays her partner, but not until she has sucked the lifeblood out of him like a true mythical succubus. Stan lived a dreamlike existence through her dream schemes. She literally takes the money and runs, leaving him in limbo, treating him even worse than he treated his carnie cronies. It is his old carnie partner who tracks him down and informs the police about his whereabouts.

Miss Lilith is the consummate *femme fatale*, the fatal female who haunted American post-war films and reflected the tensions that arose when men returned from war and encountered women who gained power while the men were away. Postwar, those women were perceived to be threats to society rather than saving graces, as they were during the war years.

Lilith's pernicious character fires a warning shot. It implies that post-war changes in society can threaten the social fabric. It makes spectators question the wisdom of welcoming European born-and-bred psychoanalysts, who were arriving en masse after the war. (Some had arrived even before the war.) Should they be arbiters of moral authority and conduits to spiritual secrets, or could they prove to be dangerous and deceitful, much like Miss Lilith? Interestingly, Los Angeles' first psychoanalytic institution opened a year before this film premiered.

In the movie, Miss Lilith dupes her collaborator Stan without a moment's hesitation. She turns him in to the authorities. As the sirens approach, he flees, while she makes off with the money. Without a partner to carry out his act, Tyrone Power has no options. And so he returns to the carnival and seeks shelter in the life he knew best.

This time around, though, he has taken to drink, much like his ex-partner's husband, who he accidentally killed by giving him wood alcohol. Now Stan is as disheveled as Zeena's late husband. In his dilapidated state, the carnival offers him a role as the "geek," and Stan begrudgingly accepts. He dives into this degrading job, and he dives further into the bottle as well. He lives out his life in a waking nightmare that is worse than the life of the man he unwittingly murdered. He lives for a drink and sleeps in a cage. The evil woman doomed the gullible man.

It is easy to appreciate the parallels between *The Cabinet of Dr. Caligari* and *Nightmare Alley*. Both have convoluted plots that take place in carnivals. Both films revolve around sham psychiatrists or psychologists who use their skills to manipulate or murder. *The Cabinet of Dr. Caligari* reflects the lingering distress of World War I and implicitly comments on the painful electrical "Kaufmannization" techniques employed by military psychiatrists who sent "malingering" soldiers back to the front. It also recollects the personal experience of its writer, who held his own grudge against the military psychiatrist who demeaned him.

One can say that the 1947 *Nightmare Alley* also reflects anxiety about a nodal point in American psychiatric practice, when psychiatrists shifted gears and turned in a very different direction. In 1947, American psychiatrists abandoned their old outposts: asylums, sanitariums, and rest homes, and turned to office-based treatments, according to Edward Shorter, historian of psychiatry. For the first time ever, more psychiatrists practiced in offices than in "institutions" such as hospitals or asylums. Was it a coincidence that this sea change occurred in the same year as *Nightmare Alley*, or was something already in the air that made it easier to make films such as this one?

By this point in time, American psychiatry was falling under the influence (or should I say "spell"?) of recently-arrived émigré analysts who were born and bred in Europe. Mostly Jewish, these analysts set sail for the Americas as they fled Hitler. Some had arrived in the U.S. shortly before the start of the Second World War, and more appeared soon after the war ended. (Some could not escape and perished.) Some settled in South or Central America. They brought their theories about dream analysis and their psychoanalytic techniques, and, of course, their authentic-sounding accents, which were intriguing to Americans but which were also threatening. (Recall how Peter Lorre's accent won him sinister roles in American films.)

A contingent of Central European analysts were welcomed into the elite Menninger Clinic, and *Spellbound*'s "Green Manors" may represent the Menninger's homelike setting. By 1947 the sanitarium setting of *Spellbound* was already an endangered species (even though it took decades before such settings fully faded away). For in 1947, office-based analysis had become readily available (for those who could afford it). "Neurotics" could seek treatment with a psychoanalyst in an office rather than in a rest home. Several films from the late 1940s reflect ambivalence about this new psychiatric setting. By the 1950s, novels that demeaned psychiatry started to appear and gained steam at exactly the same time that the movies glorified psychiatry and psychoanalysis, between 1957 and 1963.

Another film, *In Dreams* (1999), is worth mentioning in this section — not because it is a good film, but because it leads smoothly into the next chapter on supernatural psychiatrists. *In Dreams* also shows how psychiatric nurses are depicted as more diabolical than medically-trained psychiatrists or psychoanalysts. Like *Dressed to Kill*, *In Dreams* accentuates the confused mental state of its protagonist by using a gender-bender drag theme.

If we ignore the occult subtext of *In Dreams*, we see strong similarities between the drag nurse *In Dreams* and Nurse Ratched in Milos Foreman's *One Flew over the Cuckoo's Nest* (1975). We can find parallels with Kathy Bates' role as a retired nurse and an active captor in *Misery* (1990), which is based on Stephen King's novel about a writer who is stranded on a lonely mountain road.

We can find parallels between the menacing cross-dressed psychiatric nurse from *In Dreams* and the sneering male nurse in *Lost Weekend*'s detox ward. There is also a major distinction: the psychiatric nurse of *In Dreams*, played by Robert Downey, Jr., enters other spiritual planes and possesses the bodies of patients and staff from the state hospital. The male nurse in *Lost Weekend* is all-too-realistic, even decades later.

We could stretch the point even further and compare Robert Downey, Jr.'s performance to the Joker's tragic-comic role in *The Dark Knight* (2008). In that Batman film the eternally evil Joker (Heath Ledger) dons a freshly-starched nurse's uniform. He completes his drag outfit with a classic double-pointed white nurse's cap. And then he detonates the hospital as he exits. Both actors who play these evil nurses had real-life drug problems. Unlike Robert Downey, Jr., whose drug treatments were highly publicized when he was in rehab, Heath Ledger's substance abuse became known only after he died of an overdose of prescription meds. Ledger won an Oscar for this role posthumously.

In Dreams has a dreamlike, amorphous plot that is often difficult to follow — like dreams themselves. It is also a good example of the so-called "mind-f**k films" that appeared around the turn of the millennium. Those movies were intended to confuse the viewer. They distort time and logic and even place, and thus they mirror the confusion that existed as the second millennium ended and the third began. No one knew which way the world would turn. Was this the beginning of the end or just the beginning? Many people were uncertain if the world as they knew it would continue. Y2K stocks soared as brokers convinced clients that computers would stop in the year Y2K, and that new services would be needed to clean up the financial mess that followed.

In the year 2000 we were far away from the year 1000, when the medieval mentality reigned and when "millenarian" cults prophesized about the end of time, as described in Norman Cohen's classic study *The Pursuit of the Millennium* (1957; revised and expanded edition, 1970).[5] But old fears die hard, and magical thinking typically emerges in times of stress, both for individuals and for societies as a whole. So Hollywood treated us to a host of confusing films about occultism around that time. *In Dreams* was released in 1999. It arrived in time to capitalize on that overarching sense of uncertainty.

The psychiatric world had also shifted dramatically by the time the millennium ended. Managed care had begun in the early 1990s and had completely changed the way psychiatric patients were treated by the end of the decade. Hospital stays were cut shorter and shorter, and more and more treatment was conducted in offices or occasionally in "partial hospitals" that allow people to sleep at home at night while attending treatment programs during the daytime. (This innovation allowed managed care insurance companies to cut the cost of 24/7 hospital-based care.)

Asylums, or even long stays in psychiatric hospitals, had all but disappeared by the time *In Dreams* premiered. The doors of state hospitals started to close in the mid–1950s, when the discovery of phenothiazines such as Thorazine transformed treatment for schizophrenia. Horrific hallucinations could now be controlled through chemicals, and not only through ECT. By 1999, when *In Dreams* appeared, "acute care hospitals" (as opposed to "chronic care institutions") had their "average length of stay" shortened to a few days instead of the one-time-standard 30 days.

The months-long or year-long rest home retreats that were the norm when Bette Davis had her nervous breakdown in *Now Voyager* (1942) were fading into memory, fossilized in films such as *Girl Interrupted* (1999). *Girl Interrupted* was released in the same year as *In Dreams*. That film was much more popular and much more accessible to most moviegoers, and was also much more realistic. And it also starred Angelina Jolie rather than Robert Downey, Jr., in drag. But *Girl, Interrupted* was set in 1967 rather than 1997. By 1999, the idea of being committed to an indefinite stay in a state hospital was still scary. But the likelihood of that happening in 1999 was almost as low as the likelihood of ghosts inhabiting the bodies of psychiatric asylum staff and infesting the dreams of its patients.

But that's exactly what happens in *In Dreams*. In that film Annette Bening plays a suburban housewife and mother named Claire Cooper. Claire illustrates children's stories for a living. She is married to a professional airline pilot (Aidan Quinn). Her life seems idyllic — until her daughter is kidnapped and brutally murdered. For the remainder of the movie Claire is haunted by waking (and sleeping) dreams and intrusive memories of her daughter's murderer, who is a known serial killer named Vivian Thompson. The killer is played by Robert Downey, Jr.

Robert Downey, Jr., was still battling his addictions when he acted in *In Dreams*. He experienced rehabs and relapses, arrests and jail time. It was not until 2003 that he was stable enough to resume a strong career. His early comeback films were not as high quality as *Iron Man* (2008) or *Sherlock Holmes* (2009). This otherwise implausible *In Dreams* acquires a modicum of credibility because of Downey's typecasting (capitalizing on his psychiatric and substance abuse history), but even that was not enough to add cache to this bad movie. The best that can be said about *In Dreams* is that it is a good example of the occult films that proliferated at the millennium's end.

Downey reappears as Vivian Thompson in several scenes. The name of the character — Vivian — is a tip-off for what comes later, at the climax of the movie. In the meantime, Claire has visions of murders that Thompson plans to commit in the future. She consults psychiatrists. Not surprisingly, her doctors do not heed her warnings and conclude that she is psychotic. Claire is committed to a mental institution, and a horrific one at that. None of the niceties that Angelina Jolie (or Bette Davis) enjoyed are made available for poor Claire. When she has a vision of Vivian kidnapping another child, she escapes and tries to track down the killer so that she can stop him from killing again.

In one final scene we see a knife-wielding Vivian Thompson (Downey) appear in Claire's hospital room, as if out of nowhere. Vivian is dressed as a nurse. It turns out that Vivian has been invading Clair's dreams throughout her hospital stay. Needless to say, this scene does not inspire confidence in the psychiatric staff, since it shows them as collaborators in patients' delusions and in murder schemes.

This movie has some similarities to a film that arrived a few years later — *Gothika* (2003), in which Downey once again costars. This time he is the likable male lead. He plays a supportive psychiatrist who balances the unbalanced female psychiatrist who is the focus of the film. *Gothika* will be discussed in the next chapter. Until then, it is useful to note that some of the most damning characterizations of "dream analysts" ever to appear on the American screen were *not* physicians or psychiatrists or neurologists. The "consulting psychologist" in *Nightmare Alley* and the psychiatric staff nurse from *In Dreams* are far more evil than most movie MDs. Each can compete, in his or her own way, with Nurse Ratched, the time-honored villain of *One Flew Over the Cuckoo's Nest* (1975).

Robert Downey, Jr.'s character is not a *femme fatale* like Miss Lilith. But his genderbender drag performance in *In Dreams* updates the long-standing fear of murderous females and even gives new meaning to the much ballyhooed concept of "phallic women" that intrigues psychoanalysts and that receives a lengthy examination in Gabbard and Gabbard's book about *Psychiatry in the Cinema* (1999).

Later in this book I will turn to the silver screen's most extreme gender-bender sinister psychiatrist to date seen in *Dressed to Kill* (1980). But for now let's abandon our focus on the body and move on to the topic of "Spirit Possession and Supernatural Psychiatrists."

4

Spirit Possession and
Supernatural Psychiatrists

The last chapter dealt with dreams and sinister psychiatrists. The chapter immediately preceding that one focused on hypnotism. Both hypnotism and dreams share blurry boundaries with occultism and supernaturalism. Dreams are analyzed by fortune tellers who gaze into crystal balls and claim that they foresee the future. Hypnotism was — and still is — connected with the occult and with carnivals, even though some turn-of-the-century neurologists and proto-psychiatrists used hypnotic trance to relieve symptoms that had no identifiable physical origin.

Like hypnosis, dreams straddle a netherworld that includes occultism and supernaturalism, but stretches onto psychoanalysis and sleep science. Dream interpretation is indelibly linked to Freud's so-called "modern science" of psychoanalysis — which bears next to no relationship whatsoever with contemporary "sleep medicine" and is hardly considered to be a "science" today. Just the same, dream themes have such ancient origins that they never lose their links to the primitive world, when everyday life was infiltrated by supernatural explanations.

In this chapter on supernatural and sinister psychiatrists I focus on films that are directly connected to the occult but still concern psychiatry and psychiatrists. We will see how easily sinister psychiatrists substitute for those antiquated sorcerers, shamans, or "soul doctors" who either cured or caused mental disease in earlier eras. Some of these practitioners continue to ply their trade, unperturbed, in some parts of the globe and in some circumscribed societies.

Even in an industrialized country like Korea, which conducts international trade and educates many scientific professionals, traditional shamans have recognized roles and are available for consultation. An American fascination with alternative medicine and spirituality has simmered since the Sixties, when the counterculture questioned the authority of medicine and all other authority, and when the Age of Aquarius rekindled atavistic ideas about "force fields," "vibes," and beaming information from one person to the next, a la *Star Trek*.

Those counterculture concepts were distilled by New Age healers and spiritually-oriented health resorts that mushroomed in the seventies and continue to proliferate today. New Age offerings in America incorporate many magical concepts but typically substitute contemporary terminology that obscures the connection between "new" theories and antediluvian ideas. Even in the Age of the Internet, when advanced technology governs our daily lives, a Google search yields 52 million hits for "psychics." As of the autumn of 2011, "900" numbers for psychics have not been disconnected. Interestingly, spiritually-based approaches to treatment often command higher prices than scientifically-sound treatments, partly because these unproven approaches are not covered by health insurance and so reflect free market forces and public demand.

So we should not be surprised to find many movies that exploit these age-old occult connections between mental illness and magic, and movies that conflate psychiatrists with psychics and sorcerers. Maybe moviemakers know more about the "magical thinking" than scientists do, for most scientists dismiss those ideas as outdated and obsolete.

We know that moviemakers do not have crystal balls — but we also know that they employ sophisticated marketing tools that reveal who is interested in what, and how many people are interested in that "what." They also tap into when and where those hotspots of interest lie. Before we consecrate filmmakers as latter day prophets that peer into the minds of 21st century Americans as clearly as Chandu the Magician read his crystal ball in the 1930s, let's look at some other intriguing developments. If we examine some relatively recent shifts in psychiatry we can better appreciate the message in such movies, and we can also understand why there was an uptick in occultist themes near the turn of the twenty-first century, as the new millennium approached.

By the 21st century, neuropsychiatry was established as the norm in psychiatry. The pendulum had begun to swing toward "science" ten to fifteen years earlier, in the 1980s. As early as 1977, APA officials began advocating a return to psychiatry's "medical roots" (which had been uprooted by the more literary and less scientific psychoanalytic approaches that prevailed for decades). Official psychiatry journals dubbed the 1990s the "Decade of the Brain." This designation directed attention to the seismic shift that had overtaken psychiatric theory and practice as the 20th century ended, and as metapsychology and psychoanalysis fell from grace.

"Evidence-based medicine" became the buzzword for medicine in general and for "psychiatric medicine" in particular. Metapsychological terms such as "ego" and "id" were pushed to the sidelines and suddenly sounded passé, even though they had been part of the vocabularies of all educated people for years. These words were brushed under the rug, kicked behind the curtain, hidden from sight. For this was an era that used neuro-imaging tools such as PET scans, SPECT scans and ƒMRIs (functional MRIs) to identify functioning parts of the physical brain.

This "new" psychiatry — that is, neuropsychiatry — sought to distinguish itself from the armchair theorizing of psychoanalysis. Psychoanalysis was based on skewed samples and philosophical speculation and unproven pontification about single case histories. Eloquent arguments linking psychoanalysis to Romantic-era literature and philosophy were made. Henri Ellenberger's monumental *Discovery of the Unconscious* (1970) became better known in wider and wider circles, and provided voluminous background material (and nearly a thousand pages of print), while many Freud debunkers offered polemics alone. Neuropsychiatry based itself on science and fact and proven (or provable) hypotheses. More recently, respected physician and medical editor Marcia Angell, MD has questioned the science behind industry-subsidized clinical psychopharmacology studies, but the fallout from those vitriolic anti–Pharma essays published in the *New York Review of Books* is not yet known.

In spite of its many flaws, psychoanalysis made an indelible mark on the 20th century, a mark that can never be eradicated. Psychoanalysis is intertwined with culture as a whole. Psychoanalysis impacted film, art and literature in America, just as surely as Christianity impacted Renaissance and pre–Renaissance art, music and drama in Christian Europe. The Sistine Chapel would not be the same Sistine Chapel without Christianity's influence. It could have been just another building that withstood the ravages of weather and time. Michelangelo would not have known to paint angels or godheads were it not for the imagery inspired by his religious credo. It is irrelevant if his divinities actually live in the sky or breathe air into clouds. The more important issue is that these belief systems are fossilized in art, and that art endures. One need not believe in Michelangelo's Christian religion to respect his artistic achievements.

Similarly, Eugene O'Neill or D.H. Lawrence or Tennessee Williams could not have carved out their characters or their dramatic conflicts without the templates laid forth by Freud. Salvador Dalí, Max Ernst and other Surrealist artists appropriated Freud's dream theories and sexual symbolism when they produced image-laden paintings and coined their Surrealist ideology. Andre Breton, the proverbial High Priest of Surrealism and author of *The Surrealist Manifesto* (1924), and a former medical student, re-interpreted Freud's *Interpretation of Dreams* (1900) when he wrote his own art-oriented philosophy of dreams. And so on and so forth.

Roy Porter, the renowned and remarkably prolific British historian of psychiatry, referred to the 20th century as the "psychoanalytic century."[1] This term, "the psychoanalytic century" entered the annals of history, just as the appellation "Age of Reason" became interchangeable with the 18th century, and just as the "Romantic Era" refers to a good chunk of the 19th century.

By the last quarter of the 20th century, psychoanalysis came under attack. Scientific critics disdained its speculative nature. Social critics inveighed against its Eurocentric and anti-feminist politics. Even literary critics, such as Frederick Crews, wrote polemics against psychoanalysis and Freud's role in promulgating this false belief system. But psychoanalysis refused to die an easy death. It survived the ravages of the leftists during the sixties and seventies — but just barely. Already limping from the assaults of the social critics, psychoanalysis gasped and wheezed as the 20th century came to a close, as more advanced approaches to brain and mind strangulated Freud's once-upon-a-time revolution in theories of mind.

Psychoanalysts themselves continued to express undying love for psychoanalysis, in much the same way that religious martyrs hail their gods as they ascend the blazing pyre and face their deaths. Some analysts became strident and defended their ideology with the same verve as any zealot. Some practitioners quoted scientific data that support the use of psychoanalysis in circumscribed situations, but most practitioners were not so well-versed in academic studies.

In contrast, more scientifically-minded neuropsychiatrists tried to distance themselves from their profession's less scientific past. For some psychiatrists it is embarrassing to admit that non-scientific ideas about psychoanalysis shaped psychiatry for so much of the 20th century. Imagine how much more embarrassing it is to own up to psychiatry's more distant — but not all that distant — occult connections. In a way, it is easier for some to accept the occult origins of psychiatry because they are so far-removed from current conflicts.

Then again, at the time of this writing, in the summer of 2011, it is also embarrassing to admit that some (*but not all*) well-connected and well-respected neuropsychiatric researchers lined their pockets with pharmaceutical company payola. The *New York Review of Books* articles by Marcia Angell, MD were followed by *New York Times* repudiations by Peter Kramer, MD. Letters to the editor from the APA president turned this into a hot topic of discussion, which spiced up the summer's uncharacteristically wet weather. Had Hurricane Irene not disrupted the East Coast in August and cut off computer access for many, there is no doubt that even more hot air and turbulent storms would have been released during the course of these debates.

However, materialism is not on par with occultism. Accepting payoffs to skew scientific studies or selectively publish studies that are favorable to funders may be morally despicable, but there is an underlying logic to monetary motivations. Believing in devils lacks that logic.

That said, the link between supernaturalism and "soul doctors" and psychiatry is solid. That link dates back to ancient history. Biblical tales, Babylonian legend and Greek myth attribute mental derangement to divine wrath. Pre-literate societies still attribute mental distress or bizarre behavior to evil spirits or disembodied souls or the influence of dead ancestors. Some religiously-influenced sects retain related belief systems, and more and more Americans embrace Eastern ideas about reincarnation as the cause of bad karma and possible psychiatric problems.

Hippocrates and his heirs challenged those notions long ago, but only temporarily. Writing between the 5th and 4th centuries B.C.E., Hippocrates' treatise *On the Sacred Disease* discredited the idea that seizures result from spiritual afflictions. Hippocrates did not consider epilepsy any more "sacred" than any other illness, so the title of this text is ironic rather than descriptive. Hippocrates (or the group of authors who wrote under Hippocrates' name) found it necessary to write an entire essay on this subject because the opposing ideas were so pervasive and because "prophetic frenzies" were still regarded as "prophetic" rather than pathological. Greek physicians such as Hippocrates favored naturalistic explanations for mental symptoms.

Hippocrates' advances were all but forgotten over the centuries. The reign of rational Greek medicine was intentionally interrupted when Christianity swept Europe after the Emperor Constantine's conversion. In their zeal, Christians suppressed pagan ideas, whether they be about religion or medicine or science or philosophy. Ideas put forth by Hippocrates or by the Greek physician Galen or their followers were honored by medieval Muslim physicians who studied Greek precepts that the Christian West rejected. Some North African Jewish doctors (such as Maimonides) learned medicine from Muslims, and grounded their practice in Greek ideals, refusing to separate the mind from the body or the soul from the skin.

Europe had its own approaches to what is deemed to be mental illness today. Until the 18th century, doctors of the church retained jurisdiction over mental or neurological disorders. In Christian Europe, odd behavior and strange perceptions, memory problems, movement disorders, or epilepiform seizures were attributed to occult forces. Voices and visions could be divine or demonic, depending upon religious rulings. Neuropsychiatric issues were not classified as physical abnormalities or medical illnesses and so were not the concern of doctors of medicine. Medical doctors did not even inquire about the presence of such symptoms and did not bother to include them in a clinical medical history, even after they began routinely recording histories.

During the Renaissance, humanism challenged the existing order and made humans more central than the divine. The world advanced far beyond the "medieval mentality." Even so, witch hunts continued. Stillbirths, impotence, crop failures and other unfortunate incidents were ascribed to Satan. Mentally deranged women (and some men) stood accused of collaborating with the Devil. Most Americans readily recall the Salem witch trials of 1692, when nineteen women were sentenced to death. Over the centuries, some 200,000 Europeans and North Americans were executed for witchcraft. It is unclear how many died on other continents or how many people continue to experience persecution because of such accusations.

A 1922 Danish/Swedish silent film, *Häxan*, depicts the link between psychosis and witchcraft so clearly and so dramatically that the movie remains in circulation today. It is still a must-see for film students and is a familiar feature at art houses and themed film festivals. *Häxan* is better known to English speakers as *Witchcraft Through the Ages* (1922). It was made as a documentary, but its more vivid scenes resemble contemporary horror films. *Häxan* gained a cult following after its re-release in 1966, when it was narrated by William Burroughs, a bad boy of the Beat Generation whose novels *Junkie* (1953) and *Naked Lunch* (1959) anticipated the next decade's drug culture and influenced post-modernist culture many years later.

Häxan (*Witchcraft Through the Ages*) includes graphic depictions of torture, nudity, and sexual paraphilias, so much so that it was originally banned in the U.S. and was heavily censored in many countries. There are no sinister psychiatrists in *Häxan*, but the film has rich illustrations of psychosis, hysteria, and other popular mental maladies of the day, such as kleptomania and somnambulism. The filmmakers compare the medieval torture of witches (many of whom had unidentified mental illness) to the mistreatment of identified mental patients in contemporary institutions. The points made by this film from 1922 never seem to go out of date.

For many people the links between psychosis and witchcraft and psychiatry have been forgotten — except, perhaps, on Halloween, when adults and children dress as witches and ghosts and goblins and celebrate ancient beliefs that are unacceptable under other circumstances. For physicians it is a point of pride to think that virtually no one in the developed world attributes seizures or comas or psychosis to devils, demons, dybbuks or djinns, or to sorcerers or succubae. However, every so often mass hysteria lends itself to latter-day witch hunts, as occurred in the case of the Memphis Three, who were released from prison in 2011 after serving 18 years.

Psychiatrists themselves are sometimes shocked to see how often occult themes appear in the mainstream media — regardless of whether or not those occult themes have any connection to psychiatrists in particular. Statistics show that only 1 percent of the population carries a diagnosis of schizophrenia, and another 1 percent is classified as having "schizotypal disorder." Schizotypal disorder is far less severe than a full-blown schizophrenic disorder or even the less prolonged "schizophreniform disorder," which, by definition, lasts for less than six months. But schizotypal disorder is also characterized by preoccupations with the supernatural and fleeting occult-like perceptions. Misperceptions of schizotypal personalities do not turn into full-fledged hallucinations or delusions that leave them convinced that supernatural contact has occurred. One of the hallmarks of the schizophrenic spectrum disorders is magical thinking. In more advanced cases, such persons may believe that they communicate with demons or devils or angels, or that they perceive their "presence," even if they do not hear voices or see visions.

If we accept that only people with severe psychiatric pathology (such as schizophrenia or the lesser schizotypal personality disorder) should be interested in "schizotypal ideas," such as occultism, then we would predict that these films would appeal to approximately 2 percent of the adult population. We would expect these themes to attract much larger numbers of children, who, under normal circumstances, show "magical thinking" and often believe in "uncanny ideas" (such as the Easter Bunny or the Tooth Fairy). Some children have imaginary playmates that are visible to them. But children are probably prohibited from seeing these films in the first place.

Yet we can be certain that filmmakers would not spend hundreds of millions of dollars on films that are expected to appeal to such a tiny percentage of the population. Such movies would be unaffordable and unprofitable. For filmmakers (as well as for horror genre writers), rekindling the connections between the supernatural and the psychiatric is almost reflexive, since filmmakers do not answer to scientific fact or political credo. Rather, they take the pulse of the public (metaphorically, that is) and then present themes that they expect to appeal to the paying audiences. (Some "go by their gut," but most do extensive market research before investing.) It seems that moviemakers know something that scientists and psychiatrists would rather forget.

The success of late 20th century occult-horror writers such as Stephen King and Anne Rice is legendary. The fantasy-occult themes of *Harry Potter* turned that author into a billionaire. Many successful supernatural films are based on popular literature that already proved its potential to draw in audiences, thus convincing commercial filmmakers to take a chance on a film adaptation. In contrast, independent filmmakers are not so motivated by market forces.

Because occultism has proven appealing to a wide enough audience, supernaturalism is not just a skeleton that has been shoved into the back of cinema's proverbial closet. In the early days of film, cinematographers had even more motivation to exploit occult themes. Such subject matter showed off their newly-acquired camera and editing skills, which went far beyond the "trick photography" and fairy photos of the Victorian Era. Makers of moving pictures could superimpose images to show "ghosts" and "souls" entering and exiting their bodily habitats.

In Fritz Lang's second Mabuse movie, *The Testament of Dr. Mabuse* (1933), the spirit of the dead Dr. Mabuse invades the body of Dr. Baum. The same cinematographic techniques used by film pioneers are employed here. Dr. Baum became Mabuse's erstwhile psychiatrist when the evil Mabuse was locked in an insane asylum. Poor Dr. Baum tries to treat the psychotic and sinister psychiatrist, who writes and writes and writes while sitting in a cell. Eventually, Mabuse dies while in prison, but his signature crimes are still being committed. Soon we see Dr. Baum invaded by the spirit of the dead Dr. Mabuse. Baum is forced to commit evil acts orchestrated by the deceased Mabuse. It is a treat to see film negatives lift themselves from chairs to inhabit the body of poor Dr. Baum.

Such movies prove that "magical thinking" remains with us, even as we age and even as we become educated. "Magical thinking" is supposedly the province of children and primitive people and psychotics. But what should be is not always what is. Perhaps Freud was right in his own way when he wrote about *The Psychopathology of Everyday Life* (1901).

Dr. Baum (Oscar Beregi, Sr.), left, is about to be possessed by the translucent spirit of the dead Dr. Mabuse (Rudolf Klein-Rogge), right, in Lang's *The Testament of Dr. Mabuse* (1933).

The popularity of films such as *The Da Vinci Code* (2006) and *The Exorcist* (1973) and *The Omen* (1976) (and the their multiple sequels) affirms the appeal of occult themes. It seems that these ancient ideas are buried just beneath the surface and are easily accessed by a flight into fantasy or by skillful use of the silver screen.

Films about mental patients who are visited by ghosts or overtaken by Satan or controlled by *dybbuks* are too plentiful to mention here. That genre deserves a separate study. It is a well-exploited theme, with strong historical roots, given that madness was ascribed to demonic forces for so long. *Gothika*, which I will discuss at length, is but one of many, as is *In Dreams* (1999).

Films about psychiatrists or psychologists who dabble in the occult or fall victim to supernatural forces are less common but are hardly rare. Some are well-received when done well, and some gain cult followings for inexplicable reasons. The contrast between the supposedly rational psychiatrist, who tries to dissuade his/her patients from such occult "delusions" that ultimately prove true, is too appealing to bypass. Converting the psychiatric non-believer into a believer by virtue of their otherworldly experiences is a tried and true ploy.

Dead of Night (1945) and *Asylum* (1972: aka *House of the Crazies*) are but two examples that feature "rational" psychiatrists who meet horrific fates at the hands of demonic forces that they denied exist. Similarly, Jacques Tourneur's *Night of the Demon* (1957) stars Dana Andrews as a psychologist who confronts the demonic powers unleashed by a devil cult leader. Andrews narrowly escapes the very powers he intended to debunk. Tourneur's film is also known as *Curse of the Demon*, but Tourneur himself is best known for *Cat People* (1942), which I will discuss in detail in "Sex, Seduction, and the Couch Cure."

The Sixth Sense (1999) is a psychological-supernatural thriller that gained cult status at the millennium's end. M. Night Shyamalan's film focuses on a distraught child psychologist who comes to respect spiritual messages as he tries to treat a very disturbed patient who claims that he sees the dead. In the end we learn that Dr. Crowe (Bruce Willis) is already dead, and so it is fortuitous that his young patient has an ability that others lack. *The Sixth Sense* appeared the same year as *In Dreams*. In *The Sixth Sense* the sick psychologist reassures rather than scares. The rest of the film is intentionally frightening, with its focus on ghosts, hallucinations, and murderous child patients.

It should be noted that Bruce Willis plays a psychologist rather than a psychiatrist. His doctorate degree in psychology *might* be mistaken for an MD, but he surely cannot be confused with psychiatric staff nurses like Vivian Thompson or Nurse Ratched. His troubles arise as his marriage unravels because he is too dedicated to his patients and profession. Caring Dr. Crowe is the polar opposite of the proverbial sinister psychiatrist in cinema. This positive portrayal of a psychologist (rather than a psychiatrist) confirms the oft-cited statistics that non-medically trained mental health professionals *usually* receive better representations in film.

Most supernatural psychiatrists in cinema are sinister, and some turn out to be the Devil in disguise. But not all of them follow this rule, as shown by the shining example of the priest-psychiatrist in *The Exorcist* (1973). *The Exorcist* is one of the best-known films of all times and is probably the best-known film about a psychiatrist who straddles the worlds of science, psychiatry, and the spirit. The psychiatrist-priest in that film is 180 degrees from evil. This self-sacrificing man of the cloth commits himself to serving his religion and to serving his patients. He also serves science simultaneously. He offers up his own life and suicides after he invites the demon inside of him in order to free Regan (Linda Blair) from Satan's grasp.

We the audience lose some faith in psychiatrists at the same time, as we are reminded of "modern" medicine's limitations. This film was a child of its times. In 1973, accepted authority was questioned. By 1975, *One Flow Over the Cuckoo's Nest* would cast psychiatric wards in the worse possible light. We wonder, in retrospect, if *The Exorcist* anticipates 21st century claims that scientifically-based neuropsychiatry forgets the significance of "the spirit" in its zealous pursuit of science.

As fanciful as *The Exorcist* seems to be, it actually elucidates true-to-life, fact-based issues. Its allusion to the age-old link between psychosis and the supernatural is accurate. Similarly, when it hints at the competition between psychiatry, science, and the clergy, it is capturing an historical truth. Even grade-schoolers know that astronomers' discoveries were disregarded because they discredited Church teachings and challenged the notion that the sun revolves around the earth. So viewers need not study the history of psychiatry to learn about clashes between "doctors of the cloth" and "doctors of the soul." They can extrapolate from what they studied in high school, and "believe" enough of the story line of *The Exorcist* to make them "suspend disbelief" and rethink the subject once the lights go on.

The Exorcist as a film carries many more implications relevant to shifts in psychiatric theory and practice. It stands apart from the psychoanalytically-oriented films that dominated the late fifties and early sixties, and that presented nearly magical cures performed via the "couch cure." *The Exorcist* highlights the link between psychiatry and neurology, a link that was sorely neglected by American psychoanalysis (in spite of the fact that Freud began his career as a neurologist, and in spite of the fact that most early psychoanalysts were trained as neurologists and not as psychiatrists). A few years after *The Exorcist* premiered in 1973 the medical director of the APA (American Psychiatric Association), Dr. Mel Sabshin, announced the need to reestablish psychiatry's medical roots.

In *The Exorcist*, when her symptoms start, the perturbed (and possessed) young patient Regan (Linda Blair) is referred for a medical exam. She is not sent directly to a psychiatrist. She is evaluated for temporal lobe seizures, which can mimic psychosis and can also induce religious states. In true seizures (as opposed to "psychogenic seizures"), loss of bladder control occurs (if the bladder is full). The scene where the child passes water in public has a medical meaning and is not intended as comic relief. This episode of incontinence suggests that she is in a seizure state.

Regan is transferred to a psychiatrist after her medical doctors complete their neurological evaluations and are convinced that nothing is wrong with her physical being. As we know, her psychiatrist is also a priest. Yet he is reluctant to perform an exorcism, and agrees to do so begrudgingly in the hopes that this extreme measure will have a psychological impact and free her of her symptoms. Later on he realizes that his psychiatric skills are not strong enough to overcome the spiritual forces at work. By the end of the film, even the priest is defeated by the Devil. He lies dead on the ground after Satanic forces flee from the girl's body and inhabit him instead. To stop the Devil from possessing anyone else, the priest jumps from the window.

Mister Frost (1990) also deals with the Devil, and also revolves around a psychiatrist and her patient. This European-made occult thriller had a far lower profile than *The Exorcist*. It attracted a small cult following but never penetrated the mainstream. *Mister Frost* shows an equally bad outcome from psychiatric treatment, albeit for diametrically different reasons than in *The Exorcist*. The film stars Jeff Goldblum as an elusive man known only as "Mister Frost." Mr. Frost never reveals his first name. In other words, he has no "Christian name," as it is said in some circles. There is a good reason why Mr. Frost has no "Christian name"— He is the Devil.

Early in the film we meet a police detective named Felix Detweiler (played by Alan Bates). Those who have seen *King of Hearts* (1966), which was a light-hearted spoof of psychiatry and World War I, will remember Alan Bates in his lead role as the Scottish soldier. The final scene shows Bates standing stark naked and holding a bird cage in one hand (the proverbial "cuckoo's nest"). He knocks on the asylum door with his free hand in hopes of reentering the asylum as a patient and escaping from the mad, war-ridden world that lies outside.

In *Mr. Frost*, Alan Bates knocks on the door of a different sort of "asylum," one that is equally psychotic but not as charming as the Belgian asylum he encountered in *King of Hearts*. In this case, Detective Detweiler arrives at the palatial French estate of Mister Frost. He intends to investigate a report of a dead body found nearby. To his surprise, Mr. Frost cooperates completely. Mr. Frost is suspiciously cheerful. He glibly admits that he has buried many more bodies in his yard. The detective seems incredulous. Apparently he is not accustomed to such straightforward confessions. We the audience are also skeptical and expect some sort of twist, even after we see 24 bodies exhumed. There *will* be a twist, but it is yet to come.

Mr. Frost is arrested almost immediately. Eventually he is transferred to a psychiatric asylum. Two year pass without his speaking a word. (That precedent was set by Dr. Mabuse in his second film in 1933.) The police are unable to learn his true identity. The detective leaves his job during this time, but has become obsessed with Mr. Frost and the bodies in the garden.

Finally, Dr. Sarah Day arrives at the asylum and starts her new job as a staff psychiatrist. After having refused to speak to anyone for two full years, Mr. Frost suddenly confides in this young physician. He tells her that he is Satan. In a psychiatric institution such pronouncements are not so unusual and are automatically considered to be evidence of delusional ideas. Then he tells her that he plans to convince her to murder him. Again she is skeptical and dismisses this claim as yet another sign of psychosis.

However, former Detective Detweiler takes Frost's words literally. Detweiler has come to believe that Frost is "the Devil himself." He begs the young psychiatrist to beware of Frost. She dismisses the detective's warnings — until inexplicable events start to occur around her. It seems that her patients, her colleagues and even her brother have been bewitched. Dr. Day eventually concurs with Frost. She decides that Mr. Frost is telling the truth and that he is indeed the Devil. To help others avoid his harm, she agrees to kill him. It is then that she herself is possessed by the Devil. We see her face change as she prepares to do the "Devil's handiwork."

Dr. Sarah Day did not start out as a "sinister psychiatrist," and she never intended to be one. But she was just as susceptible to being possessed by the Devil as anyone else. The implied "fear of contagion" presents itself here. Those who come too close to the psychotic may become psychotic themselves, because of demonic possession or just plain "contagion" or belief in "sympathetic magic" — that like begets like. Her intentions are admirable, but her acts are not.

The theme of a good psychiatrist turning bad in an attempt to right wrongs and prevent more wrong has worked its way into other films. The theme of a good cop turning bad, or pretending to be bad, in order to right wrongs is even more popular. Even Batman occasionally pretends to be a villain, or lets the authorities believe that he is the bad guy, so that he can catch more criminals. But psychiatrists who turn into the Devil, or who collaborate with the Devil, have no hope for redemption — unless there is a sequel.

A much more celebrated film played upon this theme many years before *Mister Frost* appeared. Dr. Loomis, in *Halloween* (1978), confronts a moral dilemma that is similar to the dilemma that Dr. Day faced. Dr. Loomis makes a deliberate choice to bypass the law, professional ethics, and all known moral codes in order to thwart a greater evil. *Halloween* does not add an occult twist until its fourth sequel, and so offers a better example of a morally-ambiguous psychiatrist than a supernatural one. However, since there seems to be such a strong overlap between the "morally ambiguous psychiatrist" and the "supernatural psychiatrist," I will take the opportunity to explore this film here.

Halloween (1978) was one of the first slasher films of the seventies. (Film historians list Hitchcock's *Psycho* [1960] as the very first of the slashers.) Most people remember John Carpenter's contribution to that much-maligned genre, and for the commercial success of this low-budget film. Far fewer people recollect the supporting character-psychiatrist, played by Donald Pleasence, or his not-by-the-book approach to an inherently "evil patient."

Memories aside, this semi-supernatural film series is a morality tale in disguise, as are so many horror films. It offers provocative commentary on the alleged leniency of the juvenile justice system, the insanity plea, criminal culpability and mental capacity. Specifically, it broaches the contentious views on whether an adult should stand trial for crimes he committed as a child, or whether a child of a certain age should be held accountable for unconscionable crimes. However, it ultimately answers those questions in such a flamboyant way that the more serious issues that lie beneath the surface are lost to the less-scrutinizing spectator.

Slashers were wildly popular among adolescent audiences, who delighted in the blood and gore, and were enthralled by the conflation of sex and violence. When AIDS came to light in the very early eighties, and it became known that both blood and sex spread the HIV virus that caused AIDS, some film critics thought that they had stumbled upon a rational reason for this disturbing trend. But slashers had started well before the AIDS epidemic began.

Other critics, who were more attentive to detail, noted that the young female victims were typically sexually promiscuous substance abusers who implicitly deserved "divine wrath" for their bad behavior. And thus this sensational film functioned as a recapitulation of Deuteronomy's curses. The psychiatrist's dilemma holds special interest for those interested in clinical and forensic psychiatry and its responsibility to society. But that is not the only dilemma.

The psychiatrist is only a supporting character that helps drive the plot, wrapping things up in a final denouement. The main character is a young man named Michael Myers (who should not be confused with the comedian of the same name). The film is set in the fictional Midwestern town of Haddonfield, Illinois, a place where the main entertainment is watching the grass grow. This is a very unassuming city, one that could exist anywhere.

A Nightmare on Elm Street (1984) played upon this very same image of small-town Americana to instill the idea of the "anywhere-ness" of evil. The horrors that happen on either Elm Street — the most ordinary of streets — or in a no-name town in rural Illinois remind us of the ordinariness of evil and the banality of evil, to borrow a catchphrase from Hannah Arendt's book of the same name. The setting recollects Hitchcock's *Shadow of a Doubt* (1943), where Uncle Charlie (Joseph Cotten) returns to the small town of Santa Rosa to live with his sister and niece — until he is discovered to be the literal ladykiller that the police are looking for.

The setting of *Halloween* is intentionally ordinary, but the day on which the action opens is anything but. The story starts on Halloween, when six-year-old Michael Myers murders his older sister. His parents return home and find him in a trance-like state. His teenaged sister is lying dead, and the murder weapon is still in Michael's hand. Michael is committed to a county sanitarium, where he remains until the action opens in *Halloween*.

Fast-forward fifteen years, when Michael turns 21. He is about to be transported to court, where he will be arraigned as an adult. Dr. Loomis, his psychiatrist, arrives, along with his assistant. They will supervise Michael's transfer from the asylum to the courthouse. But Michael attacks the doctor's car and nearly kills the doctor's assistant in the process. He then steals the car and escapes from the sanitarium. Conveniently, this occurs on Halloween eve of 1978.

Michael heads home, where he stalks a teenager, played by Jamie Lee Curtis. (This was Curtis' break-out role.) In the interim, psychiatrist Sam Loomis (Donald Pleasence) gears up for action. Dr. Loomis knows Michael well, having treated him for the last eight years. But Dr. Loomis is anything but optimistic about the success of his protracted treatment. Their therapy sessions convinced this child psychiatrist that Michael is pure evil, without hope for a cure.

Dr. Loomis suspects that Michael has escaped so that he can kill again. Following his hunch, the doctor trails Michael to Haddonfield in hopes of preventing another tragedy. We have already witnessed Jamie Lee Curtis' unease when she briefly glimpses Michael. Finally, Dr. Loomis arrives and approaches the house where Jamie Lee Curtis' character (Laurie) is babysitting. Before he can enter, Dr. Loomis sees panicked children running from the house, screaming. Then he spots Michael from afar as Michael grabs Laurie's neck and tries to choke her.

Dr. Loomis shoots Michael six times. Michael flies through a window and falls off the balcony. Dr. Loomis looks over the balcony, expecting to see Michael's lifeless corpse. But Michael's body has disappeared — thanks to some supernatural fluke. This intrusion of the supernatural helps Michael and the *Halloween* franchise squeak by for yet another sequel.

Halloween avoids dabbling in the occult directly until a much later sequel. At that point the film suggests that the youthful villain Michael Myers is possessed by the Devil, and so he can live endless (evil) lives and survive gallant attempts to kill him in earlier episodes.

Dr. Loomis (Donald Pleasence), gun in hand, plans to kill his evil patient in *Halloween* (1978).

The characterization of Dr. Loomis as morally ambiguous is important. Dr. Loomis is not innately evil. His intentions are good, even though he goes far, far, far beyond his professional reach. He resorts to evil when absolutely necessary and all else has failed. His actions remind us of clichéd police procedurals where rubber-gunned cops who were suspended from the force spring into action and resort to violence, but only after the law refuses to protect the innocent and no one else is available to help. This ploy works well for police procedurals, as proven by their popularity. But no one really expects to see psychiatrists killing their patients.

One might say that Dr. Loomis is hyper-moral because he is willing to undertake actions that run counter to standard medical ethics (or rudimentary points of law or just plain common sense). To understand the psychiatrist's plan of action, we must first understand Michael Myers.

This topsy-turvy event causes a chain reaction in spectators. The attempted murder of a patient by his psychiatrist forces viewers to question their own personal values, as well as the day-to-day values of the psychiatric profession, which clearly run contrary to Dr. Loomis' choice of action. The doctor intends to kill Michael not because Dr. Loomis himself is a murderer at heart, but because Dr. Loomis has determined that Michael is pure evil and that no other force can contain him. In the end, Dr. Loomis seems more like a hero than a villain.

We can read into the subtext of the film. If a psychiatrist, who is bound by medical ethics, is willing to break the law when the law does not reach far enough, then why shouldn't an ordinary citizen also take the law into his own hands? Is Dr. Loomis simply a vigilante, despite his medical degree? But this film is not set in the Wild West — its action occurs in Haddonfield, Illinois, in contemporary times. The absurd actions of the psychiatrist imply that the laws that protect minors from full criminal responsibility are even more absurd. The insanity plea itself, something that invariably unsettles society, seems to be insane.

Halloween spawned many sequels. More importantly, this low-budget hit set the stage for the more profitable *Friday the Thirteenth* (1980). *Friday the Thirteenth* was a true moneymaker of a movie; it turned into a slasher franchise. But *Halloween* still has its fans.

Rob Zombie remade *Halloween* in 2007. In the remake, Malcolm McDowell stars as Dr. Loomis. McDowell had carved out a long career by appearing in edgy, not-quite-sane roles. His resume lists almost 200 entries. Perhaps his most memorable role is Alex in Stanley Kubrick's *A Clockwork Orange* (1972). *A Clockwork Orange* remains one of the screen's most pessimistic renditions of youth-gone-mad and society-gone-awry commentaries. *A Clockwork Orange* chronicles the lives of a youthful McDowell and his gang, who are allowed a chance at rehabilitation after they terrorize, rape, cripple and kill innocent people.

In the *Halloween* remake McDowell plays the adult doctor who attempts to kill the youthful assailant. He tries to complete the circular justice that is missing in *A Clockwork Orange*. Those who have seen *A Clockwork Orange* and bristled at the profligate absence of justice tend to applaud McDowell's decision to take matters into his own hands in his role as Dr. Loomis.

Twenty-five years earlier, McDowell starred in the 1982 remake of Jacques Tourneur's 1942 classic *Cat People*. McDowell plays the role of the cat woman's brother. He, too, is a panther-person, just like his sister. As the film progresses, we learn that McDowell's edgy character spent much of his childhood in and out of mental institutions. He attempts to consummate an incestuous relationship with his sister Irena, having explained that the two sibs cannot safely consummate a union with humans because they turn into panthers when sexually aroused. According to legend, they are descendents of an ancient people who sacrificed their women to leopards (or was it panthers?), who mated with them and produced this unusual race. Cat People look like humans but must mate with other Cat People.

In the original 1942 version, which will review in the next chapter, a sexually-aroused psychiatrist has been entrusted to treat Irena's "delusions" about her panther heritage. But the psychiatrist proves to be more sinister than the cat lady-cum-patient herself. The psychiatrist accosts his attractive panther-lady patient, but he is mauled to death because Irena the Cat Lady cannot control her claws when her libido reacts. The remake that stars McDowell omits the psychiatrist and the psychiatric sessions found in the first film, but most viewers who seek out the remake of this fabled film are familiar with the original's psychiatrist scene. So we automatically associate McDowell with morally-ambiguous psychiatrists even before seeing him play Dr. Loomis.

Clive Barker, a horror writer turned film director, conceived of a film about a sinister supernatural psychiatrist who is not so ambiguous. In *Nightbreed* (1990), David Cronenberg is not the director. Rather, he stars as the psychiatrist Dr. Decker, who is a closet serial killer who wears masks when he murders (in much the same way as *Batman*'s Dr. Crane, aka Scarecrow).

In the interim, Cronenberg's Dr. Decker treats a patient who believes that he inhabits a supernatural land of monsters known as Midian. Dr. Decker convinces this most unstable patient that the patient has been committing the murders the psychiatrist himself is responsible for. Decker drugs him with hallucinogens — but leads him to believe that he is taking Lithium, which is written on the bottle and which is a standard treatment for bipolar disorder. Decker convinces the patient to turn himself in to the police, who turn out to be even more evil than the MD.

The patient attempts suicide but fails, and ends up in a hospital. That last act may be the most plausible scene in this otherwise implausible film, which received bad reviews across the board but is nevertheless cherished by Barker and Cronenberg fans, who have awarded it cult status.

Another movie that deserves mention in this section is *Gothika* (2003). However, that film does not necessarily deserve viewing, unless the viewer is specifically interested in seeing how low "nouveau Blaxploitation" can go, and how the highest paid Black actress of the day, Halle Berry, was so badly miscast. Berry, who plays the lead female psychiatrist, has derisively been nominated as "Worst Actress" for this film. She lost that "accolade," but she did, in fact, later earn the ignominious award for her portrayal of Catwoman in the film by the same name.

In my view, it is unfair to blame Berry for bombing in this unpopular film. From the start, *Gothika* looks like a me-too version of the *Hannibal* films, made for Black audiences and for anyone with an unquenchable taste for movies about sinister or supernatural psychiatrists. As it turns out, Berry's psychiatrist husband is far more evil than she, as she seems merely silly.

Gothika is the story of psychiatrist Dr. Miranda Grey (Halle Berry), who has a car accident after swerving to avoid a girl standing in the road during a stormy night. In true ghost story fashion — and in a way that is vaguely reminiscent of Ambrose Pierce's classic

Owl Creek story—Dr. Grey gets out of her car to help the girl. But the girl turns out to be the ghost of the deceased daughter of her boss at the mental hospital that employs her. The girl then possesses Miranda's body by burning the hand that Miranda extends to help her.

The next day Dr. Grey/Miranda wakes up in the very same hospital that she works for, but now she is a patient rather than a doctor. Drugged and confused, she cannot recall what happened between the time of the car accident and when she awakened to find herself in a hospital gown. She is told that her husband, who is also a psychiatrist (and the head of the hospital), has been murdered in the interim. Not surprisingly, she is the main suspect.

She is treated by her former co-worker, a very sympathetic Dr. Peter Graham, who is convinced of her innocence, even though he avoids confirming her "ghost story." Dr. Graham is played by Robert Downey, Jr. The choice of Downey for this role as the doctor is striking, since Downey's misadventures with drugs and rehab centers were well-publicized and led to his being cast in related roles during his come-back. Downey's portrayal of a predatory nurse-ghost in *In Dreams* (1999) connects him to the occult psychiatric realm yet again.

During her stay in the hospital, Miranda acquires carvings on her arm. Words such as "Not Alone" are scratched into her skin. These cuttings resemble the self-injury that commonly occurs in young women who suffer from "borderline person disorder." Even though her behavior appears to fit the diagnostic criteria of a very specific psychiatric diagnosis, we are asked to believe that the carvings are the work of the ghost, who is communicating with Miranda. Her doctor, however, suspects that she is suicidal.

Fast-forward and we, too, eventually "see" proof of Dr. Grey's innocence. It turns out that her husband has a hidden S&M trove in a remote country house. There he tortures female victims and videotapes their suffering for future viewing. Miranda discovers this cache as she traipses around the house, trying to find out what has happened. When she learns that her husband has had unusual affairs, she suspects that one of his paramours committed the murder.

In the end Dr. Grey is released from the hospital and freed from suspicion. She claims to be free of the ghost, but she remains a medium and retains her ability to see ghosts. The "moral of the story": a psychiatrist who becomes a medium is safer or stronger than she was before. The message recollects the conclusion of *The Exorcist* and tangentially remind us of the comic book hero Dr. Strange and his magical Tibetan powers. But it's too bad the performances in this movie fail to perform magic.

We walk away from this film longing for Sidney Poitier's captivating presence in *Pressure Point* (1962), where he played a seasoned psychiatrist at a time when the Civil Rights movement was roaring ahead and when James Meredith became the first Black student admitted to the University of Mississippi. We can't help thinking that "equal opportunity" has turned into an equal opportunity to feature famous Black actors in bad films. It is curious, though, that African-Americans are underrepresented as physicians, in spite of strides made since Poitier's days. More importantly, Black MDs are especially underrepresented in psychiatry. For sure, *Gothika* will not raise the status of psychiatry in the eyes of young African-Americans who are weighing career choices.

One can universalize the message of this film and see it as a gender-based indictment of psychiatry's treatment of women in general. A woman is victimized in this film—as a doctor, as a mental patient, and as a wife. A woman's word is suspect, even if she herself is a psychiatrist and supposedly the arbiter of reason who is trained to distinguish fact from delusion. (However, expecting the audience to believe that Halle Berry is indeed possessed by ghosts also disparages the credibility of women in general and of women as professionals.)

Dr. Miranda Grey is a "woman wronged," and so this film proves that any woman — regardless of education or sophistication — can become victim of her husband's deceit. The film also shows that a man — and, in this case, a Black man — is untrustworthy and even treacherous, even if he has become the head of a hospital and a trained psychiatrist himself.

To more medically-informed and public health–minded audiences, it also implies that psychiatrists over-diagnose mental illness in people of color (a fact that has been substantiated by statistics over and over again). One can go a step further and comment on the common occurrence of culturally-insensitive treatment of Hispanics in psychiatric settings, and suggest that this film alludes to those issues as well. Among some Hispanic subgroups, belief in spirits and supernaturalism is the cultural norm. Yet such ideas, when expressed in a psychiatric setting, are often presumed to be prima facie evidence of psychosis, without considering the cultural context.

Apparently, these subterranean socially-significant messages fell upon deaf ears, for few people saw this film. The organization that seemed most impressed by the supernatural-psychiatrist played by Berry, or by the sadistic psychiatrist played by Charles S. Dutton, was the Razzie Award nominating committee. Were it not for Berry's nomination, *Gothika* might have faded into [bad] memory. Instead, it is now remembered for showcasing an example of the supernatural-psychiatrist, and of the sexually sadistic psychiatrist, and as an example of bad filmmaking and bad acting.

A much more enduring example of the supernatural psychiatrist can be found in Fritz Lang's film *The Testament of Dr. Mabuse* (1933). *Testament* was the second in a long string of Dr. Mabuse films. *Testament* made history not because of the possessed psychiatrist, but because this was the first anti–Nazi movie. In *The Testament of Dr. Mabuse*, psychotic characters mouth the words of Adolf Hitler, making a mockery of the der Führer. After Lang deliberately demeaned Hitler, he was forced to flee his adopted country, taking a train to France, where he had studied art in his youth.

The Testament of Dr. Mabuse features an excellent example of the "supernatural psychiatrist" who straddles the world of the living and the dead. The versatile Dr. Mabuse exerts his power on earth and in heaven (or hell). He manipulates the stock market, heads a criminal empire, adopts many disguises, and incites lovers and patients to commit suicide. He has an impressive knowledge of psychoanalysis as well as finance. In addition, he presides over séances, which became popular as a means of contacting the dead in the aftermath of the Great War and the influenza pandemic, when tens of millions lost their lives and even more were left bereaved.

In *Testament*, the spirit of Dr. Mabuse enters the body of his doctor as the new doctor reads the scribbled and incoherent "testament" that Mabuse compiled during his ten years of incarceration in a mental institution. Now dead, Dr. Mabuse "possesses" Dr. Baum, who was previously entrusted with his psychiatric treatment. Mabuse controls the will of that second psychiatrist and forces him to commit the evil acts that Mabuse began. In one unforgettable scene, Dr. Mabuse's body superimposes itself onto the seated figure of the unsuspecting psychiatrist. This moment reminds us of *The Student of Prague* (1926), directed by Henrik Galeen, and others.

This scene is a throwback to German Romanticism, with its preoccupations with *seele* and soul and "natural supernaturalism," as it was dubbed by Abrams. In her book about *The Haunted Screen* (1969), film historian Lotte Eisner links early 20th century German Expressionism to German Romanticism of the mid–19th century. Even though Lang's Mabuse series does not employ the aesthetic conventions of Expressionism, and falls into a stylistic class of its own, this specific scene nevertheless offers strong support for Eisner's theory.

We witness the all-powerful and all-pervasive Dr. Mabuse commandeer the supranatural realm, which is a feat in its own right, and an especially impressive one for a physician who studied medicine and psychiatry and psychoanalysis. But, then again, anyone who is familiar with Lang's screen adaptation of Norbert Jacques' serialized print source knows that Mabuse is much more than a mere man of medicine. Some say that Mabuse was a stand-in for Freud, who was gaining fame in the late teens and early 1920s. But Freud was hardly "the man of the hour" at that point in time.

It is more likely that the founder of psychoanalysis was simply a signifier for "the Eternal Jew" that roiled Nazi blood. In contrast to Dr. Caligari, who was clearly an "asylum superintendent" and was therefore a class below neurologists and psychoanalysts, Dr. Mabuse stands at a podium and proclaims himself to be a "psychoanalyst" in the very first film. Psychoanalysis was important to the Nazis in 1933, important enough for them to burn Freud's books at the start of the book burning in 1933. Psychoanalysis was the first profession banned after the Nuremberg Laws took effect. Even more to the point, the Nazis referred to psychoanalysis as "the Jewish science."

Like Freud's books, and like psychoanalysis, *The Testament of Dr. Mabuse* was soon banned by the Reich, and Fritz Lang found himself in flight. Norbert Jacques, the writer who penned the original *Mabuse* for newspaper serials, refused to leave Germany when he had the chance. Rather than joining his Jewish wife in exile, Jacques joined the Nazi party and remained in Europe. Fritz Lang's wife and long-time collaborator also remained behind. She, too, became a Nazi, while Lang eventually made his way from Paris to Hollywood.

So the story of Dr. Mabuse is as much connected with the Nazis, the Third Reich, and the Holocaust as with psychiatry and the supernatural. The evil psychoanalyst turns out to be a metaphor for a far greater evil that pervaded the world and perverted Germany after the Nazis gained power. Dr. Mabuse will also be important to the next chapter, on "Sex, Seduction and the Couch Cure," since he set the trend for psychoanalyst-seducers (in contrast to Dr. Caligari).

5

Sex, Seduction and the "Couch Cure"

The couch is a signifier of psychoanalysis. Along with a bearded man, a cigar, and a Viennese accent, the psychoanalytic chaise has become an icon. With its lush upholstery and its elongated, curving design, the proverbial psychoanalytic couch says "come hither" without having to say a word. When it is draped with sensuous Persian rugs, like the ones that Freud tossed over his own divan, it says even more. It is the Odalisque without the odalisque.

Recall "The Odalisque's" couch from museum walls or art history courses. This setting is a favorite of artists. A voluptuous woman reclines on a couch, her body partly revealed but still half-covered with exotic fabrics, perhaps some peacock plumes, and a dab of imagination. It takes little ingenuity to transport the seductive odalisque image from a 19th century Ingres painting to the standard Victorian sitting room, where psychoanalysts tended their analysands.

Associating seduction with the so-called "couch cure" is nearly reflexive. An attractive patient reclines on the couch and free associates about repressed sexual memories, while the analyst ... listens. Voila, what comes next? Seduction, for sure — at least according to some moviemakers. For who could listen to such arousing tales without becoming aroused himself?

To put it another way, the psychoanalytic couch carries the same connotation as the back seat of an automobile from the 1950s (before the Sexual Revolution started in the late 1960s). If we see a 1959 Chevy parked at the back of a drive-in movie theater, we know that the camera is telling us that two teens are having (illicit) sex in the back seat. We know this even before we see the shadowy figures sink into the seat. Similarly, a panning shot of the psychoanalytic couch says that a psychoanalyst and a patient will soon be snuggled together, side by side. Or so it goes for those cinematographers who tap into public fantasies about those once-taboo topics.

It is unfair to say that all psychiatric seductions in cinema occur on the couch. For sure, evil hypnotists, who could be physicians or charlatans or sideshow performers, were popular on the silent screen from the start. Several hypnotists from the silent screen tell their entranced subjects to disrobe. Some instruct their subjects to engage in specific sex acts, in a foreshadowing of films that will be much more graphic than the early peep shows. Recall that stage hypnotists could convince somnambulists to commit murder. (Dr. Caligari and his Cesare are the most famous examples of this recurring dramatic theme.) So it is even more credible to claim that hypnotists could lure their somnolent subjects into sexual escapades.

When psychoanalysis entered the scene, and when Freud theorized that libidinal (sexual) impulses underlie neurosis, the words "psychoanalysis" and "sex" became nearly synonymous. The very fabric of psychoanalytic theory rests on sexual conflicts and instinctive urges. Many laypersons imagine that an analyst who listens to sexy stories for hours on end will eventually lose control of his impulses and be unable to restrain instinctive reactions to such lurid tales. Some might take it a step further and suspect that the errant analyst never intended to harness his impulses, but instead deliberately chose a profession that facilitated such seductions.

The psychoanalytic couch made those seduction scenes so much more convenient, and presumably more comfortable than, say, a "romp in the woods" or a "roll in the hay" between the farmer's daughter and the cowhand (or any passing stranger). In fact, the psychoanalyst and his couch became the urban equivalent of the haystack and the farmer's daughter, and an adult version of the back seat of an automobile for teens with wheels.

Cinema psychiatrists have more screen sex than gynecologists, who are privy to more intimate views of their patients. We virtually never hear a word about urologists, and comparatively little about internists. The reason why? Perhaps the idea of "exposing" one's innermost psychological secrets is scarier than the idea of "exposing" one's physical private parts. Anatomical details vary little from person to person unless serious pathology is present. But inner secrets are distinctive and make each individual unique. Sometimes those "inner secrets" are sexual, but often they are not.

However, Freudian theory posited that even the most mundane ideas or obsessions have secret sexual origins, and so devout Freudian spectators expect to hear sexual exposés attached to each and every revelation, no matter how remote the subject matter. Considering that entire generations were reared to be "devout Freudians," and that Freudianism was at its peak from the mid–1950s to the mid–1960s, Freudianism was part and parcel of the cultural currency. Even Dr. Spock, the child-rearing expert, spoke to 1950s-era parents in Freudian terms. He trained them and their children to expect Freudian-style sexual innuendos from ordinary events. Magazines that celebrated Freud's centennial in 1956 made Freudianism even better-known and thereby educated otherwise uneducated audiences about sexually-explicit psychoanalytic theories.

Some say that psychiatric seduction scenes on screen are one more way to denounce the psychiatric profession. Those people can find ample examples of exploitative films that prove their point. However, the issue is more complex. Unlike the sadistic surgeon films that usually go straight to video and do not need artistic merit to hold the interest of buyers, "seduction-by-psychiatrist" themes appear in many respected film classics that have undisputed artistic merit. We would have to censor some of the best-made movies if we were forced to forgo all films that feature objectionable psychiatric seduction scenes.

For instance, one of the century's most renowned films is *Cat People* (1942). Directed by Jacques Tourneur and produced by Val Lewton, *Cat People* (the original) features a psychiatrist who lusts after his troubled female patient, Irena. Irena is a recently married woman who has problems consummating her marriage. She believes that she is a descendent of ancient panther people that hail from Serbia. But her belief is denounced as delusional — even though the camera shows scenes of Irena at the zoo, captivated by the large cats, and trying to communicate with them and acting as if she knows them. The spectator who has seen these shots of panthers knows something the psychiatrist doesn't.

Lobby card for Jacques Tourneur's original *Cat People* (1942), with the amorous Dr. Judd (Tom Conway) trying to seduce his psychotic patient Irena (Simone Simon) while she is still human.

Irena's new husband is concerned about her well being. He is also concerned about her refusal to share the marriage bed and have sex with him. He doesn't understand that Irena is trying to protect him because she knows that she literally turns into a raging beast when sexually aroused. Irena realizes that she can safely mate only with other panther people. We the audience know that, but men who want to bed her, like her husband and her psychiatrist, disbelieve her.

Irena attends her psychiatric sessions as scheduled. She confides in the psychiatrist and tells him about the ancient Serbian panther people that revert to their atavistic origins whenever aroused. She warns the doctor that she herself can transform into a panther.

From the start the psychiatrist considers Irena psychotic. He warns her husband about her poor prognosis. Up until that point, we the audience agree with the psychiatrist's assessment. For this film was made in 1942, long before the first effective antipsychotic medication—Thorazine—came on the American market in 1954. However, viewers from the 1940s, or even the 1950s, might believe that an earnest and skilled psychoanalyst could cure this "Panther Lady" in the same way that Freud allegedly cured "the Wolf Man." The Wolf Man was one of Freud's most celebrated cases because Freud used this case history to confirm his fledgling science of psychoanalysis.

It's worth digressing a little to discuss the Wolf Man, since that case may have been known to the original film audiences and may have garnered associations with the Panther People. Freud's "Wolf Man" is *not* the same lycanthrope made popular by Lon Chaney, Jr. in the 1941 film of the same name. Rather, the "Wolf Man" was a pseudonym for a young Russian aristocrat who was sent to Freud because he could not have a bowel movement without an enema. He also suffered from depression, which in retrospect may have had some inheritable basis, given that his sister and his father committed suicide. But the Wolf Man (whose real name was Sergei Pankejeff) gained fame for his dream about a pack of wolves. Freud linked this dream to the primal scene where a child witnesses his parents having sex in the marital bed and remains traumatized forever after.

Freud published his essay about the Wolf Man in 1918 in a collection entitled "From the History of an Infantile Neurosis." Coupled with "Irma's injection," which was Freud's own dream disguised under another name, Pankejeff's dream about wolves played a pivotal role in Freud's theory of psychosexual development. This dream reified previously published ideas about *The Interpretation of Dreams* (1899) and became one of the most important dreams in all of Freud's theories. It is an easy case to remember because of its fairy tale-like name, the "Wolf Man." Even if the details become fuzzy, or were never known in the first place, many people learned about how Freud "cured" the Wolf Man.

For our purposes, it is critical that Freud claimed success in treating the Wolf Man — even though Pankejeff later refuted this claim of a cure and debunked Freud's sexually-oriented interpretation of his dream of white wolves. Pankejeff continued his analysis for another six decades, which would have been unnecessary had he been cured by his lengthy analysis with Freud. Moreover, Pankejeff developed a psychotic delusion some years after his "cure" and was seen walking down the street, looking for holes that a doctor had drilled into his nose.

Even though next to no one now believes that Freud cured the Wolf Man through his analysis, film spectators of the 1940s were primed to believe that dreams and delusions about wild animals, such as wolves and panthers, could be relieved by psychoanalysis. So when Irena's analyst warns her husband about her incurability, his readiness to accept defeat arouses our suspicions. Why would the psychiatrist be so quick to tell the husband that his attractive wife has no hope of being cured through this presumably helpful treatment technique?

As spectators, we witness the psychiatrist's attempt to alienate her husband from his beautiful young bride. He nearly succeeds in creating a rift between Irena and her groom. Soon after, the husband begins a flirtation with another woman who shows more interest in him than his wife does. His interest in the other woman — Alice — is cut short when Irena grows suspicious and stalks Alice, tracking her down to a deserted basement swimming pool where Alice swims.

In one of the most admired scenes in film history, Alice senses that something is amiss. She leaves the pool abruptly and rushes to grab her robe, only to find it lying on the ground, shredded. She never sees a panther, and there is no blood or gore. But there is terror galore.

This swimming pool scene deserves more attention. Director Jacques Tourneur gained fame for his subtlety and for his ability to make strong statements through indirect allusions. He whispers; he never shouts (as the slashers did in the 1980s). Yet he succeeds in producing a horror classic that resonates to this day without resorting to the iconic conventions of horror.

Later in the film the psychiatrist tries to kiss Irena, even though he knows that she is married to another. Spectators realize that his profession prohibits such sexual contact, whether or not the patient consents. To make matters worse, he has already declared her to be delusional, and so she is presumably incompetent to make reasonable decisions about his unreasonable advances. Instead, Dr. Judd, the psychiatrist, tells Irena, "I'm not afraid of you. I'll take you in my arms. So little, so soft, warm perfume in your hair, your body. Don't be afraid of me, Irena."

It is interesting to consider that Tourneur's original *Cat People* premiered the same year as Michael Curtiz' *Casablanca*—1942. Both films are love stories of sorts, but *Casablanca* features a man who puts honor above personal interest, even though he has nothing to gain for himself, and even though he never presents himself as an exemplary citizen or a man of high morals.

In *Casablanca* Humphrey Bogart stars as Rick, an American drifter who opens a café in French Morocco and caters to European expats who await visas to the Americas. He receives occasional visits from Nazis that occupy Vichy France. As the film ends, Rick, the owner of Rick's Café, sends a reluctant Ingrid Bergman onto a plane to accompany her husband Laszlo, a leader of the resistance. He sacrifices the love of his life, even though he is hopelessly in love with the woman who had abandoned him in Paris and would like nothing more than to spend eternity with her. The ending takes us by surprise, since Rick presents himself as a cynic, a politically uncommitted person who enables patrons to idle away the hours at his booze-laden piano bar. We do not expect such high-minded behavior from someone who lives such a dissolute life.

In contrast, *Cat People*'s psychiatrist presents himself as an altruist who is devoted to his profession and to patient care. Then he literally jumps at the opportunity to "jump" on a confused woman who sought his counsel. The psychiatrist in this film has more in common with Fritz Lang's Dr. Mabuse, the sociopathic seducer of married women, than with Rick of Rick's Café, who bedded a woman who erroneously believed that she was a war widow.

In the end, Tourneur's psychiatrist receives his comeuppance, and no one laments his fate. Before that happens, however, Tourneur weaves an intricate web. The celebrated swimming pool scene sets expectations for what happens later. We know that Irena has been stalking Alice ever since she grew suspicious of Alice's relationship with her husband. It is hardly shocking that Irena would seek revenge, for she is a "woman wronged."

Tourneur tells us everything we need to know by supplying next to no information. His portrayal of the psychiatrist's lasciviousness is not so subtle. Ironically, Irena fears that she will succumb to her impulses and transform into a panther that preys on others. But it is the psychiatrist — supposedly the voice of reason — who succumbs to his baser animalistic desires. He makes an overture toward Irena. As predicted, Irena becomes a panther and attacks Dr. Judd.

The ending tells us about Tourneur's attitudes towards psychiatrists (and mirrors his audience's presumptions as well). For the psychiatrist shows himself to be clever and cunning, as well as deceptive and desirous. Mortally wounded by the panther, the psychiatrist makes one last attempt to assert himself. He wounds the panther with a sword that he concealed in his cane. He dies from is wounds, but the panther does not.

The wounded Irena hides outside in the shadows when the police are called to investigate the ruckus. As the film ends, Irena allows herself to be killed so that she cannot kill again. She slips away to the zoo, where she unlocks the panther cage with a key that she had previously stolen. The panther that she releases attacks her and knocks her to the ground. As she lies dead, we see the broken sword-cane protruding from her back, making it easy to identify her. The husband now knows the truth.

These final scenes convince us that the psychiatrist is indeed intelligent — intelligent enough to strategize as he lays bleeding and dying. Yet, with all of his intelligence he is unable to control his own impulses. Dr. Judd proves himself to be as animalistic as his patient, who considers herself to be an actual animal. This sort of ending turns this special film into another version of the "inmates controlling the asylum," with some sexual spark thrown in, not to mention the added allure of first-class photographic techniques and camerawork.

Jacques Tourneur's film is a tribute to his filmmaker father, Maurice Tourneur, who worked in the early years of cinema and directed the important horror short *The Lunatics* in 1913 for Éclair Studios. That film was originally known as *La Système du Docteur Goudron et du Professeur Plume*. It was adapted from a Grand Guignol performance based on Edgar Allan Poe's short story of a similar name. Maurice Tourneur's film about "the inmates taking over the asylum" predated the much better remembered *Cabinet of Dr. Caligari* from 1919. We can see elements of the "inmates taking over the asylum" motif embedded in his son's *Cat People*.

The elder Tourneur also made *Trilby* in 1915. Based on literary fiction from the 19th century, *Trilby* recounts the deeds of the evil hypnotist Svengali, who may have been modeled after Freud. Film fans who are familiar with the favored themes from Tourneur Père's early career may not be surprised to see his son follow suit in 1942.

While it is intriguing to trace the Tourneur family lineage and to look for father-to-son transmission of skepticism about psychiatrists, it is equally useful to view *Cat People* as the start of a new breed of horror film rather than as a simple statement about psychiatry per se. It is important to recall that the name of Val Lewton, the producer, is associated with *Cat People* just as much as Tourneur's, albeit for different reasons.

Cat People was Val Lewton's first production. Lewton had been a journalist, novelist and poet before he became a story editor for David O. Selznick. Then Selznick's RKO hired Lewton to make horror films on a budget of under $150,000. Universal had set the pace for horror in the 1930s, and now RKO wanted to try its hand at low-budget (high profit) productions. With horror films outlawed in Britain during the war, there was a gap in the American market.

Lewton borrowed the staircase from *The Magnificent Ambersons* (1942), and co-opted other props from his studio's high-budget films. These were war years, when money was tight and supplies were short. Some supplies, such as rubber or nylon, were unavailable altogether. Inventiveness went a long way. Lewton and his team claim credit for inventing the popular horror film technique called the "bus," which remains popular in horror films to this day.

The term "bus" comes from the scene in *Cat People* in which Irena, the panther person, walks behind Alice, the paramour of Irena's husband. The audience expects Irena to turn into a panther and attack Alice. Tension mounts, and the camera zooms in on Alice's terrified face. The silence is broken by something that sounds like a hissing panther but turns out to be nothing but a bus that has stopped to pick up Alice. This technique of creating tension—and then dispelling it, and leaving spectators with a complete sense of uncertainty about what horrors lie ahead—would become a staple of future horror films. Whenever a film includes a scene where tensions rise and then dissolve into something insignificant, it is called a "bus."

There are other ways to approach *Cat People*, as should be expected of a film that continues to elicit discussion some seventy years after its first appearance. We can read this movie as a metaphor for world war, and as a metaphor for the failure of reason to control libido, rather than as a literal commentary on psychiatry and its failings. Recall that Freud lumped aggressive urges with sexual urges when he spoke of the primitive instinctual "libido." Even if neuropsychiatry draws far finer distinctions between sex and aggression, we must nevertheless be aware that movies made in the 1940s reflect the theories that held sway during that era.

The fact that Irena is Serbian is also telling. For Serbia was the tinderbox that ignited World War I, which in turn sent sparks flying across Europe and around the globe. *Cat People* was made at the peak of the Second World War, when the most enlightened and most cultured country of all—Germany—was more out of control than the usual suspects, such as Serbia. This most cultured country—which is symbolized by the enlightened psychiatrist—proves to be more bestial than real beasts.

Of course, we can skirt metaphors and deep meaning and see this film as a simple commentary on psychiatry, its duplicity, and its failure to identify delusions or contain bad behavior because its practitioners have even less impulse control than their patients.

The stereotype of the impressively intelligent but uncontrollably impulsive and essentially animalistic psychiatrist comes to the forefront in the Hannibal series. That sort of psychiatrist is personified by Anthony Hopkins in his role as Dr. Hannibal Lecter. Dr. Lecter is stunningly smart, so much so that FBI officers like Agent Starling (Jodie Foster) visit him in prison and consult with him as he sits in his own special cell. Yet Hannibal's appetite for human flesh—and for whatever other strange sadomasochistic appetites that compel him—is so intense that his face is bound by a leather harness that looks like a cross between a dog's muzzle and an S&M restraint. His body is strapped to a hand truck whenever he is transported.

We know that Dr. Lecter harbors some odd libidinal urges. We also know that he has a strange compassion for Agent Starling. Like the slave-like Cesar in *The Cabinet of Dr. Caligari* (1919), who throws Jane over his shoulder in his attempt to rescue her from the murderous rage of Dr. Caligari, Dr. Lecter also risks life and limb for Clarise Starling. In one film he lifts her in his arms and carries her to safety. In *Hannibal* he literally sacrifices a limb—in this case, his hand—so that she can be freed from the manacles that bind the two of them together.

Hannibal the Cannibal is a latter day Jeffrey Dahmer, albeit a primarily heterosexual version. Like the crazed serial killer Dahmer, Hannibal woos his victims before they become his dinner. When Ray Liotta, playing a supervising agent, hurls sexually-insensitive insults at Agent Starling, Dr. Lecter responds in kind. The FBI agent calls Clarise a "corn-poked pussy" as the three of them sit down to a candlelight dinner. So the doctor "denudes" Liotta's skull and "reveals" the bifurcated lobes of his brain beneath the cranial bones.

The *gyri* that snake through the brain show a superficial resemblance to testicles. But most people do not eat brains and do not know what they look like, and most audience members did not perform dissections in gross anatomy lab, where students learn to identify brain anatomy by sight. So it is entirely possible that many spectators think about testicles when they see cerebral sulci. This visual similarity adds more sexual innuendos to an already bizarre sequence of events.

Rather than commenting on this coincidence, and enlightening Ray and Clarise and viewers about the obvious implications of his dissections, Dr. Lecter the psychiatrist transforms into head chef and saucier and displays another of his many talents. He fries Ray Liotta's brains in a pan, sprinkling in sherry and a few carefully selected herbs. He then ladles Liotta's brains onto a plate and serves them to the lobotomized Liotta, who is able to see everything before him but is unable to react to this startling event. In the interim, Agent Starling staggers down the stairs, as if she had been drugged. She wears that classic little black dinner dress, the kind with straps that slip off the shoulders, seductively.

In spite of the absurdity of the scene, the tacit sexual chemistry between Starling and Lecter oozes through. There is no doubt that this dinner was intended to be a classic romantic dinner, with linen tablecloth, lit candelabra and all the trappings. This meal might have been a simple "tete-a-tete" between the agent and the doctor. Instead, it turns into a very different sort of "tete-a-tete," or, better yet, a tit-for-tat, as Ray Liotta supplies his own head — or at least the brains inside it — and Hopkins avenges Liotta's sexist insults. The proverbial dinner-for-two becomes a threesome of sorts, and Agent Starling nearly chokes.

Dr. Lecter does not limit himself to Agent Starling, even though his fondness for her is evident. He gives us glimpses of his polymorphous perversity in other instances. In *Hannibal*. which premiered in early 2001 (before 9/11), Dr. Lecter has a sadistic interchange with an aging gay male pedophile, and a wealthy one at that, who comes with a complicated past. Mason Verger is a convicted child molester, and Dr. Lecter is his court-appointed psychiatrist.

Dr. Lecter uses non-traditional treatment techniques on Mason. He tells Mason to slice off his face and feed his flesh to hungry dogs. Drunk or drugged out, or perhaps even more intoxicated through sexual arousal inspired by Dr. Lecter, Mason complies. He loses face, quite literally as well as figuratively. Then he literally devotes the rest of his life to "saving face" and avenging Lecter's horrific act. We never know for sure if the amoral Dr. Lecter had a sexual liaison with this disfigured and disabled chap, or if he only hinted at it. We suspect as much but try not to think about it.

The Hannibal films are so over the top that they fail to offend many psychiatrists, who don't take the stories seriously and don't view such fanciful portrayals of the profession as jeopardizing their standing. Forensic psychiatrists may be more sensitive to these characterizations, however, since there seems to be a close correlation between the timing of the original Hannibal novels and one particularly high-profile forensic psychiatric testimony.

Specifically, public respect for forensic psychiatry reached its nadir in 1979, just two years before the publication of Thomas Harris' first Hannibal novel, *Red Dragon*, in 1981. In 1979 the much-mocked "Twinkie Defense" made headlines. It came by way of a respected but imaginative psychiatrist named Martin Blinder. Dr. Blinder's exact words were refashioned by an even more imaginative wordsmith who worked for a San Francisco daily. It was in San Francisco where Dan White was tried for the murders of Supervisor Harvey Milk and Mayor Moscone. "Twinkie Defense" entered into the vernacular, and came to mean a "meaningless but useful defense against criminal behavior."

White stood accused of assassinating San Francisco's Mayor Moscone and Supervisor Harvey Milk in 1978. White never denied that he himself pulled the trigger. Prior to standing trial for a double-murder in 1979, White had been a San Francisco Police Officer and Firefighter who became a city district Supervisor. Because White showed signs of overt depression prior to committing this act (he became slovenly when he was previously clean-cut; he traded his health food diet for sugar-laden junk food and sodas; he quit work), the psychiatrist claimed that White suffered from "temporary insanity" brought on by blood sugar fluctuations induced by junk food. These words were later "translated" as "Hostess Twinkies" and appeared in the press as such.

The judge and jury accepted the arguments and agreed that White had "diminished capacity" because of this sugar rush. He was convicted of voluntary manslaughter, acquitted of premeditated murder charges, and spared the death penalty. Riots followed, for Harvey Milk was openly gay. The relatively lenient sentencing of his assailant was seen as homophobic-based. His assassination became a cause célèbre for gay activists ever since, and became the subject of a 2008 film starring Sean Penn as the martyred Milk. The Twinkie Defense became a black eye on the face of forensic psychiatry. The fact that the Twinkie Defense originated at this politically-explosive trial made this silly psychiatric testimony even better known, both at the time it was first heard and forever after in history.

It is entirely conceivable that Thomas Harris, who wrote the series of Hannibal novels, was influenced by this trial. The Hannibal character could conceivably be a parody of a profession that seemed so capable of self-parody, if this trial was any example. But that is all speculation, for we do not know what Harris was thinking.

What we do know is that the Hannibal films are based on novels by Thomas Harris, and that the stories were not written as screenplays from the start but were adapted to the screen secondarily. Here we can draw a comparison with the Dr. Mabuse movies, which were based on very popular publications by journalist Norbert Jacques. In contrast, Dr. Caligari started out as a screenplay and was made into a movie.

Thomas Harris, the novelist, refuses to speak in public about the source of his inspiration for his Hannibal character, but it is known that he visited the FBI's newly-formed psychological intelligence unit shortly before writing his novels. That Behavioral Science unit hired Ph.D-level psychologists to perform psychological profiling on serial killers. At that point in time, serial killers were deemed to be more of a menace in America than ever before, even though history tells us that serial killers are not a uniquely American phenomenon nor are they exclusive to the late 20th century. (London's Jack the Ripper and the real-life Vlad the Impaler, inspiration for the character Count Dracula, are but two examples of earlier and cross-continental killers.)

One might say that Dr. Lecter personifies this "psychological profiling" unit of the FBI — yet there is no explanation about how an intelligence unit turned out to be so subversive and so twisted. Hannibal himself reminds us of another notorious serial killer whose evil deeds came to light in 1978, not long before Harris began his history-making Hannibal series. The trial took place in 1980, allowing just enough time for Harris to add extra touches to his tales. Both Gacy and Lecter are superficially respectable and admirable in many ways, but they are evil to the core.

John Wayne Gacy was known as Pogo the Clown when he donned clown's make-up and costumes and performed at fundraisers, parades and children's parties. He later became known as the "Killer Clown." In many ways Gacy was an exemplary citizen. He did charitable work for children, and he held public appointments for the Polish community in Chicago. He even received a commendation letter from then–first lady Roslyn Carter.

In his off-hours, Gacy raped and murdered 33 little boys, as well as some young men. He buried 26 of them in the crawlspace of his home. Others were left on his property or in a nearby river. Gacy's last crime was traced to 1978.[2] He was tried in Chicago in 1980, a year before Harris published his first Hannibal book, and just in time to add extra touches to his work. Even if Harris did not mold his character to conform to Gacy's likeness, his readers had read all about Gacy before they began reading the Hannibal books.

Other characters in the Hannibal novels and films bear striking resemblances to real-life people. Most obviously, the Buffalo Bill killer has direct parallels to Ed Gein. The fictional Buffalo Bill strips women of their skins and sews costumes for himself. Gein's actual activities were not so different from his fictional counterpart.

Gein was the bizarre Wisconsin-born loner who murdered at least two women and dug up graveyards in search of extra body parts. He made belts out of nipples and fashioned other usual outfits from skeins of human skins. Gein died in 1984, after Harris published *Red Dragon* but before *Silence of the Lambs* made it to the big screen.

Gein was tried for the murder of only one woman, Ms. Worden, because the town could not afford a more comprehensive trial. But the evidence against him in the Worden case was overwhelming. Worden owned a local hardware store, and a sales slip showed that Gein was her last customer on the day she disappeared. That prompted the police to search Gein's property, where they found Worden's decapitated body hanging upside down in a shed. She was splayed as if she were a gutted deer, with ropes at her wrists and a crossbar at her ankles.

Gein was sentenced to lifetime imprisonment but was found mentally unfit to stand trial, and so he served his sentence in a mental hospital. It was later learned that Gein wanted a sex change shortly after his mother died. His bizarre and abusive mother had been his only friend and companion, and his brother had died earlier in a suspicious fire that may well have been linked to Gein. To give vent to his transsexual leanings, Gein began to create a "woman suit" that he made from tanned skins of women. When he wore this suit he pretended to be female and danced under the full moon.

Gein became the subject of many psychological studies, and he also served as a loose inspiration for Robert Bloch's book *Psycho* (1959). Hitchcock made Bloch's book into a movie by the same name. Gein's imprint is found in the Thomas Harris' book, in the character of Buffalo Bill. Buffalo Bill similarly skins women, makes clothes of their skin, and wears these based costumes in transvestite shamanistic rituals.

It is Buffalo Bill who inadvertently draws the FBI to Dr. Lecter when the FBI seeks Lecter's professional counsel in pursuing this bizarre killer. As captivating as Gacy or Gein may be (and each became subjects of other films, documentaries and books), it is Dr. Hannibal Lecter who would claim center stage in movies made from the Harris novels — but not until a film starring Anthony Hopkins and Jodie Foster appeared several years after Harris' literary original.

In 1991 *Silence of the Lambs* premiered. Posters of a moth covering a mouth were everywhere, proclaiming the appearance of an entertaining film about evil. The movie was released in February and caused a sensation from the start. Then Jeffrey Dahmer was arrested in the summer of 1991. This coincidence added credibility to the over-the-top fictional film. Jeffrey Dahmer was a real-life cannibal and necrophiliac who abducted, raped, tortured and ate 17 young men. He kept some skulls for souvenirs. A human heart was found in his refrigerator.

News of Dahmer's horrifying deeds captivated an already cynical America. Americans had already "eaten up" details of serial murders. Details of the Dahmer deaths, dismemberments, and cannibalization convinced the public that humans are capable of committing crimes worse than what occurs in one's own nightmares. Dahmer's otherwise unbelievable acts made a fictional character like Dr. Lecter seem more real. Dahmer was tried the following year. Like Gein, he, too, hailed from Wisconsin.

In actuality, Hannibal Lecter's character bears little resemblance to Dahmer, apart from their mutual taste for human flesh and their indifference to human life. Dahmer was a loner and an alcoholic who was discharged from the service and evicted from his family's home. But John Wayne Gacy seemed to be an exemplary citizen and a charitable soul who also happened to be multi-talented. Dr. Lecter's complex character, with his amazing charm and grace, coupled with an unimaginable dark side, is closer on the continuum to Gacy.

Another explanation for the origins of the Hannibal novels can be found in a film that opened a year before Harris published his first Hannibal novel. That film is *Dressed to Kill* (1980). Like the Hannibal movies, *Dressed to Kill* revolves around a cross-dresser and strange sex. Unlike the Hannibal films, which were too removed from reality to be taken seriously — except perhaps by forensic psychiatrists — *Dressed to Kill* offended many practicing psychiatrists, simply because it added too many elements of reality and forced spectators to "suspend disbelief."[3]

Dressed made waves among the gay community as well, who objected to the demonization of persons with atypical sexual preferences. But it was William Friedkin's *Cruising* (1980) that truly fanned the flames of offensive gay stereotypes. Directed by the same man who made *The Exorcist* (1973) and *The French Connection* (1971), *Cruising* starred Al Pacino as an undercover cop who investigates a string of gay leather bar murders on the far West Side of Manhattan, in the pre-gentrified, far-from-fashionable Meatpacking District.

It is interesting to speculate about possible reactions to *Dressed to Kill* or *Cruising* had they arrived a year or two later, when AIDS reared its ugly head in America. In 1981 AIDS first appeared, but a full-scale epidemic was a way's away — or so it seemed. Memories of *Dressed to Kill* and *Cruising* were fresh, and the films were still in circulation when the so-called "gay plague" surfaced in New York and San Francisco. The region where the fictional *Cruising* murders occurred would be particularly hard hit by the merciless disease. Soon bars featured in the film would be closed by public health authorities.

AIDS would not be named "AIDS" for another few years. Before then, the deadly and disfiguring disease was known as GRID (gay-related immune deficiency) because it struck only gays — or so it seemed. Gays would soon be ostracized by those who feared the spread of contagion. Fundamentalists who believed that this fatal illness reflected divine wrath were quick to say so. Many AIDS patients were denied medical or dental care because professionals feared this ill-understood infection and did not know how to protect themselves against it. All that was known with certainty was that an AIDS diagnosis carried a death sentence. Case-fatality rate neared 100 percent, meaning that virtually everyone who contracted AIDS died sooner rather than later. (Some very rare exceptions to this rule became the subjects of intensive scientific study.)

Even though the lead character in *Dressed to Kill* is definitely not gay, he is still a "sexual atypical." He wears women's clothes and murders women to protect him from psychologically unacceptable sexual impulses. He cannot tolerate the thought of having sex with women. In many peoples' eyes, Michael Caine's character may just as well have been gay, even if he is not overtly gay. Some queer theorists argued that Caine's sexually-repressed character actually makes a pro-gay statement because it implies that "coming out" as gay is far preferable to killing women. Arguments aside, this character clearly casts a shadow on gays, cross-dressers, transsexuals, and other "sexual atypicals" by dint of association — not to mention psychiatrists.

Psychiatrists did not take to the streets in protest the way gay advocacy groups did, but many bristled in private. The film impacted the public's opinion of psychiatrists for several reasons. De Palma's *Dressed to Kill* has a very realistic setting: the Upper East Side of New York City. New York was — and still is — the bastion of psychiatry and psychoanalysis. Boston boasts more psychoanalysts, and Buenos Aires has more analytic patients per capita than most North American cities, but New York remains the capital of psychiatry in the eyes of the public.

For many moviegoers in the early 1980s, psychiatry was still something for "big city" people, and for rich people at that. The age of psychopharmacology had not dawned in the early 1980s. The "Decade of the Brain" (1990s) was still years away. Easy access to affordable mood-altering medications like Prozac would have to wait several more years. It seemed plausible to situate private psychiatrists in pricey Manhattan skyscrapers, like the one where Michael Caine's character both lives and works. ("Public" psychiatrists who tend to the poor and the psychotic in the "public sector" are generally shown in "asylums" or dingy community clinics.)

Dressed to Kill focuses on a well-heeled doctor who works in a well-furnished office and tends to the needs of well-dressed, well-coiffed women like the one played by Angie Dickinson. On the surface, everything about this New York City psychiatrist is stereotypical — until we get a glimpse of what goes on behind the scenes, and we find doubles of everything.

We learn that the socially-prominent, superficially respectable Angie Dickinson is adulterous. We see that the doctor's fancy office building also supports prostitutes, including the prostitute that gets the one-and-only glimpse of the murderer after the crime is committed. We find that Michael Caine dresses as a woman, even though he is a man who counsels women about their relationships with men. Everything turns out to be topsy-turvy. Much like the lyrics from the Gilbert and Sullivan operetta *H.M.S. Pinafore*, "Things are seldom what they seem. Skim milk masquerades as cream."

Even the film itself is a "double" of sorts. *Dressed to Kill* is often denounced as a rip-off of Hitchcock's *Psycho* (1960). Sometimes it is described as an homage to *Psycho*. Either way, the film features a cross-dressed male protagonist — a psychiatrist — who kills the stereotyped fragile blonde. Except in this case the "fragile blonde" is not so fragile. The blonde Dickinson had aged and presumably grayed, but was still remembered for her TV role as *Police Woman* (1974–78), and for her comedic role as a psychiatric army nurse in *Captain Newman, M.D.* (1963).

Importantly, the cross-dressing male is not a frightened mamma's boy like Norman Bates. Rather, he is a full-fledged psychiatrist. He is a mature professional who is entrusted to identify delusions. He helps patients differentiate reality from fantasy and deal with their impulses better than they did before. In *Psycho* the psychiatrist interviews Norman Bates after his arrest. In the film's final sequence the psychiatrist calmly explains the events that contributed to Bates' derangement, and brings a sense of closure. *Dressed to Kill* does not offer such consolation.

Michael Caine plays the role of the sexually-twisted psychiatrist so perfectly that he would be cast as an even more sinister psychiatrist in the much more gruesome *Quills* (2000). *Quills* is chronologically and geographically far removed from New York City in the 1980s — but there is an underlying similarity in spirit. *Quills* is set in Napoleonic France during the Reign of Terror, and revolves around the Marquis de Sade and his stay in an insane asylum. Compared to *Quills*, the movies covered in the "Madhouse Movies, Involuntary Incarceration (and Managed Care)" chapter look like frat party films.

Compared to *Dressed to Kill*, the love-murder triangle *film noir Shock* (1946) depicts a relatively ordinary relationship of a doctor, his nurse, a female patient, and her husband. The psychiatrist and the nurse love one another, or at least are attracted to one another, enough to conspire to kill the woman who witnessed the murder of the psychiatrist's wife. The catatonic patient and her husband love one another also, enough that the unsuspecting husband naively entrusts his speechless and motionless wife to a psychiatrist who moonlights as a murderer.

This film can be read as a commentary on absent husbands from the World War II years, and how they returned home to find their wives unresponsive to them. In this case a woman looks through her hotel window and witnesses the murder of another woman, *Rear Window* (1954) style (with some caveats). The woman sees a husband and wife fighting. She sees the man brandishing a candlestick above his wife's head, and she sees the woman fall down as if dead.

The onlooker slumps into a catatonic stupor when she realizes what has happened. Stripped of her speech, she is unable to describe the events that just occurred. One might think that the film's title, "*Shock*," alludes to her state of shock, and perhaps it does to some degree. But we will soon see that "*Shock*" really references the treatment that awaits her.

In the interim, her husband arrives at the hotel room to get his first glimpse of his wife since he returned from the war. He finds her in this uncommunicative state. Lacking any information about the cause of her condition, he concludes that she needs a psychiatrist, preferably one who owns a sanitarium. To the rescue comes Vincent Price, in his role as Dr. Cross. In retrospect, we wonder if his name was intended to tip us off to his "double-cross."

Of course, we the spectators know that a character played by horror meister Vincent Price is almost always destined to do evil (save for a few exceptions). We spectators also know that the man who stood near the window as he clubbed his wife to death is the same man who offers to treat the catatonic wife and take her to safety in his sanitarium.

The husband is grateful for this offer of treatment, for he is in a strange city and presumably does not know of other resources. So off to the sanitarium she goes, where she receives shock treatment. This is not the shock treatment we know about today (the one administered via electricity), but an older and more complicated form of shock treatment — insulin shock treatment — that was all but abandoned in America once ECT (electroconvulsive treatment) arrived in this country in 1938. A few exclusive places continued to use insulin into the early 1950s, when the protagonist from *A Beautiful Mind* (2001) sought psychiatric treatment.

Insulin shock treatment was effective, and even had its enthusiasts, but it was deemed too dangerous once other alternatives became available. A little too much insulin could cause permanent brain damage or even death. Insulin injections could kill or cripple patients in the very same way that overdoses of insulin could send diabetics into permanent comas.

As it turns out, the insulin treatments take effect, and the unfortunate woman starts to regain consciousness. At that point the nurse who works with the evil psychiatrist grows concerned. She realizes that the patient might identify the doctor once she rouses. We learn that the nurse and the psychiatrist–sanitarium owner are romantically involved, and that disposing of the psychiatrist's wife was part of their plan to clear the way for their relationship.

The nurse urges the doctor to administer a lethal dose of insulin to the unsuspecting patient. Even though she wears stiffly-starched hospital whites, the nurse is as evil as the black-garbed *femmes fatales* of other films of that era. The doctor suffers pangs of conscience. He hesitates. He cannot kill his patient — even though he recently murdered his wife. Shouting ensues, just as it did with his wife. In a perfectly symmetrical "parallel process," the psychiatrist turns on the nurse and kills her instead of his patient.

The happy ending to this dark film? The "good" husband and the loyal wife are reunited. The lieutenant who returned from the war has saved his wife as surely as he saved his country. What wonderful consolation for both the women who waited for their men to return from the front and for the men who wondered if their wives would still need them after the war.

Shock is a classic *noir* (and more), with an evil woman, a romantic triangle, and characters who prove to be more criminal than not. The catch is that the murderer is an MD, and the place of attempted murder is a posh psychiatric sanitarium with whitewashed walls and flowing curtains. This film was made in the same era as Hitchcock's *Spellbound* (1945), which is set in the stately (and presumably costly) Green Manors sanitarium.

At the Green Manors sanitarium, bad things happen. Hospital heads commit as murder. But not all rest homes of that era are horrible. Bette Davis' Aunt Charlotte spent time in a sanitarium cum rest home, but she was treated by a kind and compassionate psychiatrist (played by Claude Rains), in the beloved classic *Now, Voyager* (1942). That same year Claude Rains had a memorable role in *Casablanca* (1942), in which, as Captain Renault, he befriends Humphrey Bogart and donates travel papers as a show of support "for the cause." If that doesn't make for a trustworthy and dedicated cinema psychiatrist, then what does?

But back to *Shock*, which arrived four years after *Now, Voyager* and *Casablanca*, but is eons away in spirit. As dark and disturbing as *Shock* is, the film still shows a positive side of the psychiatrist: No matter how high the stakes, he will not harm his patient. He is willing to go to the gallows, so to speak, when forced to choose between killing his patient or letting her expose him. His patient's life is more important than his wife's life. He is "married to medicine," as the expression goes.

As for his love affair with his nurse — that is closer to what happens on *General Hospital* (1963) or any of the many TV soap operas that appeared in the next decade or two, when TVs took their place in American homes and pushed aside the entire genre of "weepies" or "women's pictures" that *Shock* fit into (albeit uneasily). Those melodramatic films were very popular with women during the war years when most men were away in the service. Some of those 1940s melodramas incorporated enough dark elements to allow them to be repackaged as *noirs* later on, when the *noir* genre gained more cache, and their rereleases sold.

Love-murder triangles remain ever-popular, not just in films but in opera, ballet and the theater. Psychiatrists also figure into this tried-and-true motif. Another film, the 1999 remake *House on Haunted Hill*, adds an adulterous psychiatrist, although the psychiatrist does not have the leading role. We learn that the psychiatrist has been conducting an affair with the wife of the wealthy amusement park owner who rents the "haunted" mansion. The mind doctor has used his medical know-how to fake the wife's death in order to set her free from her strange husband. They plan to start new lives together — after taking someone else's life, if need be.

The original *House on Haunted Hill* (1959) starred Vincent Price as an eccentric millionaire who invites money-hungry strangers to the extravagant home (or haunted house) that he leases for the occasion. He hopes to dupe one of them into killing his fourth wife, Annabelle (accidentally, of course), during their stay in this ghost-ridden palace. Each has been offered $10,000 if they survive the night. (This sum is inflated to $1,000,000 in the second film.) In both films, most of the guests die before dawn, with each death scene more gruesome than the last.

In both the original and the remake, a psychiatrist is one of several invited guests. In 1959, which lay smack in the center of screen psychiatry's "golden years," mind doctors were usually idealized on screen. This film is an exception to that trend, which lasted from 1957 to 1963. Although Dr. Trent is smart, in spite of his libidinous excesses and impulse control problems, he will become an accessory to a murder. The psychiatrist and his married lover have been plotting to frighten another guest into shooting Annabelle's husband, who hosts the odd party and who is attempting to arrange for her murder at the same time that they are scheming to have him killed. The last we see of him, the psychiatrist tries to push the presumably dead husband into a vat of acid.

The 1959 original was a

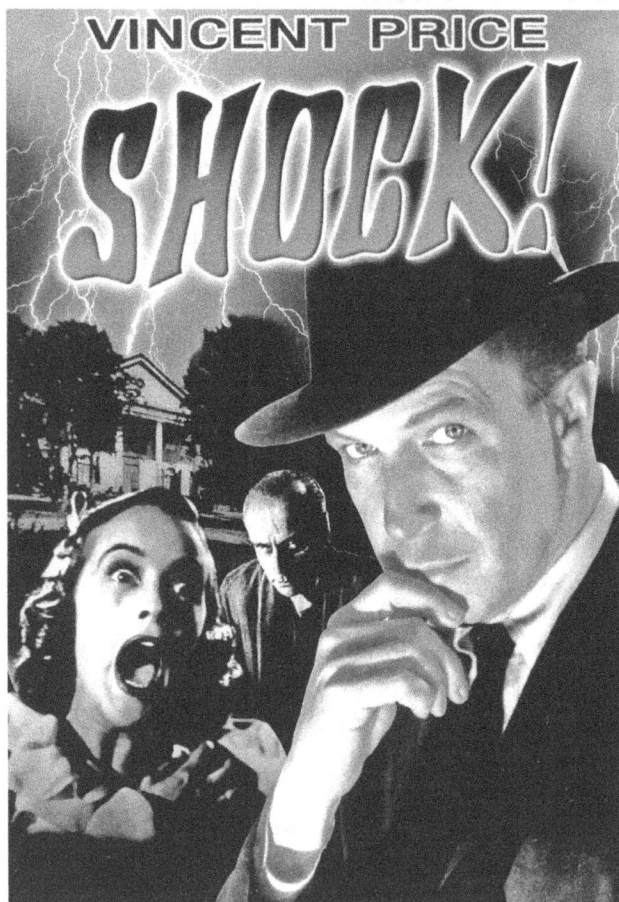

Janet Stewart (Anabel Shaw) screams after witnessing psychiatrist Dr. Cross (Vincent Price) kill his wife — then she enters his sanitarium for "treatment" in *Shock* (1946).

Poster for the original *House on Haunted Hill* (1959), in which an eccentric millionaire (Vincent Price) orchestrates the murder of his wife, who's conducting an affair with a psychiatrist.

William Castle classic, gimmicks and all. Castle was known for adding corny touches at a time when most Americans had televisions at home and were less inclined to patronize movie theaters. To entice viewers into paying for movie seats, he used a gimmick for *House on Haunted Hill* that he nicknamed "Emergo." The audience was left laughing as white paper skeletons floated through theaters, suspended overhead. The remake was not so well-received; it won Rotten Tomato awards. Yet it is relevant to this study in many ways.

In the second film the psychiatrist is still conniving and adulterous, undaunted by the idea of claiming another man's wife. He rigs a shock machine to feign his lover's death (further discussed in the "Shock Schlock" chapter). More significantly, the second film is set in a one-time psychiatric asylum. Brutal experiments were conducted in that asylum just a few years before Nazi doctors operated on Jewish and gypsy prisoners. While the movie itself falls short of expectations, this specific reference to medical experimentation on humans, and to the role of psychiatrists in the Nazi death camps, is so important that its discussion will be deferred to a chapter devoted entirely to "Unethical Experimentation."

Up till now I have not mentioned female psychiatrists in this chapter on Sex and Seduction, but that is not because there is nothing to be said. Quite the contrary, there is so much to be said about female psychiatrists in the cinema, and about seduction scenes and other boundary breaking, that I will devote an entire chapter to that topic. The next section, on "The Not-So-Gentle Gender," looks at this other side of the spectrum.

6

The Not-So-Gentle Gender

The last chapter, on "Sex, Seduction and the Couch Cure," focused on sinister male psychiatrists — the ones, who entrap, seduce, deceive, and even murder or maim their female patients, their wives or their (mostly female) nurses. Occasionally these fictional male psychiatrists harm the husbands of their female prey (as Dr. Mabuse did when he kidnapped Countess Told and then persuaded her husband, Count Told, to commit suicide). Some carry on with men as well, or they hint that they do (as with the ambiguous relationship between Dr. Lecter and Mason Verger, the pedophile who was mandated to Lecter's care). A few men dress as women when they exhibit their worst behavior.

Female psychiatrists were omitted from the last chapter on "Sex, Seduction and the Couch Cure" in order to devote this entire chapter to diabolical female doctors. I will also have something to say about female nurses (and about a few male nurses and some memorable cross-dressing male nurses) in this section.

I won't make too much fuss over the distinction between psychiatrists and psychologists in this chapter — for a very simple reason: films commonly confuse psychiatrists with psychologists, especially when both administer talk therapy. Yet movies virtually never confuse doctors with nurses. Interestingly, psychiatric nurses, who are more often female than not, have a special niche in film. It is they who are singled out for the harshest treatment of all.

Psychoanalysts are generally described as psychoanalysts because psychoanalytic expertise carries a special connotation for the film industry. Psychoanalysis and film were born within a year of one another, and so both shared the same cultural climate. But that occurred as the 19th century came to a close. Another significant event took place several decades later, when many psychoanalysts relocated to Hollywood, both before and after the Second World War. These analysts were often called in as consultants for films. Some treated industry giants — sometimes with good results, sometimes with not so good results.

Unlike medically-trained psychiatrists or administrative asylum superintendents, psychoanalysts may or may not be medical doctors. Freud decided that medical education was not needed for psychoanalytic practice, but until the 1980s American psychoanalytic institutes required an MD degree to gain admission. Analytic training was often recommended, if not also required, for completion of psychiatric training. At the very least, analytic credentials conferred enough prestige that even biologically-inclined neuropsychiatry pioneers often acquired analytic credentials when psychoanalysis was in its heyday.

That changed by the mid–1980s. By then, MDs as a whole stopped applying to analytic institutes. Faced with declining enrollments, analytic training institutions that had once demanded an MD degree from all applicants opened their doors, first to psychologists with doctorate-level degrees, and later on to candidates with MSW (master's of social work) or other mental health degrees. At present, practicing psychoanalysts are more likely to have trained as psychiatric social workers, who are much more abundant than doctorate-level psychologists.

How does this educational shift (and accompanying power shift) impact women in movies? Women were present in psychoanalytic circles if not exactly from the start, then soon after. Freud's daughter Anna founded an important school of child psychoanalysis, even though she had no medical degree and was therefore known as a "lay analyst." The Anna Freud Center remains in North London, at Maresfield Gardens.

Some female physicians were prominent in the early years of psychoanalysis. The best-recognized among them is arguably Dr. Helena Deutsch, who joined Freud's circle in 1918 after having worked at Wagner-Jauregg's clinic in Vienna. The biologically-oriented Wagner-Jauregg was Freud's competitor when it came to explanations for shell shock, although Wagner-Jauregg eventually won a Nobel Prize for his work on neurosyphilis, while Freud later earned the Goethe Prize in literature. Deutsch's work on *The Psychology of Women* was the first in the field, but her conclusions about women's inherent masochism and their "as-if" personality structure put her at odds with feminists who "rediscovered" her work in the late 1960s and 1970s.

Lou-Andreas Salomé, a lay analyst who was a paramour of Nietzsche and others, was a colorful figure of the early psychoanalytic circle. Another celebrated female analyst was Frieda Fromm-Reichmann, a German-born physician who was a contemporary of Freud but left Europe to escape Hitler. Although well-respected for her innovative treatment methods and her humanistic approach to patients, she gained her greatest fame as the idealized analyst in the semi-autobiographical novel and film *I Never Promised You a Rose Garden* (book 1964, film 1977).

Psychoanalysis was once very prominent in feature films, and was especially important to *film noir* in the 1940s and 1950s. So we would expect to find many female psychoanalysts in that subgenre of cinema. Because *film noir* often portrayed women as evil *femmes fatales*, we should not be surprised to find female psychiatrists, psychoanalysts and nurses who fulfill the function of *femmes fatales* and therefore qualify as "sinister."

In their book on *Psychiatry and the Cinema*, second edition (1999), Glen and Krin Gabbard count up the American films that feature female psychiatrists. They conclude that these women psychiatric specialists are four times as likely to be depicted badly as their male counterparts. ("Bad depictions" include falling in love with male patients, and breaking boundaries in that way, as much as causing harm to patients or other people.) The Gabbards' study covers American film exclusively, and so does not include early German Expressionist films or European silent shorts that made mincemeat of male psychiatrists, psychoanalysts and asylum superintendents.

However, we must rethink these statistics before we take them literally. As brilliant as their books are, the Gabbards do not consider the possibility that the "*film noir* factor" skews the statistics they cite. Recall that women, regardless of their profession, are often depicted as evil in *film noir*— even though there are also plenty of helpful "gal pals" in *noir*. Given that noirs are also known for their psychiatric themes, dream scenes and psychoanalytic references, it stands to reason that many female and male psychiatric professionals appear in films from that era. Furthermore, we would expect at least some female psychiatrists from *noir* films to show *femme fatale* tendencies, and hence qualify for the Gabbards' stats on female docs.

Much has been written about the *femmes fatales* who populate *film noir*'s gritty urban scenes. Even more has been written about *noir* films overall, which were shot in shadows during wartime blackouts, and show dramatic chiaschuoro contrasts that highlight the differences between black and white, and, by implication, between good and evil. Less has been written about "evil women" who appear in pre–Code cinema that pre-dates Hays' Production Code. "The Code" took full effect by the mid–1930s and cleansed films of amoral themes that glorified evil, sex, violence, or criminal activity. Some pre–Code female roles make us rethink the "received wisdom" about post-war *femmes fatales* as a commentary on wartime female empowerment.

For instance, Barbara Stanwyck starred as a self-serving, conniving, ladder-climbing, non-professional prostitute-like character in *Baby Face* (1933) a decade before she appeared as a *noir*-era *femme fatale* in *Double Indemnity* (1944), and nearly 30 years before her portrayal of a New Orleans madam in Edward Dymtryk's *Walk on the Wild Side* (1962).

Several feminist film scholars from the seventies carved out careers for themselves by claiming that *noir*'s "evil woman" embodies male anxieties about women who became empowered when the men were away in the service during World War II. During wartime, women were heading households and holding down the proverbial forts — or, more accurately, the factories. So men wondered if women would revert to "normal" upon their return, or if the traditional gender roles would remain reversed after the war ended. Rosie the Riveter posters offered a benign, even humorous, image of women who aided "the war effort" but needed goading to line up for the assembly lines. Films made a few years later added a diabolical twist to this image.

Consequently, the seductive *femme fatale* became an icon of the black and white films of the era. The *femme fatale* of film land is the much-touted "castrating female" or "phallic woman" from psychoanalytic theory — and was probably directly influenced by psychoanalytic theory, which had become more influential in America in the years when these films were in their heyday.[1] Films from the 1940s offered ample opportunities to cast women as evil and powerful. Then again, Barbara Stanwyck, one of Hollywood's most reliable "castrating women" of the late 1940s, had appeared in related roles in the early 1930s, before the Hays Code was enforced.

One of the most odious therapists ever shown on screen appears in the film noir *Nightmare Alley* (1947). Miss Lilith Ritter is not a doctor. Rather, she is a "consulting psychologist" who prominently displays the title "Miss" rather than "Dr." Those who believe that biological treatments alone receive harsh treatment from Hollywood can refer to Ms. Ritter for proof that talk therapists and dream analysts can be as venomous as lobotomists.

As mentioned in the earlier chapter on "Sweet (and Sour) Dreams," Miss Lilith Ritter is true to her name. As her name implies, Lilith invades the dreams of others. She preys upon people as they sleep. She metaphorically sucks the life blood from them as if she were a vampire. But why shouldn't she? She represents the "Lilith" of ancient Babylonian and Biblical lore. She metaphorically steals the dreams of her wealthy clients, who confide their secrets in her Michigan Avenue office on Chicago's "Magnificent Mile."

Miss Lilith records these dreams on vinyl LPs and then recounts them to Stan (Tyrone

Power), her partner in crime, who she recruited from the carnival/side-show/nightclub circuit. Stan connects with Miss Lilith's patients when he performs as a clairvoyant in nightclubs. He impresses them with privileged information and then schedules private meetings with the most distressed among them, staging séances where the bereaved can communicate with their lost loved ones.

Together they deceive her clientele. Miss Lilith also deceives Stan. She sets him up as the patsy who takes the fall for their nightclub scam. She cuts Stan loose, and Stan returns to the circus where he had performed as a "mentalist." Broke and friendless, the hapless Stan returns to the circus. Only this time around he has taken to drink and so is given work as the circus "geek" who sleeps in an animal cage by night and works in return for a bottle. Stan, the small-time carnival con man, seems almost benign compared to the diabolically cunning "consulting psychologist."

Plots about hypnotists and clairvoyants who con their wealthy clientele were popular in the 1930s and 1940s, and were not restricted to medically-trained therapists or hypnotists, or to female physicians. Otto Preminger's *Whirlpool* (1949) pits a scheming hotel hypnotist against a well-intentioned psychiatrist-psychoanalyst. More than a decade earlier the plot of the pre–Code film *The Mind Reader* (1933) parallels that of *Nightmare Alley*. *The Mind Reader* follows the rise and fall of a phony psychic, from his humble Bowery beginnings to an exclusive salon where he deceives wealthy women and relieves them of their money.

Clearly, neither psychologists nor psychiatrists are essential to this time-honored theme. Even though *Nightmare Alley*'s sinister "consulting psychologist" repulses us, *Nightmare Alley* manages to strike a sentimental chord when viewed today, largely because it revolves around a lost bit of Americana: sideshows, small-town carnivals and traveling circuses. *I, the Jury* (1982), in contrast, seems much more contemporary, even though it is based on a book that sets the action in 1944, when World War II was winding down and when *film noir* was at its peak.

Two *I, the Jury* films have been made to date. Both were based on the same Mike Hammer novel. Considering that Mickey Spillane's novel about Mike Hammer was published in 1947, the chronology is not inconsistent at all. Curiously, the Spillane novel — and the start of the Mike Hammer hardboiled detective series — appeared the same year that *Nightmare Alley* debuted. The posh urban settings of *Nightmare Alley* and *I, the Jury* parallel one another, even though they are set in different cities. Chicago's Michigan Avenue, and its elegant lakefront location, of *Nightmare Alley* holds up well when compared to Manhattan's legendary Park Avenue, where the action of *I, the Jury* occurs.

Unfortunately, the first *I, the Jury* film, made in 1953, is not available for purchase or rent at any price. If copies exist, not a soul is selling them on eBay, not even at ridiculously inflated prices. The first film is a toned down version of the novel and revolves around a Park Avenue psychiatrist who specializes in treating prostitutes in her private practice. This is not one of those socially-conscious clinics that popped up in the late '60s, where left-wing organizations such as MCHR (Medical Committee for Human Rights) and SHO (Student Health Organization) volunteered to treat the underprivileged patients. This is not a specialty clinic that treats prostitutes as "victims" of male trafficking, as some programs do today. This is an early '50s' Eisenhower-era film, when the powers that be balked at the idea of distributing Salk's non-patented polio vaccine for free because it could lead to socialized medicine.

Poster for the original *I, the Jury* (1953), based on Mickey Spillane's first Mike Hammer novel, in which Hammer (Biff Elliott) confronts a drug-dealing, disrobing, deadly psychiatrist (Peggie Castle).

Rather than addressing the social ills that contribute to her patients' psychological problems, before she treats the psychiatric problems per se, the psychiatrist in the first *I, the Jury* treats her prostitute-patients to heroin. Dr. Bennett has organized crime connections herself. In 1953 substance abuse treatment did not carry the same cache as it does today. The rise of the Betty Ford Clinic for alcoholism and drug abuse was still decades away. (The Ford Clinic opened in 1982, when the *I, the Jury* remake appeared — and so the remake was adjusted accordingly.)

Dr. Charlotte Bennett makes another mistake, one that is even more unforgivable in the eyes of Mike Hammer. She murders Hammer's war buddy, a one-time cop named Jack Williams. Williams lost an arm while in the service. He lost the arm while saving Hammer's life. The deceased ex-cop character is the "MacGuffin" that drives the film's plot.

Naturally, the rough and tough Mike Hammer will not tolerate the death of a friend, especially when he owes his life to this deceased friend and when this friend made such a sacrifice for him. He will not permit slimy insinuations about Jack's strange sexual preferences to disgrace his dead buddy, and such innuendos have surfaced through Dr. Charlotte's clinic. So the hard-boiled detective steps in — for the first time ever. This film is based on Mickey Spillane's first novel, which spiraled into a remarkable writing career and turned Mike Hammer into the quintessential "hard-boiled" hero.

In the 1982 neo-*noir* remake the setting has shifted and the times have changed. Rather than treating prostitutes' addictions with worse addictions, the psychiatrist has a new gig. Dr. Charlotte Bennett is now running a sex clinic. Dr. Bennett is played by an elegant Latina-looking Barbara Carrera. She speaks with an accent that is subtle enough to be understood but obvious enough to sound exotic. Her Spanish accent foreshadows her Cuban connections.

Dr. Bennett's current collaborator is the CIA rather than the crime syndicate. Again, private detective Mike Hammer investigates the murder of his maimed pal. The result is a bloody, gory film with excessive nudity — or so the critics said. This film suits an era that was riddled with self-indulgence, sexual excess, pricey cocaine, and overall decadence.

Almost everyone involved tries to kill Mike Hammer — for that's what Mike Hammer books and movies are all about. In the end, Dr. Bennett tries to seduce and shoot Mike Hammer in a single move. She is alone in her lavish abode, dressed in a slippery, silky robe that is about to fall off her shoulders as she beckons Hammer to come closer. As she and Mike Hammer enter into one last embrace, she reaches for her pearl-handled gun that lies behind her, hidden in a box that sits on the mantle. Before she can wrap her fingers around her gun, Mike Hammer has pulled out his own revolver. He shoots her in the gut. Mike Hammer anticipated her intentions, even though he appeared to be enraptured. As the film closes, blood streams from her falling body. No one in the audience mourns the demise of the not-so-good doctor.

This 1982 film appeared soon after *Dressed to Kill* (1980), suggesting that the early 1980s were not good years for positive representations of psychiatrists in cinema. Strange sex, mayhem and murder are the norm for films of those years. Curiously, at least two other movies about psychiatrists were released in 1982, both with all-star casts. The farcical *Alone in the Dark* (1982), with Jack Palance, Donald Sutherland and Martin Landau, focuses on a POW who develops paranoid delusions after a new psychiatrist is assigned to his unit. This innovative psychiatrist condones his patients' delusions and refers to them as "voyagers" rather than patients (as if to imply that they are taking a "trip" that is reminiscent of the once-fashionable LSD-aided therapy).

The other notable 1982 film is *Still of the Night* (1982), with Roy Scheider, Meryl Streep, and Jessica Tandy. As a psychological thriller, this film has been compared to the movies of Alfred Hitchcock. Scheider plays a psychiatrist who falls in love with the strange and possibly sociopathic mistress (Streep) of his murdered patient. The psychiatrist's mother is also a psychiatrist. She helps her psychiatrist-son decipher his dreams so that he can use them in the same way a detective utilizes clues. The movie convention of solving crimes via psychoanalysis and dreams started with Hitchcock's *Spellbound* (1945), but the convention of a cinema psychiatrist-mother helping her psychiatrist-son is novel and began with this film.

The doctor clearly breaks boundaries, but this is celluloid, not clinical practice. He falls victim to his sexual attraction but without victimizing his already deceased patient. He never breaks the law, as happened with *I, the Jury*'s Dr. Bennett or with Miss Lilith Ritter, the consulting psychiatrist from *Nightmare Alley*.

Since we are on the subject of psychological thrillers, we can turn to *House of Games* (1987), a film based on David Mamet's co-written screenplay. *Games* was directed by Mamet himself in his directorial debut. Mamet is known for focusing on themes of deception and for featuring lowlifes. This film portrays a "morally ambiguous" psychiatrist-protagonist who interfaces with Mamet's signature "lowlifes" that include a compulsive gambler, his card-playing pals and a cadre of hard-core con artists and liars.

The psychiatrist commits at least one crime, even though she intends to help her patient at the start. She takes a human life, but not until she was wronged herself. She was wronged so badly that viewers ask themselves if she was justified in pointing the gun and pulling the trigger, or if they themselves might have acted similarly in such a situation.

As the film opens, we learn that the psychiatrist has earned a significant sum from her best-selling book about compulsions. She is about to sign a second book contract. In spite of her publishing success, she continues her day-to-day clinical practice, where she treats a young man named Billy. Billy cannot overcome his gambling compulsion and so seeks therapy with Dr. Ford. Some skeptics — as well as die-hard believers in "EBM" (evidence-based medicine) — say that Dr. Ford is as much of a fraud and a con as her gambler-patient, for she treats Billy with psychodynamic methods that have never proved helpful in the treatment of serious addictions.

Billy arrives at an appointment, claiming that he needs $25,000 to pay off a debt and avoid possible loss of life. Dr. Ford arranges to bail him out (breaking standard psychiatric boundaries at the get-go). She delivers the money to a seedy pool hall called House of Games. House of Games is owned by a card player and two-bit pool shark played by the somewhat handsome, somewhat seedy Joe Montagna. Dr. Ford watches the action. She is so intrigued by these events that she wants to write a book about this underworld. She begs Montagna for the opportunity to shadow him so she can learn more about these "games" and round out her research. Montagna complies with her request and asks her to accompany him to a card game, where she will masquerade as his girlfriend. He instructs her on ways to spot the "tell" that shows who is bluffing.

It turns out that Mike (Joe Montagna) is a player in more ways than one. He seduces the psychiatrist, who believes that his interest in her is sincere, even though her initial interest in him was not. Once she is hooked by his charms, he plays her for an even bigger patsy and arranges for her to deliver even more money, allegedly to save him from a horrible fate that awaits him at the hands of crime lords.

In this scam, which is potentially worth $80,000, he makes her believe that a policeman was shot when they switched a suitcase containing the money. He implies that his life is at stake and that he has to go on the lam. Dr. Ford has fallen for Mike and wants to save him. She also believes that she may be an accomplice to a capital crime, for she does not yet know that the uniformed "cop" who was killed before her very eyes was not really a cop (and that he was not really killed), but that he was planted for this purpose and his death faked.

She would have gone along with the plan had it not been for one glitch. Her patient Billy arrives at his scheduled appointment. When he leaves, she sees him drive away in the same car that was used in the getaway scene. The psychiatrist finally figures out that everything was a ruse and that the crew, her patient included, set out to separate her from her money. Eavesdropping on the team at the House of Games confirms her suspicions. She also hears Mike say that "making love to her was a small price to pay" for the scam.

She then launches her own scheme. Having heard that Mike plans to leave town that night, she waits for him at the airport and offers him even more money if he takes her along. As per his suggestion, she agrees to meet Montagna at a remote corner of an airport loading dock before the scheduled take-off. But she comes armed both with knowledge and Billy's gun, which she had taken from Billy to prevent him from harming himself.

Dr. Ford confronts Mike, but he shows no remorse. When he turns to leave, she pulls out the gun and demands that he beg for his life. But he acts as though she is bluffing. When he walks away, she starts shooting — not once but many times, just to ensure that he is dead.

As the film ends, we see Dr. Ford gleefully lifting a cigarette lighter from another woman's bag. She shows the cover of her latest book, *Forgive Yourself*. Her happy demeanor tells us that she can forgive herself, just as she instructs her readers.

David Mamet's character comes along far too late to be considered a *film noir*–style *femme fatale*. In fact, her naiveté is the polar opposite of the scheming *femmes fatales* of 1940s and '50s era films. She is a better example of the "woman wronged" than a *femme fatale*. The fact that she is a psychiatrist tells us that even trained professionals can be duped by ill-intentioned men. Dr. Ford is more of a symbol of universal womanhood, avenging a wrong á la Carmen. However, anyone who has heard that "only a con can be conned" will wonder if Dr. Ford is simply a sociopath in the raw, waiting to be revealed for what she really is, rather than a purely innocent victim who becomes the victimizer — or is it the avenger? — in the end.

The head psychiatric nurse in *One Flew Over the Cuckoo's Nest* (1975) who victimizes Jack Nicolson and sends him off for a lobotomy has even less justification for her actions. Her authority at Oregon State Hospital has been challenged by McMurphy, a petty criminal played by Nicholson. So she convinces an unobtrusive psychiatrist to sign off on her proposed treatment plan. Nurse Ratched, played by Louise Fletcher, is by far the most evil female psychiatric professional found in film. She is more malicious than just about any female physician seen on screen (except perhaps for Dr. Bennett from the Mike Hammer film). Even in her literary form, in Ken Kesey's best-selling novel from the 1960s, Nurse Ratched is as wretched as her name sounds.

The film made Academy Awards history. It won the "Big Five" Academy Awards: Best Picture, Best Actor (Jack Nicholson), Best Actress (Louise Fletcher), Best Director (Milos Forman) and Best Adapted Screenplay (Lawrence Hauben, Bo Goldman). Commentators claim that Nurse Ratched reflected fears about the rise of feminism in the late 1960s and early 1970s.

Something is wrong with that assessment, for the book upon which the film was based appeared in 1962, several years before the women's movement officially began in 1969. The Pill was brought to market in 1962, and it surely paved the path for feminism. But who could foresee the future in 1962? They say that hindsight is always 20/20, and the aftershocks of the Pill were not foreseen but only recognized in retrospect. The book was a best-seller long before Milos Forman added his cinematic skills to the mix in 1975. However, the stage version of *Cuckoo's Nest* was also remarkably successful back in 1963, the same year Betty Friedan published *The Feminist Mystique*.

Apart from criticizing the critics for overlooking the chronology of the book, stage play, and film version, we can safely conclude that psychiatric nurses, and even other supporting figures in psychiatry, are depicted badly more often than not. In David Cronenberg's dismal film *Spider* (2002), a heartless woman runs a half-way house for persons with chronic mental disorders.

The movie is set in 1950s London, in the poverty-ridden East End. A decade or so later the controversial "anti-psychiatrist" R.D. Laing opened a very different psychiatric residence at Kingsley Hall, in the same East End area. Similar to *Spider*'s home, Kingsley Hall originally housed a soup kitchen and homeless shelter. Then it became the home of Laing's very different, "let it all hang loose" approach to the treatment (or lack thereof) of psychosis.

Actors (left to right) William Redfield, Sydney Lassick, Jack Nicholson, Christopher Lloyd, Vincent Schiavelli, and William Duell play patients in *One Flew Over the Cuckoo's Nest* (1975) just before the "I want my cigarette scene" erupts into mayhem.

In *Spider* the protagonist suffers from schizophrenia. He hears hallucinatory voices, as well as the harsh voice of the woman who runs the house. The film stars Ralph Fiennes, Miranda Richardson, and Gabriel Byrne. Their performances convey the tragedy of the situation and the coldness of the "head mistress," as poignantly experienced by her vulnerable charges. Ralph Fiennes' exemplary portrayal of the schizophrenic boarder predates his more predatory role as the psychotic "Tooth Fairy" in *Red Dragon* (2002), which was released later that year.

An odd example of a sinister psychiatric nurse can be found in *In Dreams* (1999), with Robert Downey, Jr. This film was mentioned in an earlier chapter on "Supernatural Psychiatrists." If *Spider* is a cornerstone of stark realism in the depiction of psychiatric settings, then *In Dreams* is an example of Surrealism to the point of absurdity. The psychiatric nurse in this film is a serial killer who invades the dreams of patients of a tawdry state institution. What's more, the nurse not only crosses dimensions, but s/he also crosses gender boundaries. Downey returned to acting through second rate roles such as this one after his foray with rehab for his substance abuse problems. The film showcases his acting skills and also proves that a checkered psychiatric past need not disqualify an actor from a comeback. Rather, we see how his checkered "credentials" qualify him for lead roles in films about checkered psychiatric institutions.

Oddly enough, no one bothered to compare Downey's rendition of Nurse Vivian Thompson to Caine's portrayal of the cross-dressing psychiatrist in *Dressed to Kill* (1981). But perhaps that is because relatively few people bothered to see *In Dreams* in the first place. Even De Palma's rip-off of Hitchcock ruffled more feathers than this offbeat supernatural psycho-thriller. Perhaps the difference in settings also played a role: Manhattan's posh Upper East Side skyscrapers are more appealing than dilapidated institutions in the middle of nowhere (unless a *Texas Chainsaw Massacre* takes place there). The supernatural setting of *In Dreams* also makes it inherently unreal, whereas *Dressed to Kill*'s setting brings it closer to home. *Dressed to Kill* makes the spectator believe that owners of Manhattan high rises have more to fear than heights.

There are many other examples of heartless female psychiatric nurses and heads of halfway houses to cite. There are also memorable examples of caring and compassionate ones who sometimes break boundaries in their pursuit of a cure. (*Persona* [1966]) comes to mind as an oft-cited example.) Still, it should be noted that mean male psychiatric nurses have also made it to the silver screen. One of Hollywood's most memorable films, *Lost Weekend* (1945), includes a sneering (and stereotyped) male nurse who makes patients' miserable lives even more miserable as they suffer through alcohol withdrawal. The frightening hallucinations endured in the detox ward of a city hospital are peppered by pain-inducing quips made by a man who wears whites.

In conclusion, we have seen how celluloid female psychiatrists can act as villains (or victims), and how sex and seduction figures into the plot more often than not. But female psychiatric nurses deserve their own separate study, for they are cast in an even worse light than MDs. Nurse Ratched appeared on screen decades ago, in 1975, yet she remains the most memorable female mental health worker even seen on screen. It would be hard for any female physician to reverberate as consistently as Nurse Ratched has for over a third of a century.

Lest anyone forget Louise Fletcher's Nurse Ratched, Mel Brooks etched her character even deeper into the cultural *zeitgeist*, when he spoofed her in *High Anxiety* (1977). The Mel Brooks rendition parodies Hitchcock films just as irreverently as it spoofs Nurse Ratched. In *High Anxiety*, Cloris Leachman plays a whip-wielding RN named Nurse Diesel. Her name needs no explanation. Harvey Korman is the mild-mannered psychiatrist (Dr. Thorndyke) who is tied upside down in a closet while the leather-clad Diesel expresses her anger at this "thorn" in her side. The audience responds with laughter, relieved that the tragedy of *Cuckoo's Nest* is not replayed here.

Not even Dr. Melfi (Lorraine Bracco), of the *Sopranos* (1999–2007) television show, has as much name recognition as Nurse Ratched, even though Lorraine Bracco won several Emmy nominations for her role as Dr. Melfi. Years have passed since that show ended, and mob movies and TV crime shows come and go. Few have the staying power of Coppola's *The Godfather* saga (1972), or even *Goodfellas* (1990), where Lorraine Bracco co-starred as a mobster's free-spending wife some years before she was cast as Tony Soprano's psychiatrist.

Then again, Dr. Melfi was not sinister in her own right, and she was more of a foil for James Gandolfino's crime boss character, who was her patient and occasionally her protector. Because her primary patient is so evil, her own ethics are called into question. But that is a secondary issue. Psychiatrists may debate the ethics of Dr. Melfi's decision to treat mobsters, but no one debates the extent of Nurse Ratched's evil. Nurse Ratched is a latter day devil, a she-demoness who masquerades as a helper and healer. Imagine what she might accomplish if she were first in command. But that thought is too scary to contemplate.

7

Shock Schlock

Shock therapy is the most common — and the most hackneyed — anti-psychiatry theme in film. Shock docs, as they are sometimes known, usually (but not always) become sinister by association.

I should be more specific before proceeding further. ECT (or electroconvulsive therapy), which is also known as electroshock therapy, receives the most attention in movies, for reasons that I will reveal later. But there are other kinds of "shock therapy" that are nearly forgotten by everyone save for film fans, or proto-psychiatrists preparing for board exams or historians of medicine, who remain intrigued by outdated treatments.

Insulin shock therapy was once an important form of shock therapy. In insulin shock, a patient is injected with insulin, which lowers blood sugar levels in the same way that it drops blood sugar in diabetics. Just as the blood sugar plummets to dangerously low levels and the patient falls into a coma, a nurse revives the patient with a big bolus of glucose.

Sometimes this system fails. If staff members are not as mindful as they should be, the patient runs the risk of permanent brain damage after staying in coma too long. To this day it is still not fully known how or why this risky treatment works. But it is known that insulin coma is no more — and no less — effective than barbiturate-induced coma, which is far safer.

Insulin shock faded from memory until it was featured on the popular TV show *House MD* in 2009 ("Under My Skin," Season 5, Episode 24). In that instance the ever-controversial but ever-entertaining Dr. House injects himself with insulin in hopes of fending off hallucinations induced by Vicodan withdrawal. Poor Dr. House has become addicted to self-prescribed prescription opiates and has forgotten about medical ethics. But he has not forgotten a seat-of-the-pants psychiatric treatment that most American doctors discarded decades ago.

Apart from earning an MD medical degree, Dr. House has little in common with the flawless character of Dr. Kildare that appeared in ten films from the mid–1930s through the early 1940s. Dr. Kildare has the best of intentions when he tries insulin shock on a patient in *Dr. Kildare's Strange Case* (1940). In this instance Dr. Kildare hopes to relieve a post-operative patient's neuropsychiatric symptoms that emerged after a surgical error. By curing the patient with this once-respectable technique, he also hopes to save the reputation of the surgeon who probably caused this serious side effect.

Insulin shock was still in use in 1940. This Dr. Kildare drama was but one of many Dr. Kildare films that were followed by a radio show in the 1950s and a TV series in the

1960s. All versions idealized the young intern as he learned about all medical specialties. In that era, most physicians became general practitioners — but some became curmudgeonly surgeons that contrasted with the young doctor's kindly approach.

But our main concern here is with schlocky shock therapy in cinema, where this theme was overplayed time and time again. One might say that it took a stroke of genius to represent a different sort of shock scene in *Death Wish II* (1982). In that film we witness a confrontation that ends with fatally-administered ECT (electroshock or electroconvulsive therapy). The deadly electric volts are *not* delivered by a doctor and are not part of prescribed psychiatric treatment. Rather, the ECT comes courtesy of a vigilante, Paul Kersey, who is played with relish by Charles Bronson.

In this sequel to the 1974 original, the vigilante and his daughter live in LA after leaving their native New York, where their troubles began and where the first film was based. His daughter is still recovering from her attack. She is not completely well, but at least she has come out of her trauma-induced catatonic stupor and can speak.

But this is an action film, and it is a Charles Bronson movie. So we have a pretty good idea of what is in store for us (and the characters), and we know that it can't be anything good, given Bronson's tendency to right wrongs, in the most violent ways possible, in whatever film he appears. This time around, bad things are awaiting both the housekeeper and the still-traumatized daughter.

The housekeeper is raped by a gang of punks who come to Kersey's house. That's just the beginning. Worse yet, the daughter jumps through a window while trying to escape the attackers. As she falls, she is impaled on a rail, and dies. The audience is now ready to condone whatever retaliation Charles Bronson can conjure up.

The attacker and accidental murderer of Bronson's daughter is arrested, but he is acquitted on an insanity charge and moved to a state psychiatric hospital. This acquittal shakes the credibility of forensic psychiatry and casts doubt on how well this specialty serves the interests of society as it strives to protect the interests of the individual. That is hardly a novel observation. But the ECT scene that follows makes an even stronger impression and casts shadows over the treatments currently used in psychiatric facilities.

A born avenger, Bronson tracks down the supposedly insane assailant and gives him his due — in the electroshock therapy room. Bronson enters the hospital, having stolen a doctor's ID badge. He confronts the assailant. Fists fly, and the assailant is repeatedly stabbed with a scalpel. He throws another punch, which smashes through a nearby ECT machine. Bronson then turns up the power, and electrocutes his adversary without showing the slightest sign of remorse.

ECT treatment is never blamed for this bad outcome, and, indeed, few viewers denounce this innovative use of electroshock therapy for non-medical purposes (although psychiatrists often assail the negative associations that ECT acquires in this setting). Spectators side with the vigilante. Even the peaceniks and war protestors that made up much of the audience for the original *Death Wish* from 1974 cheer him on.

A hospital orderly also understands Bronson's motivations. The orderly spots Bronson, witnesses the events, but recognizes him from photos he saw in the newspaper. When he realizes that this man's daughter died while escaping a rapist, the orderly says, "You've got three minutes to go. And then I call the cops."

Unfortunately, many psychiatrists find this film insulting to the profession in general and to ECT techniques in particular. But many film aficionados find this scene no more insulting than a scalpel scene conducted in a surgery suite. Both are violent, both are vicious, but both are simply opportunistic and have little to say about medical care.

It just so happened that the sequel to the original *Death Wish* appeared at a time that was especially receptive to sinister psychiatric themes, so that psychiatry as a profession may have been extra sensitive about more bad celluloid press. *I, the Jury* was remade in 1982, with the lead psychiatrist having turned into a sex therapist that conspires with the CIA but then dies while trying to kill Mike Hammer. Two years earlier, Michael Caine's cross-dressing psychiatrist murders his adulterous patient (Angie Dickinson) in *Dressed to Kill*. Each of those films were damning to the profession, even without ECT.

We have to wait until 1999 to see ECT depicted as brutally as it was in *Death Wish II*. (There may have been straight-to-video movies with worse ECT scenes, but we are not dealing with those films in this context.) In 1999 another remake —*House on Haunted Hill*— utilizes an ECT machine for murder (or, more accurately, for simulated murder that is extremely sadistic nonetheless). In this case, psychiatrist Dr. Blackburn is evil because he is willing to take another man's wife and use his medical know-how to fake her death. But Dr. Blackburn is nowhere near as evil as the psychiatrist who ran the Vannacutt Psychiatric Institute for the Criminally Insane, which was housed in the mansion where the film's action occurs. The back story is as important as the present-day plot.

Numerous murders occurred at the Vannacutt Psychiatric Institute in the 1930s. Ghosts of the original inmates reappear regularly to remind us (and the party guests) of the atrocities committed in the original Vannacutt Institute. Dr. Donald Blackburn has no connection to this institute, and he bears none of the blame for its doctors. But he and his married lover have conspired to fake her murder so that she can leave her wealthy husband, who has hosted this unusual Halloween and birthday party, and the two can run off together.

The host has his own plans, however. He hopes to do away with his fourth and current trophy wife, and has offered generous prizes to party guests who might aid in her demise, however unwittingly. He apparently dislikes her a great deal, although he does not suspect her affair with the psychiatrist. If it is any consolation, the wife is *not* the doctor's patient, so he has not broken those professional boundaries.

As discussed in the chapter on "Sex, Seduction, and the Couch Cure," the party guests are offered one million dollars apiece if they succeed in spending the night in the abandoned asylum that the husband has rented for his wife's gala. As an amusement park mogul, he has a wide range of tricks and special effects at his disposal. He also has large sums of money to spend.

We learn that this house became known as "The House on Haunted Hill" after several unexplained murders occurred during its restoration. It has remained idle ever since. The evening progresses, with the usual sprinkles of murder and mayhem. At one point the guests spot Evelyn, the host's wife and the psychiatrist's paramour, strapped to a bed, writhing wildly in apparent pain. She appears to be undergoing ECT. But the lever of the ECT machine is stuck. None of the guests can stop the machine to stop the torture, no matter how hard they try. Eventually someone cuts the electric supply and the machine stops. Electric sparks flash. We have seen the victim suffer for far too long. In the end, she oozes blood from her mouth, gasps, and then dies (supposedly) from excessive electroshock.

It turns out that Dr. Blackburn has staged the death. Partygoers (and film spectators) believe that ECT killed Evelyn (who was named "Annabelle" in the original version). Then the bad doctor uses his medical credentials to declare her dead — even though she remains alive. The purpose? To set her free from her husband so that the two of them can flee.

In this case, the sham ECT-induced death is but one of many daggers thrown at psychiatry. However, it is not true-to-fact. Consider the fact that the original hospital — the current *House on Haunted Hill*—housed patients in the early 1930s. The asylum has 15 ECT rooms — but ECT had not yet been invented! It would be imported to America by the Hungarian doctor Munoz in 1938, well after the invention of the EEG (electroencephalogram), which permitted monitoring of brain waves. But, of course, in cinema, good storytelling takes precedence over accurate storytelling.

Another film, a very different, socially-constructive movie, also exploits ECT to emphasize its point about psychiatric collusion with (corrupt) legal authorities. In *Changeling* (2008) we see the star, Angelina Jolie, being hosed down in a mental ward. She is about to be subjected to shock treatment against her will and against good clinical judgment (or against any clinical judgment, since her interment is a political ploy and not a professional decision).

Angelina Jolie plays a woman who is literally a prisoner of the state. As Christine, she was deemed delusional after she bucked the authorities and refused to corroborate the police chief's claims that he found her real "son," who had disappeared some time before.

The film is set in 1928, a decade before ECT became available. The shock value of shock therapy speaks for itself. This otherwise high-minded film comments on a very real event that was later condemned by higher state authorities. Apparently, director Clint Eastwood felt it necessary to embellish the psychiatric "crimes" recounted in the drama by adding an emotion-laden ECT scene that might strengthen the political points he hopes to make.

Although one would not guess from watching his *Dirty Harry* series or seeing him act in his hyper-macho cowboy roles, Clint Eastwood sports impressive feminist credentials. He plumps up his pro-woman resume with this film, even though his exploitative portrayal of ECT, and his casual indifference to historical timelines in the history of psychiatry, cost him a few points with psychiatrists. Previously, Clint Eastwood had made *Sudden Impact* (1983) as a deliberately pro-feminist film. In that movie, Dirty Harry (Eastwood) is a suspended cop who rights wrongs in his own way. He teams up with a woman who was gang-raped ten years before. When she exacts revenge on her rapists, he looks the other way and lets her flee.

In *Changeling*, Clint Eastwood deliberately comments on the co-optation of women's recently won rights in the late 1920s. In the early '20s the Suffragette movement pushed for women's right to vote, but there came a backlash after the victory. Women who defied the power structure — like Angelina Jolie's character, Christine Collins — bore the brunt of retribution. When Jolie plays the defiant Collins, she harkens back her role as a defiant young female mental patient in *Girl, Interrupted* (1999).

Changeling makes other political points as well. It focuses on the relative disempowerment of women in American society, even after they obtained the vote and even to this day. It comments on crimes against children, on capital punishment, on police corruption, and on psychiatry's behind-the-scenes collusion with corruption. For these efforts, and for its execution, it received three Academy Award and eight BAFTA Award nominations.

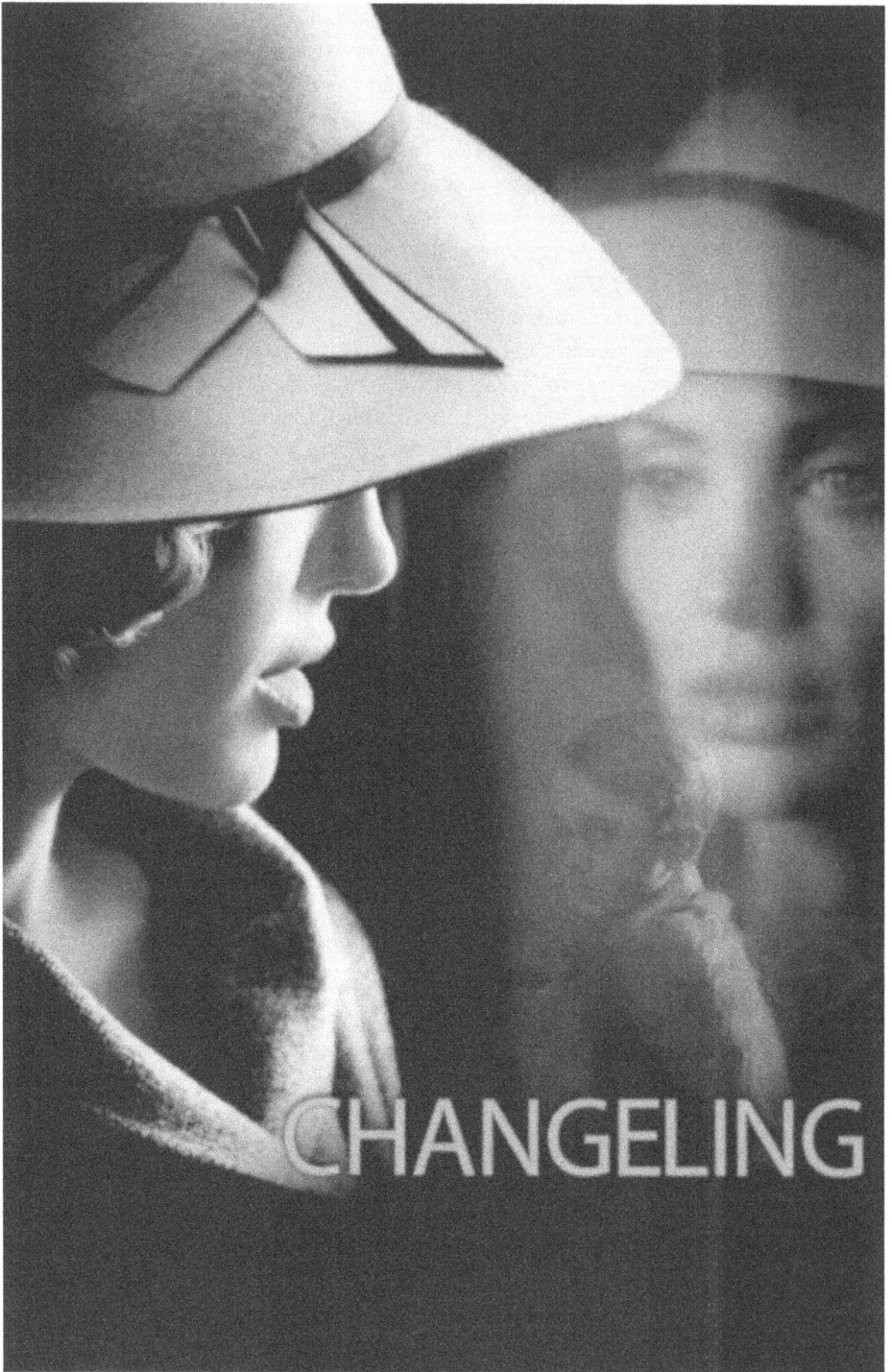

Christine Collins (Angelina Jolie) gazes at her reflection, contemplating her missing son, before she is hosed down in a mental ward and threatened with ECT in this poster for *Changeling* (2008).

The story revolves around a single mother who lives in Los Angeles in 1928. Christine Collins (Angelina Jolie) works as a supervisor of telephone operators. Telephone operators were a newly-formed female task force. They represented not just modernity but also the changing role of women in the work world. Christine roller skates down long corridors as she reviews the work of other women but confers with a male supervisor, who expresses romantic interest (in an ever-so-polite way).

Christine is also the devoted mother of a young son, whom she discovers missing. Nine-year-old Walter cannot be found, even though she searches for him frantically. Some time later the LAPD's police chief proudly announces that her missing son has been located. He calls a press conference to publicize the reunion (and to fortify his political power and name recognition).

However, Christine is certain that the found boy is *not* her son, even though the young man proclaims her to be his mother and himself to be the lost Walter. The police chief derides her but eventually concedes to a physical exam, to be performed by a doctor. But the doctor offers no help. When told that the new boy is shorter than Walter, the doctor says that trauma shrunk his spine. When told that "new" Walter was circumcised, whereas her son was not, the doctor argues that the man who took Walter had him circumcised while he was away.

At this point the LAPD bristles and tries to declare Christine an unfit mother. They wage a publicity war against Christine, but a powerful and politically-astute preacher, played by John Malkovich, steps in to offer support to Christine. In the interim, Christine is whisked away to a mental hospital. A psychiatrist shoves official-looking papers before her, telling her that she will be discharged if she signs papers in support of the police chief and if she drops her claim that the found boy is someone other than her own natural son Walter.

Christine refuses. We see her shoved into a locked ward and hosed down by orderlies. We hear another female inmate warn Christine about other women who were sent to the psych ward because they challenged the police. Soon enough, she is strapped to a slab and shoved into a small chamber that houses ECT equipment.

Christine is about to be subjected to shock treatment (which can disrupt memories as well as dislodge depression), but Reverend Briegleb's intervention proves successful at the eleventh hour. John Malkovich's clergyman character has convinced the mayor to release Christine, even though the colluding psychiatrist had claimed that she is delusional.

The denouement is both good and bad. Reverend Briegleb's theory proves to be correct. The police had planted evidence to discredit Christine, just as he predicted. Psychiatrists like Dr. Steele are patsies of the police. Thanks to the Reverend's intervention, and thanks to clues that surface about the real killer around the time of the protests, Christine is released from the L.A. County Hospital "psychopathic ward." As she exits, crowds cheer. But the end is still to come.

Over time, Christine's private theories also prove to be correct. The boy in her charge confesses that he is not the real Walter. He admits that he played along with the police chief's ploy because he needed a home, food and clothes, which he no longer had after running away from home to meet the actor Tom Mix and his horse Tony.

New leads about the disappearance of some young boys surface some time later. Detectives follow up on these leads and track the missing boys to a farm, where many boys, Walter included, were taken after being abducted. They were molested, maybe raped, and most were murdered. Some escaped, with Walter being one of them. But it is never learned where he wound up. Neither Christine nor the audience know what actually became of Walter.

What we see on screen is the true tale of the Wineville Chicken Coop case. Even though aspects of Christine's psychiatric confinement and treatment were fictionalized or overly-dramatized, there are many true-to-life facts in this film. It is a fact that the California State Legislature reacted to some of the events that were chronicled by Clint Eastwood. The legislature made it illegal for the police to commit people to a psychiatric facility without a valid warrant. The rights of "psychiatric patients" were advanced.

In this instance, Clint Eastwood has presented us with a "social problem" film, but one that is set in the past. By backdating the action to 1928, Eastwood has softened the impact of the subject. This ploy makes a touchy issue more acceptable to more people, and makes him look less like a social crusader, which might be off-putting to those who disagree with him or who seek out movies as mere entertainment rather than movies that moralize.

And so Eastwood succeeds in making his point and alerting us to his views about the continuing victimization of women by organized psychiatry. Women are still grossly over-represented among psychiatric patients and are more likely to receive ECT than male patients with similar symptoms. (Men are more likely to develop substance abuse problems, or they wind up in jail because their "bad behavior" gets them into trouble with the law.) Since ECT can cause temporary or permanent memory impairment at the same time that it offers rapid relief of depressive symptoms, this practice implies that women's minds, memories and intellect are less valued than men's memories and minds.[1]

Many of those who comment about psychiatry and the cinema reflexively conclude that ECT is *always* depicted badly, and that this treatment technique *automatically* shows psychiatry in a bad light. That is simply not true. *Fear Strikes Out* (1957) contradicts that theory headon, and bucks the usual trends in depicting ECT on screen.[2]

Fear Strikes Out fictionalizes and romanticizes (yes, romanticizes!) the ECT treatment that relieved the catatonia endured by the popular baseball player Jimmy Piersall. This film is not an accurate rendition of the triumphs and travails of the once-promising Boston Red Sox player, as the movie implies that Jimmy fared better than he did in real life. True, his catatonia lifted after his treatment in a hospital setting. That is to be expected, since ECT is remarkably effective in relieving this uncommon condition that occasionally accompanies bipolar disorder (more than schizophrenia). His mood swings persisted, however, and often interfered with his baseball career after the acute crisis ended. But when he stepped up to the plate, wearing a Beatles wig and playing "air guitar" with his bat, fans cheered him on.

Jimmy Piersall eventually carved out a niche as a baseball announcer. He disowned the film made about his life story, disagreeing with its depiction of his father. In his autobiography, which he wrote with Dick Wittingham in 1985, he says, "Probably the best thing that ever happened to me was going nuts. Who ever heard of Jimmy Piersall, before that happened?" Retrospective diagnoses determined that Piersall suffered from bipolar disorder with catatonic features, and the treatment of choice for this condition was, and still is, ECT.

Curiously, Piersall's troubled character is played by Anthony Perkins, who gained far greater fame from his role as a much more troubled young man a few years later. In 1960, Perkins played Norman Bates in *Psycho*.

It's worth mentioning a film like *Fear Strikes Out*, if only to remind readers that ECT is not universally portrayed negatively, and that psychiatric conditions and treaters are not invariably seen as dangerous or diabolical. Other films about famous people who underwent ECT have inspired mixed reactions in spectators. But recall that *Fear Strikes Out* is a film of its era, and that era was known as "the golden age of psychiatry." During that brief interlude that lasted half a dozen years, psychiatric treatment was glorified on screen rather than demonized. Even ECT fared well under those conditions.

A later movie about a famous person shows a diametrically different perspective. *A Beautiful Mind* (2001) chronicles the mental breakdown of the Nobel Prize–winning mathematician John Nash (Russell Crowe). This 21st century film shows mid–20th century shock therapy as a violent and implicitly painful treatment. It also confuses electroshock therapy with insulin shock therapy. For purists, and for historians of medicine and psychiatry, and for practicing psychiatrists, the conflation of insulin shock with electroshock is unforgivable. For anti-psychiatry activists, such blurred boundaries only proves that psychiatric treatments, whatever their form, are hurtful rather than helpful.

Overall, *A Beautiful Mind* was praised for the sensitivity it lavished on its schizophrenic protagonist — who is also a mathematical genius.[3] In spite of his brilliance, Nash could not ward off the voices and visions that interfered with his ability to distinguish fact from fantasy. His troubled existence, and his tenuous academic tenure, is beautifully rendered on screen. The filmmakers take some artistic liberties and "translate" misperceptions and auditory hallucinations into visual imagery that is more accessible to spectators and more appropriate to a primarily visual medium such as movies. But everyone who observes Nash, his wife included, realizes that his insulin shock therapy was ineffective as well as uncomfortable.

The professionally sophisticated spectator knows that schizophrenia is nowhere near as responsive to treatment — any treatment — as bipolar disorder with catatonic features. Thus, we would expect Jimmy Piersall to fare far better than John Nash, even though one was a baseball player and the other was a Nobel Prize–winning mathematician.

Those who are not trained to treat serious psychiatric illnesses might expect a brilliant person to heal faster than a professional athlete, but that is not necessarily so. The type of psychiatric condition counts for more than the patient's profession. However, a schizophrenic person with high intelligence at baseline does have a better prognosis than someone who starts out with lesser intelligence before their breakdown. But intelligence alone does not override schizophrenia or allow someone to reason his way out of hallucinations or delusions.

The professionally sophisticated spectator also knows that ECT was an improvement over the insulin shock treatment that preceded it. As we know, insulin coma, or insulin shock, ran the risk of inducing dangerously low blood sugar and an irreversible coma. A person who stays hypoglycemic, with low blood sugar, for too long a time period can suffer permanent brain damage. That means potential intellectual impairment, a vegetative state, and possible death.

The usually temporary and reversible memory impairment and confusional states that can follow electroshock treatments are mild in comparison to the risks imposed by insulin coma therapy. As a result, ECT replaced insulin shock and even metronidazole shock soon after it arrived in North America. A very few pricey and specialized sanitariums offered insulin therapy into the early 1950s, but they were few and far between.

Apart from the recent episode of *House MD* mentioned earlier, we rarely hear of the use of insulin shock after muscle relaxants made ECT less uncomfortable, and after advances in anesthesia allowed patients to sleep through the procedure safely and painlessly. However, I have personally heard psychiatrist Dr. David Kreditor's recollections of insulin shock used in a former Communist-controlled country (Estonia) that could not afford ECT equipment, which is costly compared to insulin.[4] But if we read the fine print of articles about ECT advocate Dr. Max Fink, we learn that Dr. Fink's residency began in 1952 at New York hospital, which housed a 22-bed insulin coma therapy unit. He headed that unit for six years, and later became an outspoken ECT spokesperson, as well as a researcher, educator, and practitioner of psychiatry in general and ECT in particular.

In an earlier chapter I discussed *Shock* (1946), a melodramatic *film noir* starring Vincent Price. In that movie about a classic love-murder triangle, the action revolves around insulin shock treatment. A woman has fallen into a catatonic state after witnessing a man murdering a woman. The woman does not know that the murderer is a psychiatrist, and that he will soon become *her* psychiatrist when her husband takes her to a nearby sanitarium for treatment. As it turns out, the sanitarium nurse is the secret lover of the murderous psychiatrist. The nurse fears that the patient might recognize the doctor upon awakening and identify him as the murderer. So she urges the psychiatrist to inject his patient with more insulin to send her into a permanent coma.

In *Shock* (1946), Dr. Cross (Vincent Price) hovers over his patient (Anabel Shaw), wondering if she recognizes him as the murderer, as she regains consciousness after insulin shock therapy.

Shock does not present insulin as particularly painful or harmful. It merely reminds audiences of the potential harm that it can cause when applied by untrained or untrustworthy staff. In this film it is not the treatment that is shown as sinister; it is the treater, and his accomplice and romantic partner. The female nurse in the film proves to be more dangerous than the male doctor. For the male doctor suffers pangs of conscience and refuses to murder his patient. But the nurse urges him on, only to have him turn on her instead. In the heat of an argument he kills her in the same way he killed his wife.

There is an implied warning in this film, even if the warning does not concern insulin coma. The movie reminds us that we don't really know the person who is treating us and to whom we entrust our lives. Even if they own a fashionable sanitarium, and even if they present themselves in professional ways and pretend to be altruistic, can we really trust them?

If *Shock* provided bad press for ECT or insulin shock therapy or psychiatry in general in 1946, then *Shock Corridor* ensured that audiences carried away an even worse image. *Shock Corridor* (1963) also features a catatonic patient — even though catatonia is a rare condition. A reporter who wants to investigate the goings-on at a mental hospital finds himself locked inside the ward. The stress of masquerading as a mental patient is too great, and he finds himself falling into a catatonic stupor himself.

It's besides the point that this dreadful effect is clinically improbable, and that catatonia is not the end result of severe stress but is connected to a poorly-understood neuro-biological condition. It's the action and the drama that count, rather than the details. To end the catatonic state, the reporter is strapped to a table and his limbs covered in leather bands. A wad of gauze is stuffed into his mouth. He makes a temporary recovery after ECT but relapses (as is all too common with catatonia in real life). He ends the film frozen in position and unable to speak.

Like so many movies, *Shock Corridor* reflects the era in which it was made as much as it reflects its subject matter. By 1963, the flash-in-the-pan "Golden Age of Psychiatry" was starting to tarnish. By the early 1960s, positive portrayals of celluloid psychiatrists had given way to gloomier imagery. This is one of those films that signaled that the Golden Era had come to an end, and that times and attitudes had changed. Movie monsters turned into psychotic mental patients in the Sixties and Seventies, even though they had not been so before.

By 1960, anti-psychiatry spokespersons such as R.D. Laing, Thomas Szasz and David Cooper were casting shadows over psychiatry. These psychiatrist-activists discredited accepted concepts of mental illness (albeit for different reasons). They suggested that mental illness was invented both by psychiatry and by the state for their own benefit rather than to aid the ill. Even if their views were never accepted by mainstream psychiatry, their ideas struck a nerve and provoked debate and self-reflection.[5]

In 1962, a year before *Shock Corridor* opened, Ken Kesey's novel about his job at Menlo Park Veterans Hospital was published. Kesey wrote about his work as a psychiatric aid and as a volunteer for CIA-sponsored drug trials that were conducted onsite. His irreverent account is not forgotten, even though half a century has passed since it first appeared in print. Kesey reportedly talked to patients while he was under the influence of LSD-like drugs and concluded that the patients were not insane, but that society was sick. Those sentiments were echoed across the counter-culture and by some psychiatrists as well.

In book form, *One Flew Over the Cuckoo's Nest* (1962) did not achieve the same celebrity as the film version from 1975. But the book did become a best-seller, and it did inspire a successful stage adaptation a year after its publication. The play's star, Kirk Douglas, played an important role in ensuring that the play made it to the silver screen. This book paved the way for the anti-psychiatry attitudes that came to full fruition in the mid–1970s, with the release of Milos Forman's epoch-making film based on Ken Kesey's novel.

The social and professional impact of the film version of *One Flew Over the Cuckoo's Nest* (1975) was nothing less than remarkable. Medical students who saw the movie changed their attitudes toward ECT after a single viewing. Most grew reluctant to recommend ECT to friends or family after witnessing Jack Nicolson's ordeals as McMurphy. McMurphy is a petty criminal who feigns madness so he can be moved out of his jailhouse confinement to supposedly cushier surroundings in the psych hospital.

The psychiatrists in the film are benign (and some are played by real psychiatrists). It is the head nurse who orchestrates the attack on patients and on the insolent McMurphy. Even though the psychiatric nurse is the "devil in disguise," and the psychiatrists play no part in the evil that ensues (thought they also do nothing to stop her), this one film remains the most powerful anti-psychiatry statement ever made. McMurphy is eventually lobotomized after ECT fails to control his defiant behavior. But it is the ECT, rather than lobotomy, that comes off as the more immediate threat to both patients and society.

After viewing films like *Shock Corridor* and *One Flew Over the Cuckoo's Nest*, it is easy to think that the irreverent representations of ECT on screen are a result of political motivations. While that may be true at times, there are also more benign reasons why filmmakers add scenes of electroconvulsive treatments. The reasons we see so many ECT scenes in cinema may have no relationship to clinical or philosophical attitudes toward psychiatry per se. The fact that shock therapy is visually interesting is just as important as clinical commentary. Since film is primarily a visual medium that is secondarily enhanced by sound it stands to reason that directors would insert scenes with gripping visual details. Hitchcock himself insisted on playing his films without sound, to ensure that the story could be understood from imagery alone. (Hitchcock started his film career in the silent era and learned the importance of visuals as stand-alone storytellers.)

ECT induces (supposedly) wild thrashing, at least when administered before muscle relaxants became available. Because ECT comes with a complicated mechanical apparatus, with flashing lights and mysterious knobs, and the sharp spikes and wavy lines of the constantly moving EEG (electroencephalogram), ECT scenes tell audiences that something special is happening on screen. It holds the viewer's attention.

Compare the dramatic gyrations of ECT to a hospital scene where a nurse holds a pill on a tray, along with a small cup of water. Psychopharmacology scenes cannot compare to the drama of shock therapy. Injectable medications are somewhat more interesting than pill-only scenes, but injectable medications are less commonly used. Even the surgical scenes of lobotomy are not as unique as ECT. Operations are performed on all sorts of organs, and are performed all the time. So the "surgical amphitheater" where brain surgery (and other surgeries) takes place is not particularly special. But ECT is ECT. It cannot be confused with any other procedure.

Another reason why ECT attained such prominence in film revolves around the timing. ECT was imported into America in 1938 after having been used by the Italians first. In those years there was usually a ten-year lag time between an event and its cinematic depiction. (Newsreels were far faster means of visual communication and regularly played in movie houses during the war years, both before and after featured films.) Thus, an event that occurred in 1938 had to wait until the late forties to be seen on screen. That means that late '40s films —*film noir* in particular — would be ripe for ECT scenes.

It just so happens that *film noir* incorporated many psychiatric themes and subtexts. Dream scenes and dark deeds and quasi-criminal activity (or full-fledged crime scenes) were favored motifs from the *film noir* period. So frightening ECT scenes and diabolical doctors fit perfectly into the ethos of the times. Seedy, seamy sequences laden with deep, dark secrets — which included psychiatric secrets — were ideal for this genre.

At the same time that *film noir* rose to prominence, the psychoanalytic establishment also gained a greater foothold in the U.S. Psychoanalysis had arrived much earlier in the century. Dr. Abraham Brill founded America's first psychoanalytic institute in New York in 1911, having previously translated Freud's works into English.[6] But Brill devoted his efforts to promoting psychoanalysis more than practicing it. Interest in psychoanalysis increased as psychoanalysts arrived in America, in flight from Hitler's Europe. Their continental education, their European refinement, and their first-hand familiarity with Freud made them the envy of American psychiatrists, most of who were relegated to asylum-based practices. In 1946 the Los Angeles Institute for Psychoanalysis was founded — and would be a handy influence on filmmakers.

The year 1947 marked a sea change in psychiatric practice. In 1947 the site of psychiatric practice shifted. More psychiatrists were found in private, office-based practice than in institutions, as had been the case previously. Treatments associated with institutions and asylums — such as ECT — were vilified by psychiatrists who were influenced by psychoanalysts. Because some psychoanalysts wielded influence on some Hollywood filmmakers, the analysts' antipathy toward biological treatments made itself manifest through some movies of that era.

Even a pro–ECT film of that era, such as the Academy Award–winning *The Snake Pit* (1948), pits ECT against talk therapy. *The Snake Pit* shows ECT as essential and effective, but depicts it as a prelude to the more important couch cure provided by psychoanalysis. Anatole Litvak's acclaimed film stars Olivia de Havilland as a recently-married young writer who grows depressed and enters a psychiatric institution, Juniper Hill State Hospital. Litvak himself was a refugee from Hitler's Europe and was open to the psychoanalytic esprit of fellow European émigrés.

In the film, de Havilland's psychiatrist administers a total of three ECT treatments instead of the standard 8 to 12 treatments that have since been shown to relieve depression. At that point the psychiatrist deems de Havilland's character to be cured enough to start the essential element of psychiatric treatment: talk therapy. A psychiatric nurse disagrees with this strategy, but to no avail. The nurse's pro–ECT stance sets the stage for a very different film that followed in the mid–70s: *Cuckoo's Nest.* However, by today's standards, the (female) nurse in *Snake Pit* was correct, while the (male) doctor was wrong.

Besides viewing *Snake Pit* as a debate about the merits of ECT versus talk therapy, we can also see it as a commentary on gender roles and gender-based authority in the immediate post-war years. The female nurse's authority is trumped by the decision of the male psychiatrist, implying that men who return home from war will once again rule the roost and override the authority that was temporarily enjoyed by women a few years earlier.

By the 1990s, feminist revisionists derided this film's traditionalist commentary on women's roles, even though psychiatric reformers praised the movie for spearheading much-needed reforms in the treatment of mental patients. For the patient is considered to be cured when she returns to her role as wife and abandons dreams of being a professional writer. We will discuss other aspects of this film in greater detail in the last chapter, on "Madhouse Movies and Involuntary Incarceration."

Until then, it is clear that the plot of *The Snake Pit* concerns itself with much more than psychiatric treatment or illness. Like most films, it reflects the social climate and the political concerns of its era, and intertwines those concerns with clinical issues.

8

Lobotomies and the Like

Hands down, lobotomies are the most extreme psychiatric procedure available. Lobotomies are irreversible. Even ECT — shock therapy — is time-limited. Adverse effects that follow ECT usually wear off within weeks, if not days or hours. Only a small minority of people describe persistent memory problems. Likewise, the curative effects are not permanent, but they tend to be long-lasting. ECT is still the fastest and most effective way to relieve depression, catatonia, and some psychotic symptoms.

Once the frontal lobes of the brain are severed — with an instrument as simple as an ice pick — no currently available procedure can reconnect them. What can be scarier or more sinister than a lobotomy, especially if it is not needed? And especially if it can be completed with an ordinary kitchen tool, and with just a jab near the eye?

If cinema's goal is to prove that psychiatrists are instinctively sinister, or that they are agents of the state who are willing to exert social or political control upon request (as some psychiatrists have suggested), then there should be far more movies about medical lobotomies. But we find relatively few medical lobotomy entries in film history. There are vast numbers of other movies about brain damage or mind control or brain chips or whatnot, and there is a whole subgenre dealing with brain exchanges. But lobotomies, or even leucotomies, are in short supply, even though some films that feature psychosurgery have gained prominence and even received Oscar awards or nominations (such as *Cuckoo's Nest* and *Frances* [1982]).

Psychiatry-themed films are much more likely to revolve around psychotherapy or psychoanalysis. Even horror films favor shock therapy over psychosurgery, although there is a subgenre dubbed the "medsploitation film," which seems to be on the rise recently.

A casual look at film lists reveals many entries about ape-human brain exchanges but surprisingly few about general psychosurgery. Human-ape brain exchanges were popular in the early days of cinema, when Darwinian influences were strong and when the concept of human evolution from apes still shocked large segments of society. Early in the 20th century, audiences were reverberating from Dr. Moreau's human-animal experiments, as described in H.G. Wells' book about *The Island of Dr. Moreau* (1896). Later on a lobotomy scene appeared in a century-shaping ape-human film, *The Planet of the Apes* (1968). That movie will be discussed in detail below.

Even zombie films outnumber lobotomy themes many times over. Zombies are stripped of their brain functions (and their brains) and lose human will. Their transformation from free-willed beings with functioning frontal lobes to shell-like bodies without souls is *not* necessarily connected to medical experiments. Every so often, however, zombies are produced by MDs (*Astro-Zombies* [1969], *Dr. Butcher, MD* [aka *Zombie Holocaust*, [1982]). More often than not, though, non-physicians create zombies. In turn, zombies eat the brains of their victims, and sometimes eat the bodies as well. Sometimes direct contact can create zombies, paralleling the process by which vampire bites turn unsuspecting victims into blood-sucking vampires themselves.

Zombies are more appealing in some eras than others. Literary zombies soared in popularity in the early 21st century. Zombies are currently repopulating movies and television series, almost as though they were spread by an epidemic. Brad Pitt is scheduled to star in *World War Z* (2012), for instance. But it was George Romero's 1968 groundbreaking *Night of the Living Dead* that deserves credit for bringing zombies to the forefront of film. Romero's stylistic depiction set a precedent for future zombie movies. Many people read race-based political meanings into Romero's film because it stars an African-American man. Yet Romero insists that he based his casting choice on the best performance and was not swayed by tacit political intentions.

Romero movies aside, brain-deprived zombies often act as metaphors for puppets of political oppression — in much the same way that some psychiatrist films function as political metaphors about authoritarian regimes and repression, and state dictatorship. In a 1943 *Batman* serial, a "Japanazi" named Dr. Daka creates zombies via his brain machine, and thereby makes a potent political statement about totalitarianism and the Axis forces.

Sci-fi cinema offers another variation on this theme: aliens that possess the brains of human beings. Alien brain-eaters and brain-drainers flourished during the Sputnik years, as the "race-to-space" colored sci-fi films from the late 1950s and early 1960s. *Brain from Planet Arous* (1957) is an example of a genre that thrived at drive-in theaters of that era, as is *Invaders from Mars* (1953). Sometimes atomic creations, like *Fiend Without a Face* (1958), stake a claim on human brains. Even though the glory days of alien brain-suckers faded to grey long ago, such creatures are still more plentiful in cinema than psychiatrists who perform lobotomies.

So let's brainstorm a bit about the reasons why lobotomy is so low on the list of "sinister psychiatrist cinema." Considering how frightening this operation is to most people, why don't we see more "sinister psychiatrists" performing (or ordering) such a dastardly procedure? There are several reasons why lobotomy docs are underrepresented in cinema (and there are more reasons why we can expect a proliferation of such procedures in the not-too-distant future).

For one thing, psychosurgery per se does not make for a very interesting film. It can't compete with the drama of the couch cure. It can't even compete with the exotic scenery found in sci-fi films about alien brain-eaters. A single surgical scene is second-rate compared to the dramatic thrashing of bound victims and the panic-producing spiking lines on EEG strips that invariably accompany ECT scenes on screen.

Equally importantly, lobotomies are usually performed at institutions. However, transorbital lobotomies can be office-based procedures, or they can be done in "lobotomobiles" (like the one that belonged to Dr. Walter J. Freeman II, who promoted them in the 1950s). Either way, they are surgical procedures performed by surgeons who operate on the recommendations of psychiatrists. Even though Dr. Freeman was a co-founder of the American Board of Psychiatry and Neurology, and was a member of the American Psychiatric Association, he had other medical training that made him the exception rather than the rule. Even he was eventually barred from performing surgery (but not because he lacked surgical skill). Let me stress this important point again: psychiatrists *do not* perform lobotomies themselves — although films often confuse medical specialties and professional jurisdictions, particularly in the case of psychiatry. So we may encounter some screen psychiatrists who take liberties with medical procedures as they deprive their patients of their personal liberties.

Because these procedures are done in hospital settings, the responsibility for ordering or performing psychosurgery usually shifts away from the medical staff and onto the institution. Films of this sort can be categorized as "asylum thrillers" or "mental hospital movies," which are sometimes said to be a subgenre of prison movies, and are even related to hotel films, where guests check in and out, so the setting serves as a backdrop for interactions between characters. Often, the "evil institution" is a setting for mean-spirited medical staff members. At other times the evil institution corrupts the innocent. If the institution appears more powerful than the individual physicians or psychiatrists who staff it, then the "transference" is diffused (as they say in psychiatric parlance). Emotions that were initially directed toward an individual doctor can be displaced onto a bigger and broader institution with which the individual is affiliated, or vice versa. So spectators can cast a wider net when they want someone or something to blame for bad outcomes in institutional settings.

That was certainly true for *One Flew Over the Cuckoo's Nest*, where Oregon State Hospital shifts to the sidelines, compared to Louise Fletcher's unforgettable performance as the evil head nurse. *Cuckoo's Nest* brings up an even more important point: the psychiatrist is not necessarily the most villainous member of the staff. In *Cuckoo's Nest* the head nurse is the prime mover and shaker. She manipulates everyone and everything, patients and psychiatrists included. There has yet to be another film about psychiatry, psychiatric institutions, ECT or lobotomy that is as damning as *Cuckoo's Nest*.

In this film (and the book that begot it), hospital heads and the most highly trained professionals act as conduits for the rage and revenge of one woman who wears white. This nurse is not the docile and undemanding nurse of yesteryear. She is not cast in the mold of the self-sacrificing Florence Nightingale, or even Sue Barton, the student nurse who starred in a series of pre-teen novels published between 1936 and 1952. In *One Flew Over the Cuckoo's Nest*, the docs do not call the shots. The roles are reversed, with the message being that "even the meek can destroy the earth." The compassion that is ordinarily associated with nursing care is turned upside down in these psychiatric wards. Perhaps that is one reason why the film is so riveting.

It is well-known that the main psychiatrist in the movie was played by a real psychiatrist who worked at the hospital. Even some patients "played themselves," acting as extras and receiving stipends for their work. The real-life psychiatrist-in-chief was proud of the fact that the film brought income and a moment of fame for the mentally ill men who lived at Oregon State. Nurse Ratched was played (to the hilt) by a professional actress, Louise Fletcher. Her prime opponent, and the film's protagonist, was Jack Nicholson. He also achieved lasting acclaim for his portrayal of the slick and sociopathic but still likeable McMurphy.

Another salient fact about this film revolves around gender role reversal. In real life — and in reel life — women are more likely to be "victimized" by sinister psychiatrists. During the heyday of psychosurgery, most lobotomies were performed on women — by male MDs. Yet it is Jack Nicholson, who is a "man's man" and a man who belittles women, who is shorn of his frontal lobes in *Cuckoo's Nest.* This takes place at the hands of a woman who wields power that exceeds both her skills and her stature in the hospital hierarchy.

Because the twisted grooves (gyri) of the brain's frontal lobes remind some people of testicles, the lobotomy functions as an ersatz castration scene, engineered by the proverbial "castrating female," Nurse Ratched. (I detailed another instance of the lobotomy-as-castration analogue a few chapters earlier when I focused on the Hannibal films.)

The lobotomy scene in *Cuckoo's Nest* is striking, as is everything that leads up to it and comes after it. McMurphy attacks Nurse Ratched after she goads another patient to suicide. McMurphy is summarily lobotomized. When he returns to the ward after the procedure, he is little more than a zombie. Many post-lobotomy patients need continuous custodial care because they lose other mental functions and become unable to care for themselves or interact meaningfully with others. But McMurphy meets a different fate. Fellow inmate Chief Bromden is upset to find McMurphy unresponsive; but when he sees the surgical scar on his friend's forehead, he is unwilling to let him live in this state. And so he puts a pillow over his face and smothers him.

Leaving off the irony that the "worst" lobotomy film on record revolves around a psychiatric nurse rather than a psychiatric physician, we can still find a few notable examples of lobotomy films that involve psychiatrists. *Hannibal* (2001), *Suddenly, Last Summer* (1959), *A Fine Madness* (1966), and *Frances* (1982) all deserve mention. The *Manchurian Candidate* remake recollects the behavioral psychologist of the original but substitutes punitive psychosurgery for Pavlovian conditioning. I will discuss some of these classics in the next few pages.

Planet of the Apes (1968) is in a class of its own, partly because its "behaviorist" or psychologist is an ape herself. To be specific, Zira the behaviorist is a chimpanzee in this class-stratified society where primates rule and where humans are treated as, well, "sub-human." The commentary on race relations and racial oppression in the U.S. is primary to this film, which was released in the same year that both Senator Robert Kennedy and Reverend Martin Luther King, Jr. were shot. Also in 1968, Apollo 8 was launched.

In the film, three astronauts crash-land on what appears to be an alien planet. The planet is governed by apes. The astronauts are taken captive. One is killed and stuffed and put in a museum display. Another (Charlton Heston) is locked in a zoo with feral humans, where his behavior is observed by the psychologist. The third, Landon, is lobotomized, presumably so he cannot reveal the falsehoods embedded in the "official" sanctified ape history. Like many films and books of its era, this movie depicts this extreme psychiatric technique as a repressive measure used to maintain political and social control.

Before proceeding, I should mention an odd film that appeared in 2011, *Sucker Punch.* This strange movie is easily forgettable, except for the fact that its director has impressive credentials in films adapted from comic books, graphic novels, and zombie classics. In 2007, Zach Snyder made *300,* based on Frank Miller's Dark Horse Comics series. The film was a box office hit and won him the opportunity to direct the much-anticipated superhero film *Watchmen* (2009). *Watchmen* adapted Alan Moore's cutting edge and controversial graphic novel. Synder is also responsible for the 2012 reboot of the *Superman* film series. His first film was the 2004 big-budget remake of the standard-setting zombie movie *Dawn of the Dead.*

For comic book fans, Snyder's works are interesting. Those who wonder why *Sucker Punch* looks like a music video that morphed into a video game can look to the director and his aesthetic preferences. For those who are trying to make sense of this nonsensible storyline, well, they are still trying. The plot is confusing and off-putting. But the film does end with a lobotomy scene, which may be real or may be imagined.

In *Sucker Punch* a 20-year-old woman named Babydoll is committed to a decrepit mental institution in Brattleboro, Vermont. There is no physical resemblance between this facility and the sprawling, country-like campus of a real psychiatric hospital in the area, Brattleboro Retreat. Her stepfather has blamed her for the death of her sister and is intent on obstructing her inheritance. So he bribes the orderlies to forge the signature of the head psychiatrist, who is a dark-haired woman with an exotic but unidentifiable Eastern European accent.

In Babydoll's fantasies she is living in a brothel rather than in the women's ward of a psychiatric asylum. The psychiatrist substitutes for the madam, and the orderlies act as pimps who procure young women for loathsome old men who watch them dance. Babydoll plans her escape in true comic book fashion but is eventually lobotomized. In the interim, she and other young woman inmates fire steam-powered World War I weapons, storm a castle that is protected by a fire-breathing dragon, disarm a bomb, and ambush the asylum's cook after he attempts to rape one of the young women.

For video game players this absurdist, a-chronological quest is part of the fun. For those of us wondering what this far-out film has to say about psychiatry, women in psychiatry, institutional psychiatry in the 1960s, and lobotomy, the task is more difficult. One thing is sure: backdating a psychiatric hospital film has become essential in our times, given that hospital stays are so short and that so many legal protections against involuntary commitment are in place.

Were this a more engaging film, it might make us wonder if strong enough protections are in place to stop the use of unauthorized lobotomies and inappropriate admissions to mental hospitals. But it seems that the visuals, the music, and, above all, the sexual innuendoes (or direct statements) of the erotic dances and skimpy costumes are more important than plot. Reading meaning into this movie is probably meaningless.

Dr. Hannibal Lecter is a different story. Dr. Lecter (Hannibal the Cannibal) is the most recent arrival among the "real" lobotomy docs, and arguably the most memorable. Dr. Lecter teaches us everything we need to know about the so-called kitchen-table lobotomy. Lobotomies are connected to kitchen equipment because of the ease with which they are performed, and because an ordinary ice pick substitutes for a surgical scalpel. During their heyday, simple lobotomies were performed during lunch hours. Being a gourmet who doesn't cut corners, Hannibal opts for the more complicated procedure and removes the top of the skull itself to reveal the "sweat meats" inside.

In *Hannibal* (2001) the ever-clever Dr. Lecter excises Ray Liotta's forebrain with a simple swipe of his scalpel. He has already separated the skin of the scalp. He lifts the boney cranium with amazingly little effort. The procedure, from start to finish, is almost bloodless, and even painless (both in the movie and in actual neurosurgery). Still, many spectators wince and squirm as they watch Dr. Lecter separate the frontal lobes of the former FBI agent's brain before placing the body parts into a sauté pan (copper-bottomed, of course). The gourmet meal that results from these efforts resembles sweetbreads, or pancreas, which is another organ meat that was once the fare of the poor but has since become a luxury item.

Hannibal's approach to psychosurgery is campy and borders on parody — except for the fact that the film itself also functions as a serious murder mystery. By the time we see Dr. Lecter fry the brains of the insolent FBI agent in retaliation for the insults he hurled at Hannibal's female protégée, we already know that Hannibal delights in eating human flesh.

The lobotomy scene adds some impressively correct medical details to a meticulously rendered mise-en-scène, where lit candelabras, shiny silver dinnerware and a luminous linen tablecloth make for a picture-perfect table setting. But we as spectators know that Ray Liotta's lobotomized brain could easily turn into another enemy's fleshy cheeks the next day. We are not that impressed that this represents bad medical practice, so much as we are struck by the fact that Hannibal the Cannibal is at it again, and that he has pursued his tasteless but tasty culinary passion with his usual zest.

Should we have any doubt that Dr. Lecter's brain-eating scene is motivated by childhood exposure to cannibalism, and that it is *not* a deliberate attempt to twist psychiatric practice, we can watch *Hannibal Rising* (2007), the prequel to the Hannibal series. *Hannibal Rising* the film is based on Thomas Harris' book, likewise called *Hannibal Rising*. This attempt to explain the motivations of the brilliant psychiatrist, gourmet cook, art collector and all-around esthete appeared seven years after the *Hannibal* film.

The film *Hannibal Rising* focuses on Hannibal as a boy and young adult. We are introduced to a youthful Hannibal and his younger sister. The time is wartime, the place is Lithuania, and the setting is a makeshift camp set up by a ragtag group of Nazi sympathizers. The Lecter sibs have been removed from their elegant home and have been taken captive. Their parents have already been murdered by the children's captors.

We watch the vile commandos compliment Hannibal's sister — before they boil her into a soup and serve her as a meal. When we see Hannibal retaliate in future films and rip into cheeks with his teeth, we realize that we are watching an advanced version of the Biblical axiom "an eye for an eye, and a tooth for a tooth."

From there, we see Hannibal progress through adolescence. We witness his affairs with women in his early adulthood. While living in Europe he meets a beautiful Japanese woman. When she is insulted by a racially-insensitive and sexually-inappropriate slur, Hannibal defends her honor — by decapitating the offender and ripping off his cheeks with his teeth.

Given his history of trauma that is delineated in *Hannibal Rising*, Hannibal is destined to live a life of "repetition-compulsion." We now understand why he is overpowered by the urge to devour human flesh from time to time, in spite of his professional promise and his many other talents. So he embarks on a dual career. He is a brilliant psychiatrist by day, but he moonlights as a serial killer whenever the opportunities arise. In spite of these moral shortcomings, he does not lose sight of the intellectual side of his psychiatric responsibilities, although sometimes he confuses his clinical care with his true passion — namely, murder and dismemberment.

The *Hannibal* series is too over-the-top and too implausible to make us believe that forensic psychiatrists still perform tabletop lobotomies in real life (even though we know for a fact that some lobotomists used kitchen table tools in the 1950s). The remake/reimagining of *Manchurian Candidate* (2004), which features a science fiction–like psychosurgery scene, lacks credibility for other reasons (and it also lacks the charm of the *Hannibal* films). When the remake of *Candidate* substitutes psychosurgery for the brainwashing, behavioral conditioning and hypnosis scenes of the original, it tries to update the psychiatric techniques and put the film trajectory on "fast-forward" rather than "rewind." But in making this move (and in making many other modifications), the remake obfuscates the political context of the original film and overrides the historical parallels that made the first movie so poignant. The director, Jonathan Demme, dismissed the significance of political references and claimed that the presence of profit-driven companies like Halliburton infuses sufficient meaning into his film.

Let's recall that when soldiers in the original movie were brainwashed, they were brainwashed by Manchurian doctors who practiced at the Russian-influenced Pavlov Institute in Manchuria. Manchuria symbolizes North Korea, where American POWs expressed sympathy for Communism after exposure to similar brainwashing techniques. Pavlovian conditioning speaks of Russian-ness and Communist influences as much as it refers to a psychological theory.

In the original film, innuendos were everywhere. The statue of Abraham Lincoln ("Honest Abe") plants clues about the lies and truths that percolate beneath the surface. The secret playing card of the Red Queen refers to the Communist mother or the upside down universe of Alice-in-Wonderland, where the Red Queen imposes psychotic rule. Even "Korea 1952" has many meanings. For instance, it can be read as a commentary on racial integration in the military, which occurred in the middle of the Korean War near the end of 1951.

The remake stays on the surface and adds a psychosurgery scene where a brain chip is implanted in a soldier. The soldier becomes the patsy of a multi-national corporation rather than a cog in a Communist conspiracy. The implant tells the soldier to kill on command (in much the same way that auditory hallucinations of some schizophrenics tell them to hurt themselves or others). This brain chip lacks the rich history of the Russian-related brainwashing scenes.

This procedure is not a lobotomy or even a leucotomy, which preceded lobotomies. The chip resembles the "influencing machine" described in Viktor Tausk's classic psychoanalytic paper of 1919, which was published the same year as his suicide. In a paper that goes by the same name, Tausk describes "influencing machines" that commonly appear in schizophrenics' delusions, even though there was no real-life equivalent for such a device at the time.

The psychiatric influences have been updated in the remake and have been fast-forwarded to some time in the not-so-far-off future. The mind-control scene shifts to more up-to-date "invasive psychiatric techniques." This turns the film into a sci-fi version of the original Cold War drama.

The remake pushes races issues from the sidelines to center stage because it stars Denzel Washington in the hero-soldier role that Frank Sinatra made famous. From a commercial standpoint this is a good move because Denzel Washington is a box-office draw. But this tactic deracinates the ground-breaking contribution made by black actor Joe Adams, who played a psychiatrist and a commissioned army officer.

The original *Candidate* arrived as the Civil Rights Movement was about to boil over. Although no one could predict it at the time, the Reverend Dr. Martin Luther King, Jr. would be assassinated in 1968. When Joe Adams played an army psychiatrist in the 1962 *Candidate*, his presence made a subtle yet strong statement. He showed that black MDs could represent the "establishment" (specifically, the U.S. army) at a time when blacks were disenfranchised and without full civil rights, and when black physicians were not admitted to the AMA. Adams' role is minor compared to the drama that unfolds, but his symbolic importance is major.

Setting the action in "Korea 1952" may be sending subtle messages about American racial relations in general. For "Korea 1952" was the first year that American military troops were officially desegregated since the Civil War. But it didn't start out that way. When the Korean War started in June of 1950, most black soldiers served in segregated support units and were stationed in the rear. The remainder served in segregated combat units.

The first months of the Korean War witnessed some of the worst disasters in U.S. military history. American soldiers, and U.N. troops, were driven off the North Korean peninsula. Having to contend with overwhelming losses in white units, ground commanders began accepting black replacements, thereby integrating their units by default. Several high-ranking officials were skeptical.

When the Army high command finally became convinced that integrated combat units could perform under fire, the U.S. Army formally announced its plans to desegregate on July 26, 1951, exactly three years after President Harry Truman had issued an Executive Order to do the same. Thus, the caption about "Korea 1952" proclaims the start of a groundbreaking era in race relations, and shows support for the desegregation marches that were underway when the original movie was in production.

Casting noted black actor Denzel Washington as the lead in the remake can be seen more as a commercial decision than an ideological one. This choice capitalizes on Washington's star status and his draw for audiences. The fact that Denzel Washington made his name through his portrayal of slain Black Muslim activist Malcolm X suggests that a political statement is waiting in the wings, and perhaps a subversive one at that. But that statement is watered down, compared to the strength it had in 1962. (Washington's previous sensitive portrayal of an uncharacteristically sensitive military psychiatrist in the tearjerker *Antwone Fisher* [2002] contributes to the confusion about the intentions behind the remake. *Antwone Fisher* was based on the real-life story of a troubled enlistee who found solace through treatment by military psychiatrists and interventions by social workers.)

Liev Schreiber is credible as the bad guy, Sergeant Shaw, in the *Mancurian Candidate* remake, and he is credible in his role as a buddy or platoon mate. He often plays the bad guy, or the bad brother (*X-Men Origins: Wolverine* [2009], *Defiance* [2008], and he has come to represent capitalist exploitation *Repo Men* [2010], which we will discuss below).

Given all these "ersatz" representations in the newer film, spectators fail to "suspend disbelief." We are not convinced that either the corporate raiders or the brain chips or the Iraqi soldiers are anywhere near as pernicious as the politically-motivated Manchurian captors of the original. For the Soviet-influenced Manchurians of North China used Russian-born Pavlovian conditioning to the max in the original *Manchurian Candidate*: they chose the soldier-son of an aspiring political wife and clandestine political operative as their subject. They turned this son, Raymond Shaw, into a cold-blooded murderer, unbeknownst to even Raymond Shaw. Shaw is expected to fire the shot that kills the U.S. presidential nominee, so that his Communist-puppet of a stepfather can step up to the plate and take over. In the end, Shaw points the gun at his mother and stepfather. He pulls the trigger and kills the people who pulled his strings and turned him into a puppet. Then he uses the same gun to shoot himself in a final act of suicide that frees him from mind control.

As the *Manchurian Candidate* remake ends, we come away with the feeling that we could have been watching *any* futuristic sci-fi film about brain chips and mind control. David Cronenberg's *eXistenZ* (1999) or *Total Recall* (1990), perhaps? Not that that is such a bad thing, given the success of *Bladerunner*-type themes over the years. But it is disappointing, considering that our expectations were turned up so high.

Had the original Soviet setting been retained for the remake, and had the psychiatrists declared political dissidents to be insane before incarcerating them for years on end and subjecting them to brain-damaging psychiatric treatments that stop their political protests, the remake might have provided a modicum of political clout, even though it would be too outdated to make much of a splash in the 21st century. That topic would have worked well some twenty or thirty years earlier, when it was well-known that psychiatrists from the FSU (Former Soviet Union) discredited dissidents by declaring them psychotic.

As it stands, this bastardized remake does not function as an indictment of unethical psychiatric treatments in the FSU or in contemporary China. It doesn't even make a political point (although one could argue retrospectively that casting Denzel Washington as the officer-in-charge foreshadows the election of Barak Obama as America's first black president—but even that subtext is light years away from the original intent).

If anything, the remake of *The Manchurian Candidate* has more in common with Batman movie serials from 1943. In the latter years of World War II, short serials screened before top-billed feature films. Batman was popular, but he could not yet be declared to be America's reigning superhero, as he is today. In the serials we encounter an evil Dr. Daka who uses brain machines to strip subjects of their wills. The contraption turns them into zombie-like creatures that do the bidding of the "evil empire." Dr. Daka's exact medical credentials are never specified in the sixteen chapters. We know that he is a "Japanazi" (which was comics' shorthand for a cross between a Jap and a Nazi). Dr. Daka is an agent of the enemies who attacked Pearl Harbor and who continue to kill American and other Allied troops in the South Pacific.

The actor who plays Dr. Daka is clearly a Caucasian. His name was J. Carrol Naish, and he was Irish. Yet we know that he represents Asians because his eyelids have been altered through special effects so that he appears to be "Oriental." He also speaks in stilted and stylized English to imply that he is a native Japanese speaker. His disguise derives from that Charlie Chan–style, Hollywood shorthand for "Asian" that was once so prevalent but is now so politically incorrect.

Dr. Daka may be either a psychiatrist or a neuroscientist or both—that is unclear. But it is completely clear that he represents more than just "Japanazis." He is the "Yellow Menace" that pre-dated World War II and the Japanese bombing of Pearl Harbor. He is a direct descendent of Ming the Merciless (who was the villain from *Flash Gordon* serials from the 1930s, which become a TV serial in the early years of broadcast television). Dr. Daka anticipates the much more malevolent Dr. No (1962) from the James Bond book and film. He continues in the tradition of Dr. Fu Manchu, the fictional Asian scientist from thirties-era films that is credited with inspiring a host of Yellow Peril characters, including Dr. Yen-Lo of *The Manchurian Candidate*.

Dr. Fu Manchu was far more versatile than Dr. Daka. Dr. Daka's skills are limited to draining the brains of Batman, Gotham City's newspaper editor and other luminaries. Dr. Fu Manchu generated much more controversy than Dr. Daka. Indeed, Fu Manchu movies

Poster for *The Batman* serial (1943), where evil "Japanazi" Dr. Daka grins, standing to the far right of the seated Batman (Lewis Wilson), whom he turned into a zombie via his brain machine.

and novels could not be published during the Second World War because Dr. Manchu demonized Chinese, who were America's allies against the Japanese. The "Japanazi" character of Dr. Daka was perfectly permissible under the circumstances.

Dr. Daka is important to our discussion of sinister psychiatrists who use "lobotomies and the like" to control their subjects and thereby misuse their medical skills. But Dr. Daka is by no means the *only* evil scientist/psychiatrist found in Batman comics, films, cartoons, TV shows, and, most recently, video games. Batman stories feature so many sinister psychiatrists, who have so many different ways of effecting evil, that the comic book character's controversial psychiatrists deserve a book all of their own. Indeed, Dr. Hugo Strange, Dr. Harlene Quinzel (Harley Quinn), Dr. Jonathan Crane, Dr. Jeremiah Arkham, Dr. Amadeus Arkham, medical student Alyse Sinner (Alice Synner), the neuroscientist Mad Hatter, and, to a lesser extent, Dr. Chase Meridian, all merit mention.

It is important to point out that not all cinematic brain surgery scenes are sinister, and that some of them bear no connection to medicine at all. In *Total Recall* (1990), a film directed by Paul Verhoeven and starring Arnold Schwarzenegger and Sharon Stone, the doctor who attempts to administer the second "brain bolus" is well-intended. He is practicing a form of "cosmetic psychiatry" or "recreational psychosurgery" that has yet to be introduced into common clinical practice. He provides affordable vacations for those who might not otherwise be able to buy action-adventures in pricey getaways like Mars.[1]

The story is set in 2084, an obvious play on Orwell's classic *1984*. The film was based on a novelette by sci-fi great Philip K. Dick. Dick's novella, *We Can Remember It for You Wholesale*, was published in 1966, at the dawn of the psychedelic era. At that time experimentation with altered states of consciousness and perception had already attracted public attention, thanks in large part to a *Life* magazine spread about G.W. Wasson's adventures with "magic mushrooms" in Mexico. But the blossoming of a full-fledged "counterculture" was still a few years away. Dick's story reflects society's concerns about these "head trips," and also draws on Dick's own dabbling with drugs.

Rather than focusing on the LSD "trips" that were making headlines in those years, Dick introduces the concept of a "brain bolus" that sends a mild-mannered construction worker on a cost-effective excursion to Mars. Unlike with LSD, which was notorious for the unpredictability of the "mind trips" that followed ingestion, a company called "Rekall, Incorporated" allows clients to pick their vacation spot of choice as simply as if they were picking paint colors for their walls. The "brain bolus" is inserted intra-nasally in the same way that neurosurgeons operate on the pituitary gland that lies at the base of the brain. This bit of scientific fact brings the fantastic tale closer to reality and makes us wonder if such feats actually await us in the distant future.

The story becomes more interesting when we learn that Arnold Schwarzenegger's character, Douglas Quaid, already has an implanted brain bolus in place — but he doesn't know it. This bolus blocks the implantation of a new bolus. It also blocks his past memories and replaces them with false ones. Since his true memories have been eradicated, he has no way of knowing about his past history of surgery. He doesn't even know his true identity or his prior profession or his political connections (or enemies).

When he consults the Rekall Company, he expects to acquire false but fun memories of an action-adventure vacation on Mars. Part of the plan is to act as a secret agent on Mars rather than an ordinary vacationer who idles away time by basking in the ruddy glow of the red planet. Little does he know that he really *was* a secret agent before he was surgically robbed of his memories. And so the drama begins.

In the film we do not get a glimpse of the "bad" brain doctor who acted as a government operative when he "changed the memory card" in Quaid's brain and erased recollections of Quaid's days as a government operative. But our own "memory" of that doctor remains intact when we watch the remake of *The Manchurian Candidate* and imagine a Philip K. Dick look alike doctor operating on Denzel Washington's stranded platoon.

Even in the *Total Recall* retelling of Dick's "We Can Remember It for You Wholesale" we lose the context of the political paranoia that was present when Dick wrote his original 1966 story. But both the novella and the film center on a philosophical concept that has endured far longer than of-the-moment political intrigues. As Dick himself pointed out when talking about his writing, he deliberately plays upon the theme of reality versus delusion. He is less concerned with current events than with eternal questions. Dick repeatedly asks: "Which is the real truth?" And thus his works connect to Aldous Huxley's *The Doors of Perception* (1954) and related queries evoked by hallucinogen use. At the same time, they footnote Plato's allegory of *The Cave*.

In *The Cave*, prisoners sit in a cave, facing inwards, and see only shadows of passersby from the "real world" outside. When the prisoners are released and exposed to the "real" objects that cast the shadows they have been watching, they continue to believe that the shadows are the "real" objects. They doubt that the "real" people they see are as real as the shadows they have observed throughout their lives. It has been said that all of philosophy footnotes Plato, and so Philip K. Dick's philosophy follows this tradition.

Total Recall stars Arnold Schwarzenegger — before his election as governor of California. As Douglas Quaid, Schwarzenegger is an "everyman" who is kicked around by the state, but then turns the tables and kicks around the agents of the state. This twist makes up for the loss of the political context of the novella, and may have helped Schwarzenegger's later campaign for office as much as his wife's political connections (and his bodybuilding image). (I am at a loss to explain his more recent election loss.)

Total Recall won an award for the Best Science Fiction film of the year and was recently remade in 2012. *Repo Men* (2010), on the other hand, did not reap many accolades from film critics, but it deserves mention for its intriguing treatment of brain death. The film portrays a remarkably bleak take on the future of for-profit organ transplantation. It stars Jude Law and Forest Whitaker as the "repo men" who repossess organs when payments are overdue.

Liev Schreiber heads the heartless organization that promises new lives to those whose original organs have failed. It then dispatches "repo men" to remove those same organs when fees are late. Schreiber, of course, had co-starred as the would-be soldier-assassin in the *Manchurian Candidate* remake. Schreiber displays his usual psychological intensity when performing his role in *Repo Men*. Liev Schreiber has become known for his portrayals of the "bad brother" or "evil twin." It is noteworthy that Schreiber's own maternal grandmother was lobotomized when his mother was twelve. His mother was in and out of mental hospitals during his youth. Some of Schreiber's own youth was spent at a commune in New York's drug (and probably vermin)-infested East Village. He also lived on the lam after his affluent father kidnapped him from his mother's commune. Other locales that he lived in sound more like movie settings than real-life living quarters, but he recalls his mother fondly.

His mother, a one-time flower child and current iconoclast, is reported to live on an ashram at present. In spite of this family turmoil, Schreiber received an excellent education. One can infer that his acting is informed by the chaos that he witnessed first-hand while growing up. It is ironic that his steely-cold character in *Repo Men* performs just one kind act, and that is to provide a brain bolus, of sorts, to brain dead Jude Law after he sustains a serious on-the-job injury.

Thanks to the company's largess, Jude Law's comatose character is treated to an unending memory loop of joyful days on the beach, spent with his best friend and long-time work buddy, played by Forrest Whittaker. Beside him is the new woman in his life, played by Alice Braga. It is only as the film ends that we learn that the reverie enjoyed by Remy (Jude Law) takes place via a neural network that implants fantasies into the unconscious character's consciousness. His pal, Jake (Whittaker), feels guilty and is grieving because he caused this injury during a fist fight. So he paid for a brain implant that lets his best buddy spend his remaining years in a fantasy life.

In this film the corporation is clearly bad, but its intents are not evil per se, but profit-oriented, without regard for humanity. However, the evil corporation is so de-medicalized that any doctors involved are closer to stage props than decision-makers. We don't even see a psychiatrist, neurologist or neurosurgeon; we only see evidence of their handiwork at the end.

It is the sales people, like Liev Schreiber, who appear sinister, even more sinister than the by-the-book repo men who perform organ-salvaging surgery in makeshift settings. The sales people are slimy because they knowingly deceive desperate people into buying over-priced organs and then forcing them to leverage their life savings to meet an impossible payment plan.

One can say that this film is a commentary on medicine's takeover by big business, and on the state of affairs that will result if financial interests supersede humanitarian considerations and come to dominate the health care industry. On a brighter note, the film suggests options that could become available to people with traumatic brain injuries or who are at risk for Alzheimer's disease or other dementias of older age. Given the numbers of Baby Boomers who are aging into Alzheimer's high risk groups, and given the rates of TBI (traumatic brain injury) reported by returning veterans, these groups are growing in both numbers and importance. This final scene of the film should make anyone who is aware of the epidemiology of these neuropsychiatric disorders think long and hard.

Psychiatrists are not singled out as sinister in *Repo Men*. Rather, the film suggests that sending brain-injured patients into pleasant fantasy states is preferable to allowing them to languish in despair or some other form of oblivion. Given that other organ transplants are used for exploitation, we come away concerned that such neuropsychiatric innovations will be subject to the same pre-conditions should these techniques be developed in the first place.

Eternal Sunshine of the Spotless Mind (2004) is another sci-fi film, albeit one that doubles as a romantic comedy. As such, it is much more light-hearted than the dark and gloomy *Repo Men*. Yet it also raises the possibility that neuropsychiatry and industry will some day team up to offer non-invasive, non-pharmacological elective procedures that remove painful memories. This futuristic possibility offers promise for the treatment of PTSD (post-traumatic stress disorder), and for stopping flashbacks of abusive childhoods or sexual exploitation. It also offers opportunities for profiteering or philandering physicians.

In *Sunshine* the doctor is neither deceptive nor exploitative toward his clientele (who are not his patients). But he does cheat on his wife with his office assistant. When the wife learns of his affair, he conveniently erases all memories from the brain of his assistant at Lacuna, Inc. (lacuna is the Latinate term for "hole," like the holes that run through Swiss cheese, or like the holes in the superegos of sociopaths). She will never testify against him.

It would be a mistake to lump Dr. Mierzwiak of Lacuna with other unethical experimenters or ignoble medical men or women who lopped off patients' brains. But it would be just as much of a mistake to forgive Dr. Mierzwiak for his ethical lapse in dealing with his office staff, and for his misuse of his medical tools. This lapse serves as a reminder that loosening the safeguards that protect everyone, employees included, can put patients at risk of dangerous procedures like memory erasure.

When explaining how "targeted memory loss" works, Dr. Mierzwiak assures the aggrieved Joel (played by comedic actor Jim Carrey) that this painless procedure is nothing more than a mild form of brain damage comparable to "a night of heavy drinking." With such reassurance, Joel chooses to delete all memories of Clementine, the eccentric woman who left him. But he loses the good memories as well as the bad ones, and he forgets all scenes from the past in which she played a role. Stripped of all those memories, he suddenly realizes how much her presence injected itself into his thinking, into his very being.

Interestingly, when I discuss *Conspiracy Theory* in a later chapter, we will encounter documented government-sponsored experiments from the 1950s which were intended to accomplish goals that are similar to the comedic goals of *Spotless Mind*.

Eternal Sunshine of the Spotless Mind ends well, as a romantic comedy should. *Suddenly, Last Summer* (1959), which stars Montgomery Clift, Elizabeth Taylor and Katharine Hepburn, is as bleak — but it could have been bleaker, had the psychiatrist agreed to lobotomize young Elizabeth Taylor, as her shrill aunt (Katharine Hepburn) insisted. *Suddenly, Last Summer* is worth mentioning here not just because it is a brilliant well-acted film based on a Tennessee Williams story (influenced by Williams' reactions to his own sister's lobotomy), but because it revolves around a lobotomy that *does not* occur. Instead, a kind and wise (though young) doctor refuses to bend to the will of an evil-minded woman, played by Katharine Hepburn.

Dr. John Cukrowicz (Montgomery Clift) goes so far as to challenge his department head at the state hospital. His superior prefers to placate the wealthy benefactor, Violet (Hepburn), when she demands psychosurgery for her beautiful but irascible niece, Holly (Elizabeth Taylor). She promises to make a generous donation in his honor in return for the favor. Hepburn's request for a quid pro quo makes today's practice of changing hospital names in exchange for huge cash infusions sound perfectly moral.

There is a reason why Violet wants Holly's memories erased. Holly has witnessed the horrific death and dismemberment of her cousin Sebastian, who is Violet's son. Holly's closeted homosexual cousin was castrated by boys that he pursued on the beach. Holly was so traumatized by this event that she needed to be institutionalized. Her aunt (Sebastian's mother) wants to wipe away all traces of her son's death and the events that led up to it, even if that means wiping away the emotions and memories and intellect of another young human being.

Rather than conceding to Violet's demands, Dr. Cukrowicz administers sodium amytal (truth serum) to Holly. This releases a flood of memories that "cures" Holly. The information supplied via "truth serum" assures Violet of the truth of Holly's account. Holly is spared surgery, and the young neurosurgeon who postponed the operation assumes heroic proportions.

In real life, Tennessee Williams' disturbed sister did not fare as well as Elizabeth Taylor's Holly, for Williams' sister *was* lobotomized. Joseph Mankiewicz' 1959 film is based on Williams' play, but the drama is set in 1937, the year before ECT arrived in America. Lobotomies were employed since 1935, a few years before electroshock therapy became available. Lobotomies fell out of favor by the mid–1950s, when the first anti-psychotic medication, Thorazine, was introduced and when concern about over-use of psychosurgery mounted.

Note that this film was made in 1959, a few years after phenothiazine medications like Thorazine became available in 1954. Soon after, lobotomies became almost obsolete and seemed comparatively barbaric. The use of amytal in this film is an example of "narco-synthesis" cures that appeared in movies from the late 1940s and 1950s, and that are thought by some to be the progenitors of contemporary psychopharmacological treatments. It is interesting that truth serum was used to recover memories around the same time that Thorazine entered the American market and proved useful in suppressing schizophrenics' delusions and hallucinations. One might say that the use of this outdated med emphasizes the fact that the plot is backdated, but this "coincidence" also highlights the importance of distinguishing fantasy from reality. It also demonstrates that doctors must ultimately decide to release or suppress painful memories. The relative value of these different approaches in treatment of PTSD (post-traumatic stress disorder) is still being studied to this day.

I am tempted to say that this classic film proves that psychiatrists who recommend lobotomies, and psychosurgeons who perform lobotomies, are not universally ill-intended. However, there are some caveats to consider before coming to this conclusion.

For one thing, the heroic doctor who favors good patient care over favors from wealthy patients is not a psychiatrist. Rather, he is a neurosurgeon.

Secondly, his superior, who is a psychiatrist, demonstrates the same evil motives that cheesier films exploit. The possibility that some people are willing to sacrifice their principles for financial gain is so well-known that it barely bears repeating — but it is still worth viewing when woven into an interesting plot. Thirdly, this film was made in 1959, during the "golden age" of psychiatry in cinema. A disproportionate number of films from that era cast a favorable light on psychiatry and psychiatrists. Remember, even *Fear Strikes Out*, a movie about shock therapy, features compassionate psychiatrists who administer ECT to a catatonic ballplayer. The attitude in this film reflects the era's *zeitgeist* more than anything else.

As we have seen in so many other movies discussed here, it is not the subject matter per se that determines the attitude toward psychiatric treatments, treaters, diagnoses, and diseases. Rather, the deciding factor is the tenor of the times. In *Suddenly Last Summer* we meet a knowledgeable and ethical doctor who performs a comprehensive "differential diagnosis" prior to recommending a permanent and potentially damaging treatment. Good intent triumphs over bad principles. Montgomery Clift's acting is memorable, and his role is admirable.

A few years later, Montgomery Clift would portray Freud in John Huston's *Freud: The Secret Passion* (1962). By that time Clift's substance abuse had snowballed. His intoxication led to a motor vehicle accident that left him disfigured. He was left with a limp and a tremor. His handsome face was scarred. Even though Freud is apotheosized in the script,

Huston's efforts to glorify the founder of psychoanalysis take on an aura of parody, for the actor who plays the master of the mind does not have the slightest mastery over his own mind. Clift's same-sex dalliances had become the topic of tabloids, further calling Freud's now outdated ideas about same-sex attractions into question.

John Huston may not have intended to be dismissive of psychoanalytic theory or treatment, but his film inadvertently made a mockery of Freud's promises to relieve the "psychopathology of everyday life." Clift's chemical dependency and its tragic results reminded us of Freud's earlier cocaine days, and eclipsed his accomplishments. Ironically, a film that was intended to lionize psychoanalysis accidentally discredited its founder.

9

Diabolical Drugging (and Other Deceptions)

If the anti-psychiatry themes in film reflected reality-based concerns and nothing more, then there should be a surge in movies about psychopharmacology and its discontents. For psychopharmacology has become the mainstay of early 21st century psychiatric treatment.

Psychopharmacology was once a supplement to psychotherapy for all but the most indigent, or for chronic and "incurable" patients in state hospitals. But the latest data, reported by the American Psychiatric Association in January 2011 and posted on the organization's website, shows that it's the other way around. More often than not, psychopharmacology is the only treatment offered.[1, 2]

Electroshock therapy is still available in 2011. What's more, its use is increasing, according to a *New York Times* article from January 23, 2011.[3] About 100,000 people a year received ECT as of 2010. But ECT is used only as a last resort, after other treatments failed or when time is of the essence because of imminent suicide risk, or when certain medical conditions (such as pregnancy) make the use of certain medications too risky.

Psychoanalysis is alive and well in Off-Broadway plays. Productions about *Freud's Last Session* enjoyed longer runs than expected. Offstage, psychoanalysis entered its sunset years well before the 21st century began. The "couch cure" that was so common in the mid–20th century has become uncommon. Even more generic "talk therapy" was not used by the majority of persons who sought psychiatric treatment in 2010.

Referrals for psychosurgery are next to non-existent, even though studies about surgical treatments for OCD (obsessive-compulsive disorder) are still being done in Denmark and are published in prestigious journals in the U.S. However, other "invasive techniques" that require surgery, such as vagal nerve stimulation and electronic brain pacemaker implantation, are on the horizon. At present, studies of vagal nerve stimulation remain unimpressive, so it is not likely that we will see an uptick in these procedures too soon, unless some improvements are made in the process itself or in pinpointing patients who can benefit from this approach.

However, psychosurgery's success in minimizing the motor symptoms of Parkinson's disease is striking. Parkinson's affects mood and cognition as well as movement and speech, and so this disease overlaps with psychiatric disorders, even though neurologists have the lion's share of responsibility for treating PD. It may be just a short time before medicine deploys related treatments for otherwise impossible-to-treat psychiatric symptoms.

TCMS (trans-cutaneous magnetic stimulation) is currently too expensive to be concerned about whether or not it is effective, but there is a possibility that those financial facts will change. But if the success of TCMS treatments improves, and if its benefits prove to outweigh its risks, costs, and inconvenience, this statement will need revision.

In the meantime, the movies have essentially neglected mood medications, which are the psychiatric treatment *de jour*. Yet print media, such as newspapers and medical journals, detail bitter debates about right and wrong ways to use psychopharmacology. Internet articles on this subject seem to multiply by the minute. Patient advocacy groups have opined on psychotropic medication matters for decades, and Scientologists attempted to outlaw Prozac when it was introduced in the late 1980s. But fringe groups with biased opinions are not alone in speaking out for — or against — psychopharmacological treatments. Even the *New York Review of Books* chimed in with its opinions in 2011. An article by Dr. Marcia Angell, who once was an associate editor for the well-respected *New England Journal of Medicine*, reviewed three anti-psychopharmacology books for a journal that caters to the professorial crowd.

Some of the most heated debates on mood medications occur in Washington, D.C., but not necessarily at the F.D.A. headquarters, where the administration of approvals of "foods and drugs" (or the revocation of some) officially occurs. (The acronym "FDA" stands for "Food and Drug Administration.") Congressional hearings, especially those conducted by Senator Grassley, have challenged psychiatric standards of practice in pharmacology — at a time that psychopharmacology *is* the "standard of practice." These hearings and recent legislation condemn manufacturers who transmit information about psychiatric medications to the MDs who prescribe them to patients.

Ironically, direct-to-consumer (DTC) advertising was legalized some years ago. As a result, ads for mood medications appear in women's magazines alongside promotions for new deodorants or diapers. When checking Internet weather reports in the summer of 2011, one is barraged by banner ads that promote stimulant-based ADHD medications to mothers of teens. It is of concern that stims are often abused, and are commonly resold as study aids on college campuses or sometimes used by the mothers themselves rather than by the children who receive the prescription. To date, there has been no attempt to reign in those ads, which are intended to increase patient demand for newer, better — and more expensive — meds. Many believe those DTC ads are even more influential than promoting those same medications directly to MDs, and it is likely that manufactures and advertising agencies are privy to proprietary information that proves it.

Senator Grassley's challenges to psychopharmacology in general, and to Big Pharma in particular, deserve special mention, if only because his attacks are well-formulated and his data is usually (although not always) well-documented. Grassley points out that one out of three psychiatrists received money (not just trinkets, pens, coffee mugs, and clocks, but actual cash) from drug manufacturers in the first decade of the 21st century. Psychiatrists, much more than any other medical specialty, were supported by Pharma grants, speaker's fees, consulting payments, book deals, and the like.

In many cases, the sums received were significant. Some psychiatrists earned hundreds of thousands of dollars through pharmaceutical consulting. Many more earned tens of thousands just for discussing new products with other doctors over dinner. Many of those doctors lacked the academic credentials or publication track records that bestow credibility. Even some of those with academic credentials did not disclose their payments to their universities, and some of them conducted highly-publicized and highly-influential studies that may have been biased by such payouts. Some payouts amounted to $1,000,000 or more.

As of June 2011, three renowned Harvard psychiatrists who specialize in the study of ADHD were censored for receiving — but not reporting — more than a million dollars of income from drug companies.[4] But hotshots are not the only psychiatrists that benefit from Pharma's largesse, and 21st century psychiatrists are not the first generation of psychiatrists to receive subsidies. I stress that not all psychiatrists accept cash from pharmaceutical companies and must remind readers that two out of three are *not* on Pharma payrolls.

Sometimes some of the high earners hail from the most modest of places. Psychiatrists who work in nursing homes can be treated to trips to exotic locales and made to feel more important by cloying drug reps that recognize their prescribing power. In most nursing homes, Medicaid pays for meds, and high-volume prescribing was once unmonitored because no one paid out-of-pocket and patients were often too demented to question their extra prescriptions. Likewise, some medical directors of community clinics rely upon Pharma funding to boost their bottom lines and to compensate for the lower-than-average salaries supplied by non-profit clinics.

Articles about commercial contamination of psychiatric research periodically appear in nationally prominent publications such as the *New York Times*, the *Washington Post*, and the *Wall Street Journal*. The Boston area press gets especially vitriolic when reporting Harvard-related events.[5] Websites such as http://www.ProPublica.org publicize these and other such socially-detrimental occurrences. *ProPublica* hosts a special subsection entitled "Dollars for Doctors."

Of course, fringe groups such as Scientologists opposed Prozac when it was introduced in the late 1980s, and they promote their own pricey prayer techniques as antidotes for mental distress instead. Scientologists typically picket annual APA conferences. Yet these fringe groups have been dwarfed by more credible critics of psychopharmacology who cite statistics about monetary payoffs and research fabrications rather than espousing their religious beliefs.

Unless one has been actively engaged in treating patients with medications, and has personally witnessed advances in treatment that have taken place over the decades, it is indeed tempting to dismiss all of Pharma's claims about new drugs out of hand. Pharma's hype often sounds like pure commercialism and a thinly-veiled attempt to exploit vulnerable patients. However, most of those who have had first-hand experience in practicing psychopharmacology over the years (myself included) agree that a great many new treatments offer benefits over older approaches.[6, 7] That said, few (if any) practicing psychiatrists concur that *all* innovations are preferable to older treatments. Anyone who automatically says "newer is better" — without evaluating the data — is automatically open to suspicion.

Standing alongside Senator Grassley and other aspiring politicians are patients' rights groups and parents' groups. They, too, express skepticism about the free-wheeling prescribing of mood medications to psychiatric patients. They show special concern about medications provided to very young patients in particular. Data shows that pediatric prescriptions for psychotropic medications skyrocketed in the course of a few short years. Because the expensive medications prescribed for children produced serious medical side effects (such as obesity and sluggishness), critics accused Big Pharma of promoting these medications needlessly.

Social advocates point out that foster children are much more likely to be medicated than kids who live in more intact households where parents can advocate on their behalf.

In the 1960s there had been concerns about excessive prescribing of stimulants for what was then known as "minimal brain dysfunction." In some cases teachers, rather than doctors, were allowed to diagnose their pupils and to recommend medications to MDs. Today most concerns revolve around overly-enthusiastic prescribing of anti-psychotic medications that dull the senses and add adipose tissue.

Psychiatry has always borne the brunt of popular criticism, and the populace has long felt itself qualified to comment on psychiatric treatments and diagnoses. Perhaps that is because "diseases of the soul" were not always the province of medicine and have historically lain in disputed territory, where the boundaries are not clearly demarcated. Bizarre behavior, mental distress and unusual perceptions — and even seizures and strokes — fell under the jurisdiction of the clergy until the 18th century. With this background it is no surprise that the diagnosis and treatment of psychiatric symptoms are still vulnerable to "squatters' rights," and that those who arrive first feel entitled to express their opinions most loudly. And those who arrive later feel equally justified in expressing their contempt for the original "squatters." But there are other reasons why the general public has become knowledgeable about this new breed of mood med.

By the second decade of the 21st century, psychotropic medications have become so popular — and so effective — that it is nearly impossible for the public *not* to take a stand. A quarter of all Americans consume mood meds. Names like Prozac, Ritalin, Adderall, Zoloft, even Abilify, Seroquel and Zyprexa, are almost as well known as iconic Fifties-era home remedies such as Geritol, Pepto-Bismol and Alka-Seltzer. Attorneys advertise class action lawsuits against many pharmaceutical manufacturers, sometimes in the very same venues where the drug makers promote their products.

The implication is that the drug companies deliberately *deceive* the public — and even physicians — about the new mood meds. The underlying dishonesty and duplicity are as important as the side effects of psychotropic meds. If this were not a concern, why would the "Sunshine Act" have gone into effect in 2011? This federal law requires Pharma manufacturers to post their payments to physicians online so as to inform medical consumers of potential bias and conflicts of interest. Even this stringent policy is not necessarily effective, as proven by recent revelations about million dollar payouts to a select cadre of Harvard facility members.[8]

As a side note, the "Decade of the Brain" of the 1990s may have cemented the era of modern psychopharmacology, but the new medications of that era — SSRIs (selective serotonin reuptake blockers) such as Prozac, and AAPs (atypical anti-psychotics) — were not the first mood medications ever prescribed. The Sixties brought Librium and Valium, as well as the Rolling Stones' song about "Mother's Little Helper" (1966). The Stones parodied the overuse of these medications by housewives, even though they themselves were known as the "bad boys" of the early rock era, and one band member was arrested for heroin possession. Jacqueline Susann's novel about *Valley of the Dolls* (1966) was a runaway best-seller. A film based on the book followed a year later (1967) and captured the ethos of that unfortunate era.

The Fifties introduced Thorazine, the first "major tranquilizer" (also known as a "neuroleptic"). Thorazine provided severely ill patients with "chemical restraints" rather than physical restraints (that often came in the form of straitjackets). Thorazine paved the path to the emptying of the asylums because it freed schizophrenics from the frightening hallucinations that incapacitated them and required full-time custodial care.

Thorazine also produced the "Thorazine shuffle" and the soulless stare. It arrived shortly before *Invasion of the Body Snatchers* (1956), a film about empty shells — "pod people"— that displace the real human inside. Alien mind control movies were also popular during that time, which overlapped with the era of space discovery and Sputnik. So we cannot attribute those films to this med alone, but it does make one wonder about the inspirations for all those brain-eating aliens that danced across the drive-in screens of the day. The Fifties were also the McCarthy era, when Senator Joe turned the American public into automatons because they feared being accused of cooperating with Communist conspiracies or harboring leftist leanings that led to Communism.

If we want to complete our "popular history of psychopharmacology," we must mention the bromides that were used to calm people down until their long-term side effects became better known. The term "bromide" entered the English language as a word that refers to something that is placating, perhaps falsely so. Bromides (such as those used in the once-popular Bromo-Seltzer) produce a sense of artificial calm. Bromides also cause a medical condition known as "bromism" when used to excess. The skin lesions and mental changes of bromism brought a halt to the use of this once-popular psychotropic medication.

Bromides should not be confused with barbiturates, which are sedating (and also addictive) and potentially deadly, as we learned from the untimely deaths of Marilyn Monroe and Judy Garland. Barbiturates help epileptics avoid seizures, but they also cause seizures when stopped suddenly. "Barbs" were superseded by benzodiazepines like Librium and Valium (and, more recently, Xanax, Ativan and Klonipin). Benzodiazepines remain popular with the public because they relieve anxiety symptoms quickly — and because some irresponsible people enjoy taking excess doses "for fun." However, abrupt withdrawal of benzodiazepines is more dangerous than stopping alcohol or even heroin.

Given the long history of sedating medications that robbed patients of their wills and left them confined to asylums, sometimes in stupors, we would expect to see "diabolical drugging" scenes in far more films than we do. We have to ask ourselves why such scenes are relatively rare, compared to other varieties of "sinister psychiatrist" scenes detailed elsewhere in this book. Why has this genre not proliferated in the recent past, and why had it not soared skyward in the present, when psychopharmacology is king?

Before I comment on these questions, let me introduce an odd little detail that might derail us. The concept of "diabolical drugging" by a psychiatrist was introduced in the very early days of film through a "comedy" by Victor Fleming. Fleming became much better known for directing *The Wizard of Oz* (1939), *Gone with the Wind* (1939), and *Dr. Jekyll and Mr. Hyde* (1941), with Spencer Tracy and Ingrid Bergman. But seeds of his genius can seen in his silent film *When the Clouds Roll By* (1919). I should add that the seeds of contemporary pharmaceutical advertising, and the Nexium ("purple pill") commercials in particular, can likewise be found in this charming 1919 movie.

In this film the culprit is not a chemical but, rather, foods — foods that induce bad dreams. That might sound preposterous were it not for a few facts that add credibility to this claim. For one thing, Freud's book on the *Interpretation of Dreams* was being read and reprinted at that time, and so more attention was being paid to the scientific basis of dreams.

It had long been thought that certain foods — overripe cheeses in particular — caused bad dreams. That folk wisdom was still in good standing when this film was made — and perhaps there is some truth to it. For overripe cheeses are high in natural tyramine, which is a stimulating neurotransmitter that interacts with anti-depressant medications such as MAOIs (monoamine oxidase inhibitors).[9]

When the Clouds Roll By was made in America in the very same year that *The Cabinet of Dr. Caligari* was made in Germany. Its intertitles make it easy to capture the train of thought of its star psychiatrist, who sports a distinctly Germanic name. But we cannot hear his accent because this is a silent film with intertitles only. Yet we hear it in our minds, thanks in part to the "psychic acoustics" and dramatic overacting that made silent films "speak" so loudly.

The movie begins by telling us that "Guinea pigs and rabbits are often sacrificed for scientific purposes. But here is a new one...." The film continues: "Before a clinic of mystery, Dr. Ulrich Metz propounds a fantastic theory of evil design." An illustration of a skull in hand appears in between the intertitles. Through the written word, Dr. Metz proceeds to tell us that "I mean to take a human life in the cause of science, but this must remain a professional secret with us.... Other scientists experiment with animals, but I have selected a human being — as my work concerns the human mind."

Metz continues: "The power of suggestion can destroy both mind and body. But first I weaken the power of resistance within my subject by implanting psychic germs of fear, worry, superstitions and kindred annoyances.... For three months I have directed my experiment upon a normal young man, but he is unaware of his fate."

In the next scene a confederate informs Dr. Metz, "I gave him the food that you directed. He will soon be in the throes of another horrible nightmare." Metz answers, "Ghostly fingers now stirring in his troubled mind will make him an easy victim for my experiment." The two continue their unspoken dialogue, describing the clinical Case of Daniel Boone Brown: "77th Day: Health — Failing; Sleep — Restless; Disposition — Nervous, Irritable; Work — Continually Late.... Remarks: Case progressing satisfactorily; Nightmares — acute nervousness; Superstitions causing constant worry."

Then an intertitle reads "The stuff that dreams are made of," alluding to the Shakespearean play. This line precedes an elaborate Hieronymus Bosch–like dream sequence in which Boone is attacked and chased both by imaginary beasts and the food that he ate. The seventh art was barely out of its infancy in 1919, and contemporary audiences were captivated by moving images that seem silly to more sophisticated spectators.

The spinning-room scene reminds us of the more recent film *Inception* (2010). The magical animated beasts mirror Méliès' magical characters and their cartoon-like qualities. The imaginary beings of *Clouds* prepare us for the work of wonder that Fleming would direct two decades later, in 1939, when he made *The Wizard of Oz* (1939).

How interesting it is that such an early film captured the ethos of diabolical drugging. At that time some foods were believed to be psychoactive, and nightmares were blamed on cheese that was eaten late at night. Feeding such food to an innocent was akin to dosing him with dangerous drugs. This theme recollects European psychiatric practices from World War I when psychiatrists administered painful electric shocks to soldiers.

There were more serious reasons for concern about foods, good and bad. Dementia induced by dietary deficiencies became a hot topic of public debate in the years preceding

Clouds. Around the same time that Fleming made his film, Dr. Joseph Goldberger was making waves about the cause and cure of pellagra. It had been believed that the illness known as "the 4 Ds" ("diarrhea, dermatitis, dementia, death") was spread by infection. In 1914 the U.S. Surgeon General assigned Goldberger to investigate the source of the pellagra epidemic in the American South. Entire mill towns, orphanages, and mental hospitals were struck by this scourge.

Goldberger theorized, and ultimately proved, that pellagra resulted from niacin deficiency caused by the maize-heavy diet of poor Southerners. He stepped on many toes with his contrarian but correct explanation. He was ridiculed, and he never won the Nobel Prize, even though he was nominated five times. Goldberger experimented on prisoner-volunteers, feeding them maize only and depriving them of other proteins. They complained bitterly about the depression and bad dreams and pains that ensued. Many begged to stop the experiment before it finished. Their symptoms disappeared swiftly once their diets changed.

To fortify the proof of his theory, he, his wife, and his assistant swallowed pills of pellagrin scabs or injected themselves with pellagrin-tainted blood. They never developed the disease. He proved beyond a doubt that pellagra was a dietary disease and not an infectious one. Dr. Goldberger amplified his research over the years. He also incited public debates about pellagra. This information was "in the air" when Fleming made his film (though it is uncertain if Fleming's imagination was sparked by these tales of food-borne woes in Southern mill towns).

There may be many more tidbits of history that can be linked to *When the Clouds Roll By*, but my focus is on "diabolical drugging." Let me conclude by saying that that it is curious to find a film about "diabolical drugging" in the early years of the moving image. Yet, in our own era, when a panoply of psychoactive medications are available, there are comparatively few films on this compelling subject; theoretically, there should be many — if movie motifs do indeed mirror reality. And we already know that that is not so, for if it were, there would be no more madhouse movies because so few "madhouses" remain in 21st century America.

Let's look for some reasons why there is a dearth of "diabolical drugging" examples. For one thing, many of those drugged-out scenes occur during the course of involuntary incarceration in mental hospitals or asylums or sanitariums. When that happens, the "mental hospital" part of the "mental hospital movie" is much more memorable than the drugging scene. Low-budget horror films often capitalize on such scenes because they are so easy to stage.

More importantly, the medication aspect of the mental hospital is less memorable than the larger setting. Offering a patient a container of pills is not very dramatic and so does not meet the needs of the movie industry, which prefers high drama rather than subtle suggestion. Seeing a phalanx of patients meandering near the nursing station, wearing scraggly standard-issue bathrobes and disposable paper slippers as they wait for their morning meds, cannot hold the attention of spectators for more than a second or two.

Injections of medications have slightly more dramatic appeal, but even that is limited, for "shots" last only a few seconds. If a few orderlies are needed to restrain a flailing patient who resists the injection, or to lock them into a straitjacket (as we will see when I discuss *The Jacket* below), there is more movie potential. But watching a psychiatric patient sit alone in a locked and empty "quiet room" is flat out boring.

So to create an attention-grabbing medication scene, films must focus on meds that can be injected rather than ingested. That limits the options. For instance, Lithium, which is used for bipolar disorder, comes in capsules only. Bipolar disorder can make for an interesting movie scene, but shots of charts that document the ups and downs of laboratory values for lithium levels (or kidney or thyroid functions) are hardly entertaining. Those graphs of laboratory values are drawn every few weeks or months and lack the dynamism of constantly moving EEGs (electroencephalograms) that are monitored during ECT (electroshock therapy).

Another point to consider: medications such as Valium, Xanax, barbiturates, and various sleeping pills produce pleasant "highs" that makes them desirable to patients, and also make them subject to overuse and abuse. Many people seek out these tabs or caps or sticks. Far fewer fear them. Medications that produce pleasant sensations are unlikely to become "predator pills." Even the "narco-synthesis" scenes from the late 1940s and early 1950s focused on the good that can come from the use of truth serum, such as sodium amytal, as seen in *The Snake Pit* (1948).

Thorazine injections, on the other hand, went from being perceived as a miracle in the mid–1950s to a menace by the early 1960s. By 1960, anti-psychiatrists such as R.D. Laing spoke out. Books such as Ken Kesey's *One Flew Over the Cuckoo's Nest* (1962) became best-sellers soon after. Dr. David Cooper coined the word "anti-psychiatry" right around then. Ken Kesey witnessed the early days of Thorazine when he worked as an aid at the VA Hospital in 1959 (and when he himself volunteered for CIA-sponsored hallucinogen experiments). Other important (and less edgy) novels from the Fifties expressed fears about "diabolical drugging," the rise of lobotomies, and various hazards of psychiatric care. But most films of that era still lionized psychiatrists, stressing the "couch cure" and skirting psychopharmacology scenes.

Again, let us return to the present and reconsider allegations made against certain psycho-pharmaceutical manufacturers, not to mention the lawsuits levied against them for false or misleading advertising, and the huge settlements — in the hundreds of billions of dollars range — imposed by government regulatory bodies. In the news we read about more and more indictments of physicians who accept money from drug companies, misrepresent their research, or spin their statistics to show better than expected results that favor the parties that pay them.

Given the grave concerns raised by Senator Grassley et al. in Congress, these are *au courant* issues. If these controversies are in the air, why we do not see *more* films about diabolical drugging — or about the long-term side effects of medications that were concealed from physicians and patients alike? Again, the answer is simple: films are a form of drama. They are intended to be entertaining rather than educational. If viewers learn something new from films, or find their opinions challenged, so be it. That is gravy, not the meat of the matter.

More likely than not, films that do *not* confirm the tacitly-agreed-upon cultural belief system have a harder time finding a responsive audience. A little controversy is good and helps promote a product. But too much controversy puts cinema off-limits.

In general, film themes reflect internal fears more than they reflect external realities. They tap into conscious or unconscious concerns that impact enough of the paying public to interest investors and make these commercial enterprises worthy of their attention. There are independent films and there are some documentaries that bypass this step; sometimes they make a splash, but more often than not they sink without a ripple.

To top it off, these subjects must be communicated in a visually dramatic manner because movies are primarily a visual medium. If a concept is better expressed through words, then the end result is a book. A book about psychiatric issues (such as Ken Kesey's *One Flew Over the Cuckoo's Nest*) must stand up to visual translation and dramatic representation if it is to succeed as a film and appeal to the moviegoing public. As a matter of fact, the film version departed so much from the Kesey novel that Ken Kesey disowned it. Financial disputes with the filmmakers embittered Kesey even more.

Curiously, Freud objected to films about psychoanalysis very early on because he recognized that abstract concepts had to be communicated pictorially, and he doubted that this was possible. Freud never believed that film as a medium would succeed at all. In that, he was so wrong — but his recognition that cinema prioritized visual imagery over theoretical ideas was so right.

Occasionally a film reveals previously untold secrets and reflects public health concerns, inspiring social change in response. *The Snake Pit* (1948) was one of those films that focused attention on conditions in state mental hospitals. *One Flew Over the Cuckoo's Nest* (1975) inflamed viewers and provoked legislation against ECT, although many practitioners believe that California's all-or-nothing anti–ECT legislation did not serve the public's best interest because that law eliminated choices of treatments.

Oddly enough, the best example of "deceptive drugging" in this era of presumed deception by drug makers can be found in films that were inspired by a 1939 comic book. (Recall that ECT had arrived in the U.S. in 1938, which was only one year before the first *Batman* comic; and Freud died the same year the first *Batman* hit the stands in 1939.) The psychiatrist character we meet in 21st century movies existed long, long ago.

In *Batman Begins* (2005), Cillian Murphy portrays a psychiatrist named Dr. Jonathan Crane. Dr. Crane is better known in the comic book world as "Scarecrow." In the film, Dr. Crane heads a forensic hospital that houses the criminally insane. The asylum gained greater fame after the 2008 release of the video game by the name of *Arkham Asylum*. Until then, Scarecrow was the nom de plume of a born-evil doctor who condoned the misdeeds of the Joker and Dr. Tommy Elliott, an evil surgeon.

The Joker is one of the highest profile villains of the comic book world. His green and purple garb makes him instantly identifiable. His hideous grin was influenced by an expressionist film from 1928, *The Man Who Laughs* (1928). Dr. Elliott is less well-known than the Joker. Dr. Elliot is a surgeon who rigged his parents' car when he was a boy. He murdered his father and crippled his mother in the process, but he missed the opportunity to inherit the family fortune because he had to provide for the mother who survived the accident. Dr. Crane admires Tommy Elliot's youthful handiwork because he admires evil in general.

In *Batman Begins* we witness but one of Dr. Crane's many malevolent tricks. Here he sprays mind-altering drugs into the air as he interviews an incarcerated mobster. Dr. Crane pulls a hideous mask out of his briefcase and places it over his own face. Combined with the drugs, this trick convinces the criminal that he has hallucinated a monster and has gone mad. This act elicits an extreme emotional outburst from the mobster and makes the mobster-patient appear insane in front of others. The mobster is then committed to the institution that Dr. Crane controls. But no one has witnessed Dr. Crane's actions (except those of us who sit in the audience).

A different tactic is taken by the psychiatrist involved in the treatment of the protagonist

In *Batman Begins* (2005), Batman (Christian Bale) beats up bad psychiatrist Dr. Crane (Cillian Murphy) after Crane sprays hallucinogenic gas to make people think they have become psychotic.

in *The Jacket* (2005). Adrian Brody plays Jack Stark, whose convoluted story is sadder than sad. The plot is intentionally disjointed, as so many turn-of-millennium films were. As the second millennium approached, no one knew whether we were coming or going, or whether we would encounter a new era or meet an apocalyptic end. Some said that the world as we knew it would cease to exist. The more practical-minded worried that computer clocks would fail and that banks and stock trading would go awry. Films of that era mirrored this confused mindset and became known as "mindf**k" movies because they "mess with the mind" and recollect the chaos of the times.

The Jacket is one of several films where time and reality shift to the point that viewers are confused about what happened when and what happens next. Chronology and logic fall by the wayside. *Donnie Darko* (2001), *eXistenZ* (1999), *Memento* (2000), *Fight Club* (1999), and even *Jacob's Ladder* (1990), which arrived a decade before the millennium's end, captured this same sentiment and employed related post-modernist techniques.

Jack Stark's story in *The Jacket* is told in bits and pieces, in flashbacks and in flash forwards. The film's screenplay is based on a 1915 story by Jack London, who gained greater fame through his novel *The Call of the Wild* (1903). The Jack London story "The Star Rover," revolves around extra-corporeal time-travel by a man who is strapped in a tight straitjacket. Film director John Maybury said that London's tale was "loosely based on a true story of Ed Morrell, who told Jack London about San Quentin prison's use of tight straitjackets."

Regardless of the truth about the origins of the story, *The Jacket* tells the tale of a hapless Gulf War vet who was shot in the head long before we see him hitchhiking on a highway in Vermont. Jack was declared dead on the spot after he was shot. He was transported as a corpse but was then re-examined by a doctor who saw him blink his eyes while lying in the morgue. From that point forward Jack Stark is alive — but the life that he leads after that time turns out to be a strange and sad life indeed.

Psych aids stuff poor Jack Stark (Adrian Brody) into a morgue box at the behest of a drug-addled doc (Kris Kristofferson), who injects Jack with other drugs. All the while, Jack wears the straitjacket that lends its name to the film. While in the box, and even before being stuffed into the box, Jack (Brody) suffers from recurrent bouts of amnesia that interfere with past memories but allow him to see his (bleak) future.

But the story is nowhere near so straightforward. When we put the pieces together chronologically, we realize that Jack left the military after having suffered serious head trauma. Miraculously, he survived, but he endures repeated bouts of amnesia. Once he is discharged from the service he heads home to Vermont. On the road he spots a woman who stands besides her stalled car, her young child by her side. Jack (Brody) stops to help and then moves on. In the interim a cop pulls over and is shot by a passerby. Jack's amnesia about the event makes him unreliable, and he is blamed.

Unable to offer a credible alibi, Jack is arrested, tried and convicted, but he is not remanded to prison. Instead, he is sent to a hospital for the criminally insane because he was talking about time travel at the time of his arrest, and because he has a documented history of head trauma (which is now called "TBI" or "traumatic brain injury"). In the asylum he is injected with an experimental hallucinogenic drug by a disheveled doctor played by Kris Kristofferson. Kristofferson struggled with his own substance problems off screen and so seems especially credible in this unscrupulous role. Sadistic aids lock Jack in a straitjacket (hence the name of the film: *The Jacket*) and shove him into drawer. He endures flashbacks and flash-forwards that provide pieces of the film's disjointed plotline.

In a flash-forward, Jack meets a dissolute young waitress. The two feel an inexplicable pull toward one another and end up spending time together in her room. The waitress shows Jack a dog tag, not knowing that this is the very same dog tag Jack lost at the accident scene. He then realizes that she is the young girl from the auto accident, now grown up.

Everywhere he turns, poor Jack Stark meets one roadblock after another. He is victimized by drugged out doctor and subjected to "diabolical drugging"—but this is just one of his many ordeals on his Calvary-like trek through the forensic mental health system. Recall that this drugging scene occurs during involuntary hospitalization in a mental institution. It is up to the viewer to decide which of his lot is worse: the war injuries, wrongful conviction, involuntary hospitalization, straitjackets, abuse by staff, drugging or unethical experimentation.

The Jacket is clearly post-modernist and post-millennial, but we can see antecedents of this some fifteen years earlier, in 1990, with *Jacob's Ladder* (1990). Like *The Jacket*, *Jacob's Ladder* zooms in on combat wounds. Like *The Jacket*, the beginning, middle and end of *Jacob's Ladder* are hard to decipher. Both *The Jacket* and *Jacob's Ladder* involve psychiatric experiments conducted on military personnel or by military personnel. Each includes scenes of "diabolical drugging." Even more incredibly, some of these fictional drug experiments in these films contain a kernel of truth, as will be detailed in the next chapter, "Unethical Experimentation."

Jacob's Ladder begins in 1971 Vietnam, where Jacob Singer (Tim Robbins) is stationed, along with his platoon. Helicopters pass overhead, loaded with supplies. Unexpectedly, Jacob's unit is bombarded by heavy fire. The soldiers scramble for cover, but some behave strangely for no particular reason. Some seize and shake and froth at the mouth. Jacob attempts to escape but is stabbed by a bayonet that belongs to someone off screen. We never learn the identity of his assailant.

It is not until the end of the film that we realize that Jacob died on the battlefield, and that the kaleidoscopic memories that populate the movie were deathbed hallucinations of events that probably never happened. Or the hallucinations could be drug-induced, for rumor has it that the men ingested an experimental hallucinogenic agent that was concealed in their food supply. This rumor is confirmed by a dialogue with a chemist who was recruited to synthesize mind-altering medications for the military.

We see Jacob whisked through the halls of a decrepit hospital that looks like Brooklyn's Kings County Hospital. Yet he never returned to his home base of Brooklyn. Instead, he traveled through the "Bardos" of Tibetan Buddhist lore and confronted monsters that wait at different stages after death. The "Ladder" alluded to in the film's title has several meanings. It refers to the same "Jacob's Ladder" that is mentioned in the Biblical book of Genesis (Genesis 28:12). The ladder is a meeting place between Heaven and Earth where angels ascend and descend. This theme is illustrated beautifully by the Bible-obsessed visionary artist William Blake. But "the Ladder" also refers to a drug that brought users down to the lowest ladder of hell.

Just as his hallucinations grow progressively stranger, a former army buddy contacts Jacob and attempts to tell him about his own hallucinations. When this buddy dies in an unexplained car explosion, Jacob's paranoia mounts. The possibility of a conspiracy increases.

Platoon mates in Vietnam, Jerry (Brent Hinkley) and Paul (Pruitt Taylor) sit and smoke before becoming dangerously psychotic from "Ladder"-laced food in *Jacob's Ladder* (1990).

At his buddy's funeral, surviving platoon-mates confess to Jacob that they, too, have been subject to horrible hallucinations. (We are reminded of *The Manchurian Candidate*, where fellow soldiers discover that they dream the same dreams.)

Jacob is then approached by someone named Michael Newman (Craven). The youthful Newman claims that he was a chemist who worked in the Army's chemical warfare division in Saigon. The chemist offers details about the drugs and confides his own personal criminal history. He was arrested for manufacturing LSD in his home lab, but government agents arranged to drop the charges if he cooperated with their secret studies. He explains that he agreed to continue his chemical experiments after being corralled into this clandestine and completely unofficial plea bargain. Once in Vietnam, he synthesizes a drug that increases aggression.

We the spectators believe that Newman is a chemist, and we somehow know that he is not a clinician. He wears a white lab coat, and he tinkers with Bunsen burners and beakers. But it is somehow implied that someone with psychiatric know-how is pulling the strings behind the scenes. During his short encounter with Jacob, the chemist blurts out some details. He confirms that the drug was code-named "the Ladder" because it takes people straight to their primal urges. He says that tests were performed on monkeys first and then piloted on a group of enemy POWs, all with horrific results. Later, small doses of "the Ladder" were secretly added to the food that belonged to Jacob's battalion. Instead of attacking the enemy, the men in Jacob's unit attacked one another while under the influence of "the Ladder." After hearing this revelation, spectators start to suspect that Jacob was stabbed by a fellow soldier in base camp before he had a chance to die on the proverbial battlefield.

The last scenes of the movie show Jacob returning to the apartment building that he once shared with Sarah, his real wife (not his nightmarish, imaginary wife who works in the post office). As he rummages through a box of memorabilia, he is greeted by his little son Gabe, who had died in a car accident before Jacob was drafted. Gabe takes his hand and leads Jacob up the stairs, where the two disappear into the light. The dead Jacob and the long-deceased son can now spend eternity together. Like the angels in the Biblical story about Jacob's Ladder, the two step upwards, approaching heaven together.

By the time the film ends we realize that Jacob never left Vietnam. We see his body lying in an army triage tent, surrounded by two surgeons. He is dead, and the events that he (and we) just witnessed were deathbed hallucinations. Before the credits end, a title card appears on screen, telling us that the U.S. Army allegedly experimented with a hallucinogenic drug called BZ, but that this claim was denied by the Pentagon.

Military conspiracy themes and CIA conspiracy themes have been popular for decades and tend to revolve around Vietnam, which took place during the height of the counter-culture movement. While it is tempting to attribute these "urban legends" to the counter-culture's antagonism toward "the man" and the "establishment," there is some basis for the notion. Recent psychiatric journals published by the American Psychiatric Association now acknowledge that Dr. Cameron, a Canadian psychiatrist, did in fact collaborate with the CIA and did indeed conduct unapproved LSD studies on their bequest. Those studies would be considered unethical by current psychiatric standards. Films like *Jacob's Ladder* may still be far-out fantasies, and science may never be ready to confirm the existence of life after death, but recent revelations about Cameron's LSD studies from the 1960s suggest that it is still too soon to close the book on rumors about unethical experiments and diabolical drugging.

Of course, we cannot undo the past. But we can impact the future. And there is a strong likelihood that recent revelations about Dr. Cameron's connections with the CIA, and the unethical experimentation conducted, will be translated into more film fare. Then again, maybe more pointed data will *not* lead to more movies, since a little bit of mystery makes for a more gripping film. Sometimes knowing too many of the facts removes the fantasy element of cinema, and detracts from our own imaginative powers, which fill in the gaps and add more color.

10

Unethical Experimentation

We just learned that Victor Fleming directed *When the Clouds Roll By* in 1919. In that year — the same year that Robert Weine completed *The Cabinet of Dr. Caligari* across the Atlantic — the American public viewed this silent short as a comedy. Judging by comments found on http://www.imdb.com, American audiences found it funny when Dr. Metz introduced his ideas about human experimentation.

The intertitles of the American-made silent film discloses the details: "Guinea pigs and rabbits are often sacrificed for scientific purposes.... Before a clinic of mystery, Dr. Ulrich Metz propounds a fantastic theory of evil design."

An illustration of a hand holding a skull appears, and then Metz says, "I mean to take a human life in the cause of science, but this must remain a professional secret with us.... Other scientists experiment with animals, but I have selected a human being — as my work concerns the human mind."

Fantastic imagery decorates the screen and reminds us of Hieronymus Bosch. Turnips and radishes have human legs and romp through the fields. Surrealistic, slow-motion sequences of acrobats entertain us. This funny film is almost a prelude to Fleming's directorial masterpiece twenty years hence, when his *The Wizard of Oz* (1939) appears.

Today virtually no one disagrees that Victor Fleming is a master director, but virtually no one in our own era laughs at the thought of human experimentation, whether conducted by a psychiatrist or some other scientist. A theme that seemed funny back in 1919, shortly after the First World War ended, would inspire placards and protest marches, if not a congressional hearing or two, in the 21st century. Sensibilities have changed, perhaps because time and World War II have proven that human beings, physicians included (and psychiatrists in particular), are capable of the most inhumane acts.

Our attitudes toward unethical experimentation have changed dramatically, and our criteria for distinguishing "ethical experimentation" from "unethical experimentation" have shifted over time. Those changes are seen on screen, in courts of law, in professional debates about medical ethics, in journalistic exposés about violations of those laws, and even in book choices made by the American public. We can look to best-seller lists to see which issues are important to readers in the 21st century. (Granted, book readers are not necessarily the same population as moviegoers, but their book purchases still tell us something about issues that intrigue people in the second decade of the second millennium.)

It's safe to say that members of the public are morbidly afraid of being conscripted into unethical experiments, and are wary of participating in medical experiments in general.

163

Consider the recent rise in parents' refusals of standard childhood immunizations. The movement to forego immunization of school-age children is based on anecdotal tales, and on a single medical journal article that was subsequently retracted because of gross inaccuracies.

Consider the fact that Rebecca Skloot's book about *The Immortal Life of Henrietta Lacks* (Random House, 2010) has been on the best-seller list for more than a year at the time of this writing in 2011. That book examines the ethics of using dead and discarded cells that were cultured from a woman's tumor. No actual experiments were performed on the patient, who expired long ago. Yet many people consider the use of lab tests derived from her cells to be inhumane.

More evidence about the public's fear of medical experimentation comes from data derived from drug companies and medical device makers. It is common knowledge that approvals of new medications are often delayed because it is so difficult to recruit participants in controlled studies needed to confirm the benefits (and weigh the risks) of these novel treatments. Patients are reluctant to enroll in these clinical studies. Interestingly, researchers report that some cancer patients are more frightened by the prospect of being assigned to the "control group" that uses dummy pills instead of the experimental med, for fear that they will miss the opportunity to try promising but unproven treatments. It is not surprising that people who have no other options left — and who will die without new treatments — are more willing to take their chances on experimental methods, provided that the testing source is reliable and well-respected.

For persons receiving psychiatric care, fears about unethical experimentation fly higher — and for good reason. The idea that doctors stealthily select patients for secret studies in locked laboratories sounds paranoid on the surface, and persons who are known to be paranoid frequently express such ideas without any prodding. Anyone who has heard of Dr. Moreau or Dr. Jekyll has the seeds of such fears planted already. Yet there are important historical facts to consider before we dismiss such fears outright, and consider them to be presumptive evidence of psychiatric illness and nothing more. Later in this chapter, I will review ignominious events in North American history that will make us think twice, and I will reference articles in the *JAMA* (*Journal of American Medical Association*) and elsewhere that catalogue actual events.[1, 2, 3, 4]

Let's try to understand why persons receiving psychiatric treatment (voluntarily or involuntarily) have special concerns. Recall that people who are deemed to be dangers to themselves or others, or who are unable to care for themselves, can generally be admitted to mental institutions against their will and held there for one to three days. Specific regulations vary from state to state, and the exact guidelines differ according to locale, but involuntary commitment is possible in most places in the United States.

In the distant past, people could be committed to asylums for more reasons and for longer time periods. It's not all that long ago that people did not return after they entered a state hospital. On Friday, November 4, 2011, an obituary appeared in the *New York Times*. This obit announced the death of Ricky J. Wyatt, who died at age 57 while living in a trailer next to his mother's house. It's no small feat to merit three long columns in the *Times*' obituary page, along with a three-inch photo and a caption that reads "A legal challenge resulted in new standards."

Wyatt had been committed to an Alabama state hospital at age 14 — not because he was psychotic but because he was a "hell raiser" whose mother was serving time in prison. He was dosed, and overdosed, with Thorazine, and subjected to inhuman indignities before being chosen to be the "poster boy" of a state hospital system gone awry. He was the lead plaintiff in a class action suit that led to a landmark judgment in 1971, a few years before the film *Cuckoo's Nest* appeared. Ricky Wyatt's story confirms some of our worst fears about involuntary commitment, unethical experimentation, and diabolical drugging. His obituary shows that such practices are not relics of a distant past, but that their victims live on (or die off) to this day.[5]

Alabama's laws were changed, but similar practices persist in other countries. Some countries, such as the People's Republic of China (PRC) or FSU (former Soviet Union), have had much laxer laws, and were accused of incarcerating political prisoners in psychiatric asylums or of misusing psychiatric labels to justify detention of dissidents. Such practices have come under the attack of the American Psychiatric Association and often make headlines in professional publications.

Given these circumstances, a reasonable person would worry about the types of treatments administered in such places. A person who is already prone to worry would worry even more. By extension, it's not so far-fetched to wonder if people are admitted involuntarily to mental hospitals to "fulfill quotas" needed for experimental subjects, for either pharmaceutical studies, psychological techniques such as brainwashing or stimulus deprivation, or even testing out ECT (electroconvulsive therapy) equipment. This question is commonly asked by patients.

In our current era we wonder about the impact of pharmaceutical companies that fund experimental studies and pay their research teams or host universities handsomely, even, perhaps, adding a little more incentive under the table. We quiver when we read about Harvard-based psychiatrists who do not disclose their million dollar–plus payments from drug companies. What else are they hiding from the public, from patients, and from other professionals, who rely upon such prestigious research for their own decisions?[6]

We question if such partisan financial backing influences the conclusions drawn by those studies. We ask if the studies are constructed in ways that favor the interests of the industries that subsidize them. We have many other studies to show that researcher bias does occur, and that the studies that favor their funders are more likely to be published in journals that accept advertising from those industrial funders. In November 2011, newspaper articles about fudged psychology experiments appeared, and those studies had no connection to medicine or pharmacology.

Given that these concerns continue in contemporary society, it makes sense that "unethical experimentation" has been a recurring theme in films about sinister psychiatrists. This is a popular topic for horror films in general. Horror films, good and bad, have a knack for tapping into the anxieties of the era, and so can be impressively psychologically informative at the same time that they can be grossly offensive.

A special category of film — medsploitation — deals with more generic medical experimental topics. As its name implies, many of these movies are cheesy, straight-to-video releases, but a few have cinematic merit that attracts interest beyond their core cult audience. Virtually all can be lumped under the rubric of horror. As audiences grow more jaded, moviemakers push boundaries, and some produce even edgier products, including the emerging genre of "torture porn," which can be considered a close cousin of "medsploitation." Some of these films go mainstream, even though they would have been "back alley" fare in the past. For instance, a recent movie about an evil surgeon who creates *The Human Centipede* (2009) was popular enough to merit a second version a little more than a year later, even though the first began as an art house–only release.

Unethical experimentation is not the sole province of horror films, Grade–B melodramas or bootlegged DVDs that are illicitly sold on Canal Street. Unethical experimentation holds a hallowed place in literary history. Some of the most enduring tales from the 19th century revolve around unethical experimentation. Dr. Moreau, Dr. Frankenstein, and Dr. Jekyll and Mr. Hyde remain fresh in our memories and are still among our favorites more than a century later. These fictional beings lived second, third, maybe even twenty or more lives in movies, video games, toys, lyrics and plays of the 20th and 21st centuries. It is entirely possible that the names of Dr. Moreau, Dr. Jekyll, and Dr. Frankenstein are better-recognized today, in our media-saturated 21st century, than they were when they first popped up in print.

Each of these characters dabbled in areas related to brain chemistry, brain anatomy or brain-based behavior, although none of them was a psychiatrist per se. Dr. Jekyll was a compassionate doctor who toiled in London's charity clinics. He prioritized the treatment of poor patients over the care of the affluent paying patients (to the dismay of his future father-in-law, whom he murders after he transitions into the evil and lascivious Mr. Hyde).

There are many, many film versions of Stevenson's story about Dr. Jekyll, not to mention stage adaptations. So I will discuss the most acclaimed, which also happens to be my favorite. The pre–Code version was released on December 31, 1931, and is listed with a release date as either 1931 or 1932 (in much the same way that *Interpretation of Dreams* was published in November 1899 but lists "1900" as its official date of publication). Mammoulian's pre–Code film, with Fredric March, escaped the censorship of the Motion Picture Production Code of 1930 (also known as the Hays Code) because "the Code" was not fully enforced until 1934.

Dr. Jekyll was a humanitarian of the highest degree. But he also dabbled in drugs that change brain chemistry and unleash animalistic instincts that lie buried beneath social skills and Victorian etiquette. Dr. Jekyll references Darwinian evolutionary ideas when he regresses to an ape-like appearance after ingesting neuro-active chemicals from his vials. He also spoofs Victorian society, with its strict social and sexual mores. He dramatizes the dangers inherent in complete repression of animal instincts (or libido) and shows how "either-or" thinking fails society.

One might say that *Dr. Jekyll and Mr. Hyde* also acts as a morality tale against self-experimentation. Even though Jekyll uses his experimental potions on himself, and does not distribute them to patients, one of his patients indirectly meets her maker because of those experiments. That loose lady in question sang in disreputable dancehalls and was polar opposite of Dr. Jekyll's polished lady love. The improper dance hall performer made Jekyll aware of the beast inside of him as he tended to her injury. Her brazenness kindled "improper instincts" that the doctor repressed in the presence of his elegant fiancée.

In the end, the dancehall singer becomes his victim rather than his patient because of his self-experiments. For Dr. Jekyll transforms into the hideous murderous being known as Mr. Hyde and eventually strangles the woman who tried to seduce him (in the form of Dr. Jekyll) while he tended to her medical needs.

Many, many, many versions of *The Strange Case of Dr. Jekyll and Mr. Hyde* have

Fredric March casts a scary shadow after transforming into Hyde, who represents Dr. Jekyll's "shadow self" of repressed instincts, in Mammoulian's *Dr. Jekyll and Mr. Hyde* (1931).

appeared on stage and screen over the years. Robert Mammoulian's 1931 version is considered to be the classic rendition. Fredric March won an Oscar for portraying the handsome and refined Dr. Jekyll, as well as his coarse and ugly counterpart, Mr. Hyde. Ingenious theatrical lighting, rather than make-up or special effects alone, turned one character into another on the movie screen. This version was pre–Code, but it might have passed the Production Code's standards because the evil woman is murdered and the lustful doctor dies at the end. When the play made it to Broadway in the 1990s, fan clubs formed spontaneously. Audiences as devoted as Trekkies evolved in response to this compelling story.

Admittedly, *The Strange Case of Dr. Jekyll and Mr. Hyde* raises many enduring questions. According to Henri Ellenberger's magnum opus about *The Discovery of the Unconscious: The History and Evolution of Dynamic Psychiatry* (Basic Books, 1970), Stevenson's 1886 novella foreshadowed Freud's century-shaping theories about ego, id, and superego. So this classic cannot be considered as an example of "unethical experimentation" and nothing more. It holds an important place in the history of psychoanalysis and psychiatry, and in their literary antecedents. And yet it definitively speaks about unsupervised self-experimentation in medicine and the potential adverse and unforeseen consequences for patients. It is thoroughly modern with respect to such concerns.

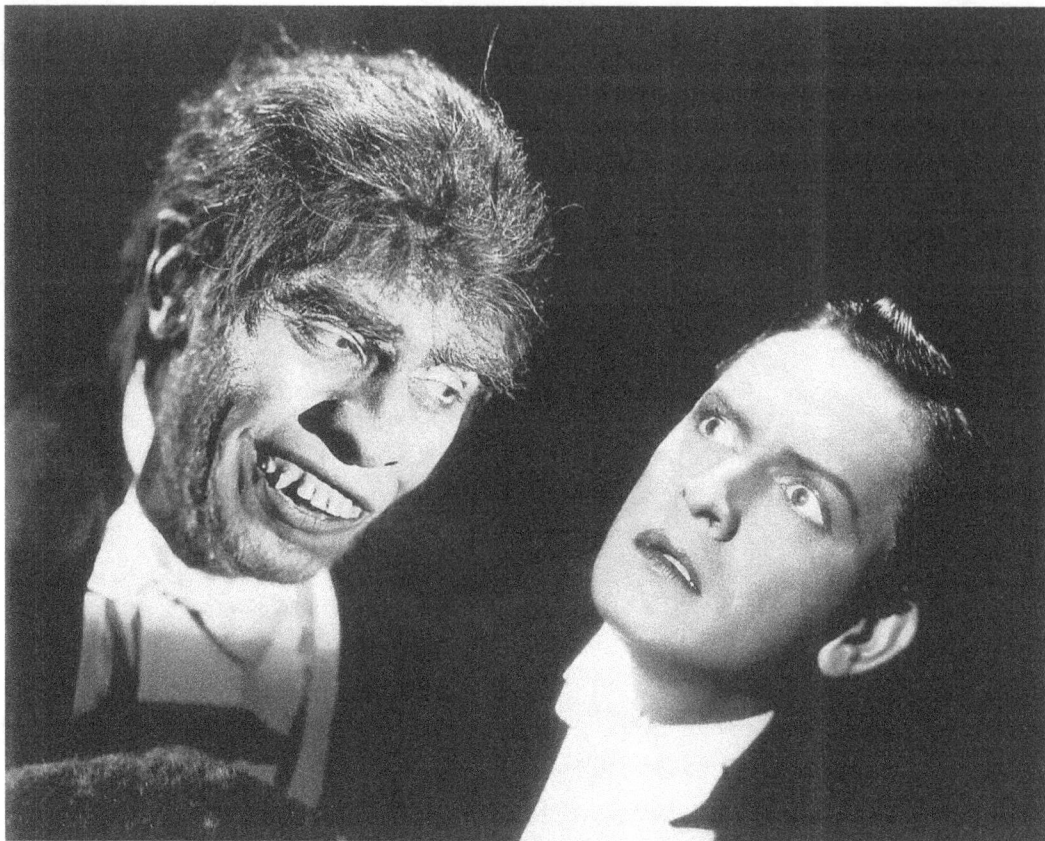

In *Dr. Jekyll and Mr. Hyde* (1931), Fredric March morphs between good Jekyll and bad Hyde thanks to lighting tricks, make-up, costumes, acting skills, and a fictional chemical.

In fact, Jekyll's colleague vehemently objects to his self-studies. In the last scene of Mamoulian's 1931 version, it is this medical confidant who aims his gun at the disturbed Dr. Jekyll (who has assumed the appearance of the hideous Mr. Hyde and bears no resemblance to his handsome counterpart). The other doctor recognizes Hyde for who he is because he has heard Jekyll's story. He alone realizes that Hyde is Jekyll transformed. He shoots Hyde from a distance. In a very dramatic ending, the dying Hyde morphs back to his original physical form and assumes the appearance of Dr. Jekyll.

Dr. Moreau bears little-to-no similarity to Dr. Jekyll, who was a good man before bad drugs turned him into a bad human being, and his good intentions morphed into terrible mishaps. Dr. Moreau possesses no such redeeming qualities. Moreau has no higher aspirations for humanity. Moreau experiments on animals and trains them to act more human. He performs operations that make them more human-like and that give them the ability to speak and stand upright. He also causes extreme pain to his subjects, as he disrupts the natural order and disregards the inborn tendencies of his menagerie. Moreau's operating room is located in the aptly-named "House of Pain."

Dr. Moreau's fictional story is retold in *The Island of Lost Souls* (1932), which premiered the year after Mamoulian's definitive version of *Dr. Jekyll and Mr. Hyde* (1931), and one year before Hitler was appointed as Chancellor of the Third Reich. The first anti–Jewish Nuremberg Laws went into effect in 1935. In a strange foreshadowing of the future, the inhumane experiments on Dr. Moreau's island mirrored experiments that the Nazi doctors would soon conduct on humans.

Don Taylor directed another movie version of *The Island of Dr. Moreau* in 1977. Two decades later, in 1996, yet another remake of the enduring tale appeared, this time starring Val Kilmer as Montgomery and an aging Marlon Brando as Dr. Moreau. This later remake was directed by John Frankenheimer, who was responsible for the original *Manchurian Candidate* in 1962. In *The Manchurian Candidate*, brainwashing experiments conducted on captive soldiers feature prominently in the plot. Dream scenes reveal the details of the experiments conducted on unwitting and unaware subjects, and provide the film's most visually interesting imagery.

While few people believe that Moreau-like animal experiments could ever impact their daily lives,

In *The Island of Lost Souls* (1932), Dr. Moreau (Charles Laughton) is a proto-psychiatrist who experiments on animals, like Panther Woman Lota (Kathleen Burke), to make them look and act human.

many people have been intrigued by the concept of turning humans into apes or vice versa. Chimps dressed in human clothes are ever-popular circus attractions. *Planet of the Apes* was a spectacular success and spawned several sequels, although the film functions as a social metaphor more than as a pro-primate treatise. In the early years of cinema, movies about ape-man brain transplants were common. Those shorts were applauded by audiences that were still shocked by the discoveries of Darwin but were also intoxicated by recent advances in science. Moving pictures were just one of the many scientific advances of the nineteenth century's end.

Freud's experimental sessions with his psychoanalytic patients were receiving attention in the first decade of the 20th century. His emphasis on the animalistic libidinal urges reinforced the fin-de-siècle's infatuation with the interchangeability between human and ape. But Freud's cathartic talking cures were nowhere near as scary as the surgical scenes from early silent shorts. The concept of being confined to a couch in a Victorian sitting room does not compare to the terror of being strapped to an operating table, with a surgical scalpel waving overhead. But any change involves some degree of experimentation, and perhaps that is another reason why change itself is scary.

One film that pulls no punches about medical experimentation is the remake of *House of Haunted Hill* (1999). The original *House of Haunted Hill*, from 1959, stars Vincent Price, whose characters always have their charms (for horror audiences at least). Two years after the release of the first *House on Haunted Hill*, Stanley Kramer's film *Judgment at Nuremberg* (1961) made the general public more aware of the horrors of the Holocaust, as did the Eichmann Trial, which was televised worldwide from Jerusalem that same year.

Before those mass media events, far fewer people knew the details of the Nuremberg Trials that prosecuted Nazi war criminals from 1945 to 1946, immediately after World War II ended. The huge Baby Boom generation that came after the war were infants or had not yet been born when the trials were held. It is unclear how many Americans of that generation were aware that the Doctors' Trial was the first of twelve Nuremberg Trials held in postwar Germany.

The Doctors' Trial tried twenty-two men and one woman. Twenty were physicians, including the sole female, who had worked at Ravensbruck, a camp for women. The other defendants were Nazi officials. Eighty-five witnesses testified. Almost 1,500 documents were introduced as evidence. Sixteen of the doctors were found guilty. Seven were executed. It was said that some were recruited by the CIA, even after they were found guilty of crimes against humanity. (Rumors about Operation Paperclip still circulate and are hard to prove or disprove, although it is known that NASA was staffed in part by Paperclip recruits.)

The original *House on Haunted Hill* was produced by William Castle, who remains one of the most memorable horror masters of all time. His cute-but-corny touches included paper skeletons that floated through movie theaters. The *House on Haunted Hill* remake is the first film produced by Dark Castle Entertainment, which hoped to capture the classic Castle kitsch, and which then went on to make remakes of other horror classics, such as *House of Wax* (which also starred Vincent Price in the original).

The second *House on Haunted Hill* film draws on Nazi war crimes and medical experiments that came to light during the Doctors' Trial at Nuremberg, and were alluded to in *Judgment at Nuremberg* in 1961. But the second film spices up these true tales with the psychiatrist seduction scene discussed in an earlier chapter, and adds an extreme example of "shock schlock" (as detailed in the chapter of the same name).

Of course, a host of ghoulish touches, special effects and unlikable characters are sprinkled throughout the *House on Haunted Hill* remake, so that philandering psychiatrists and psychiatric treatments used as torture techniques turn out to be little more than sidebars in this over-the-top supernatural horror tale. But the backdrop of human experimentation that was once conducted in psychiatric asylums and in official Nazi medical experiments deserves attention, since these details are based on more than a kernel of truth. However, by including these scenes in a film about ghosts and supernatural visitations, the historical truth is softened, and the spectator may leave the movie theater convinced that allegations of unethical psychiatric experiments are just as unreal as the ghost story itself.

In the 1999 *House on Haunted Hill* the action unfolds in an abandoned asylum known as the Vannacutt Psychiatric Institute for the Criminally Insane. Many murders were committed at the asylum, mostly in the 1920s, when the chief of the asylum, Dr. Richard B. Vannacutt (Jeffrey Combs), performed grotesque experiments and medical procedures on patients. Many died as a result. The Nazi experiments on concentration camp inmates did not begin until the late 1930s.

The hospital was closed in 1931, which was a few years before Hitler took power in 1933. In the movie timeline, 1931 was the year that the Vannacutt patients escaped, but not until they killed most of the staff and burned the hospital to the ground. The iron gates that Vannacutt had built around the asylum to prevent the patients' escape remained in place after the fire. Attempts to reconstruct the facility were made, but several unexplained deaths occurred in the process. The abandoned building became known as "The House on Haunted Hill."

The old asylum lay idle until an amusement park mogul leases it for a lavish Halloween party planned for his hateful wife (whom he plans to murder at the party). The iron gates that had been built to contain the asylum inmates will now be used to imprison his party guests and to prevent them from leaving the House on Haunted Hill. The amusement park mogul is well-versed in spook house special effects, and he plans to exploit those skills at the party. As smart as he is, he is apparently unaware that ghosts still inhabit the old asylum and that those ghosts have tampered with his guest list and invited only five people. It turns out that the five are complete strangers and were not even mentioned in the original two-page guest list. Later we learn that the new guests were hand-picked by the asylum's ghosts, who knew that they are descendents of the asylum's original sadistic staff. They are welcomed in, nevertheless, and the host offers each guest $1,000,000 if he or she endures the night in the House on Haunted Hill.

The guests start dying off, one by one, each by more gruesome means than the last. The details of the deaths in the remake are geared toward the tastes of post-slasher audiences and are much gorier than in the original. We the spectators and the other guests are tricked into believing that the host's current wife (who is his fourth wife and also the secret paramour of the psychiatrist) has been shocked to death by a faulty ECT machine.

The remaining guests struggle to find their way out of the darkened mansion. As we follow their attempted escape from the old asylum, we are led through a basement that houses the remains of patients who are strapped to tables, gyrating in agony, as they endure unimaginable experiments. The fact that these are just ghosts of the original patients, rather than real, living people, does not make the viewing any easier.

Those of us who have seen photographs from concentration camps, or early documentary films such as *After Mein Kampf* (1961), are reminded of Dr. Mengele's horrific twin studies, and of surgeries performed without anesthesia on concentration camp inmates. We are also forced to recall the German psychiatrists who decided which mental patients did not lead "lives worth living" and which were "hereditary degenerates" that deserved to die (according to Nazi standards). Those unfortunates were shunted to gas chambers that were built specifically for such purposes. Those very same gas chambers would be repurposed and used for Jews and gypsies after Christian clergy from around the world protested the murder of mental patients.

Should there be any doubt about the willing participation of physicians, and of psychiatric physicians in particular, one can Google articles about the Doctors' Trial, or one can read Robert J. Lifton's now-dated book about *The Nazi Doctors* (1986), or we can find archives of the U.S. Holocaust Memorial Museum exhibition about Nazi pseudo-science and racial hygiene online or in a *New England Journal of Medicine* review.[7] Some of us, myself included, saw the exhibit itself, which was surprisingly sanitized compared to the source material or compared to Jerusalem's Yad Vashem. Yet it was still gut-wrenching in its own right, even in a watered-down version.

Bans on Nazi-like experiments on non-consenting humans or on humans who are incapable of providing informed consent gave rise to the Nuremberg Code for medical research ethics. The Nuremberg Code bears the name of the city that housed the infamous Nuremberg Trials that brought these horrific medical experiments to light. Inexplicably, some inhumane experiments that violated the Nuremberg Code persisted in America, and some were even sponsored by the government-run Public Health Service. Studies on residents of homes for the mentally retarded, mental hospital inmates, prisoners, nursing home patients, Black men from Tuskegee, Alabama, or Guatemalans, ran through the early-to-mid-seventies.

Should a movie based on the 1972 *Luke Cage* comic book be made, we will have a chance to learn more about unethical prison experiments that persisted through the mid-seventies. Those studies were alluded to in Marvel's blaxploitation comic book about a Black man who is unfairly convicted for a crime and sentenced to prison, where he willingly consents to participate in strange medical experiments in exchange for early parole.

Until then, let's consider the fact that hepatitis studies were conducted on profoundly retarded residents of the Willowbrook School between the years 1956 and 1972. The details of those studies came to light in 1972 and became better known after former Beatle John Lennon performed a benefit concert for the victims. Lennon was inspired by Geraldo Rivera's groundbreaking investigative reports about Willowbrook, which inspired outrage in their own right. When Luke Cage asks his doctor if he is about to be "injected or infected," he reminds readers of Willowbrook.

Dr. Beecher had called attention to the Willowbrook research in his 1966 *New England Journal of Medicine* article[8] in a far less flamboyant way than John Lennon or Geraldo Rivera, or even Senator Kennedy, who visited the facility himself. The *NEJM* article reached scholarly medical audiences though perhaps it also infiltrated the cultural currency of the counterculture that was percolating in 1966. The Beecher article made a political point, but it was dispassionate in the way it avoided pointing the finger of blame on "the establishment" only. The article tells us that the children's parents signed away the rights of their retarded progeny and allowed them to be infected with hepatitis so that vaccine studies could be conducted on them.

Some parents later claimed that they felt coerced into consenting, fearing that their children would be denied a place in the residence if they refused to participate. Others suggested that the children whose parents pre-signed consents for experiments were granted preferential admission to the Staten Island school. Whatever the truth may be, this experiment, and other experiments conducted on psychiatric patients who lack the ability to provide informed consent, opened up a whole new avenue of ethical inquiry. If a retarded child or a demented adult cannot understand the purpose of an experiment, can that person provide properly informed consent? Of course not. But who can, if anyone?

This question turned out to be relevant in other ways during those years. In Illinois, psychotic patients housed in state hospitals were used as test subjects. In Sixties-era Brooklyn, doctors injected live cancer cells into demented geriatric patients in hopes of learning more about cancer transmission. These subjects lacked any understanding and had no ability to consent or refuse.

The most widely-publicized "episode" of unethical human experimentation that came to light in those years was the Tuskegee syphilis study, which was conducted on Black men who lived in Tuskegee, Alabama. Because this study focused on neurosyphilis, which causes severe psychiatric symptoms, among other things, it can be counted among the "unethical experiments" conducted in the name of neuropsychiatry. In this shameful episode in public health history, poor Black men from Alabama who were known to be infected with syphilis were denied curative treatment even after penicillin was proved to be effective in 1947. Researchers observed their subjects over a course of years, collecting data about the natural progression of untreated syphilis. They recorded their findings without informing their subjects about newly-available treatments.

Untreated subjects — as well as some wives of the subjects and the children born to those women — developed a wide range of cardiac, cardiovascular, visual, bone, neurological and dermatological problems. Some became blind or psychotic. Death rates were higher than expected, which might not have happened with early intervention.

Those studies were stopped in 1972 after the *New York Times* published a front page article on studies that were conducted by none other than the U.S. Public Health Service, which is supposedly in place to protect the public good. Articles in the *Washington Post* appeared soon after. But there was one glitch: the study that was stopped in 1972 had had a forty year run. When asked to defend their actions in the aftermath of the Nuremberg Code (which came about around the same time that penicillin was proven to stop the progression of syphilis), the American public health doctors involved with the study claimed that they thought that the Nuremberg Laws against prisoner experimentation applied to German doctors only. Their shallow defense was disturbing.

Equally disturbing recent data from 2010 and 2011 shows that Guatemalan men were used in related American-sponsored studies, with the difference being that their plight did not become known for another forty years. *New York Times* articles about these past events did not create the same stir that occurred in the early 1970s, however.

The uproar that resulted from revelations about the experiments on poor Black men in Alabama resulted in increased scrutiny of the already-suspect prisoner studies. Most prisoners did not fare as well as the fictional comic book character of Luke Cage, who developed iron-hard muscles that broke through bars as a result of an experimental error.

Most states stopped prisoner studies soon after the Tuskegee studies were revealed, especially since a disproportionate number of American prisoners were Black. By 1976, prisoner medical experiments — such as the kind that Luke Cage underwent — were banned in federal institutions. Luke Cage's imagined experiences were now relics of the past.

But does that mean that all unethical psychiatric experiments stopped forever after? To the contrary, other ongoing government-sanctioned studies about psychopharmacology and behavior modification gained steam in this era. Congressional committees and speeches by Senator Ted Kennedy addressed these issues in 1977.

Even the Canadian government proved to be complicit in some unauthorized LSD studies. Dr. Cameron, the Scottish-born psychiatrist who once headed the World Psychiatric Association, was implicated in some of the most notorious studies. Cameron had been president of both the Canadian Psychiatric Association and the American Psychiatric Association, and was once at the top of his profession. A 2011 article in *Psychiatric News*, a monthly newspaper published by the American Psychiatric Association, commented on Cameron's studies and on the shifts in ethical standards.[9]

In the May 17, 2011, issue of *Psychiatric News* is a photo of the current APA president handing a plaque to Professor Andrea Tone, Ph.D, who lectured about "Spies and Lies: Cold War Psychiatry and the CIA." Professor Tone won the Benjamin Rush Award for her research on the Central Intelligence Agency's Cold War project MK-ULTRA, which was conducted at Canada's McGill Medical School and elsewhere, with the express purpose of developing strategies for manipulating mental states and altering brain function.

Although the *Psychiatric News* article does not mention it, Professor Tone has published extensively on psychopharmacology and society. She sometimes writes for non-professional audiences. One of her better-known books was reviewed by Oprah in 2009: *The Age of Anxiety: A History of America's Turbulent Affair with Tranquilizers* (Basic Books, 2008).

At her APA lecture, Tone explained that Dr. Cameron was commended for his studies in the 1950s and '60s but was condemned by later generations, largely because social and cultural standards had changed. Also, the definition of "medical ethics" had shifted. This intriguing notion of CIA studies has been the subject of much discussion, some of it credible but much of it conspiratorial. It is difficult to tease out fact from fantasy, especially since the primary sources (CIA officials) either destroy their documents or refuse to disclose them, fearing for national security. This shroud of secrecy leaves ample opportunity for speculation, but it also makes many authors (myself included) veer away from the subject for fear of quoting spurious sources.

Not everyone reads *Psychiatric News* or other academic publications that delve into the details of psychiatric experiments and medical ethics. But many people watch movies. Sometimes movies publicize issues that might otherwise remain neglected or confined to a select cadre of scholars. *Conspiracy Theory* (1997) is a film that serves this function. But it also functions as a bone fide action adventure film, with a light romantic subplot geared toward Julia Roberts fans. Few of said fans, however, can guess at the truth that lies beneath the movie's surface.

Conspiracy Theory stars Mel Gibson as a pseudo-psychotic taxi driver. His character reminds us of DeNiro's role as a ranting and raving *Taxi Driver* in the mid–1970s. Curiously, Gibson's real-life recorded racist rants to his estranged wife (which are readily available on YouTube.com) recollect his unhinged character from *Conspiracy Theory*. But that is not entirely surprising, considering that the director had Gibson ad lib when he related his conspiracy theories to passengers in his New York City yellow cab.

The plot begins to unfold when Gibson's Jerry Fletcher meets the comely Julia Roberts. Roberts is an lawyer who works for the U.S. Attorney's office. When not performing her "day job," Roberts investigates the unexplained death of her father. It is through that coincidence that the two characters' paths intertwine. Her father's murder is the MacGuffin of the movie, as much as MK-ULTRA is.

The film's director, Richard Donner, brought solid action-adventure credentials to the project. He previously filmed both *Lethal Weapon* (1987) and *Lethal Weapon II* (1989), which were hard-hitting films about hard-hitting men. There is little on Donner's film resume that makes him a likely candidate to direct a political polemic (other than the fact that he directed *Superman* in 1978, and we all know that Superman stands for "Truth, Justice, and the American Way").

If we knew nothing about the once-secret government experiments mentioned by the lead character, we would assume that this thriller is intended as light entertainment only, something to sell movie tickets and plenty of popcorn to munch during exciting chase

Poster for *Conspiracy Theory* (1997), starring Julia Roberts as the romantic interest of Mel Gibson, who was subjected to the botched experiments of a CIA psychiatrist (Patrick Stewart, not shown).

scenes and daring escapes. We would never dream that this is a Cassandra-like cinema that reveals untold truths. The fact that the cab driver is clearly psychotic makes him an unreliable narrator—in much the same way that the men who tell the story of *Caligari* discredit their tale after they reveal that they are inmates of the very asylum they deride, and may be giving voice to "excursions of their imaginations" (aka delusions).

However, enough details about the CIA-run project MK-ULTRA have become available over the decades to make us rethink Mel Gibson's crazed conspiracy theory that he shares with cab passengers, government officials, and prospective paramours alike. Project MKULTRA, or MK-ULTRA, which is mentioned in the movie, was the code name for a covert, illegal CIA human research program run by the CIA's Office of Scientific Intelligence. It is not a fiction invented for the sake of this film. It existed, just as Operation Paperclip existed.

This official U.S. government program began in the early 1950s and continued through the late 1960s. Both U.S. and Canadian citizens were used as test subjects for studies on brain function, psychedelic drugs, hypnosis, and the overall manipulation of mental states. Sensory deprivation, isolation, and verbal and sexual abuse were added to the armamentarium of techniques tested to break down defenses and make subjects reveal information, or cause psychotic-like behavior that would make them subject to ridicule and discredit their political theories or rational abilities. These surreptitious studies revolved around psychiatry, psychology, and the still fledgling field of neuroscience.

Project MKULTRA attracted public attention in 1975 when the Church Committee and the Rockefeller Commission presented the findings of their investigations to Congress. Their efforts were partly thwarted when CIA Director Richard Helms ordered the destruction of all MKULTRA files in 1973. From then on, the investigators were forced to rely on the sworn testimonies of participants and a few surviving documents. Then, in 1977, a cache of another 20,000 documents relating to project MKULTRA was retrieved. This led to

Senate Hearings in 1977. More recently, most information regarding MKULTRA was declassified and is available on the Internet.

Ted Kennedy entered into the discussions about the secret psychedelic experiments. Speaking on the Senate floor in 1977, Senator Kennedy said, "The Deputy Director of the CIA revealed that over thirty universities and institutions were involved in an 'extensive testing and experimentation' program which included covert drug tests on unwitting citizens 'at all social levels, high and low, native Americans and foreign.' Several of these tests involved the administration of LSD to 'unwitting subjects in social situations.' At least one death, that of Dr. Olson, resulted from these activities."

Dr. Olson's death was highly publicized in scientific circles, largely because he himself was a scientist, and was one of many military and government scientists and doctors who were dosed with LSD. Dr. Olson jumped out of a window while under the influence of the drug, and while under the supposed supervision of another doctor, who said he had fallen asleep at the time the tragic incident occurred. Dr. Olson's wife did not accept the CIA's explanation and contended that her husband was murdered because he had had a change of heart about the secret experiments and threatened to expose them. The government never confirmed Ms. Olson's more dramatic claims, but it did admit to administering the LSD and paid out $750,000 for a wrongful death lawsuit.

It would have been shocking enough if these North American studies arose de novo in a bungled attempt to produce an American version of *The Manchurian Candidate*. During the Cold War years there was intense interest in countering the success of the North Korean and Chinese Communists who supposedly brainwashed captive American military men. There was neck-and-neck competition with the Soviets, for the Soviets inherited the legacy of "Pavlovian conditioning" that was discovered by the Russian scientist Pavlov. Pavlov's studies on dogs' salivation won him a Nobel Prize in physiology in 1904.

Concern about Soviet spies was important to these studies, important enough to rename the project "MKSEARCH" in 1964. This time around the goal was to produce a perfect truth drug for use in interrogating suspected Soviet spies during the Cold War. Other types of mind control were also considered.

Alas, the Americans did not borrow that much from the North Korean Communists or the Soviet Communists (or even from the Manchurians who occupy land between the two countries). The American government deployed the skills of Nazi scientists who had worked for the Reich before and during the Second World War. These scientists were recruited via Operation Paperclip and were relocated to the U.S. It has been said that some of these scientists studied torture and brainwashing, mind control, interrogation, behavior modification and related topics, and that some had been identified as war criminals during the Nuremberg Trials. It has also been said that NASA owes its existence to Operation Paperclip, a notion that Jerry's paranoid character may be hinting at in *Conspiracy Theory* when he rants about NASA's plan to assassinate the U.S. president.

There is voluminous information available about these government studies and mind control experiments on unwitting and non-consenting subjects (that included, but were hardly limited to, mental patients). Sometimes the academic researchers being funded through grants from CIA front organizations were unaware of the purpose of their work. Eventually it was determined that 44 American colleges or universities; 15 research foundations or chemical or pharmaceutical companies, including Sandoz (which is now known as Novartis) and Eli Lilly; 12 hospitals or clinics (in addition to those associated with universities); and three prisons had participated in MKULTRA. Sandoz Labs is better-remembered for Dr. Albert Hoffmann's discovery of LSD on its premises, and for marketing medicinal ergot-based precursors of LSD that are used as migraine meds. Ken Kesey, author of *Cuckoo's Nest*, admitted to his participation in those studies — and boosted his counter-culture credibility several notches in the process.

One could write an entire book comparing popular psychiatric conspiracy theories to real-life covert government-sponsored projects. But this is not that book. So we will have to jump-cut to *Conspiracy Theory* and revisit the plot. We will also reconsider the research of political scientist Michael Barkun, who addresses cinema's influence on conspiracy theories in his book about *A Culture of Conspiracy: Apocalyptic Visions in Contemporary America* (2003). Barkun argues that films introduced the idea that the U.S. government is controlled by a secret team in black helicopters. This view was originally confined to right-wing extremists but entered into the cultural currency thanks to the movies.

Conspiracy Theory is one of many films and TV shows that added to this trend. In *Conspiracy Theory* a New York City taxi driver sermonizes about his conspiracy theories to his passengers. He goes to the Justice Department, where he encounters Alice Sutton, played by Julia Roberts, who was then Hollywood's reigning box office queen. Coincidentally, Sutton is preoccupied with solving the mystery of her father's murder, although she works for the U.S. Attorney's office.

Jerry shares his many odd and implausible ideas with the remarkably patient Alice, who feels pity for him. He insists that NASA is trying to kill the President and that it has access to a secret weapon that can trigger earthquakes. While walking down the street he identifies some random men as CIA operatives. He follows them into a building where he is captured and somehow rendered unconscious. When Jerry awakens he finds himself in another unidentified building, but now he is bound to a wheelchair with duct tape.

Then the sinister psychiatrist enters the room. The doctor, played by Patrick Stewart, tapes Jerry's eyes open and injects him with a drug he calls "gravy for the brain" (LSD). Dr. Jonas uses strobe lights and water torture while interrogating Jerry about his contacts. The scene is reminiscent of *Marathon Man* (1976), when the "White Angel" Nazi conspirator tortures Dustin Hofmann in a makeshift dentist's chair hidden beneath the Brooklyn Bridge. It also foreshadows Patrick Stewart's filmic roles as Professor X in *X-Men* (2000), *X2* (2003), and *X-Men: Last Stand* (2006). Professor X is also a medical doctor that interfaces with the CIA, though Professor X is benign and protective of his charges.

We realize that Jerry is not fully delusional when he starts to show the effects of his injection. As the LSD enters his brain, Jerry sees scary cartoons and mumbles. Dr. Jonas moves closer, hoping to hear more details, but Jerry bites the doctor's nose. This leaves a telltale sign that eventually proves that his conspiracy contentions are correct. Then he makes a daring escape, still bound to the wheelchair. He shuttles down the stairs in the chair and drops into a laundry truck. The truck drives away, but not before showing us a sign that indicates the unidentified building is a mental hospital. Jerry finds Alice and babbles about biting someone's nose.

While visiting Jerry in the hospital, where he is handcuffed to the bed and drugged asleep, Alice encounters a mysterious Dr. Jonas, whose nose is bandaged. Dr. Jonas explains that his dog bit his nose, but Alice knows that Jerry bit some doctor's nose.

More action occurs, enough to make the movie interesting (albeit unbelievable). After much ado and many adventures, and any number of near-death escape scenes, Alice shoots the psychiatrist dead, but only because the psychiatrist has already shot Jerry. Luckily, Jerry does not die, but he is whisked off in an ambulance. He stays conscious long enough to hear Alice tell him that she loves him. He also remembers how Alice's father died, and so he solves the mystery that has been driving the plot since the start.

As an epilogue to this convoluted plot, we learn that Jerry is still alive, and that he is still rounding up Dr. Jonas' subjects and will reconnect with Alice once he has completed his mission. The light romantic comedy closure helps us come to terms with the meat of the story, which revolves around serious psychiatric ethical infractions.

Conspiracy Theory has a very different feel than the remake of *I, the Jury*, even though both involve CIA conspiracies and psychiatrists. *Conspiracy Theory* includes a light-hearted romance that is sandwiched inside a fast-paced action-adventure thriller. There is nothing sweet or endearing about *I, the Jury*, however, which is decadent to the core, with its shady CIA-run sex clinic and its murderous female psychiatrist, Dr. Bennett. But the remake of the Mike Hammer movie may be playing upon recently revealed information about the CIA-psychiatry studies. The remake appeared in 1982, not long after Ted Kennedy spoke to Congress in 1977 about the agency's covert drug and sex studies.

As if it weren't enough to accuse the CIA of conducting unethical experiments involving psychedelic drugs and other mind-control techniques on prisoners, psychiatric patients, CIA staff, students, and scientists, it was also revealed that some drug studies were performed on men who patronized prostitutes. In Operation Midnight Climax, the CIA set up brothels in San Francisco in order to connect with male experimental subjects who would be too embarrassed to reveal the details of the experiments or how they were conscripted for such studies.

The men were given LSD, which was legal in the U.S. until October 6, 1966. According to John Marks' 1979 book *The Search for the Manchurian Candidate* (Times Books, 1979, pp. 106–7), the brothels came equipped with two-way mirrors. Sessions were filmed for study. The motif of the second *I, the Jury* film bears some similarities to these stories about the CIA, although it's worth recalling that the movie is loosely based on Mickey Spillane's first Mike Hammer book, which was set in 1944 and published in 1947.[10]

After these documented CIA sex and drug scandals, it seems mundane to mention the conspiracy theory about Vietnam-era experimentation retold in *Jacob's Ladder* (1990)—but I will mention it again. In *Jacob's Ladder* we never see a psychiatrist on screen. The closest we come to a medically-minded "informant" is a young chemist who confesses his participation in government-sponsored studies of "the Ladder" and explains why he agreed to collaborate in these unethical experiments. The fact that the real brains behind the scenes are shielded from the screen makes the conspiracy aspect even more believable, and highlights how unethical these experiments are.

The chemist informs Jacob that he had a choice between prison and military service after he was busted for synthesizing LSD in his home laboratory. Understandably, he chose to avoid incarceration and enlisted instead, agreeing to the terms. Once in the army he synthesized a chemical that was intended to bring out the basest instincts of humankind and take them on a trip down "the Ladder."

Though proved worrisome when the chemical caused severe aggression in monkey models, the study proceeded just the same, and Jacob's platoon was exposed to the chemical through their food supply. Because he already knew of its effects on primates, the young chemist was not surprised that the drug turned the soldiers into murderers that killed their comrades even before the enemy entered their lines of sight.

In *Jacob's Ladder*, mental patients are not targeted for unethical experimentation; soldiers are the subjects, and it is unclear who is controlling these studies. Are there psychiatrists behind the scenes, or are there biochemists like Dr. Olsen, who died during an LSD experiment? Have the military masterminds garnered enough information to conduct studies without the aid of professionals? It doesn't really matter because this film is reinforced by revelations from real life, and by later films like *Conspiracy Theory*.

Even if we forget about the films and their influence on public opinion and awareness, and even if we overlook some obvious breeches in propriety over the decades, it is fair to say that psychiatry, bioethics specialists, and medicine in general have not forgotten about the ethical implications of medical experiments. Strict laws are in place about who can provide consent and under what circumstances. Psychiatric patients, and several other vulnerable populations, are afforded extra protection under these laws.

Specifically, the National Institute of Health guidelines on research involving human subjects include a special section on "Research with Vulnerable Populations." "Vulnerable populations" that are at risk of exploitation are defined as Pregnant Women, Human Fetuses and Neonates, Prisoners, Children, Persons at Risk for Suicidality, and Persons with Impaired Decisional Capacity. As a casual reader can plainly see, two of these five "special populations" include psychiatric or neuropsychiatric patients. When a proposal to revise these ethical guidelines appeared in July of 2011, the topic made front page news in the *New York Times*, and was sent out as a bulletin to all members of the American Psychiatric Association and the American Medical Association (and perhaps to other interested associations as well).

Considering how seriously these ethical guidelines have been breached since the Nuremberg Code was enacted, and considering the horrifying acts that propelled the enactment of the original Nuremberg Code, it is hardly surprising that many people fear unethical experimentation. And it is not surprising that persons seeking psychiatric services have even greater fears for their safety. Even though this might sound paranoid on the surface, there are realistic reasons to harbor such fears. As they say, "Just because you're paranoid doesn't mean they're not out to get you."

Movies about unethical experimentation allow the general public to revisit such worries in a safe setting. Those who claim that cinema sets off such fears and incites baseless antipsychiatry sentiment have not read the history books. If psychiatrists are unwilling to examine historical evidence, then their patients will supply the data for them. The public is more likely to give credence to fictional films like *Conspiracy Theory*, and to other conspiracy theories out there, if an unwillingness to discuss their concerns inflames said concerns even further.

11

In Control or in Cahoots

According to cinema, sinister psychiatrists can be in control or they can be in cahoots. They may act alone, as independent agents, as we have seen in earlier chapters. Alternatively, some sinister cinema psychiatrists interface with various nefarious forces. Maybe they head evil empires themselves, or they act as agents of the state. Some function as fronts for crime syndicates or other subterranean special interest groups.

The concept of "control" is a recurring theme in films about psychiatrists. The French philosopher, social theorist, and historian of psychiatry Michel Foucault could have predicted the importance of control in such movies, had he included 20th century film history in his surveys. Instead, Foucault combed the archives of libraries and turned his attention to the Middle Ages. He relied upon literature and art to support his theories. He wrote about the Ships of Fools that set sail with a cargo of psychotics who were unwanted in their own ports. He also wrote about the history of prisons and sexuality and mental hospitals (in separate volumes that shared interlocking themes).

Foucault compared the control in psychiatric institutions to the control in prisons. Included among his many books were *Madness and Civilization* (unabridged version, French 1961; abridged version, French, 1964; English translation, 1964), *The Birth of the Clinic* (French, 1963; English translation, 1973), and *Discipline and Punish: The Birth of the Prison* (French, 1975; English translation, 1977). He attributed society's sudden disdain for non-income-producing individuals (re: psychotics) to the rise of capitalism. According to Foucault (but not necessarily according to other historians of psychiatry, most of whom found flaws in his conclusions), mercantilism produced a seismic socioeconomic shift. Psychotics could disrupt the social order and interfere with the machinery of money-making, and so they had to be kept under control, even if that meant warehousing them in institutions under inhumane conditions. Previously, psychotics had been allowed to roam free.

There were philosophical reasons why European society lost its tolerance for the free-wheeling antics of psychotics and their lack of awareness of social norms. The Age of Reason had arrived. "Reason" was now sacrosanct. People who "lost their reason" violated the most esteemed values of the Age of Reason, and so they were brought under control by an otherwise "reasonable" society. Other eras might have accused those same individuals of demonic activity or suspected that they were possessed by spirits and deemed them unclean. Plato might have wondered if a post-seizure psychosis should be classified as "prophetic frenzies." But the Age of Reason had intellectual, not spiritual, reasons for trying to tame and contain the mentally ill.

Foucault's complicated theories have been challenged, and a thorough examination of his ideas goes far beyond the bounds of this study. Yet his influence is lasting (even if his name is not familiar to many persons outside of academia or who were educated after the 1970s). He reminds us of the connections between social control and psychiatry. Films that appeared after the publication of Foucault's first French language edition of *Madness and Civilization* (published as *Folie et de Raison: Histoire de la Folie à l'Âge Classique*, 1961) often incorporate his ideas, although not necessarily consciously. The abridged English language edition of Foucault's book in 1964 widened the reach of Foucault's influence.

It was no coincidence that Foucault's *Madness and Civilization* came at the heels of R.D. Laing's anti-psychiatry treatises from 1960 — or that Ken Kesey's best-selling novel *One Flew Over the Cuckoo's Nest* (1962) arrived a year later. The term "anti-psychiatry" was coined by Dr. David Cooper a little later, in the early 1960s.

French films such as *Head Against the Wall* (1958) express Foucault's philosophy even before Foucault formalized his ideas in book form. This movie functions as much as a documentary as a fictional or feature film. Indeed, the director, Georges Franju, had been a documentary filmmaker before he gained fame for the controversial horror classic *Eyes Without a Face* (1960). In this film a respectable-looking surgeon who lives in a large mansion arranges for the abduction of attractive young women. He then surgically removes their faces so that he can graft their skin onto the disfigured face of his own daughter.

Head Against the Wall represents Franju's transition from educator to entertainer, and his transition from documentary-maker to drama-maker. Yet both of these films demonstrate the director's antipathy toward doctors and the "medical establishment." Each shows how medical skills and medical authority can be misused by an individual and by an institution.

Foucault's ideas indirectly seeded the counterculture that fermented in the early sixties and fulminated by the late sixties. Unbeknownst to many Americans, the student protest movements that shook the States began in France before they spread to the U.S. The counterculture's overall irreverence toward tradition — and its pointed anti-authoritarian attitudes — led to a sea change in society's attitude toward psychiatry, and toward anything else that was associated with social control or restriction of individual liberties. Cops, judges, CEOs — and shrinks — were lumped in the same category as high-ranking military officials who made war.

Foucault was not the only anti-psychiatry academian who gained cultural currency at that time. Erving Goffman's more dispassionate sociological study of *Asylums* (1961) reinforced Foucault's basic tenets. Goffman's writings were much more accessible to English-speaking students because they were written in plain English by an American professor and did not need translation. Goffman and others confirmed that inmates of asylums, be they prisons or mental institutions or army barracks or concentration camps, start to show similar conformist behavior over time. This finding will be explored in the subsequent chapter on "Madhouse Movies and Involuntary Incarceration."

Understanding the sociological impact of philosophers such as Foucault, or sociologists such as Goffman, or anti-psychiatry psychiatrists such as Laing, Szasz, or Cooper, helps us understand why films of the counterculture era emphasize themes of control. But this information does not help us understand why sinister cinema psychiatrists were linked to themes about control long before the counterculture emerged. Let's backtrack a bit to understand the function of film in general so that we can better understand how psychiatric themes fit into the greater whole.

For our study of film it is important to recall that the roles played by screen psychiatrists must first fulfill a dramatic function, even when there is a political undercurrent or a philosophical point to be made. Otherwise, those films start to sound like documentaries, as Franju's *Head Against the Wall* does.

Equally importantly, even if the filmmakers have political agendas in mind when making their movies, those political points do not necessarily need to have a direct relationship with the practice or theory of psychiatry. That is true even when the plot revolves around psychiatry, and even when psychiatrists or other psychiatric personnel are central to the story. Rather, the psychiatrist or the psychiatric asylum may be a "signifier"— or a stand-in — for other individuals or for abstract concepts that are difficult to explain via a visual medium that is pieced together scene by scene. Or perhaps those ideas would be censored if they were expressed more directly.

As usual, the goal of a commercial film is to capture the audience's attention, enough to make them watch the movie and recommend it to their friends and families. Occasionally we encounter filmmakers who are more motivated by their personal philosophical or political ends than by their artistic vision or their investors' interests. When that happens, I will point that out, so we can see how such factors modify more straightforward economic determinism or interplay with an individual's psychodynamic need to succeed, be it in cinema or in any other endeavor. Apart from independently-financed films or movies that are subsidized by special interest groups, most commercial films express a "collective consciousness." They amplify a society's underlying anxieties. So cinema can be read as a cultural commentary at the same time that it is a work of (the seventh) art.

Having mentioned psychodynamic needs, let me digress into a discussion of paranoid themes and the psychology behind them. We can say that any conspiracy theory — be it about psychiatrists or government agencies or police forces or whatnot — represents paranoid thinking by definition. Everyone is in it together, whether they are players or pawns. The bottom line is that outside forces push the action for purposes that are unrelated to the spectator or the star of the show. Those forces interact behind the spectator's back. Or they operate outside of the protagonist's field of vision. In other words, they conspire.

Often the star of the show, the protagonist, is but a hapless victim in the midst of the action, his or her life swayed by forces beyond their control or outside of their conscious awareness. Occasionally the opposite occurs in cinema, and only the "paranoid" person sees reality for what it is — until the end, when "sane" people suddenly realize that "crazy" people were correct in the first place. (*Conspiracy Theory* is a prime example of this motif.)

But spectators (formerly known as "members of the audience") are as much a part of the action as the actors on screen or on stage. The so-called "omniscient spectator" sees everything that takes place on screen (or even behind the screen), and so has "privileged information" about what's happening behind the scenes and about what is planned for the next scene. The omniscient spectator hears private conversations between royalty and butlers, between prima donnas and chamber maids, between patients and psychiatrists. Sometimes such spectators have already read letters addressed to others before those letters reach their destination.

This tried-and-true ploy creates tension in the spectator, for the spectator cannot share this information with the actors, and cannot help the players avoid harm or solve crimes or escape the forces that are about to be put into play. At other times the incompletely-informed spectator must search for clues to untangle the drama. This technique engages spectators in another way: it turns them into active participants in the plot rather than passive observers, even though these spectators sit alone in the audience, far from the events shown on screen and cut off from contact with the cast.

Paranoid themes are wonderful plot-driving devices. They push the action and explain how otherwise unexplainable events occur over the course of the drama. Such paranoid plots keep viewers glued to their seats, nervously grabbing for popcorn as they await the next twist and turn. There is great value in paranoid plots, and there is even greater reason to star psychiatrists in such proven plots.

For one thing, we would be bored if all paranoid plots revolved around police procedurals and spy stories. Plus, psychiatrists probe the human mind and search for secrets, which they uncover through clever questions or insightful observations that elude those who are less trained in scrutinizing behavior. They act as surrogates for the paranoid plot driver. Psychiatrists on screen also remind us of the distinction between reality and nonreality, since their job is to ferret out the possible from the paranoid and decide who is sane versus who is insane.

There were eras when paranoid undercurrents were especially common. During the McCarthy Era, in the mid–Fifties, the Hollywood Ten were singled out for Senator Joe's Inquisition. At that time paranoia became a fact of life rather than simply a state of mind. Conspiracy-themed films proliferated in the Fifties and for good reason. *Invasion of the Body Snatchers* (1956) was one of those films.

In those Cold War years, Senator Joe McCarthy convinced Americans that card-carrying Communists and Commie wannabes were lurking everywhere, and such bad seeds should be uprooted for the sake of American democracy and for the safety of Americans. McCarthy sensed that the Communist fungus grew deep among filmmakers. He intuited that this fungus had mushroomed among scriptwriters in particular. McCarthy aimed to stifle the seeds of discontent in post-war America (and to promote his own political power perhaps more than anything else). He tried to destroy Communist sympathizers, even if it meant driving some suspects to suicide, and blacklisting and bankrupting others.

Because Hollywood was so hard hit by the Senator's efforts, Hollywood filmmakers experienced extra anxiety. They expressed those fears in their choice of movie themes. Films from the 1950s reek of fear and hatred of McCarthyism. Paranoia pervades Fifties-era cinema and colors the plots almost as intensely as the newly-minted Technicolor hues color the screen.

A decade later, in the 1960s, the anti-war movement flowered. Student protests against American participation in the Vietnam War shook college campuses. A different form of conspiracy theory came into being and made itself felt on film. Again, Big Government was to blame. But this time around the focus was not on one self-serving senator. Rather, a bigger and broader "military-industrial complex" wielded more force than McCarthy's one-man mission. Covert government agencies and stealthy military operatives are in full view in films of that decade. They remain prominent in later films that reference the Vietnam era that spanned the 1960s and 1970s. Spy films and TV shows were extremely popular. Spymasters such as James Bond, Flint, The Man from U.N.C.L.E., and Maxwell Smart became household names. Their life stories were more familiar to viewers than the mundane lives of their next door neighbors.

By then there was no need for subterfuge or symbolism, as there had been during the heavily-censored McCarthy era. Sixties filmmakers commented on conspiracy theories openly. The public's fascination with conspiracies never fully faded away, not even after Vietnam involvement ended. By the 1970s the espionage themes of the Cold War were thawing, but there were newer renditions of that same old paranoid thought process.

By the early eighties, which was an era of excess, self-indulgence, and self-centeredness, one filmmaker spiced up his movie with CIA-sponsored sex clinics run by psychiatrists (and by a female psychiatrist, no less). That film is *I, the Jury* (1982), which is a remake of an earlier Mike Hammer film from 1953.

CIA conspiracies involving psychiatrists persisted and popped up periodically over the years as evidenced by the big budget Mel Gibson-Julia Roberts-Patrick Stewart film *Conspiracy Theory* (1996). Stewart plays the film's sinister CIA psychiatrist — and credibly at that, with his billiard-ball head and epicanthal folds that recollect Ming the Merciless, Dr. No, Fu Manchu and other relics of the "Yellow Menace" of old.

Even though the turn-of-the-millennium *Conspiracy Theory* is set in the same era in which it was made, it recollects documents and books that first surfaced in the 1970s during the counterculture years. Parts of the film remind us of John Marks' *The Search of the Manchurian Candidate*, a book that was first published in 1979 and then reprinted as a Norton paperback in 1991. Related information is now accessible on the Internet. The emotional state of the world was tenuous in 1996, when *Conspiracy Theory* was made. The public was ruminating about conspiracies that could come to pass when the clocks and computers changed at midnight to start the year 2000.

As popular as paranoid conspiracy theories have been at various times, films that were made during the counterculture years do not necessarily revolve around conspiracies — although several high-profile movies made *about* the counterculture years focus on conspiracies. Psychiatrists and other scientists play different roles in those films, for any number of reasons. For one thing, psychiatry's locus of control was shifting — very slowly but surely — as the counterculture gained power in the late '60s and early '70s. In retrospect, we can see sparks of the sea change that would sweep the profession by 1990 when the Decade of the Brain began.

In the 1970s the prestige of psychoanalysis had not yet crumbled, in spite of repeated attacks made by behaviorists in the 1960s. But the walls surrounding the Freudian establishment were starting to crack under the weight of the burgeoning anti-psychiatry movement. The youth culture pilloried and pummeled the Victorian invention called psychoanalysis, and dismissed it as yet another fossil of Hapsburg authoritarianism and Old World elitism. Feminists in particular railed against Freud's "phallocentrism," his anti-woman stance and "anatomy is destiny" ideas.

Over the next several years a cottage industry of academically-minded Freud detractors emerged. Many of them added their methodical research to histrionic campus protests that preceded them. Others, such as Henri Ellenberger, who published his tome on *The Discovery of the Unconscious: The History and Evolution of Dynamic Psychiatry* in 1970, did not start out as an anti–Freud activist. Yet he linked 19th century literary conventions (such as Stevenson's *Jekyll and Hyde*) and Romantic era philosophy to Freud's psychoanalytic "inventions," and so fueled the anti–Freud fires that had already been kindled.

In the 1970s, more American MDs undertook post-graduate specialty training in psychiatry than ever before — or ever since. As historian of psychiatry Edward Shorter tells us, office-based psychiatric practice became commonplace, at least on the East Coast, in major Midwestern cities such as Chicago, and in Los Angeles. Psychoanalytic training was well-regarded in that decade. Many residency training programs recommended personal analysis for their residents' professional growth, and many put pressure on residents to start this expensive treatment. Some even required it (unofficially) for credentialing.

In spite of this persistent pro-psychoanalysis sentiment, the concept of "better living through chemistry" had been introduced by Harvard psychologist Timothy Leary and his colleagues in the early 1960s. A drug culture congealed in response to Leary's battle cry. Fittingly, chemical conspiracy theories gained steam at this time, and stories about clandestine military-sponsored LSD experiments circulated. Some of those stories turned out to be true.

As we know, Ken Kesey, author of *One Flew Over the Cuckoo's Nest*, had worked as a psych aid at a V.A. hospital and personally participated in government-sponsored LSD studies. The film version of Kesey's best-selling novel went in very different directions, to the point that Kesey disowned it, but the film's success also called attention to the CIA studies.

Those drug studies held sway through the 1990s, with *Jacob's Ladder* (1990) being an excellent example of a full-length feature film on this subject. *Conspiracy Theory* uses these secret drug studies to flesh out an action-adventure film that comes complete with high-speed car chases and shoot-out scenes. The movie would be fun even if it did not contain a kernel of truth.

To those of us who were reared on Hollywood films, it may seem as though the American movie industry has an exclusive on paranoid-tinged themes inspired by government policies. But I must point out that the German film industry (UFA) was arguably more skilled in the use of propaganda films than any industry before or since.

At the very least, the aftershocks of Nazi German propaganda cinema shook the world in a far different way than Hollywood's commercial films. Film, and media in general, were critically important to the Third Reich's mission. In the 1930s, when the Nazis claimed power, television was two decades away from taking over "prime time." Radio lacked the mesmerizing power of the visual image, even though purely aural media ignited the imagination more. "Talkies" had just come into being in the late 1920s and were exploited for all they were worth by the early '30s. Newsreels about current events were screened at movie theaters before the features.

Goebbels, Hitler's minister of propaganda, was said to have watched a film every night. It was Goebbels who commissioned Leni Riefenstahl to produce heroic movies like *Triumph of the Will* (1935). Riefenstahl mesmerized audiences with her panning camera and made them believe that Hitler was more than a mere human — that he was closer to the mythical sky gods of Aryan Volkish lore. She silhouetted Hitler's likeness against clouds soaring in the skies, thereby elevating der Fuhrer to a deity-like status among the Germans. *Triumph of the Will* is one of the best known propaganda films in history.

Another moviemaker produced *The Eternal Jew* (1940) at Goebbels' insistence. Fritz Hippler's documentary-like film derides Jews by comparing them to rats, and reminds the German public of the "Jewish conspiracy" that controls banks, media, subversive political movements (such as socialism), sexual liberation, "degenerate" modern art, "pseudo-science" (like Albert Einstein's theory of relativity), psychoanalysis, and so on. *The Eternal Jew* appeared shortly after the Nazi occupation of Poland began and just before mass extermination of Jews in gas chambers became official policy in 1941.

The Eternal Jew was so odious — yet wielded such influence — that one would think it inspired "sinister cinema psychiatrist" films that hinted at the Jewish origins of psychoanalysis. Somewhat surprisingly, both the first and second Dr. Mabuse movies preceded Hippler's overtly anti–Semitic film. *Svengali*, a book, play, and film about an evil hypnotist who is an "Oriental Israelite," appeared even earlier, before the 20th century began. Yet it is easy to see how this characterization progressed over time and was embellished by Hippler.

The Mabuse films are the paradigm of conspiracy/control themes, with the psychiatrist serving as the kingpin in the plot. In 1922, Fritz Lang began making Mabuse films (which were based on Norbert Jacques' novels). He stopped making Mabuse movies in 1960, although European spin-offs of the Mabuse theme continued until 1970. The first film was a silent entry, while the next version (in 1933) was a talkie. Dr. Mabuse, the psychiatrist-protagonist, is an all-knowing, all-controlling — and all-evil — figure who manipulates the stock market, steals portfolios, makes stocks plummet, drives competitors broke, and, in his spare time, kidnaps a countess, treats her husband, and convinces both the count and his own lover to commit suicide.

Since he is a psychoanalyst (rather than an asylum superintendent like Dr. Caligari), Lang's Dr. Mabuse clearly represents Freud, the founder of psychoanalysis. Freud, in turn, represents the so-called "Jewish science," as the Nazis disparagingly described psychoanalysis. Ergo, many critics contend that the original hooked-nosed Dr. Mabuse recollects Jews in general, and Jewish financial and intellectual influence in particular, which became a focus of Nazi propaganda. So Nazis like Goebbels admired Lang's films (which also included a cinematic rendition of the *Nibelungen* and chronicled the German national myth).

Lang did an about-face and parodied Nazi ideology in his second Mabuse movie, *The Testament of Dr. Mabuse* (1933). That film premiered the same year Hitler became Chancellor of Germany. In that second Mabuse movie, a psychotic person parrots the words of Hitler. By using this ploy, Lang disparages Hitler and Nazi ideology and the Third Reich. Not surprisingly, he fell from grace. The film was banned (but viewed privately by Goebbels, who remained a secret admirer of Lang's cinema artistry). Lang fled Germany for Paris. (The timetable of his escape from Germany has been questioned by scholars who scrutinized details of his departure and found disparities in the stamps on his passport — but that is another issue.)

Lang's tenure in Europe was cut short, but he left Europeans with an enduring horror figure, one who became as familiar to German-speaking audiences as Frankenstein was to American viewers. To this day it is difficult to imagine a more sinister cinema psychiatrist (or a more multi-talented psychiatrist) than Dr. Mabuse. Dr. Mabuse has even greater reach than his closest cinematic competitor, Dr. Lecter, who is an American invention and who reflects America's obsession with serial killers in the 1980s, and America's disenchantment with the "insanity plea" and the far-reaching science of forensic psychiatry.

Dr. Lecter can jump continents and escape prisons, but Dr. Mabuse's conspiracy reaches from beyond the grave. The bad doctor dies in *The Testament of Dr. Mabuse* (1933), but he dies in body only. Dr. Mabuse is so powerful that he occupies the bodies and co-opts the minds of doctors who try to treat him (such as Dr. Baum). What can be more controlling than that?

In *Dr. Mabuse the Gambler* (1922) we met the psychoanalyst while he was presiding over a card game. He holds all the cards, both literally and figuratively. Each card shows a different disguise used by the devilishly clever doctor. He reminds us that he has as many different guises as the proverbial Devil, who can masquerade as anyone. He shuffles through the deck, dealing out fate as if he were a divine force rather than a human physician.

By 1922, psychoanalysis was well-known enough to the public to be featured in a film. Sigmund Freud enjoyed public renown by then, having impressed his colleagues and the world at large with his recommendations about the cause and treatment of "shell shock" during World War I. Although Freud's writings about *The Interpretation of Dreams* (1900) and *The Psychopathology of Everyday Life* (1901) reached broad audiences within a few years after publication, it was his accuracy in predicting the psychological (rather than biological) underpinnings of shell shock that increased his stature and set him apart from his competitors. Such perspicacity suggested that psychoanalysts could control the world. At the very least they could read minds.

While Dr. Mabuse employs many people to carry out his bidding, and manipulates others into acting as his pawns or patsies, many other cinema psychiatrists are shown as mere functionaries of a much more extensive system. They, too, connect to paranoid systems of control, even though they are players rather than kingpins.

36 Hours (1965) is an interesting example of power relationships that develop between psychiatrists, governments and military commanders. This implausible film is based on a short story by Roald Dahl, who also wrote charming children's stories such as *James and the Giant Peach* (1961) and *Charlie and the Chocolate Factory* (1965), both of which were made into films.

In *36 Hours* an otherwise wholesome-looking German psychiatrist drugs an American military officer, renders him unconscious, and then tries to wrangle military secrets from him, using an unusual and innovative experimental technique that he himself devised. James Garner stars as U.S. Army Major Pike. Garner had played the immensely popular *Maverick* character on TV from 1957 to 1962, and hence he is credible in his role as an adventurer sent to Europe to meet a German double agent. Major Pike awakens in what looks like an American hospital — but spectators know that he has not left Europe and that the war has not ended. He hears doctors and nurses speaking American-accented English, but spectators hear that same staff conversing with one another in German when not in the presence of Major Pike.

A psychiatrist (Rod Taylor) tells the American major that he has suffered episodic memory loss, but that his blocked memories should resurface fairly soon with a little treatment. To prove his point, he shows the major letters from home and introduces him to his "wife," who is actually a nurse at the hospital. The nurse is a real nurse, but she was conscripted from a concentration camp. Naturally, the major does not remember marrying Eva Marie Saint, but his amnesia about his wedding is used as further proof of the time has that passed since he fell into a coma.

The psychiatrist figures prominently in both the movie plot and the conspiracy plot. He is a commissioned officer — and a major, at that. Major Gerber is under the control of Nazi officials, but we later learn that it was his own decision to return to his native Germany

Nazi psychiatrist Major Gerber (Rod Taylor) sits as his American patient, out-of-uniform Major Pike (James Garner), inspects photographs, a cigarette dangling from his lips, in *36 Hours* (1965).

when he realized that the Nazi-controlled Fatherland needed his skills. The German-born psychiatrist speaks perfect English because he was reared in America, where he acquired appropriate accents and American idioms.

We also learn of the psychiatrist's plot to convince his patient that time skipped ahead and the war is over, with D-Day having passed. Gerber plans to use this ploy to trick Pike into chatting about American military strategies and revealing where American troops had "landed" so that the Germans can prepare an offensive for the real D-Day.

The psychiatrist has been granted thirty-six hours — a day and a half — to prove his tenuous theories are correct and obtain the vital information. The film title refers to this timeframe. During this time he devotes a surprising amount of time to placating a skeptical SS officer who doubts that the scheme will succeed. As the portly SS officer berates the doctor and belittles his theories, viewers learn the details of the plans and hear what goes on behind the scenes.

We learn that the psychiatrist has a dual agenda. Besides being involved in counter-espionage activities at the hospital, he has been laboring to treat soldiers who develop what we now call PTSD (post-traumatic stress disorder) but which he refers to as "amnesia." The German psychiatrist believes that he can cure his patients if he convinces them to turn back time and believe that the traumatic event has passed. We will hear more about these theories when the psychiatrist explains himself to the American military man he almost duped.

Dr. Gerber works with a nurse, played by Eva Marie Saint, who brings her own illustrious acting resume. Six years before, Eva Marie Saint starred in Hitchcock's *North by Northwest* (1959), but it is her role as a very different kind of nurse in the staunchly Zionist film *Exodus* (1960) that has the most bearing on this film. Audiences remember her as the mysterious female helpmate in *Northwest* and as the non–Jewish Nurse Kitty in *Exodus*, who volunteers at an internment camp on Cyprus, and then helps Holocaust survivors and Jewish orphans in pre-partition Palestine.

Unlike the psychiatrist, who willingly returned to Germany to support the Reich, the nurse is an inmate from the all-female concentration camp Ravensbruck. She accepted this hospital assignment to escape internment at the camp, and has now been coerced into pretending to be the American major's wife. Ravensbruck was the only concentration camp where Jews were interred with non–Jews, and it was also the only all-female camp.

We know that Major Gerber, the psychiatrist, has no intention of "treating" his American captive. Instead, he hopes to use his medical expertise to weasel sensitive information from his presumptive patient. The major is his test subject in an experiment that is nowhere near as vile and sadistic as Dr. Mengele's experiments on human subjects. But the experiment involves non-consenting human subjects nonetheless.

Major Pike is convinced that years have passed. His hair has been dyed grey to make him believe that he has aged. He now needs reading glasses (thanks to belladonna eye drops that interfere with his vision). The letters from home also further the ruse.

Major Gerber uses his psychiatric skills to encourage Major Pike to recollect, telling him that remembering is part of the therapy needed to overcome his amnesia. Gerber almost succeeds in winning Pike's trust. The two majors reminisce about events that occurred early in the war. They even talk about D-Day, which is the goal of Gerber's plan.

Then the observant Major Pike notices one detail that shakes his faith in his physician. He sees that he has a paper cut, which he acquired the day before his capture and which we in the audience witnessed. The cut is still in the same place, unchanged and unhealed. Doubt is cast on the web of deception that has been woven around the major.

When challenged, both the doctor and the nurse own up to the deception. The plot thickens as Pike, Gerber, and Gerber's SS overseer, Schack, wage a mental war to determine if Major Pike revealed or concealed the truth about American military strategies. Much happens, but the important point (for our purposes) is that Major Gerber frees both the American major and the nurse, with the proviso that they carry his research papers with them. He wants to ensure that his studies on amnesia will not be lost and will be available to benefit future patients. Realizing that he will be shot as a traitor by the SS, the psychiatrist poisons himself and dies before the SS officer has a chance to kill him.

The ending is sentimental, and even sickeningly reminiscent of Hitler's own suicide. It also evokes memories of Jewish doctors interred in the Warsaw ghetto who continued to collect data on patients as both they and their charges died of starvation because the Nazis restricted their food supply. To ensure that their research studies survived and lived beyond them, they arranged for their records to be smuggled out of the ghetto even though they themselves could not escape.[1]

Some viewers may wish to believe that the psychiatrists who worked with Nazis had the greater good in mind when they actively engaged in Nazi experiments or when they cooperated with "racial hygiene" policies and selected mental patients to die in the gas chambers for the sake of cleansing the German race of inheritable impurities. But the fact of the matter is that those doctors were Nazis who embraced Nazi ideology. Their mental states were studied by psychiatrist Robert Jay Lifton, MD, who published his results in *The Nazi Doctors: Medical Killing and the Psychology of Genocide* (1986).[2] (Dr. Lifton wrote another book, mentioned earlier, on brainwashing in China.) It would be reassuring if other researchers traced his steps and corroborated Lifton's conclusions. But the fact remains that many doctors participated in Nazi extermination and experimentation, so much so that a separate Doctors' Trial was held at Nuremberg. Twenty-three were tried at the Doctor's Trial. Twenty of the 23 defendants were MDs, with the remaining three being military overseers or administrators. Seven were acquitted; seven were sentenced to death. The rest were sent to prison. Some who escaped the death penalty used clever legal twists to spare their lives, comparing their experiments to Dr. Joseph Goldberger's groundbreaking pellagra studies that were conducted on prisoner-volunteers in the American South.

It is unclear what the filmmakers expected to accomplish when they added this strange angle to *36 Hours*. In some ways this unexpectedly sentimental representation of the Nazi psychiatrist, and his last minute change of heart, represents a "wish fulfillment fantasy" rather than a true-to-fact chronicle on psychiatrists' participation in Nazi atrocities. This final scene does not convince the viewer that such things happened, but it softens the painful edge by turning the psychiatrist into a humanist at the end. This provides the proverbial "happy ending" to a very sad story. Not surprisingly, next to no one remembers this film, not even psychiatrists who are film aficionados themselves.[3]

The psychiatrist in Clint Eastwood's movie, *Changeling* (2008) is involved in a different sort of "conspiracy." Rather than being a prime mover, this psychiatrist follows orders and does the bidding of political powerhouses. When he is told that Christine (Angelina Jolie) is delusional, he admits her to his hospital against her will and prepares to administer ECT (even though ECT was not yet available at the time this movie was set). He also offers her the opportunity for release, provided that she sign a paper denying her allegations against the LAPD and admits that her "misperception" led her to accuse the police chief of substituting another boy for her son. When the psychiatrist is told to release Christine at the very last minute, he complies as readily as he complied with his original order. Given the complexity of the case, it is difficult to believe that the psychiatrist is entirely unaware of the events that led to Christine's incarceration. And it is hard to believe that he is unaware of the debt that he owes to political powers who appoint him as the state hospital administrator.

I reviewed the plot of *Changeling* in the earlier chapter on "Shock Schlock." Suffice it to say here that even more "action" takes place after the story ends, when it comes to politics and public reform. A printed epilogue appears as the film ends. We learn that Christine sued the police department twice and won the second lawsuit. The two perpetrators from the police department were forced to leave their posts (but were later reinstated). The California State Legislature later made it illegal for the police to commit someone to a psychiatric facility without a warrant, as had happened in Christine's case. That proviso stuck.

Clint Eastwood, who directed the film, is open about his political intentions. *Changeling* is not an "anti-psychiatry" movie per se, but it is a film that openly comments on crimes against children, capital punishment, police corruption, and the co-optation of women's

In *Where Is My Child?* (1937), Celia Adler, doyenne of Yiddish cinema, plays an impoverished widowed immigrant woman who looks longingly at her son's photograph before she is involuntarily institutionalized for protesting his adoption by a wealthy, childless family.

recently won rights, as well as contemporary female disempowerment. It also comments on psychiatry's collusion with police corruption — but it cites an actual event instead of generalizing or sermonizing.

Where Is My Child? (1937) is a very different movie, yet it shares certain similarities to *Changeling*. *Where Is My Child?* is an American-made Yiddish film with subtitles. It was shot during the short-lived "Golden Age of Yiddish Film" (1936–1939). Celia Adler, doyenne of the Yiddish stage, stars as the movie's heroine. *Where Is My Child?* is unique among the Yiddish films of its era, as it confronts contemporary social problems directly, without retreating to faraway fantasy. Its sentimentalism, however, is typical of Yiddish film.

The movie's heroine arrives in New York in 1911 at the height of mass Jewish immigration from Europe to America. She is newly widowed, having lost her husband in transit. She is also friendless and impoverished — and the mother of a newborn baby boy. Fearing that she cannot care for a child, she brings the infant to an orphanage. There she consults with the medical director, who promises to rear the boy himself. She agrees to leave the baby with the doctor, hoping to bring him home with her some day. She quickly regrets her decision, however, and tries to retrieve the boy, but learns that she was deceived by Dr. Reisner, who had a wealthy childless couple waiting in the wings. The baby boy was immediately adopted by the gloating couple.

Obsessed with the hope of reuniting with her son, she pines for him. A "letter carrier" (as a "postman" is known in Yiddish) alerts her to her son's whereabouts. The "letter carrier" performs the same function as a letter that reveals the plot, but he adds a human touch.

The boy grows up amidst affluence. He becomes a doctor but somehow learns that he was adopted. The finale does not occur until he graduates from medical school, finishes his psychiatry training, and starts his first full-fledged position as a psychiatrist.

His biological mother, in the meantime, has led a very different life. She was literally carried off by the "men in the white coats" after she returned to the orphanage and challenged the director, Dr. Reisner. She was then involuntarily committed to a sanitarium, where she has spent the last 25 years.

In one of the film's more memorable scenes, Dr. Reisner of the adoption agency phones his psychiatrist colleague at the sanitarium to arrange for Celia Adler's admission to an asylum. When his assistant questions if the psychiatrist will comply with his request, Dr. Reisner says of the psychiatrist, "He'd sell his own mother for money." Then there is some repartee about the doctor not being a "real doctor" but, rather, a doctor who purchased his degree at a diploma mill. There is no doubt that the psychiatrist is as unscrupulous as the orphanage's medical director.

The proverbial men in white coats arrive and cart the crying Celia away from Dr. Reisner's office. They deliver her to the mental hospital, where she is declared delusional (like Christine in *Changeling*). Whereas Angelina Jolie's Christine Collins is freed from her confinement thanks to the intervention of a Protestant minister, Celia Adler's waiflike immigrant woman languishes in her locked quarters for another quarter of a century. She sits in her room, cradling a bundled up blanket in her arms, singing to it as if it were a baby.

When the young psychiatrist arrives at his new position he is introduced to this grey-haired woman who harbors a long-lasting delusion about her stolen baby. But he has already heard stories about his unusual adoption through the letter carrier. The two of them count the years, compare his age to hers, and put two and two together. Almost immediately they realize that he is her long lost son, and that she is his mother. Tears of joy (and sorrow) are shed in true Yiddish film tradition.

Although the film seems cynical, to say the least, and although it is dismissive of psychiatric doctors (as well as orphanage directors) and accuses them of buying degrees at diploma mills, it capitalizes on a fact that was well-known to medical reformers of the era. Recall that the action in *Where Is My Child?* Starts in 1911, even though it was made in 1937. A year earlier, in 1910, Dr. Abraham Flexner published his still-famous "Flexner Report."[4] Although Flexner was a research scholar, his report was primarily directed at the public. Flexner found that a high percentage of medical schools sold diplomas to anyone who could afford their fees. Doctors of that era were not automatically respected because it was well-known that those who could pay the price could obtain a license that would enable them to earn a living. In the wake of the Flexner Report, a quarter of all existing medical schools were closed, and a new era of medical education began.

Those who are not familiar with this important historical detail might be inclined to see this film as an indictment of doctors (as well as a condemnation of the exploitation of immigrants and of immigrant women in particular). However, like many — but not all — of the "sinister psychiatry" films discussed in earlier chapters, this unkind characterization has its roots in reality. One wonders if the Wineville case portrayed in *Changeling*, and the ordeals endured by the real-life Christine Collins throughout the 1930s, somehow influenced *Child*'s filmmakers as well, as they labored in the 1930s. Unfortunately, that data is not available now.

On the surface, *Where Is My Child?* seems to be a film about the proverbial Jewish mother whose love stops at nothing. At least that his how the *Yiddish Film World* website from Massachusetts describes it. Without a doubt it is a movie about the rupture and restoration of family ties, a subject that was near and dear to the heart of Yiddish film fans. It is also a film that is set in the past, and that is intended to reassure anxious audiences that times were once worse that they were in 1937. It reminded viewers that they survived and thrived in spite of the hardships endured during those challenging days of early immigration. Indeed, there was great need to reassure audiences in 1937, when this film was made. Anti-Semitism peaked in America during the "Roosevelt Depression" (1937–8). Father Coughlin preached his hateful diatribe on the radio. Some German-Americans voiced support for Nazis oversees. The Lindbergh kidnapping case, and the anti–Semitism it inspired, added to the furor.

Most importantly of all, Hitler was well-established as Chancellor of Germany. The Nazis were in power and had passed increasingly oppressive Nuremberg Laws that limited Jewish participation in commerce, professions, arts, and education. The official start of the Holocaust was still one year away, but some worried Jews from Central Europe trickled into America, having read the handwriting on the wall. Psychoanalysts were among the first to emigrate, largely because they were banned from practicing their profession as early as 1933. Consequently, awareness of psychiatry increased.

For sure there are many ways to "read" this film, and there are several subtexts, each of which deserves attention. For many viewers (and for many Yiddish film aficionados), *Where Is My Child?* is a movie about the stereotyped Jewish adage of "My Son, the Doctor," which was rumored to be "every Jewish mother's dream." But not even Borscht Belt comedians joked about "My Son, the Psychiatrist," even though a disproportionate number of

American Jewish medical students chose to specialize in psychiatry in the second half of the 20th century. This film may represent an unspoken fantasy described by some psychiatrists who hope that their studying psychiatry would somehow free their own mothers from the confines of mental illness.

Doctors are singled out as a privileged class that is in a position to exploit poor immigrants, but spectators from the 1930s had reason to distrust many different professionals and business people. Recall that the banks had confiscated homes and farms only a few years before, and that the Stock Market Crash of 1929, and years of record-high unemployment, left many people standing in long bread lines.

The payoffs to professionals in *Where Is My Child?* reflect generic populist concerns that permeated the Depression era (and that were rekindled during the Roosevelt Depression of 1937–1938). This film carries a left-leaning message. It reminds 30s-era Yiddish speakers that danger lurks on all sides, and that the vulnerable can be exploited by rich and powerful members of one's own group (as was proven all too well by the tragic Triangle Shirtwaist Fire early in the century). It reminds viewers that obvious anti–Semitism is not the only danger, but that profiteering professionals can be equally evil. Had this movie appeared in 1957 rather than 1937, Senator Joe McCarthy might have seen a Communist message hiding inside this populist plot.

The psychiatrist and the orphanage doctor in *Child* are independent operators in a conspiracy that persists because other professionals pitch in and lend their skills (in the same way that mobsters use their mob ties for specialized services, such as fencing and money laundering). But there are many variants of "conspiracy themes" in sinister psychiatrist cinema. *Behind Locked Doors* (1948) shows a psychiatrist who does not just act like a criminal but is in cahoots with obvious criminals. The plot of *Behind Locked Doors* is fairly thin, although its camerawork is among the finest in *film noir*. Luckily, a romance fleshes out the film and adds an unexpected twist to the hour-long feature.

The plot focuses on a corrupt judge who is in cahoots with a psychiatrist who owns a sanitarium. The judge intends to go underground until the heat is off. So he hides out in the sanitarium, where the doors are locked and where identities are kept confidential. The possibility that psychiatric hospitals can be used as criminal hideaways makes perfect sense. In fact, some of us who have practiced in psychiatric hospitals know that an occasional gambler feigns psychosis or suicidal ideation, in order to gain admittance to locked wards and escape creditors (who may have ties to organized crime).

In *Behind Locked Doors* a suspicious female reporter drives the plot forward. She has a hunch about the missing judge and hires a detective to track him down. But the only way to gain admittance to the sanitarium is to enter as a patient. To pursue his quarry, the detective pretends to be psychotic — and then has a horrific time trying to escape. To make matters more interesting, and to add to the sense of subterfuge, we see classic *film noir* shots of Venetian blinds casting striated shadows on long corridors. Sinister-looking stairways are shrouded in darkness that is pierced by the tiniest slivers of light. The "light" at the end of the proverbial tunnel comes when the female reporter and the male detective find love brewing between them, and also find their prey hiding in the psychiatric asylum.

Besides offering an example of a psychiatrist who is in cahoots with the criminal element, and who subverts his treatment facility for nefarious purposes, *Behind Locked Doors* (1948) is an example of the "Asylum B" subgenre. That genre started with *Bedlam* (1946) two years earlier. As we will see in the next chapter, "Madhouse Movies," the asylum genre is a metaphor for the madness of the outside world. It is a classic *film noir* topic, given that *film noir* viewed the world as a whole as evil, and saw evil lurking in the most innocent of shadows.

Significantly, no attention is paid to the inner workings of the patients themselves. They are seen as mere silhouettes rather than as individual humans. The patients are little more than stage props that populate the halls of the foreboding mansion that houses the asylum. Later films such as *Twinkle, Twinkle, "Killer" Kane* (1980), which is also known as *The Ninth Configuration*, portray patients very differently. Even higher quality "asylum thrillers" such as *Spellbound* (1945) make a point of detailing the nuances of patients' (and psychiatrists') personalities, setting each one apart from other characters.

Behind Locked Doors can be seen as a precursor to Samuel B. Fuller's better-known *Shock Corridor* (1963). In *Shock Corridor* a reporter again feigns insanity to learn about the inner workings of a psych ward. Rather than finding romance, as happened to the reporter and the investigator in *Behind Locked Doors*, *Shock Corridor*'s reporter ends up incurably catatonic himself. The film is quite unrealistic, given what we know about the rare condition of catatonia. But it is still entertaining. It is not so much an indictment of the horrors of mental hospitals as much as it is a warning about the perils of pursuing secret knowledge that should stay off-limits.

If *Behind Locked Doors* is gritty and grim *film noir*, then *I, the Jury* (the 1982 remake) is exactly the opposite. With its flashy colors, its over-the-top décor, and its opulent mental hospital sets that look like an offshoot of Las Vegas' Cesar's Palace, the settings of *I, the Jury* bears little resemblance to anything in real life. Its lavishness dwarfs the stately Green Manor of *Spellbound*.

Ironically, the story of a real-life midtown Manhattan psychiatrist who promoted the use of "sex surrogates" (and billed for such services as bone fide psychiatric treatments) came to light by the mid–1980s. His office was raided and he was arrested for promoting prostitution through his ads in the *Village Voice*. But the story behind the psychiatrist in the *I, the Jury* remake glosses over the use of sex surrogates (even though its cameras add panning shots of salacious orgy scenes). In *I, the Jury* the more offensive aspects of the psychiatrist's conduct revolves around her involvement with the CIA, her willingness to be an accessory to murder, and her attempt to murder Mike Hammer herself.

I, the Jury is so over the top that it is hard to believe that it found a credulous audience. But it was (re)made in the 1980s, in an age of excess, when cocaine was king, when money flowed freely, and when sexual license had not yet been curtailed by the arrival of AIDS. In fact, the film appeared at a time when over-the-top sex scandals about psychiatrists were in full bloom. Two years earlier, Brian De Palma's *Dressed to Kill* (1980) featured a cross-dressing psychiatrist who kills his female patient in the elevator of his elegant Upper East Side Manhattan skyscraper.

De Palma's psychiatrist is an independent agent, a collaborator with his own twisted desires, and nothing but. *I, the Jury*'s psychiatrist is a CIA operative. (In the original film, and in the original Mike Hammer hard-boiled novel, the psychiatrist is in cahoots with organized crime and a heroin distribution ring.)

In all versions of *I, the Jury* the psychiatrist makes the mistake of victimizing Mike Hammer's war buddy, a man named Jack Williams, who lost an arm while saving Mike

Poster for William Peter Blatty's *Twinkle, Twinkle, "Killer" Kane* (1980), also known as *The Ninth Configuration*. Stacy Keach, Scott Wilson, and Jason Miller star in this film about a Vietnam vet (Keach) who represses memories of the day he killed 14 "Cong" and came to be known as "Killer Kane."

Hammer's life when the two were in the service together. Williams was a one-time cop who presumably sought treatment at a Park Avenue sex clinic run by Dr. Bennett (Barbara Carerra).

Dr. Bennett uses her clinic as a cover-up for her Cuban connections and the CIA's involvement in Cuba's underground activities, in the same way that the sanitarium in *Behind Locked Doors* is a smokescreen for criminal activities. Like the mansion in *Behind Locked Doors*, Dr. Bennett's "clinic" offers real psychiatric treatment and is not simply a front. In her case, the sex surrogate services are presented as standard medical procedures (which they once were). But Dr. Bennett also records activities for the CIA, and thus reminds us of rumors about the way the CIA collected intimate information about influential political figures (such as the Rev. Dr. Martin Luther King, Jr.), and that it ran experiments on men at brothels.

Does Dr. Bennett's portrayal of psychiatrists disrespect psychiatrists? Does it foreshadow the fall of a much-publicized Manhattan psychiatric sex surrogate service in the mid–1980s? Does the sex clinic in the *I, the Jury* remake recollect Masters and Johnsons' serious attempt to use sex surrogates to treat sexual dysfunction — and the willingness of the medical establishment to accept this technique, at least temporarily? Or is this plot-driving device simply a sensationalistic ploy to update the original Mickey Spillane story that was set in 1944 and published in novel form in 1947? The answer to all questions is probably "yes." For our purposes here, however, this film stands as an excellent example of the "in cahoots" conspiracy films about psychiatrists.

In *The Ninth Configuration* (1980), the disturbed Colonel Vincent Kane (Stacy Keach) heads a military psychiatric hospital until he learns it is his brother (not he) who is the real psychiatrist.

On a different note, sometimes cinema psychiatrists participate in an elaborately staged conspiracy that is conducted for the good of the patient. The 1962 homage to *The Cabinet of Dr. Caligari* (which resembles its namesake not at all) falls into this category, as does *Twinkle, Twinkle, "Killer" Kane* (aka *The Ninth Configuration*, 1980) and *Shutter Island* (2010). In the latter two instances, psychiatrists stage elaborate hoaxes in hopes of curing their patient of PTSD or speeding the recovery of repressed memories.

The Ninth Configuration is far less polished than Martin Scorsese's *Shutter Island*, but the principle is the same. In *The Ninth Configuration* everyone is involved, from the hospital patients, the testy drill sergeant, and Killer Kane's brother, who is the true psychiatrist. All pretend that Kane is the psychiatrist in charge of the hospital rather than a patient at the hospital, and all because Kane (Stacy Keach) cannot come to grips with his monstrous deeds in Vietnam.

It was rumored that Kane killed 14 VietCong with his bare hands, thus earning himself the epithet "Killer Kane." Actor Keach's real face shows scars from multiple surgeries for correcting a cleft palate, making him look like someone who may indeed have engaged in hand-to-hand combat. In contrast, Kane's brother is a practicing psychiatrist who hopes to restore Kane's repressed memories. He plans to bring about a cathartic cure by pushing those repressed memories into consciousness.

As part of the hoax, Kane is led to believe that he is the head psychiatrist at the soldiers' mental hospital. We do not learn that the brother is the real psychiatrist until the film is almost over, although we wonder early on why Kane's muscular build is bursting out of his uniform, even though he has a desk job. (When we see Stacy Keach acting the role of Mike Hammer a few years later on TV, it is easy to connect the tough guy Hammer character to Killer Kane.) In spite of these good intentions, the plan fails. Kane takes his own life in the end, once he realizes who he is and realizes that he cannot live with the memories of his wartime acts.

Shutter Island has a similar goal: to help Leonardo DiCaprio's character, Teddy Daniels, recall the events surrounding the drowning deaths of his two children and the subsequent murder of his wife. In this case the psychiatrist pretends to be the partner of the hard-drinking U.S. Marshall Daniels. The two men travel to a secluded island that houses a hospital for the criminally insane, with Daniels believing that he and his partner are on a mission to find a missing patient — who also happens to be a murderess. Throughout their travails, Daniels experiences flashbacks of his wife, his children, and his World War II experiences, when he was among the soldiers who liberated the death camps in post-war Poland.

Only at the film's end do we learn that the man who accompanies Marshall Daniels is his doctor and not the government agent he claims to be. In the interim, we are led to believe that a vast conspiracy of crimes and unethical experimentation occur on the island, and that Daniels, his partner, and the patients are endangered. At the conclusion we are still uncertain if these events occurred within the deluded mind of DiCaprio's Marshall Daniels or if every detail was indeed concocted by the hospital staff as part of their last ditch effort to restore Daniels' memory and help him confront his repressed crime. But it really doesn't matter because the film is so gripping and the plot so perfectly constructed.

To sum up, there is no shortage of conspiracy-themed movies about sinister psychiatrists. It stands to reason that paranoid undertones ring true in films about false memories and sick minds. It makes sense that the same spectators who show interest in movies about mad or bad mind doctors will also be drawn to stories based on paranoid plot lines. No wonder there is an enduring market for films with this twist.

12

Madhouse Movies, Involuntary Incarceration (and Managed Care)

This is a book about "sinister cinema psychiatrists," but this chapter concerns itself with "madhouse movies." Clearly, these two topics sometimes intersect, but often they don't.

This chapter focuses on films that show the psychiatrist (or the pseudo-psychiatrist) as the "star of the show" and not simply as a stage prop in an institution that is more evil than any single individual could ever aspire to be. An entire book could — and should — be written about "madhouse movies" or "asylum thrillers," as they are known in the trade. Some academic historians of psychiatry, such as Porter, Scull, Shorter and others,[1] have explored the topic of madhouses from sociological and historical points of view. Those books are listed in the bibliography. But I do not know of a book that is solely devoted to "madhouse movies."

At first glance one is inclined to ask if a madhouse can be a madhouse without a psychiatrist running the show. Theoretically, an asylum needs a psychiatrist in the same way a ship needs a captain. At least that's the way things used to work before budget cuts and health care "reforms" shrunk professional staff and lightened licensure requirements for institutional heads.

I will not delve into the ever-changing details of psychiatric administrative policies, or the politics or economics behind them. That is too daunting a task, and not nearly so interesting as cinema and psychiatry. But I can say with certainty that a madhouse that lacks a psychiatrist, where the inmates take over the asylum and push the psychiatrist aside, or prove that the doctor is an impostor or even more insane than they are, can make for a very interesting movie. Those topsy-turvy films may be more engaging than the standard-brand docudramas about sanitariums, rest homes, retreats or insane asylums. Similarly, movies such as *Mutiny on the Bounty* (1935, 1962) prove that ships without captains can generate more excitement than ships *with* captains at the helm.

Alternatively, there are many important movies where non-psychiatrists run the show, either because other staff have overpowered the psychiatrist or operate beneath the radar of the psychiatrist. Maybe they duped the doctor, who is either dumb or drunk or suffers from some other serious flaw that interferes with his or her ability to function. Films such as *One Flew Over the Cuckoo's Nest* and *Sucker Punch* show what can happen when weak-willed, drugged-out or indifferent doctors allow hateful nurses or unruly orderlies to take charge.

Frustrated with "the system" that squelches their personal power, disgruntled support staff may displace their anger onto more disempowered patients. Then they override the pre-set hierarchy and undermine the chain of command that ordinarily imposes order and demands accountability for one's actions.

Film history shows how well these alternative approaches to asylums work for movies, for the "inmates have taken over the asylum" storyline is a recurring movie motif. In fact, almost anything that turns the existing order upside down can become a compelling drama or a funny farce. There is a dramatic advantage to films that show "parallel processes" occurring among staff and patients. When the usual hierarchy is flipped or scrambled, and when chaos overtakes order, we find parallels to the state of madness itself. Picturing those two dual processes simultaneously creates a double impact. When well-executed, those films are especially hard-hitting.

This well-worked psychiatric theme did not begin with film. If anyone deserves credit for the idea, it is Edgar Allan Poe with his story "The System of Doctor Tarr and Professor Feather [Fether]." Poe wrote it in 1845, starting this trend several years before the Civil War shook the United States and called the legitimacy of the "existing order" into question. Poe opens his story by saying, "During the autumn of 18 —, while on a tour through the extreme southern provinces of France, my route led me within a few miles of a certain Maison de Sante or private mad-house, about which I had heard much in Paris from my medical friends."

Considering that Poe created so many "genres," including detective stories, horror stories, and murder mysteries, it is not surprising that he also coined this time-honored theme of the "lunatics taking over the asylum." Given that the story is set in France, it is not surprising that a French production company turned Poe's short story into a silent short film. Éclair's *Le Système du Docteur Goudron et du Professeur Plume* (1913) is fairly true to Poe's original, even though the movie was adapted from the much more gruesome version presented by the Parisian Grand Guignol. The French film translates the names of Poe's main characters into French, which makes for a rather awkward read for English-speakers. The short was later renamed "*The Lunatics.*" The new title is much easier to remember, but it also obscures the literary origins of the story and makes it easy to overlook Poe's contribution to the plot.

Interestingly, the director of Éclair's silent short was none other than Maurice Tourneur, the father of Jacques Tourneur. Jacques Tourneur's *Cat People* still stands as a classic in horror film history, and also features an excellent example of a deceptive and seductive psychiatrist. The elder Tourneur had an impressive film resume of his own, and his oeuvre is in no way obscured by the giant shadow cast by his son. The older Tourneur also directed *Trilby* in 1915, which is a film about the evil hypnotist Svengali, who shares some superficial similarities to Freud. But Maurice Tourneur is far better remembered for *The Last of the Mohicans* (1920) than for the psychiatric themes that punctuated his early cinema career.

Even before Éclair's French production company interpreted the Poe story, Edison's *Lunatics in Power* (1909) offers a comedic interpretation of this theme. This film was directed by J. Searle Dawley, whose one-reel *Frankenstein* (1910) has gained greater recognition than *Lunatics*, perhaps because devout Frankenstein fans track every movie ever made about their favorite monster. Dawley began his entertainment career in vaudeville, where he wrote and acted. He later claimed credit for becoming the first film director at a time when cameramen were still in charge of moviemaking.

Lunatics in Power appeared one year after the publication of Clifford Beers' autobiographical book *A Mind That Found Itself* (1908). Beers' book was influential to mental hospital reform, which became known as the "mental hygiene movement." Beers probably suffered from manic-depression (bipolar disorder). After his three year stay in an asylum, he used his endless energy to campaign against abuses and indignities inflicted on mental patients. Jimmy Cagney movies from the 1930s reified Beers' pleas in favor of social reform (and against "reform schools"). It is equally possible that contemporary comedies like *Lunatics in Power*, which poked fun at asylum directors, fortified accusations made by Beers the year before and made the public wonder if foxes were indeed guarding the henhouse.

In spite of the important precedents cited above, Robert Weine's *The Cabinet of Dr. Caligari* is typically cited as the starting point of the "inmates take over the asylum" theme. *The Cabinet of Dr. Caligari* rightfully deserves a great deal of credit for many things, being the brilliant film that it is and being such a beautiful example of German Expressionism, not to mention being an important after-the-fact commentary on psychiatric treatments during the first World War. Still, the French film that was modeled after Poe's American short story in 1913 earns the accolade of being Number One. Even Edison deserves some kudos here as well, because of his one-reel comedy directed by Dawley, which eliminated horrific elements from the Poe story to make it funny.

But there is little value in arguing about which was the first "madhouse movie," or which was the first cinematic adaptation of the "inmates take over the asylum" motif, when there has been such plethora of madhouse movies over the century, with one more sinister or scarier or sillier than the next. This theme has so much potential. It can even be twisted into pseudo-psychiatrist plots, such as the ones found in *The Ninth Configuration* or *Shutter Island*.

The same can be said for the 1962 film *The Cabinet of Caligari*, which is not in any way true to the original *Caligari* (1919) but was based on a screenplay by Robert Bloch. Bloch also authored the novel, *Psycho* in 1959, a year before Hitchcock adapted it to the screen. The 1962 film's use of the title *Caligari* refers solely to the framing device from in the original 1919 film rather than to its content. As the movie ends we see that the "sinister psychiatrist" was an illusion, and that most of the characters had been morphed into malevolent forms, as in *The Wizard of Oz* (1939).

Let's take a moment to review the history of madhouse movies, which have been a staple of cinema almost since the start of filmmaking. Houses in general are cinematic staples, for several reasons. Houses provide scene and setting. They can be background or center stage. Each room is a unique place where the plot pushes forward and where the characters reveal their unique personalities and predilections.[2]

Because houses come in all shapes, sizes, and styles, they are interesting for that reason alone. Houses are also familiar to everyone. Everyone knows what a house is. Filmmakers need familiar objects — called "fetishes" by film scholars — to make their movies identifiable as a member of its genre and therefore marketable to the masses. In "madhouse movies" it is the madhouse itself that is the star of the show. The madhouse, be it the physical dwelling place or the institutional control that it represents, is held responsible for whatever happens within.

In this book I emphasize the status of the "sinister psychiatrist," whose power and control may be diminished if the institution itself overpowers said psychiatrist and chooses to violate the rights of patients sequestered inside. The institution may decide to allow unethical experiments or offer unbridled opportunities for diabolical drugging, seduction or even rape, as well as confinement via straitjackets, cells, or even morgue-like lock boxes.

In keeping with my emphasis on the treater rather than on the place of treatment, I must give short shrift to the broader genre of madhouse movies, and will gloss over details that deserve more thorough discussion in a book devoted exclusively to this topic. For now, let's just say that madhouses have a special significance psychologically and signify much more than psychiatric treatment gone awry. Houses can become unfamiliar–or "unheimlich," to use Freud's German word–when they become "un-house-like" and inhospitable. To fully understanding madhouses' function in movies, we would do well to review Freud's essay 1919 on "The Uncanny" ("Der Unheimlich," literally "the un-homey"). One need not agree with other aspects of Freudian psychology to appreciate the value of this essay, which is still assigned in most film studies classes and in many literature courses to this day.

Like all of Freud's essays, this piece was written in German and later translated into English. The German title "Unheimlich" deserves scrutiny — but it does not deserve mistranslation or approximation, because the German word conveys so much meaning. "Unheimlich" is difficult to render into English. Entire academic articles are devoted to this word alone, as Prawer's intriguing book about *Caligari's Children* (1980) demonstrates. *Caligari's Children* focuses on horror films and examines the concept of "unheimlich" with respect to "haunted houses." But his approach can be extrapolated to several other areas. The literal translation of "unheimlich" is equally applicable to our study of madhouses in movies.

Freud's essay alludes to the creepy-crawly psychological sensation that we describe with the English term "uncanny." Even our English word is difficult to define. But Freud's original word, "unheimlich," literally means "un-home-like." Without the "un" prefix, "heimlich" means "home." "Mad houses" are *heimlich* (homelike) and *unheimlich* (un-homey) at the same time, and so they serve a special function in film, and in horror cinema, in particular.

Let me explain further. Freud struggled to identify the elements that contribute to the sensation of strangeness or eeriness or uncanniness that German-speakers know as *unheimlich*. He went on and on before concluding that a scene or a setting or a sensation that is as familiar as a home will cause a distinctively disturbing sensation when something is slightly out of kilter — but is not out of kilter enough to render the setting unrecognizable or unfamiliar.

Freud mentioned marionettes and automatons–or dreams and madness — as examples of "the uncanny" or the "unheimlich." For marionettes and automatons are close enough to real human forms to resemble humans and to remind us of humans. But they are different enough to induce a sense of unease and discomfort and a feeling that something is awry. The Salzburg Marionettes premiered in Austria in 1913, shortly before Freud wrote his essay, and so these amazing works of art may have inspired some elements in his essay.

Similarly, madness is close enough to ordinary human behavior to resemble daily activity, but the actions of a "madman" are also different enough from the activity of the average person to make "madness" an example of the "uncanny." We can apply this same principle of familiarity/unfamiliarity to "homes" and "mad homes." "Madhouses" automatically become "unheimlich" because they are similar to ordinary homes that house ordinary human beings. Yet madhouses have been adapted to house madmen and mad people and mad doctors. Madhouses do not house friends or relatives or even wayfarers. Madhouses are homes to people who are already out-of-kilter and who are themselves "unheimlich."

Now that we understand why madhouse movies appeal on such a deep level, we can turn to another old adage and see what we can learn from an often repeated expression about "the fox guarding the henhouse." In other words, the henhouse (or madhouse) is nowhere near as interesting as the predatory fox (or sinister psychiatrist) who is in charge of the vulnerable hens (or patients). In these films and stories that follow this formula, the psychiatrist is typically sicker than the patients, and the madhouse (henhouse) simply provides a setting that dramatizes the depth of the psychiatrist's own disturbance.

Bedlam (1946), a horror film about a horrific mental hospital, stars Boris Karloff. Boris Karloff's name is synonymous with horror. The movie acquires more horror cache because of its very name, as the word "bedlam" has entered our everyday vocabularies, referring to a state of disarray or loss of control. The real "Bedlam" (short for "Bethlehem") was the first mental hospital in England. "St. Mary's of Bethlehem" still exists in Beckenham, Kent.

In *The Snake Pit* (1948), patient Virginia Cunningham (Olivia de Havilland) sits between whitecapped Nurse Davis (Helen Craig) and psychiatrist Dr. Kik (Leo Genn), with patients at their sides.

In 2011 the BBC launched a popular television series entitled *Bedlam*, but the TV show bears no relationship to the American horror *noir* mentioned above. The BBC program is set in modern day U.K., where the old asylum has been converted into a stylish new housing complex, Bedlam Heights. In spite of its stunning décor and attractive tenants, Bedlam Heights is haunted by ghosts of the original inmates, who remind new residents of old horrors.

Another mental hospital movie that appeared two years after *Bedlam* (the film) changed history because of the reforms and legislation it inspired. In 1948, Anatole Litvak made *The Snake Pit* (1948). *The Snake Pit* stars Olivia de Havilland as an unfortunate young woman who finds herself in an overcrowded, understaffed mental hospital that she calls "Juniper State Hospital" (instead of Rockland State Hospital). She cannot recall how she arrived, but she *can* recall the shock therapy, the failed attempts at hypnotherapy, the hallucinations and the relapses.

She can also recall her pipe-smoking psychiatrist, Dr. Kik (Leo Genn), who "helps" her return to her "normal" role in life as a wife. Dr. Kik is portrayed positively, but the hospital itself is horrendous. Although the film has a happy ending, feminist critics later deconstructed the perceived "cure" in *The Snake Pit* and objected to the value-laden definition of therapeutic "success." In the film, de Havilland's character abandons her dreams of being a writer and returns to her role as a wife. In post-feminist society, which had already read and reread Ibsen's *A Doll's House* (1879), the idea of locking a woman into the institution of marriage and forcing her to forfeit her personal and professional goals is nearly as bad as locking her into a mental institution.

The film is based on a true story that was published in novelized form in 1947. Much of the movie's plot is revealed via flashbacks, as was commonplace among psychoanalytically-inspired films of the late forties. The recollections are spurred on by a process known as "narco-synthesis," which used sleep-inducing drugs and sodium amytal ("truth serum") to free up associations and penetrate repressed secrets. Narco-synthesis was popular in late 1940s cinema but remains little more than a distant memory (and a bad one at that) in the minds of contemporary psychiatrists. It also includes nefarious variants, as seen in *Conspiracy Theory* and other brainwashing films.

The Snake Pit won the Academy Award for Best Sound Recording, and received nominations for Best Actress in a Leading Role (Olivia de Havilland), Best Director, Best Music Scoring of a Dramatic or Comedy Picture, Best Picture and Best Screenplay. The film also won the International Prize at the Venice Film Festival in 1949, and was described as "a daring inquiry in a clinical case dramatically performed." Though he did not win the Oscar, perhaps director Anatole Litvak's personal experiences with two different totalitarian governments sensitized him to the totalitarianism inherent in mental asylums. For Litvak was a Russian-born Jew who left Communist-controlled Russia for Germany in the 1920s after Russian theaters were nationalized. He fled Germany in the 1930s, just before the Nazis took power.

The Snake Pit was a high-profile film, even before its aftershocks were felt. The conditions depicted in *The Snake Pit* may have been shocking, but the fact that such an acclaimed movie attracted the attention of both cinemaphiles and social reformers is not. Another work added to the legal and medical aftershocks set off by *The Snake Pit*. Albert Deutsch's book *The Shame of the States* (1948) was published by Harcourt Brace while *The*

Snake Pit was still in production. Deutsch's work deserved attention on its own. While the author of the novel that became *The Snake Pit* did not directly demonize the doctors, Deutsch's depiction of state mental hospitals was scathing. Deutsch fortified his journalistic style with statistics and photographs. His strong words and vivid descriptions jarred readers who were still recoiling from the horrors of the Holocaust. But it was not a personal memoir and so did not resonate with the public in the same way as the first-hand account found in *The Snake Pit*.

Albert Deutsch was the medicine and social welfare columnist of the *New York Star* and was well-equipped to document accurate data. He had already written a related book on *The Mentally Ill in America—Their Care and Treatment from Colonial Times* (Doubleday, 1937). His media connections insured that his book received attention from other magazines and journals, as well as reviews in the scholarly press. *Time* magazine's coverage of the book added to the uproar.[3] Unlike anti-psychiatry activists of later eras, Deutsch did not blame psychiatrists for the inefficiencies of the system. Rather, he argued that state hospitals did not hire sufficient numbers of psychiatrists or trained nurses or other professional staff.

Deutsch claimed that patients were essentially warehoused in state hospitals like "Juniper Hill." His words were as dramatic as Litvak's movie. Deutsch wrote in first person, stating that "I was reminded of the pictures of the Nazi concentration camps at [Bergen] Belsen and Buchenwald.... I entered buildings swarming with naked humans herded like cattle and treated with less concern.... I saw hundreds of patients living under leaking roofs, surrounded by moldy, decaying walls, and sprawling on rotting floor for want of seats or benches."[4,5]

Deutsch extended his argument well beyond his home state of New York, where "Juniper Hill" (Rockland State) was located. He noted that not a single state spent the $5 a day per patient on treatment, food and housing that was recommended by the American Psychiatric Association as a bare minimum. The national average was $1.25 a day. Deutsch blamed the low recovery rates from mental illness on insufficient funding, which in turn led to inadequate training of staff and delays in hiring trained psychiatrists. For those who did not want to read the entire book, *Time* magazine summarized Deutsch's impressions. These summaries are readily available online.

Deutsch made a compelling case, but it was *The Snake Pit*'s cinematic depiction of conditions in mental hospitals that directly prompted reforms. In response to *The Snake Pit*, 26 states passed legislation requiring procedural shifts at the state hospitals for the mentally ill. Once again, a picture was worth a thousand words, and a moving picture can be worth even more. Anatole Litvak was proud of his achievement, which extended beyond cinematic success.

Again, history tells us that films are indeed compelling. Movies can change attitudes toward science and sociology far more quickly and intensely than pure text. Some decades later, Milos Forman's film *One Flew Over the Cuckoo's Nest* (1975) altered attitudes toward ECT (shock therapy), probably unintentionally. In response to the movie, the state of California outlawed ECT altogether. Even well-educated medical students changed their minds about electroconvulsive treatment after seeing this film. The book on which the movie was based, which was written by Ken Kesey in 1962, did not incite such intense reactions in readers, even though the book became a best-seller that soon inspired a successful Broadway play.

Over the next few years the reforms inspired by *The Snake Pit* met an even more formidable foe, totally unexpectedly. In 1954 the antipsychotic agent Thorazine (chlorpromazine) became available in the United State and soon produced near-miraculous changes in mental patients who had been "warehoused" in asylums for years. Thorazine stopped the voices of persons suffering from schizophrenia. It decreased their aggression and made it possible for many formerly psychotic people to leave their long-term hospitals and return home.

The zombie-like "Thorazine shuffle" is evident early in treatment, so that the informed onlooker is well aware that the person is on strong anti-psychotic medication. When it was learned that more serious side effects can surface years later, the use of Thorazine (and related meds) was discouraged, and the search for safer medications started. Still, compared to the horrific conditions in state hospitals that were detailed by Deutsch and shown on screen in *The Snake Pit*, Thorazine offered the hope of help, or at least the hope of returning home.

Within a few years this optimism engendered by Thorazine's success in the treatment of schizophrenia led to brand new mental health policies. Now that the most serious psychiatric symptoms could be contained by potent pharmaceuticals, the goal of treatment became "deinstitutionalization." Patients who lived in state hospitals were sent packing.

Some of them adapted and were welcomed back by their families and neighbors. More often, however, they landed in heartless and decrepit "adult homes," like the one that we see in Cronenberg's eerily correct *Spider* (2002), which is set in the U.K. rather than the U.S. *Spider* stars Ralph Fiennes as a hapless and hopeless schizophrenic man. His life revolves around his internal hallucinations, which are often difficult to distinguish from the harsh voice of the matron who runs his post-hospital halfway house. (This same year Fiennes played the floridly psychotic killer Francis Dolarhyde, aka "The Tooth Fairy," in the Hannibal film *Red Dragon*.)

While very, very few former patients became violent or turn into a Francis Dolarhyde, many wound up even worse than they were before they were "freed" from the asylums. Some lived on the streets, using street drugs in lieu of their "miraculous" prescription meds. Tent cities sprang up in urban areas. Subway tunnels filled with former inmates of mental hospitals camping out alongside hard-core criminals, dedicated drug users, and varied and sundry drifters. Today the largest mental hospital in the world is located on Riker's Island, the New York City jail located near Queens, across a bridge that connects the island to the city. And it has become next to impossible to differentiate mental patients from career criminals now that so many of them end up at the same place.

Years after policies about "deinstitutionalization" were put into place, the psychiatrists who pushed for this policy admitted that this plan was the greatest regret of their careers. So many mental patients did worse, rather than better, without trained staff to care for them, and without receiving assistance in their daily activities or help with securing housing.

Mental hospital movies were the worse for wear, also. As more and more legal constraints against involuntary hospital commitments were put in place, and as more safeguards against sadistic treatments were established, asylums ceased to be the threats they once were. So the fears induced by asylum thrillers grew weaker.

Theoretically, the genre might disappear once it became less socially relevant. Or it might be reinvented. But let's see what happened with women's films, or weepies, which had been so popular during the World War II years before fading away when the war ended, and when husbands and fathers and brothers returned home from the front. The need for those over-the-top tearjerkers theoretically dissolved, especially when television soap operas appeared in the next decade. But there is one glitch — women's films and weepies of the 1940s had *already* been reinvented and revitalized. Weepies first appeared in the silent era, when "emotional acoustics" substituted for words, and when the wounds of World War I were still fresh. That genre plays on universal emotions that are inherent in most people but are intensified by certain social conditions. Could the same thing happen for asylum thrillers, even if social circumstances shift?

As a matter of fact, motifs about mental hospitals and involuntary incarcerations did not disappear from the silver screen, even though the immediate reality of involuntary incarceration and the likelihood of being carted away by "the men in the white coats" became less and less likely as the years passed. Horror films about escaped mental patients became popular after 1961 (partly because of the success of Hitchcock's *Psycho* [1960], and partly because mental patients really were on the loose). Films about psychosis — with or without psychiatrists — became the dominant horror theme by 1980,[6] suggesting that many people fear going crazy, and many have a reflexive fear of involuntary incarceration and losing control to the powers that be.

Many laypersons suspect that the hypothetical sinister psychiatrist waits at the end of the hospital corridor — even though it is unlikely that they will ever enter such a hospital at all. In much the same way, police films still exist because enough moviegoers still fear imprisonment by police, even though safeguards were put in place to avoid police brutality or false arrest. (Admittedly, those safeguards are not failsafe, and breeches still occur.) Yet police procedurals did not disappear, even though police procedures changed. But the themes did change over time, and such films often feature police officers who themselves are victimized by high-ranking bureaucrats or investigation units. Mental hospital movies do not parallel the exact same shifts found in police procedurals, but they adapted themselves to the changing times in their own way, as we will see.

If a single individual has an unrealistic fear, then that fear is said to be a phobia, or possibly even a form of paranoia. That fear can be called a psychosis if the fear is deep enough and unrealistic enough, and does not disappear in the face of "reality testing." When many members of society share the same fear, a cultural shift results, which is then mirrored in the arts of that era. Film is the seventh art, and is quite capable of dramatizing these fears and acting as a medium to dispel them (although sometimes it strengthens such fears). The upshot is that many members of the public patronize movies about involuntary admission to mental asylums because this is a fairly common fear. As long as some minor plot modifications are made to reflect the realities of the day, this time-honored horror theme survives and stays plausible.

To accommodate these new trends in de-institutionalization and to acknowledge the limitations placed on psychiatric services, several significant changes occurred. Newer mental hospital movies began to blend supernatural elements with standard asylum settings. *In Dreams* shows the dagger-wielding psychiatric nurse (played by Robert Downey, Jr., in drag) entering the dreams of disturbed patients, and traipsing between the real world and the netherworld.

Gothika (2003) also adds an obvious supernatural touch to an otherwise sensationalized film. This 21st century blaxploitation film stars Halle Berry in a role that won her a Rotten

Tomato nomination. Berry plays a psychiatrist who is visited by a ghost but is presumed to be psychotic because of the messages that are carved on her arms (by the ghost). Everyone other than her personal psychiatrist and former colleague at the mental hospital (Robert Downey, Jr., again) is convinced that her cuts are self-inflicted rather than messages sent from beyond the grave. Dr. Miranda Grey's sadistic psychiatrist-husband turns out to be a worse fiend than the ghouls that torment her.

But supernatural-psychiatrist themes attract a limited audience. To expand the appeal of sinister psychiatrist and madhouse movies beyond the dedicated supernatural thriller crowd, Hollywood filmmakers added a very clever touch. This switch may be a response to even more changes that came in the wake of the "managed care" movement of the early 1990s.

Another tried and true technique is the abandoned asylum. Video games about *Silent Hill*, even more than the 2006 film based on the video game, revolve around abandoned asylums. In the remake of *House on Haunted Hill* (1999), which appeared the same year as the *Silent Hill* (1999) video game, the action occurs in a long abandoned (and haunted) asylum.

Session 9 (2001), another turn-of-the-millennium thriller, also takes place in an abandoned mental hospital. A cleaning crew struggles to remove asbestos but meets unexpected challenges. That film was set and shot at Danvers State Hospital, which is located in the rural town of Danvers, Massachusetts. The hospital is believed to have been the inspiration for some H.P. Lovecraft stories, which, in turn, inspired "Arkham Asylum" in the Batman world.

There are good reasons for the proliferation of "abandoned asylum" films around the turn of the millennium, but those reasons have little to do with the millennium itself and much to do with the economic, political, and administrative changes that had come to pass in the decade before the 20th century ended. Half a century had elapsed since "deinstitutionalization" began as an earnest effort to free patients from abusive and isolating conditions at state hospitals. Financially-motivated managed care dealt the final blow to the "asylum" or "sanitarium" or "rest home" or "retreat." MCOs (managed care organizations) arrived in the early 1990s. MCOs came to be the standard of mental health care delivery by the latter 1990s, in spite of the objections of most hospitals and doctors. The millennium was irrelevant. Psychiatry was not singled out for belt-tightening, but psychiatric institutions felt the squeeze more than many other medical fields because psychiatrists care for a disproportionately high number of chronic patients who remain in custodial care. Some say that the trend to hospitalize acting-out adolescents for years at a time contributed to the rising census in psychiatric hospitals, and that managed care made its greatest inroads by limiting otherwise lengthy hospital stays for troubled teens.[7]

In retrospect, some cynical critics now suspect that the deinstitutionalization movement was also financially motivated, and that it was not exclusively ideologically-driven. But we would need more detailed studies to confirm or refute such claims. In the case of managed care, the monetary motivations were articulated from the start. Although some seriously ill people were deprived of needed hospital care as a result of these administration shifts, it should be noted that encouraging independence among those who are capable of using that independence constructively can have great clinical advantages over fostering dependency on "the system."

Some former psychiatric patients appreciate the length-of-stay limits imposed by managed care (as per Linda Andre's narratives in *Doctors of Deception* [2009] and other tales told on the long-defunct radio show *Madness Network News*, which was produced by self-described "psychiatric survivors").[8] Some anti-psychiatry activists boast about helping their hospitalized comrades to call their insurance companies covertly to inform them that they are not receiving sufficient treatment to justify reimbursement for the hospital stay. The reluctant patient is more likely to be discharged once the hospital learns that it will not be reimbursed.

Sometimes those antics invite a chuckle from others who are not directly involved. But the financial upshot of managed care is no laughing matter. No one expected that managed care companies would siphon off about one-third of medical payments while cutting overall costs. One out of every three dollars goes toward administrative expenses needed to restrict access to treatment. As a result, there has been little to no net financial gain from limiting hospital admissions, decreasing hospital lengths of stays, or rationing psychiatric care. Some of those managed care and insurance companies went bankrupt, but many others flourished, and their stocks have soared.

When it became known that insurance carriers commonly refuse patients' requests for admission to hospitals, and divert them to "partial hospitals" or "intensive out-patient programs," where they sleep at home and live with families, "asylum thrillers" ran the risk of losing their edge. Producers were concerned with maintaining credibility and ensuring that their viewers could "suspend disbelief" long enough to enter into "movie mode" and partake in the plot. To do that they could set mental hospital movies in the past, when such risks were more real. And so many 21st century films about sinister asylums (and sinister psychiatrists who staff them) are backdated, even though they are presented as though the action is taking place in the present.

An excellent example of this is *Changeling*, directed by Clint Eastwood, and starring Angelina Jolie and John Malkovich. As previously discussed, this film shows how an unscrupulous psychiatrist bows to the demands of politicos who want to discredit Jolie's character, Christine. The psychiatrist is an otherwise unimportant player in the plot, yet he locks her away in a mental ward and demands that she sign false statements if she wants to be released. He is ready to subject her to ECT (electroconvulsive therapy), even though ECT was not available when the action occurs. The action is set in 1928 and continues into the mid–1930s.

Other films fit this bill equally well. Many of those movies were covered in earlier chapters because their plots pertain to other themes. *The Jacket* (2005), starring Kris Kristofferson as a drugged-out doctor and Adrian Brody as the hapless veteran who ends up in a time warp and then a morgue-like box in a state hospital basement, may be the most disturbing film of the lot. In this movie, the orderlies are more directly abusive than the indifferent psychiatrist. Yet it is the doctor who presumably orders the drug studies, solitary confinement, and straitjackets. This proves another point: one never knows if the abusers will come from the bottom of the hospital hierarchy or from the top. In asylum cinema, nothing is sacred, and there is no one to help.

Perhaps the most memorable sinister psychiatrist in a sanitarium or rest home (which is worlds away from Adrian Brody's hideous institution for the criminally insane) is Leo G. Carroll's character in *Spellbound*. *Spellbound*'s Green Manor is magisterial. It treats its patients well, and it treats them to analytic sessions with a wide range of trained staff. It treats them to lovely living quarters, with maids, waitresses, butlers, and doormen. But the aging hospital head pulls a gun on Ingrid Bergman after she accuses him of murdering the missing doctor.

A more recent asylum film that is unlikely to have the staying power of *Spellbound* is *Sucker Punch* (2011). In this movie, a female chief psychiatrist has an exotic accent and an even more exotic wardrobe. She wears skirts that are slit to the hip as she speaks to the young women in her ward. In their deluded minds they imagine that the psychiatrist is the madam of a brothel, where the young women are sexually exploited by leering onlookers, orderlies, paying customers and even an enormously obese cook who works in the kitchen and attempts to rape a patient. When not in the throes of their delusions, incarcerated women like Baby Doll see only the peeling grey paint on the walls and the grim barracks-like beds where they bunk.

Baby Doll is scheduled for a lobotomy with the male doctor who performs operations when he visits the institution. It turns out that Dr. Vera Gorski's signature was forged by an underling who was bribed by Baby Doll's abusive stepfather upon her admission to the hospital. The stepfather wants to ensure that she cannot tell her side of the story when he co-opts her inheritance. The psychiatrist is helpless to stop the procedure after the order is set in motion.

It seems likely that the sexual motifs that run through the plot exist in the disturbed imaginations of the asylum inmates only, except that the story is narrated by several narrators who tell essentially the same story. If the plot were not confusing enough, and if the whole host of institutionalized narrators were not so unreliable from the start, the disjointed time line of the film makes it even more confusing and inaccessible. And maybe that's what it's meant to be.

The comic book quality of the visuals is interesting, albeit uninformative. The time-lessness of the sci-fi renditions of World War I war equipment, used by young women dressed in contemporary clothes, is even more disorienting. What we have is a music video in film's clothes. Perhaps the filmmaker intended to take the asylum setting out of chrono-logical context in order to tell a timeless story about exploitation of female patients in mental institutions. Such stories date back to Charlotte Perkins Gilman's *The Yellow Wallpaper*, which was first published in *New England Magazine* in 1892. The sixties and seventies produced many books and films about women's abuse in mental hospitals and by psychiatrists. Clint Eastwood addresses a related, but less sexually-explicit, theme in the 21st century with *Changeling*.

Alas, it is more likely that the filmmaker Zack Snyder aspired to make a sexually-titillating story with graphics that could compete with his other comic book–inspired stories, such as *Watchmen* (2009) and his *Superman* film. He says that he planned to write and direct a movie about "*Alice in Wonderland* with machine guns." The mental hospital part of the film seems to be secondary to the short, short skirts and fetish fashions. Like in so many movies, sinister psychiatrists and malevolent mental hospitals simply serve as the scene and setting, and are not terribly significant in their own right.

Since we are on the topic of comic books and mental hospitals, I would be remiss not to mention the *Arkham Asylum* video game. References to the Arkham Asylum for the Crim-inally Insane also appear in Joel Schumacher's *Batman Forever* (1995) and *Batman and Robin*

Psychiatrist Harlene Quinzel falls for the Joker and abandons her post at Arkham Asylum for the Criminally Insane to become the acrobatic Harley Quinn in the *Arkham Asylum* video game (2009).

(1997), and in Christopher Nolan's *Batman Begins* (2005), *The Dark Knight* (2008) and *The Dark Knight Rises* (2012). There has yet to be a complete film about Arkham Asylum, and, considering that the second video version of *Arkham Asylum* was renamed "Arkham City," it is unlikely that we will see a full film about this awful mental institution in the near future.

The sinister psychiatrists who populate Arkham Asylum, both as staff psychiatrists and as patients, are almost too numerous to mention. In this case the institution of Arkham IS important, and is named for the fictional city mentioned in H. P. Lovecraft's story "The Dunwich Horror," among others. In the *Batman* comics, and in several films based on the comics, we are told that Arkham is named for the Arkham family, which includes several psychiatrists who have inherited a gene that causes psychosis in later life. Such genes do exist in real life (and also occur in Edgar Allan Poe's story "Fall of the House of Usher"). One can speculate about several inheritable disorders that cause such symptoms, but some things we know for sure. According to the story line, Dr. Amadeus Arkham is the patriarch of this clan. He murdered his own mother, perhaps as a mercy killing after she became demented.

Arkham houses the "criminally insane" villains of the Batman stories. The Joker is one of the inmates. In the 1990s cartoon, a psychiatrist named Dr. Harleen Quinzel becomes infatuated with the Joker, even though he abuses her and tries to strangle her. Her character became popular enough to make its way from cartoons to the small screen via a short-lived TV series called *Birds of Prey* (2002–3). She has not yet made it to the big screen. Quinzel abandons her position as staff psychiatrist at Arkham and helps the Joker to escape. She taps into her skills as a high school gymnast and morphs into the carnivalesque character "Harley Quinn," who performs acrobatics. She accompanies the Joker on his evil escapades and functions as a villain. She is eventually committed to her own institution as a patient, thereby following a tradition begun by Dr. Caligari in Germany. Dr. Quinzel's saga goes on and on, in true comics tradition, with no end in sight.

For those who are more familiar with films than comics or video games, there is Dr. Crane, also known as the Scarecrow, played by Cillian Murphy in *Batman Begins*. As discussed in the chapter on diabolical drugging, Dr. Jonathan Crane sprays nerve gas, wears a scary mask, and induces nightmarish "visions" in everyone who sees him. He uses this technique when he interviews a mobster who was remanded to his mental hospital. The mobster does not realize that Dr. Crane's unethical antics can compete with the tactics used by the Mafia itself.

Although the film does not tell us the backstory behind Dr. Crane, the Batman comics reveal Dr. Crane's long history of evil. He appeared in very early Batman comics. As a young psychiatrist and professor, Dr. Crane evaluated a boy who deliberately killed his father and crippled his mother by rigging the family car (he intended to murder both parents, but the plan failed and the mother lived on). That horrid little boy grew up to be Dr. Tommy Elliot, an evil surgeon who is also known as Hush. From the start, the perceptive Dr. Crane realized how evil little Tommy was, but the bad doctor wanted to see how a truly evil child matures. So he gave Tommy a clean bill of health that released him from the psychiatric facility.

In the films we get only fleeting glimpses of Dr. Jonathan Crane. We see nothing of Dr. Amadeus Arkham or Dr. Jeremiah Arkham, or even Alice (Alyce) Sinner, the misguided medical student who cavorts with Dr. Jeremiah Arkham in his guise of the Black Mask.

The Batman comics, and, to a lesser extent, the Batman movies, are a treasure trove of sinister psychiatrists who function in even more sinister institutions. The Arkham Asylum for the Criminally Insane touches on a popular and recurring subgenre of "mental hospital movies." Some of Dr. Hannibal Lecter's five films are excellent examples of this genre. *Halloween*, both the original and the remake, with Donald Pleasence or Malcolm McDowell as the psychiatrist, also interfaces with forensic psychiatric issues. However, the *Halloween* psychiatrists are not inherently evil. Rather, they are pushed into committing evil acts in an attempt to prevent even worse evil being perpetrated by Michael Meyers. Martin Scorsese's recent film about *Shutter Island* is another movie of this ilk. On the surface, *Shutter Island* shows us something that looks like an "old-fashioned funny farm." This isolated island seems to be as far away from civilization as the proverbial Devil's Island, which once housed the world's most dangerous criminals. In reality (or in the film's reality), Shutter Island hosts the Ashecliffe Hospital for the Criminally Insane. The genteel inmates who tend the garden in the opening scene are anything but benign.

Interestingly, some say that mental hospital movies are a subgenre of prison films (even though mental hospital movies predated prison films). This subgenre that blends both prison and psychiatric settings has proven to be a formula for success when presented well. And directors as skilled as Martin Scorsese (*Shutter Island*) and Jonathan Demme (*Silence of the Lambs*) can definitely deliver on their promises. Because forensic psychiatric facilities are the last institutions that admit involuntary inmates only, lock their gates, and do not permit "passes" outside, they validate any fears about involuntary incarceration that remain with us.

Fortunately, the presumably sinister psychiatrists in *Shutter Island* reveal themselves to be "pseudo-sinister psychiatrists." They are well-intended but are misperceived in the deluded mind of U.S. Marshall Teddy Daniels. Daniels is a drinker who has flashbacks. He may have been in the throes of the D.T.s (delirium tremens), or alcohol withdrawal, which causes hallucinations, shakes and seizures, or he may have PTSD. He is a World War II vet who is still reeling from the trauma of liberating Dachau, where he saw cadaverous bodies that clutched at barbed wire fences. Images appear before his eyes. He has many reasons to hallucinate, and much to recall.

In spite of these vivid memories, Teddy cannot remember that he murdered his wife after learning that she drowned their children. He believes that he has been sent to Shutter Island to find a patient-prisoner who went missing. As far as he is concerned, he is functioning in his official capacity as a U.S. Marshall when he arrives at the island. Neither he, nor we, realize that his government agent "colleague" who accompanies him to the island is actually his psychiatrist. The crypto-doctor hopes to jar Teddy's memory by using this ruse.

Shutter Island's bald psychiatrist Dr. Cawley (Ben Kingsley) speaks to a skeptical U.S. Marshall, Teddy Daniels (Leonardo DiCaprio), while Marshall Aule (Mark Ruffalo) stands in the background.

Teddy believes that drug studies and other procedures are conducted at the island's remote "Lighthouse," where the most intractable patients are treated. He may be alluding to the lobotomies performed in the 1950s, when Dr. Freeman drove around in his loboto-mobile, advertising his psychosurgery. After all, the action is set in 1954, when Thorazine, the phenothiazine miracle drug, arrived in America and soon enough changed mental health care.

Not all forensic psychiatry films revolve around "pseudo-sinister psychiatrists" like the ones featured in *Shutter Island*. Some forensic psychiatric films, such as the Hannibal series, focus on psychiatrists whose bad behavior is beyond belief. But the theme of the "pseudo-sinister psychiatrist" appears often enough in the history of film, and plays upon the confusion between reality and fantasy that mark a psychotic state, that it is worth exploring further.

As I conclude this book, it is useful to recall that not all sinister psychiatrists in cinema are really as sinister as them seem. Some of those sinister psychiatrists signify something other than clinical concerns. And some cinematic depictions of sinister psychiatrists in film were responsible for instigating much-needed reforms, while some sinister cinema psychiatrists from the past mirrored problems that have long since been forgotten or corrected. If sinister cinema psychiatrists were all so straightforward, this theme would not be intriguing enough to keep repeating. For films are, above all, about entertainment and keeping audiences intrigued.

Conclusion:
Evil Sorcerers, Mad Scientists
and Sinister Psychiatrists

Let's turn back in time to the late 19th century, when Romantic era ballets like *Swan Lake* starred evil sorcerers (who have since been resurrected by Disney). As I suggested in the chapter on "Supernatural Psychiatrists," sorcery and psychiatry are historically connected by a dotted line, so it is no surprise that one was superseded by the other (in entertainment at least).

It didn't take long before evil sorcerers were pushed aside by mad scientists (in film, that is, and often on the stage as well). Moreau, Jekyll, and Frankenstein, who were invented on the printed page in the 19th century, made way for Fu Manchu, Rotwang (*Metropolis*, 1927), and Lex Luthor (*Superman*) as the 20th century progressed. In other words, *Swan Lake*'s sorcerer Rothbart transformed into the mad and malevolent scientist Rotwang in Fritz Lang's science fiction masterpiece *Metropolis*.

Sinister psychiatrists appeared early in film history, but, clearly, they are the "Johnny-come-latelies" of the mad, bad crowd. Mad scientists took center stage, both *on* the stage and on the celluloid screen, for a long time. They prevailed in horror films until 1960. From the '60s onward, however, perhaps because of *Psycho*'s success in 1960, psychotic villains multiplied. Some were sinister psychiatrists, but most were psychiatric patients. Many were escaped mental patients.[1]

Ironically, in those years anti-psychiatrists such as Laing and Szasz and Cooper preached in earnest that "mental illness" did not exist. They claimed the concept of mental illness was manufactured, or that psychosis was a sane reaction against a sick society. Somehow it seems that cinema viewers — who represent society at large — did not agree with these arguments (nor did most psychiatrists). Instead, they voted with their ticket stubs when they patronized films about psychotic villains. Much later in time, 21st century psychiatrists were left wondering how the trend toward demonizing mental patients in movies began.

By the 1980s the majority of horror films featured psychotics. Mad scientists were pushed aside after the race to space ended, and after the threat of nuclear holocaust (engineered by mad scientists) dimmed. Mad scientists had once seemed so pernicious, but now they were nowhere near so threatening (or so interesting) as mental patients or psychiatric practitioners. Andrew Tudor cites statistics to this effect in his book on *Monsters and Mad Scientists* (1987).[2]

Again that shift may reflect the commercial success of *Halloween* in 1978, and the tendency of moviemakers to ape success rather than take a chance on unproven commodities. Or it may be a reflection of the fact that historians described the 20th century as the "psy-

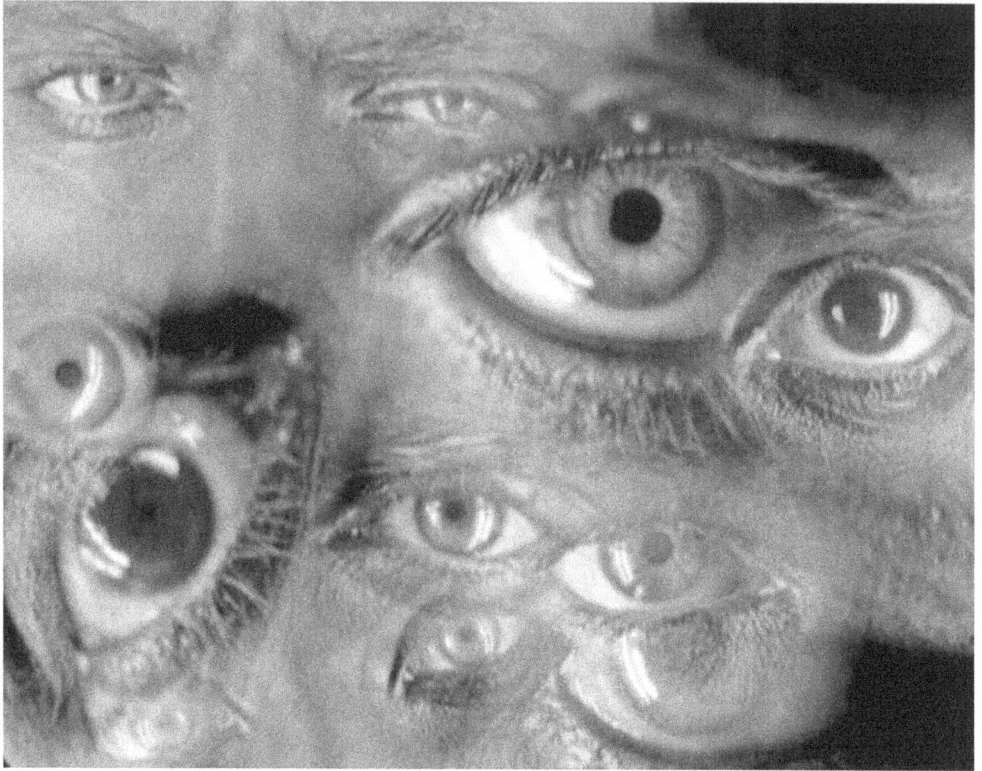

In Fritz Lang's futuristic *Metropolis* (1927), Freder (Gustav Frohlich) has a fever dream of the automaton Maria (Brigitte Helm) dancing as the Whore of Babylon while all eyes stare at her.

choanalytic century," so that an unraveled mind and the person who possesses it (or the man or woman who unravels the mind or puts it back together again) assumes greater significance to such a society.

Shifts in psychiatric practice may have contributed to this shift in cinema characters. Deinstitutionalization of the mentally ill began in 1955 and was well underway by the 1960s. The sight of discharged mental patients living homeless in the streets was a fact of life by 1980, when psychotics became the most common antagonists in American horror cinema.

The reasons behind this shift in villains deserve in-depth exploration. This merits its own separate study, which must be deferred at this time. Suffice it to say for now that sinister celluloid psychiatrists have persisted on the big screen — and will soon appear on the small screen as well. This book is ending, but the book has not closed on the subject of "sinister psychiatrists." For NBC announced in November of 2011 that *Hannibal* is coming to TV. Dr. Hannibal Lecter, America's most recognized movie villain, will soon grace the small screen, where he can be your dinner companion every week. That's quite the accomplishment for a cannibal, whether he's a credentialed psychiatrist or a forensic expert. Apparently, America has welcomed Hannibal the Cannibal into their homes just as surely as they invited the benign but remarkably popular radio psychiatrist *Frasier* into their living rooms from 1993 to 2004.

Surely that says something about American tastes (pun intended) and how those tastes have changed in less than a decade. Perhaps the nodal point was 9/11, but perhaps not. That will become obvious in retrospect, even if it is not quite clear right now. In the meantime, let's look at some similarities (and dissimilarities) between the two psychiatrists.

Like Hannibal, Frasier did not maintain his own clinical practice. Unlike Frasier, who hails from the working class, Hannibal is clearly upper crust. He is a European aesthete and a descendent of nobility. As for family relationships, Hannibal once had a sister, who remains in his memories — every time he takes a chunk out of someone's cheek.

Frasier also had a family, but of a very different sort. He has a father, a brother, and a mean-spirited ex-wife (also a psychiatrist — named Lilith, no less). His father is a retired police detective who was wounded in the line of duty. Brother Niles is also a psychiatrist and a man of impeccable taste who likes fine wine (like Hannibal).

But that's where the similarities between Hannibal and Frasier end. For Hannibal has other "gourmet" tastes as well. It will be interesting to see what happens when the American public gets a "taste" of Hannibal's antics in their own homes. Maybe that will be a good time to open this book and end the evening with a different take on Hannibal's history.

Filmography

After Mein Kampf (1961): Ralph Porter
Alone in the Dark (1982): Jack Sholder
Analyze That (2002): Harold Ramis
Analyze This (1999): Harold Ramis
Annabel Lee (2001): George Higham
Annie Hall (1977): Woody Allen
Antwone Fisher (2002): Denzel Washington
Arkham Asylum [videogame] (2009): Sefton Hill
Arkham City [videogame] (2011): Sefton Hill
Artist's Dream, The (1898): Georges Méliès
Astronomer's Dream, The (aka *the Man in the Moon*) (1898): George Méliès
Astro-Zombies (1968): Ted V. Mikels
Asylum (2005): David Mackenzie
Attic Expeditions, The (2001): Jeremy Kasten
Avenging Conscience, The (1914): D.W. Griffith
Asylum (2008): David R. Ellis
Asylum (aka *House of the Crazies*) (1972): Roy Ward Baker
Baby Face (1933): Alfred E. Green
Batman and Robin (1997): Joel Schumacher
Batman Begins (2005): Christopher Nolan
Batman Forever (1995): Joel Schumacher
Batman serials (1943): Lambert Hillyer
Beautiful Mind, A (2001): Ron Howard
Bedlam (1946): Mark Robson
Beetlejuice (1988): Tim Burton
Beggar's Dream, The (1898): Georges Méliès
Behind Locked Doors (1948): Budd Boetticher
Black Cat, The (1934): Edgar G. Ulmer
Black Pit of Dr. M, The (1959): Ramon Obon
Boys from Brazil, The (1978): Franklin J. Schaffner
Brood, The (1979): David Cronenberg
Brain from Planet Arous (1957): Nathan Jaran
Bugsy (1991): Barry Levinson
Cabinet of Caligari, The (1962): Roger Kay
Cabinet of Dr. Caligari, The (1919): Robert Weine

Captain Newman, M.D. (1963): David Miller
Casablanca (1942): Michael Curtiz
Cat in the Brain, A (1990): Lucio Fulci
Cat People (1942): Jacques Tourneur
Cat People (1982): Paul Schrader
Cavalier's Dream, The (1898): Edwin S. Porter
Cell, The (2000): Tarsem Singh
Cendrillon [Cinderella] (1899): Georges Méliès
Chandu the Magician (1932): William Cameron Menzies, Marcel Varnel
Changeling (2009): Clint Eastwood
Charlie and the Chocolate Factory (2005): Tim Burton
Chinese Opium Den, A (1894): Thomas Edison (producer)
Christmas Dream, The (1900): George Méliès
Clockmaker's Dream, The (1904): George Méliès
Clockwork Orange, A (1971): Stanley Kubrick
Convicted by Hypnotism (1912): Éclair (production company). Victorin-Hippolyte Jasset
Crimes and Misdemeanors (1989): Woody Allen
Cruising (1980): William Friedkin
Curse of the Crimson Idol (1914): Phoebus (production company)
Curse of the Demon (aka *Night of the Demon*) (1957): Jacques Tourneur
Curse of the Hindoo Pearl (1912): American Standard (production company)
Curse of the Jade Scorpion (2001): Woody Allen
Curse of the Scarabee Ruby (1914): Gaumont/Eclipse/Urban (production companies)
David and Lisa (1962): Frank Perry
Da Vinci Code, The (2006): Ron Howard
Dangers of Hypnosis, The (1923): Hugo Werner-Kahle
Dark Knight Rises, The (2012): Christopher Nolan
Dark Knight, The (2008): Christopher Nolan

Hypnotic Violinist, The (1914): Warner Brothers (production company)

Hypnotic Wife, The (1909): Pathé (production company)

Hypnotism (1910): Lux (production company)

Hypnotist at Work, The [*Le Magnetiseur*], (1897): Georges Méliès

Hypnotist's Revenge, The (1909): Georges Melies

I Confess (1953): Alfred Hitchcock

I Never Promised You a Rose Garden (1977): Anthony Page

I, the Jury (1953): Harry Essey

I, the Jury (1982): Richard T. Heffron

Inception (2010): Christopher Nolan

Intolerance (1916): D. W. Griffith

Invaders from Mars (1953): William Cameron Menzies

Invasion of the Body Snatchers (1956): Don Siegel

Invasion of the Body Snatchers (1978): Philip Kaufman

Ipcress File, The (1965): Sidney J. Furie

Iron Man (2008): Jon Favreau

Island of Dr. Moreau, The (1977): Don Taylor

Island of Dr. Moreau, The (1996): John Frankenheimer

Island of Lost Souls, The (1933): Erle C. Kenton

Jacket, The (2005): John Maybury

Jacob's Ladder (1990): Adrian Lyne

Jade (1995): William Friedkin

Judgment at Nuremberg (1961): Stanley Kramer

King of Hearts (1966): Philippe de Broca

Klute (1971): Alan J. Pakula

Last of the Mohicans, The (1920): Maurice Tourneur

Lethal Weapon (1987): Richard Donner

Lethal Weapon II (1989): Richard Donner

Lilith (1964): Robert Rossen

Lost Soul, The (aka *The Dangers of Hypnosis*) (1923): Hugo Werner-Kahle

Lost Weekend, The (1945): Billy Wilder

Lunatics in Power (1909): Thomas Edison

M (1931): Fritz Lang

Madhouse (2004): William Butler

Malcolm X (1992): Spike Lee

Maltese Falcon, The (1941): John Huston

Man from U.N.C.L.E. [TV series] (1964–68)

Man on Fire (2004): Tony Scott

Man Who Knew Too Much, The (1956): Alfred Hitchcock

Man Who Laughs, The (1928): Paul Leni

Man with the Golden Arm, The (1955): Otto Preminger

Manchurian Candidate, The (2004): Jonathan Demme

Manchurian Candidate, The (1962): John Frankenheimer

Mandrake the Magician (1939): Norman Deming, Sam Nelson

Manhunter (1986): Michael Mann

Mansion of Madness (1973): Juan Lopez Moctezuma

Marnie (1964): Alfred Hitchcock

Match Point (2005): Woody Allen

Matrix, The (1999): Andy Wachowski, Larry Wachowski

Max Hypnotisé [*Max Hypnotized*] (1910): Max Linder

Mayor of Hell, The (1933): Archie Mayo

Memento (2000): Christopher Nolan

Metropolis (1927): Fritz Lang

Midnight Cowboy (1969): John Schlesinger

Milk (2008): Semih Kaplanoglu

Mind Reader, The (1933): Roy Del Ruth

Minority Report (2002): Steven Spielberg

Mister Frost (1990): Phillipe Setbon

Mummy, The (1932): Karl Freund

Naked Lunch (1956): David Cronenberg

Next (2007): Lee Tamahori

Night of the Demon (aka *Curse of the Demon*) (1957): Jacques Tourneur

Night of the Hunter, The (1955): Charles Laughton

Night of the Living Dead (1968): George Romero

Nightbreed (1990): David Cronenberg

Nightmare Alley (1947): Edmund Goulding

Nightmare on Elm Street (1984): Wes Craven

Ninth Configuration, The (aka *Twinkle, Twinkle, "Killer" Kane*) (1980): William Peter Blatty

North by Northwest (1959): Alfred Hitchcock

Nosferatu (1922): F. W. Murnau

Now, Voyager (1942): Irving Rapper

One Flew Over the Cuckoo's Nest (1975): Milos Forman

Pandora's Box (1929): George Wilhelm Pabst

Partie de Cartes, Une (1896): George Méliès

Planet of the Apes (1968): Franklin J. Schaffner

Planet of the Apes (2001): Tim Burton

Police Woman [TV series] (1974–78): created by Robert L. Collins

Possessed (1947): Curtis Bernhardt

Pressure Point (1962): Hubert Cornfield

Prime (2005): Ben Younger

Psycho (1960): Alfred Hitchcock

Psycho (1998): Gus Van Sant

Purple Rose of Cairo (1985): Woody Allen

Quills (2000): Philip Kaufman
Rajah's Dream, The (1900): Georges Méliès
Rear Window (1954): Alfred Hitchcock
Repo Men (2010): Miguel Sapochnik
Requiem for a Dream (2000): Darren Aronofsky
Return of Chandu, The (1934): Ray Taylor
Return to Oz (1985): Walter Murch
Rise of the Planet of the Apes (2011): Rupert Wyatt
Rope (1948): Alfred Hitchcock
Rosemary's Baby (1968): Roman Polanski
Session 9 (2001): Brad Anderson
Shadow of a Doubt (1943): Alfred Hitchcock
Sherlock Holmes (2009): Guy Ritchie
Shock (1946): Alfred L. Werker
Shock Corridor (1963): Samuel Fuller
Shutter Island (2010): Martin Scorsese
Silence of the Lambs (1991): Jonathan Demme
Silent Hill (2006): Christophe Gans
Sixth Sense, The (1999): M. Night Shyamalan
Snake Pit, The (1948): Anatole Litvak
Spellbound (1945): Alfred Hitchcock
Spider (2002): David Cronenberg
Still of the Night (1982): Robert Benton
Strangers on a Train (1951): Alfred Hitchcock
Student of Prague, The (1913): Paul Wegener, Stellan Rye
Student of Prague, The (1926): Henrik Galeen
Sucker Punch (2011): Zack Snyder
Sudden Impact (1983): Clint Eastwood
Suddenly, Last Summer (1959): Joseph L. Mankiewicz
Superman (1978): Richard Donner
Svengali (1931): Archie Mayo
Sybil (1976): Daniel Petrie
System of Dr. Tarr and Professor Fether, The (1912): Maurice Tourneur
Système du Docteur Goudron et du Professeur Plume, Le (1913): Éclair (production company)
Tales That Witness Madness (1973): Freddie Francis

Testament of Dr. Mabuse, The (1933): Fritz Lang
Texas Chainsaw Massacre, The (1974): Tobe Hooper
Three Faces of Eve (1957): Nunnally Johnson
Till the Clouds Roll By [stage] (1946): Jerome Kern
Tingler, The (1959): William Castle
Topper [TV series] (1953–55)
Total Recall (1990): Paul Verhoeven
Trainspotting (1996): Danny Boyle
Trilby (1915): Jacques Tourneur
Triumph of the Will (1935): Leni Riefenstahl
Two Evil Eyes (1990): Dario Argento, and George A. Romero
Valley of the Dolls (1967): Mark Robson
Vertigo (1958): Alfred Hitchcock
Walk on the Wild Side (1962): Edward Dymtryk
Ward, The (2011): John Carpenter
Watchmen (2009): Zach Synder
When the Clouds Roll By (1919): Victor Fleming
Where Is My Child? (1937): Abraham Leff, Henry Lynn
Whirlpool (1949): Otto Preminger
Willy Wonka and the Chocolate Factory (1971): Mel Stuart
Witchcraft Through the Ages (aka *Haxan*) (1922): Benjamin Christensen
Wizard of Oz (1939): Victor Fleming
Wolf Man, The (1941): George Waggner
Woman in the Window (1944): Fritz Lang
World War Z (2012): Marc Forster
X-Men (2000): Bryan Singer
X-Men Origins: Wolverine (2009): Gavin Hood
X-Men: Last Stand (2006): Brett Ratner
X2 (2003): Bryan Singer
Young Frankenstein (1974): Mel Brooks
Zelig (1983): Woody Allen
Zombie Holocaust (aka *Dr. Butcher, M.D.*) (1980): Marino Girolami

Chapter Notes

Introduction

1. See websites by Roland Atkinson: http://www.AtkinsonOnFilm.com; http://www.psychflix.com. See also Atkinson's article on "Film, Fame, and the Fashioning of an Illness" in *Clinical Psychiatry News*, July 01, 2009, and the heated discussions generated about DID (dissociative identity disorder) in subsequent journal issues.

2. See articles by Marcia Angell, MD, former editor of *New England Journal of Medicine*, in *New York Review of Books*, August 2011, as well as her responses to the letters to the editor.

3. Glen and Krin Gabbard, *Psychiatry and the Cinema, Second Edition* (Washington, DC: American Psychiatric Press, 1999).

4. See Burt Hanson, *Picturing Medical Progress from Pasteur to Polio* (New Brunswick, NJ: Rutgers University Press, 2009) for a detailed discussion of comics and medical discoveries. See also Sharon Packer, *Superheroes and Superegos: The Minds Behind the Masks* (ABC-Clio, 2010) for a psychiatrically-oriented approach to this topic.

5. Anton Kaes, *Shell Shock Cinema: Weimar Cinema and the Wounds of War* (Princeton, NJ: Princeton University Press, 2009).

6. Non-commercially biased data is published on government-sponsored websites that include http://mentalhealth.gov/statistics; http://www.nimh.nih.gov/statistics; and http://www.ptsd.va.gov/professional/pages/epidemiological-facts-ptsd.asp. Detailed statistics about trends in pharmaceutical prescribing is also available through various financial websites, market research firms, and http:www.ProPublica.org.

7. www.cdc.gov/nchs/fastats/drugs.htm; http://articles.cnn.com/2007-07-09/health/antidepressants_1_antidepressants-high-blood-pressure-drugs-psychotropic-drugs?_s=PM:HEALTH (accessed online 10-16-11).

8. A few farm-like residential treatments facilities remain open in rural areas, and some drug rehabs include horse therapy, but these pricey places are rarely reimbursed by third party payers (insurance) and so are generally reserved for the wealthy.

9. Http://www.treatmentadvocacycenter.org/component/content/article/622 (accessed online 10-23-11).

10. Jonathan Gregg, "Will the Real Andrew Goldstein Take the Stand," *Time*, March 3, 2000. Accessed online on 10-18-11 at http://www.time.com/time/arts/article/0,8599,40257,00.html#ixzz1bBYxafL0.

11. The *New York Times* ran dozens of articles on this topic on a course of years. Articles include, but are not limited, to: Julian Barnes, "Judge Allows Lesser Charge in Trial of Subway Pusher," *New York Times*, March 22, 2000; Julian Barnes, "Second Murder Trial Opens in Subway Shoving Case," *New York Times*, March 4, 2000; David Rohde, "For Retrial, Subway Defendant Goes Off Medication," *New York Times*, February 23, 2000; Michael Winerip, "The Nation — Behind One Man's Mind," *New York Times*, December 26, 1999; Anemona Hartocollis, "Nearly 8 Years Later, Guilty Plea in Subway Killing," *New York Times*, October 11, 2006; Anemona Hartocollis, "A Subway Nightmare Will Be the Focus of Yet a Third Trial," *New York Times*, May 23, 2006.

12. Deborah Sontag, "A Schizophrenic, a Slain Worker, Troubling Questions," June 16, 2011.

13. Deborah Sontag, "Teenager's Path and a Killing Put Spotlight on Mental Care Published," *New York Times*, August 2, 2011.

14. Bruce Japsen, "Out from Behind the Counter," New York Times, October 21, 2011.

15. Stefan Andriopoulos (translated by Peter Jansen and Stefan Andriopoulos), *Possessed: Hypnotic Crimes, Corporate Fiction, and the Invention of Cinema* (Chicago: University of Chicago, 2008).

Chapter 1

1. See Robert Genter, "'Hypnotizzy' in the Cold War: The American Fascination with Hypnotism in the 1950s," *The Journal of American Culture* 29 (2006).

2. See Sharon Packer, *Dreams in Myth, Medicine and Movies* (Westport, CT: Praeger, 2002).

3. See chapter on "Paranoia and Post-War PTSD" in Sharon Packer, *Movies and the Modern Psyche* (Praeger, 2007).
4. See S. S. Prawer, *Caligari's Children* (Oxford: Oxford University Press, 1980); and David Robinson, *Das Cabinet des Dr. Caligari* (London: BFI Publishing, 1997).
5. See David Soren, *The Rise and Fall of the Horror Film* (Baltimore: Midnight Marquee Press, 1997); and Lottie Eisner, *The Haunted Screen: Expressionism in German Cinema* (Berkeley: University of California Press, 1969).
6. Mark Salisbury, *Burton on Burton* (New York: Faber and Faber, 1995).
7. See Anton Kaes, *Shell Shock Cinema* (Princeton, NJ: Princeton University Press, 2009).

Chapter 2

1. See Thomas Elsaesser, *Weimar Cinema and After* (London: Routledge, 2001); and Tom Gunning, *The Films of Fritz Lang* (London: BFI, 2000).
2. Emanuel Rice, *Freud and Moses: The Long Journey Home* (Albany: State University of New York, 1990).
3. Some of Sandor Gilman's many books on Freud, Judaism, and psychoanalysis examine Freud's status as a Jewish "outsider" who hailed from the less sophisticated and less educated Eastern European Jews ("Ostjuden").
4. See S. S. Prawer, *Caligari's Children* (Oxford: Oxford University Press, 1980); and David Robinson, *Das Cabinet des Dr. Caligari* (London: BFI Publishing, 1997).
5. See Allan Beveridge, *Portrait of the Psychiatrist as a Young Man* (Oxford: Oxford University Press, 2011).
6. Nathan Kravis, "James Braid's Psychophysiology: A Turning Point in the History of Dynamic Psychiatry," *American Journal of Psychiatry* 14, no. 10 (October 1988): 1191–1206.

Chapter 3

1. Compare Carl Jung's *Psychology and Religion* (New Haven: Yale University Press, 1966) to Sigmund Freud's *The Future of an Illusion* (New York: Norton, 1950).
2. Edward Shorter, *A History of Psychiatry: From the Era of the Asylum to the Age of Prozac* (New York: Wiley, 1997). Interestingly, Shorter's book ends with the Age of Prozac (which begins in the late 1980s) and does not extend to 21st century psychiatry, when a shift in practice setting occurred in the opposite direction. By 2002 the majority of psychiatrists were employed by publicly-funded clinics or institutions, and only a minority make private practice the mainstay of their practices. See detailed statistics in Jules M. Ranz, Michael J. Vergare, Joshua E. Wilk, Sigurd H. Ackerman, Richard C. Lippincott, W. Walter Menninger, Steven S. Sharfstein, and Ann Sullivan, MD, "The Tipping Point from Private Practice to Publicly Funded Settings for Early- and Mid-Career Psychiatrists," *Psychiatric Services* 57 (November 2006): 1640–1643.
3. Jules M. Ranz, Michael J. Vergare, Joshua E. Wilk, Sigurd H. Ackerman, Richard C. Lippincott, W. Walter Menninger, Steven S. Sharfstein, and Ann Sullivan, "The Tipping Point from Private Practice to Publicly Funded Settings for Early- and Mid-Career Psychiatrists." *Psychiatric Services* 57 (November 2006): 1640–1643.
4. See Laurence J Friedman, *Menninger: The Family and the Clinic* (Topeka: University of Kansas, 1992), for a rich discussion of the trials and tribulations of Menninger's émigré analysts.
5. Norman Cohen, *The Pursuit of the Millennium* (Oxford: Oxford University Press, 1970).

Chapter 4

1. Roy Porter, *Madness* (Oxford: Oxford University Press, 2002).

Chapter 5

1. *The Human Centipede* (2010) seems to be an exception to this trend; a sequel to what was labeled "the barfiest movie" was scheduled because of its success.
2. The search to identify more Gacy victims has not yet ended as of this writing. On October 28, 2011, Monica Davey wrote an article for the *New York Times*: "Sheriff Hopes to Identify John Wayne Gacy Victims Using DNA."
3. Highlights from a workshop run by psychiatrist Major Steven Pflanz appear in "Positive Psychiatry Portrayals: A Rarity in Hollywood Psychiatric News," *Psychiatric News* 37, no. 15 (August 2, 2002): 10–10.

Chapter 6

1. See David Sievers' *Freud on Broadway* (New York: Hermitage House, 1955) for an illuminating discussion of prominent playwrights and screenwriters who self-consciously incorporated Freudian themes. In some psychoanalytically-oriented psychiatric training programs, some training analysts pointed to those plays as "proof" of the universal applicability of Freudian theories — without apparent awareness of the writers' influences.

Chapter 7

1. Author Linda Andre describes her crusade against ECT in her 2009 book *Doctors of Deception: What They Don't Want You to Know About Shock Treatment* (New Brunswick, NJ: Rutgers University Press, 2009).
2. See Gabbard and Gabbard's discussions of ECT; as well as A. McDonald and G. Walter, "The portrayal of ECT in American Movies," *Journal of ECT* 17, no. 4 (2001): 264–274; and B. O'Shea, and A. McGennis, "ECT: Lay Attitudes and Experiences — a Pilot Study," *Irish Medical Journal* 76, no. 1 (1983): 40–43.
3. "Psychiatrists Invited to Peer Inside 'A Beautiful Mind.'" *Psychiatric News* 37, no. 9 (May 3, 2002): 32–32.
4. Personal communication from David Kreditor, MD, PhD, about his early experiences as a psychiatrist in Estonia.
5. For a comprehensive and thoughtful review of Laing's early influences, see Allan Beveridge, *Portrait of the Psychiatrist as a Young Man: The Early Writing and Work of R.D. Laing, 1927–1960* (Oxford: Oxford University Press, 2011).
6. Arnold D. Richards and Paul W. Mosher, "Abraham Arden Brill, 1874–1948," *American Journal of Psychiatry* 163 (2006): 386–386.

Chapter 8

1. To read about the potential medical implications of this film, and how this relates to the looming epidemic of dementia and possible treatment approaches, see Sharon Packer, "Recalling *Total Recall*," *MDng Magazine*, Psychiatry/Neurology Edition (February 2011). Retrieved on November 10, 2011, at http://www.hcplive.com/publications/mdng-Neurology/2011/february_2011/psych_in_film.

Chapter 9

1. Rich Daly, "Cost Concerns Likely Driving Drop in Psychotherapy Use," *Psychiatric News* 46, no. 1 (January 7, 2011): 8; "National Trends in Outpatient Psychotherapy" is posted at http://ajp.psychiatryonline.org/cgi/reprint/167/12/1456, quoted in *Psychiatric News* (January 7, 2011), accessed online October 10, 2011; "The Changing Face of U.S. Mental Health Care" is posted at http://ajp.psychiatryonline.org/cgi/content/full/167/12/1419, quoted in *Psychiatric News* (January 7, 2011), accessed online October 11, 2011.
2. Gardiner Harris, "Talk Doesn't Pay, So Psychiatry Turns Instead to Drug Therapy," *New York Times*, March 5, 2011. Unlike the references cited above, which are quoted by the American Psychiatric Association, this article is inflammatory and is a part of a series that finds fault with current changes in the practice and administration of medicine.
3. Duff Wilson, "F.D.A. Is Studying the Risk of Electroshock Devices," *New York Times*, January 23, 2011.
4. Scott Hensley, "NYT: Harvard Psychiatrists Under Fire for Drug-Company Funding," *Wall Street Journal*, June 9, 2008.
5. See Boston.com, "White Coat Notes," by Elizabeth Clooney.
6. John Oldham, MD, President, American Psychiatric Association (August 18, 2011), in response to "The Illusions of Psychiatry," *New York Review of Books*, July 14, 2001; and "The Epidemic of Mental Illness: Why?" *New York Review of Books*, June 23, 2011.
7. John Oldham, Daniel Carlat, Richard Friedman, and Andrew Nierenberg, reply by Marcia Angell (2011, August 18) to "'The Illusions of Psychiatry': An Exchange," *New York Review of Books*. In response to "The Illusions of Psychiatry" from the July 14, 2011, issue; "The Epidemic of Mental Illness: Why?" *New York Review of Books*, June 23, 2011.
8. Lest it seem as though psychopharmacologists are the only behavioral health practitioners or researchers who bend data, and lest it seem as though American research is the only research in the world that ever runs afoul of regulations, see this article about psychological research that appeared in the *New York Times* as this book was being proofed: Benedict Carey, "Fraud Case Seen as a Red Flag for Psychology Research," *New York Times*, November 2, 2011.
9. There is no data that indicates overripe cheese alone acts as a stimulant or antidepressant, but there is ample data that cheese, when combined with MAOIs, can cause deadly serotonin syndrome. See Sharon Packer and Stephen Berman, "Linezolid in the Induction of Serotonin Syndrome," *American Journal of Psychiatry* 164 (2007): 346–347; or any basic psychopharmacology text for more data. For a visual representation of an MAOI-related death that inspired changes in legislation governing residents' work hours, see painting by Sharon Packer, "A Lily for Libby" (illuminated obituary about Libby Zion's death), in *Southern Medical Journal*, 2000.

Chapter 10

1. Preeti Malani, "*Dark Medicine: Rationalizing Unethical Medical Research* (Book Review)," *JAMA* 300, no. 10 (September 10, 2008): 1217–1218.
2. Jochen Vollmann, Rolf Winau, "Informed Consent in Human Experimentation Before the Nuremberg Code," *British Medical Journal* 313 (December 7, 1996): 1445.

3. Thomas R. Frieden and F. Collins, "Commentary. Intentional Infection of Vulnerable Populations in 1946–1948," *JAMA* 304, no. 18 (2010): 2063–2064. Published online October 11, 2010.

4. Credible references published in reputable medical journals are far too numerous to catalogue here and can be found in specialist publications on medical ethics and history of medicine. The few citations included here represent but a tiny number of a vast body of literature.

5. Obituary written by Douglas Martin, "Ricky J. Wyatt, 57; Led Mental Care Suit." *New York Times*, November 4, 2011.

6. See chapter on "Diabolical Drugging" for citations about Big Pharma–supported research.

7. Richard Hunt, "*Hitler or Hippocrates: Medical Experiments and Euthanasia in the Third Reich* (Book Review)," *New England Journal of Medicine* 328 (May 13, 1993): 1429.

8. Henry Beecher, "Ethics and Clinical Research," *New England Journal of Medicine* 274 (August 28, 2008): 1354–60.

9. Mark Moran, "When Ethical Lines Were Crossed in Service to the Nation," *Psychiatric News* 46, no. 12 (June 17, 2011): 16.

10. John Marks, *The Search for the Manchurian Candidate* (New York: Times Books, 1979, 106–7).

Chapter 11

1. Lecture by Myron Winick, MD, about his book *The Final Stamp: Jewish Doctors in the Warsaw Ghetto* (November 13, 2008, New York Academy of Medicine).

2. Robert Jay Lifton, MD: *The Nazi Doctors: Medical Killing and the Psychology of Genocide* (New York: Basic Books, 1986). Dr. Lifton also wrote about brainwashing in China.

3. When presenting my chapter on "Mad Bad Military Mind MDs" at Grand Rounds at the Brooklyn VA Hospital in 2010, I showed clips from this film and was surprised to learn that none of the psychiatrists or other psychiatric staff in attendance had heard of this movie, much less seen it, even though many audience members were very familiar with many other military psychiatry–themed movies.

4. See Andrew H. Beck, "The Flexner Report and the Standardization of American Medical Education," *JAMA* 291, no. 17 (2004): 2139–2140. Also see Molly Cooke, David M. Irby, William Sullivan, and Kenneth M. Ludmerer, "American Medical Education 100 Years After the Flexner Report," *New England Journal of Medicine* 355 (September 28, 2006): 1339–1344.

Chapter 12

1. W. F. Bynum, Roy Porter, Michael Shepherd (eds.), *The Anatomy of Madness: Essays in the History of Psychiatry, Volume 3* (London: Routledge, 1988). Also see Roy Porter and David Wright (eds.), *The Confinement of the Insane: International Perspectives, 1800–1965* (Cambridge: Cambridge University Press, 2003); Roy Porter, *Madmen: A Social History of Madhouses, Mad-Doctors and Lunatics* (Tempus, 2006); Andrew Scull, "Book Review: The Confinement of the Insane: International Perspectives, 1800–1965," *Medical History* 49, no. 1 (January 1, 2005): 109–110; Andrew T. Scull, *Madhouses, Mad-Doctors, and Madmen: The Social History of Psychiatry in the Victorian Era* (Philadelphia: University of Pennsylvania Press, 1981); and Edward Shorter, *A History of Psychiatry: From the Era of the Asylum to the Age of Prozac* (New York: Wiley, 1997).

2. Sharon Packer, *Movies in the Modern Psyche* (Westport, CT: Praeger, 2007); S. S. Prawer, *Caligari's Children* (Oxford: Oxford University Press, 1980); Sigmund Freud, "The Uncanny" (1919).

3. Http://www.time.com/time/magazine/article/0,9171,799558,00.html#ixzz1USq1VOdk.

4. Albert Deutsch in *The Shame of the States* (New York: Harcourt Brace, 1948).

5. For unusual images of asylums, see http://www.abandonedasylum.com/booklist.html.

6. Andrew Tudor, *Monsters and Mad Scientists* (Oxford, UK: Basil Blackwell, 1987).

7. Personal communication from Mel Thrash, MD, Medical Director of Magellan Health Services in NYC in 2001.

8. Linda Andre, *Doctors of Deception* (New Brunswick, NJ: Rutgers University Press, 2009).

Conclusion

1. Jeffrey William Bullins, *Sound Design for American Horror Films* (unpublished MFA thesis), Savannah College of Art and Design, 2008.

2. Andrew Tudor. *Monsters and Mad Scientists* (Oxford, UK: Basil Blackwell, 1987).

Bibliography

American Psychiatric Association. *DSM-III (Diagnostic and Statistical Manual),* 3rd ed. Washington, DC: American Psychiatric Association Press, 1980.

_____. "National Trends in Outpatient Psychotherapy." Retrieved online October 10, 2011, at http://ajp.psy-chiatryonline.org/cgi/reprint/167/12/1456.

Andre, Linda. *Doctors of Deception: What They Don't Want You to Know About Shock Treatment.* New Brunswick, NJ: Rutgers University Press, 2009.

Andriopoulos, Stefan (translated by Peter Jansen and Stefan Andriopoulos). *Possessed: Hypnotic Crimes, Corporate Fiction, and the Invention of Cinema.* Chicago: University of Chicago Press, 2008.

Angell, Marcia. "'The Illusions of Psychiatry': An Exchange." Reply to letters from John Oldham, Daniel Carlat, Richard Friedman, and Andrew Nierenberg. *New York Review of Books,* August 18, 2011.

Arnheim, Rudolf. *Film as Art.* Berkeley: University of California Press, 1957.

Atkinson, Roland. "Film, Fame, and the Fashioning of an Illness." *Clinical Psychiatry News,* July 1, 2009.

Bartov, Omer. *The "Jew" in Cinema.* Bloomington: Indiana University Press, 2002.

Bazin, Andre (ed. Francois Truffaut). *The Cinema of Cruelty.* New York: Seaver Books, 1982.

Beck, Andrew H. "The Flexner Report and the Standardization of American Medical Education." *JAMA* 291, no. 17 (2004): 2139–2140.

Beecher, Henry (1966). "Ethics and Clinical Research." *New England Journal of Medicine* 274 (1966): 1354–60.

Beers, Clifford. *A Mind That Found Itself* (1908). Retrieved November 11, 2011, from questia.com.

Bergfelder, Tim, Erica Carter, and Deniz Gokturk. *The German Cinema Book.* London: BFI, 2002.

Bergstrom, Janet (ed.). *Endless Night.* Berkeley: University of California Press, 1999.

Bernstein, Matthew, and Gaylyn Studlar (eds.). *Visions of the East.* New Brunswick, NJ: Rutgers University Press, 1997.

Berrios, German, and Roy Porter (eds.). *A History of Clinical Psychiatry.* London: Athlone Press, 1999.

Beveridge, Allan. *Portrait of the Psychiatrist as a Young Man.* Oxford: Oxford University Press, 2011.

Biesen, Sheri Chinen. *Blackout: World War II and the Origins of Film Noir.* Baltimore: Johns Hopkins University Press, 2005.

Bould, Mark. *Film Noir: From Berlin to Sin City.* London: Wallflower, 2005.

Bourde, Raymond, and Etienne Chaumeton (trans. Paul Hammond). *A Panorama of American Film Noir: 1941–1953.* San Francisco: City Lights, 2002.

Brown Edward M. "Why Wagner-Jauregg Won the Nobel Prize for Discovering Malaria Therapy for General Paresis of the Insane." *History of Psychiatry* 11, no. 44 (2000): 371–382.

Budd, Mike (ed.). *The Cabinet of Dr. Caligari.* New Brunswick, NJ: Rutgers University Press, 1990.

Bynum, W. F., Roy Porter, and Michael Shepherd (eds.). "The Asylum and Its Psychiatry." In *The Anatomy of Madness: Essays in the History of Psychiatry, Volume 3.* London: Routledge, 1988.

Ceram, C. W. *Archaeology of the Cinema.* New York: Harcourt, Brace and World, 1965.

Chadwick, Gary. "*The Oxford Textbook of Clinical Research Ethics* (Book Review)." *New England Journal of Medicine* 359 (2008): 982–983.

Channan, Michael: *The Dream That Kicks,* 2nd ed. London: Routledge, 1980.

Charney, Leo, and V. R. Schwartz. *Cinema and the Invention of Modern Life.* Berkeley: University of California Press, 1995.

Clarens, Carlos (Introduction by J. Hoberman). *An Illustrated History of Horror and Science Fiction Films.* New York: Da Capo Press, 1991.

Cohen, Elizabeth. "CDC: Antidepressants Most Prescribed Drugs in U.S." Retrieved October 16, 2011, from www.cdc.gov/nchs/fastats/drugs.htm.

Cohen, Norman. *The Pursuit of the Millennium*, rev. and expanded ed. Oxford: Oxford University Press, 1970.

Conraad, Peter. *The Hitchcock Murders*. London: Faber and Faber, 2000.

Cooke, Molly, David M. Irby, William Sullivan, and Kenneth M. Ludmerer. "American Medical Education 100 Years After the Flexner Report." *New England Journal of Medicine* 355 (September 28, 2006): 1339–1344.

Cosgrove, L., and H. J. Bursztajn. "Pharmaceutical Philanthropical Shell Games: Has Industry Removed the Transparent and Replaced It with the Opaque?" *Psychiatric Times* 27, no. 3 (2010): 20.

_____ and _____. "Undue Pharmaceutical Influence on Psychiatric Practice: Steps That Can Reduce the Ethical Risk." *Psychiatric Times* 27, no. 5 (2010).

Coyle, Jake: "The New Western? The Mind Is Latest Movie Frontier." *AP Entertainment*, July 14, 2010 (retrieved online).

Craddock, Jim (ed.). *Videohound's Golden Movie Retriever 2007*. Detroit: Thomson Gale, 2006.

Daly, Richard. "Cost Concerns Likely Driving Drop in Psychotherapy Use." *Psychiatric News* 46, no. 1 (January 7, 2011): 8.

DeMijolla, Alain. "Freud and the Psychoanalytic Situation on the Screen." In *Endless Night*, edited by J. Bergstrom, 188–199. Berkeley: University of California Press, 1999.

Digby, Anne. *Madness, Morality, and Medicine: A Study of the York Retreat, 1796–1914*. Cambridge: Cambridge University Press, 1985.

Dixon, Wheeler Winston: *A History of Horror*. New Brunswick, NJ: Rutgers University Press, 2010.

Domino M. E., E. C. Norton, J. P. Morrissey, and N. Thakur. "Cost Shifting to Jails After a Change to Managed Mental Health Care." *Health Services Research* 39, no. 5 (October 2004): 1379–401.

Eberwein, Robert T. *Film and the Dream Screen*. Princeton: Princeton University Press, 1984.

Eisner, Lotte. *Fritz Lang*. New York: Da Capo, 1976.

_____. *The Haunted Screen*. Berkeley: University of California Press, 1952.

Elsaesser, Thomas. *Fassbinder's Germany*. Amsterdam: Amsterdam University Press, 1981.

_____. *Weimar Cinema and After*. London: Routledge, 2001.

Everson, William K. *Classics of the Horror Film*. New York: Citadel, 1974.

Ezra, Elizabeth. *Georges Méliès*. Manchester: Manchester University Press, 2000.

Fakhourya W., and S. Priebea. "Deinstitutionalization and Reinstitutionalization: Major Changes in the Provision of Mental Healthcare." *Psychiatry* 6 (August 2007): 313–316.

Frank, Frederick, and Anthony Magistrale. *Poe Encyclopedia*. Westport, CT: Greenwood, 1997.

Frazer, James. *The Golden Bough: A Study of Magic and Religion* (1890). Oxford: Oxford Paperback, 2010.

_____. *The Roots of Religion and Folklore*. Oxford: Oxford Paperbacks, 1981.

Friedan, Betty. *The Feminine Mystique*. New York: W. W. Norton, 1963.

Frieden, Thomas R., and F. Collins. "Commentary: Intentional Infection of Vulnerable Populations in 1946–1948." *JAMA* 304, no. 18 (2010): 2063–2064. Published online October 11, 2010.

Friedman, Laurence J. *Menninger: The Family and the Clinic*. Topeka: University of Kansas, 1992.

Gabbard, Glen, and K. Gabbard. *Psychiatry and the Cinema*, 2nd ed. Washington, DC: American Psychiatric Press, 1999.

Gabler, Neal. *An Empire of Their Own*. New York: Anchor Books, 1988.

_____. *Life: The Movie—How Entertainment Conquered Reality*. New York: Vintage, 2000.

Gay, Peter. *Weimar Culture*. New York: Norton (paperback), 2001.

Gerani, Gary (Introduction by Roger Corman). *Top 100 Horror Movies*. Korea: Fantastic Press, 2010.

Giannetti, Louis, and S. Eyman. *Flashback*, 4th ed. Upper Saddle River, NJ: Prentice Hall, 2001.

Gifford, Denis. *A Pictorial History of Horror Movies*. London: Hamlyn, 1974.

Goldman, Eric A. *Visions, Images and Dreams: Yiddish Film—Past and Present*. Teaneck, NJ: Holmes and Meyer, 2011.

Gordon, Mel. *The Grand Guignol: Theatre of Fear and Terror*. New York: Amok, 1988.

Gould, Michael. *Surrealism and the Cinema*. London: Tantivy Press, 1976.

Greenberg, Harvey Roy. *Screen Memories*. New York: Columbia University Press, 1993.

Greenberg, Joanna. *I Never Promised You a Rose Garden*. Paperback, 1964.

Gunning, Tom. *The Films of Fritz Lang*. London: BFI, 2000.

Haddad, Peter. "The 'Evil' Psychiatrist and Modern Cinema." *Psychiatric Bulletin* 15 (1991): 652–653.

Halpern, Leslie. *Dreams on Film*. Jefferson, NC: McFarland, 2003.

Hammond, Paul (ed. and trans.). *The Shadow and Its Shadow*, 3rd ed. San Francisco: City Lights, 2000.

Hansen, Bert. "Medical History for the Masses: How American Comic Books Celebrated Heroes of Medicine in the 1940s." *Bulletin of the History of Medicine* 78, no. 1 (Spring 2004): 148–191.

_____. *Picturing Medical Progress from Pasteur to Polio.* New Brunswick: Rutgers University Press, 2009.

Hardy, Phil (ed.). *The Overlook Film Encyclopedia.* Woodstock, NY: Overlook, 1999.

Harris, Gardiner. "Talk Doesn't Pay, So Psychiatry Turns Instead to Drug Therapy." *New York Times,* March 5, 2011.

Harris, Thomas. *Red Dragon.* New York: Dell, 1981.

Hayward, Susan. *Cinema Studies,* 2nd ed. London: Routledge, 2000.

Heard, Mervyn. *Phantasmagoria.* Hastings, UK: The Projection Box, 2006.

Heath, Stephen. "Cinema and Psychoanalysis." In *Endless Night,* edited by J. Bergstrom, 25–56. Berkeley: University of California Press, 1999.

Hensley, Scott. "Harvard Psychiatrists Under Fire for Drug-Company Funding." *Wall Street Journal,* June 9, 2008.

Hill, Geoffrey. *Illuminating Shadows: The Mythic Power of Film.* Boston: Shambala, 1992.

Hoberman, J. *The Dream Life.* New York: The New Press, 2003.

_____, and Jeffrey Shandler. *Entertaining America.* Princeton: Jewish Museum with Princeton University Press, 2003.

Hollywood Auction 30 (catalogue). Calabasas Hills, CA: Profiles in History, December 13–14, 2007.

Hollywood Auction 31 (catalogue). Calabasas Hills, CA: Profiles in History, March 27–28, 2008.

Hollywood Auction 32 (catalogue). Calabasas Hills, CA: Profiles in History, July 31–August 1, 2008.

Howard, K. I., C. V. Davidson, M. T. O'Mahoney, D. E. Orlinsky, and K. P. Brown. "Patterns of Psychotherapy Utilization." *American Journal of Psychiatry* 146 (1989): 775–778.

Hunt, Richard. "*Hitler or Hippocrates: Medical Experiments and Euthanasia in the Third Reich* (Book Review)." *New England Journal of Medicine* 328 (May 13, 1993): 1429

Hyler, Steven H., Glen Gabbard, and Irving Schneider. "Homicidal Maniacs and Narcissistic Parasites: Stigmatization of Mentally Ill Persons in the Movies." *Hospital and Community Psychiatry* 42 (October 1991): 1044–1048.

Induck, William: *Psycho Thrillers.* Jefferson, NC: McFarland, 2003.

Insdorf, Annette. *Indelible Shadows: Film and the Holocaust,* 3rd ed. Cambridge UK: Cambridge University Press, 2003.

Jones, Gerard. *Men of Tomorrow.* New York: Basic Books, 2004.

Jung, C. G.. *Psychology and Religion* (based on the Terry Lectures delivered at Yale University, 1938). New Haven: Yale University Press. 1966.

Kaes, Anton. *Shell Shock Cinema: Weimar Culture and the Wounds of War.* Princeton, NJ: Princeton University Press, 2009.

Kalat, David. *The Strange Case of Dr. Mabuse.* Jefferson, NC: McFarland, 2001.

Kalman, Thomas, and Martin A. Goldstein. "Satisfaction of Manhattan Psychiatrists with Private Practice: Assessing the Impact of Managed Care." *Journal of Psychotherapy Practice Research* 7 (July 1998): 250–258.

Kaplan, E. Ann (ed.). *Psychoanalysis and Cinema.* New York: Routledge, 1990.

Kardish, Laurence. *Weimar Cinema, 1919–1933.* New York: Museum of Modern Art, 2010.

Killen, Andreas. *Berlin Electropolis: Shock, Nerves, and German Modernity.* Berkeley: University of California, 2006.

Kinnard, Roy. *Horror in Silent Films.* Jefferson, NC: McFarland, 1995.

Koch, Gertrud (translated by Jeremy Gaines). *Siegfried Kracauer: An Introduction.* Princeton, NJ: Princeton University Press, 2000.

Kolker, Robert. *A Cinema of Loneliness,* 3rd ed. New York: Oxford University Press, 2000.

Kracauer, Siegfried. *From Caligari to Hitler.* Princeton: Princeton University Press, 1947.

_____. *From Caligari to Hitler: A Psychological History of the German Film* (edited by Leonardo Quaresima). Princeton: Princeton University Press, 2004.

_____. *Theory of Film.* Princeton: Princeton University Press, 1997.

Kravis, Nathan. "James Braid's Psychophysiology: A Turning Point in the History of Dynamic Psychiatry." *American Journal of Psychiatry* 145, no. 10 (October 1988): 1191–1206.

Kuenzli, Rudolf E. (ed.). *Dada and Surrealist Film.* Cambridge, MA: MIT University Press, 1998.

Langdale, Allan (ed.). *Hugo Munsterberg on Film.* New York: Routledge, 2002.

Langford, Barry. *Film Genre: Hollywood and Beyond.* Edinburgh: Edinburgh University Press, 2005.

Lapsley, Robert, and M. Westlake. *Film Theory: An Introduction.* Manchester: Manchester University Press, 1988.

Lebeau, Vicky. *Lost Angels.* London: Routledge, 1995.

_____. *Psychoanalysis and Cinema*. London: Wallflower, 2001.

Lichtenfeld, Eric. *Action Speaks Louder*. Westport, CT: Praeger, 2004.

MacDonald, Heather. "The Jail Inferno." *City Journal*. Retrieved July 27, 2009, from http://www.city-journal.org/2009/19_3_jails.html.

Macfie, Alexander Lyon. *Orientalism: A Reader*. New York: New York University Press, 2000.

Magno, Julie, Zito, Daniel J. Safer, Susan dosReis, James F. Gardner, Myde Boles, and Frances Lynch. "Trends in the Prescribing of Psychotropic Medications to Preschoolers." *JAMA 283*, no. 8 (2000): 1025–1030.

Maisel, Albert Q. (1946, May 6). Bedlam 1946. *LIFE Magazine*, 102.

Malani, Preeti. "*Dark Medicine: Rationalizing Unethical Medical Research* (Book Review)." *JAMA 300*, no. 10 (September 10, 2008): 1217–1218.

Makari, George. *Revolution in Mind: The Creation of Psychoanalysis*. New York: HarperCollins, 2008.

Manchel, Frank. *Terrors of the Screen*. Englewood Cliffs, NJ: Prentiss-Hall, 1970.

Marks, John. *The Search for the Manchurian Candidate* (Introduction by Thomas Powers). New York: Norton paperback, 1991.

Mast, Gerald, and Marshall Cohen. *Film Theory and Criticism*. Oxford: Oxford University Press, 1985.

McCarthy, John. *Movie Psychos and Madmen*. New York: Citadel Press, 1993.

McDonald, A., and G. Walter. "The Portrayal of ECT in American Movies." *Journal of ECT* 17, no. 4 (2001): 264–274.

McGinn, Colin. *The Power of Movies*. New York: Pantheon, 2005.

McGowan, Todd, and S. Kunkle. *Lacan and Contemporary Film*. New York: Other Press, 2004.

Meduna, L. J. "Autobiography of L. J. Meduna." *Convulsive Therapy* 1, no. 1 (1985): 53.

Mitry, Jean (translated by Christopher King). *The Aesthetics and Psychology of the Cinema*. Bloomington: Indiana University Press, 1990.

Moran, Mark. "When Ethical Lines Were Crossed in Service to the Nation." *Psychiatric News* 46 (June 17, 2011): 12: 16.

Morris, Peter. *David Cronenberg: A Delicate Balance*. Toronto: ECW Press, 1999.

Naremore, James. *More Than Night: Film Noir in Its Contexts*. Berkeley: University of California Press, 1998.

Neugroschel, Joachim (ed. and trans.). *The Dybbuk and the Yiddish Imagination*. Syracuse, NY: Syracuse University Press, 2000.

O'Brien, Geoffrey. *The Phantom Empire*. New York: Norton, 1993.

Oldham, John. "The Epidemic of Mental Illness: Why?" *New York Review of Books*, July 14, 2011.

_____. "In response to: *The Illusions of Psychiatry*." *New York Review of Books*, June 23, 2011.

Oliver, Kelly, and Benigno Trigo. *Noir Anxiety*. Minneapolis: University of Minnesota Press, 2002.

Osborne, Jennifer. *Monsters*. New York: Del Ray Books, 2006.

O'Shea, B., and A. McGennis. "ECT: Lay Attitudes and Experiences — a Pilot Study." *Irish Medical Journal* 76, no. 1 (1983): 40–43.

Packer, Sharon. *Dreams in Myth, Medicine, and Movies*. Westfield, CT: Praeger, 2002.

_____. *Movies and the Modern Psyche*. Westfield, CT: Praeger, 2007.

_____. "Recalling *Total Recall*." *MDng Magazine*, Psychiatry/Neurology Edition (February 2011). Retrieved on November 10, 2011, at http://www.hcplive.com/publications/mdng-Neurology/2011/february_2011/psych_in_film.

_____. *Superheroes and Superegos: The Minds Behind the Masks*. Santa Barbara, CA: ABC-Clio, 2007.

Parkinson, David. *History of Film*. New York: Thames and Hudson, 1995.

Pennington, Jody. *The History of Sex in American Film*. Westport, CT: Praeger, 2007.

Pirie, David. *A Heritage of Horror. The English Gothic Cinema, 1946–72*. New York: Equinox (Avon), 1974.

Poe, Edgar Allan. *Great Tales and Poems of Edgar Allan Poe*. New York: Pocket Books, 1951.

_____. "The System of Doctor Tarr and Professor Feather [Fether]." Retrieved online at questia.com.

Polan, Dana. *Power and Paranoia*. New York: Columbia University Press, 1986.

Porter, Roy. *Madmen: A Social History of Madhouses, Mad-Doctors and Lunatics*. Cambridge: Tempus, 2006.

_____ and David Wright (eds). *The Confinement of the Insane: International Perspectives, 1800–1965*. Cambridge: Cambridge University Press. 2003

Prawer, S. S. *Caligari's Children*. Oxford: Oxford University Press, 1980.

Ramsaye, Terry. *A Million and One Nights*. New York: Simon and Schuster, 1954.

Ranz, Jules M., Michael J. Vergare, Joshua E. Wilk, Sigurd H. Ackerman, Richard C. Lippincott, W. Walter Menninger, Steven S. Sharfstein, and Ann Sullivan. "The Tipping Point from Private Practice to Publicly Funded Settings for Early- and Mid-Career Psychiatrists." *Psychiatric Services* 57 (November 2006): 1640–1643.

Rausch, Andrew J. *Turning Points in Film History.* New York: Citadel Press, 2004.

Rees, A. L. *A History of Experimental Film and Video.* London: BFI, 1999.

Reinhart, Mark S. *The Batman Filmography: Live Action Features, 1943–1997.* Jefferson, NC: McFarland, 2005.

Robinson, David. *Das Cabinet des Dr. Caligari.* London: BFI, 1997.

Rochefort DA. "Origins of the 'Third Psychiatric Revolution': The Community Mental Health Centers Act of 1963." *Journal of Health Policy Law* 9, no. 1 (Spring 1984): 1–30.

Rothman, David. "*The Treatment: The Story of Those Who Died in the Cincinnati Radiation Tests* (Book Review)." *New England Journal of Medicine* 347 (December 19, 2002): 2089–2090.

Salisbury, Mark. *Burton on Burton.* London: Faber and Faber, 1995.

Schelde, Per. *Androids, Humanoids, and Other Science Fiction Monsters.* New York: New York University Press, 1993.

Scherl D. J., and L. B. Macht. "Deinstitutionalization in the Absence of Consensus." *Hospital and Community Psychiatry* 30, no. 9 (September 1979): 599–604.

Schneider I. "The Theory and Practice of Movie Psychiatry." *American Journal of Psychiatry* 144, no. 8 (1987): 996–1002.

Scull, Andrew "*The Confinement of the Insane: International Perspectives, 1800–1965* (Book Review)." *Medical History* 49, no. 1 (January 1, 2005): 109–110.

_____. *Madhouses, Mad-doctors, and Madmen: The Social History of Psychiatry in the Victorian Era.* Philadelphia: University of Pennsylvania Press, 1981.

Shorter, Edward. *A History of Psychiatry: From the Era of the Asylum to the Age of Prozac.* New York: Wiley, 1997.

Sievers, W. David. *Freud on Broadway.* New York: Hermitage House, 1955.

Silver, Alain, and Paul Ursini. *Film Noir Reader 4.* New York: Limelight Editions, 2004.

_____ and _____, with Paul Duncan (ed.). *Film Noir.* Los Angeles: Taschen, 2004.

_____ and Elizabeth Ward. *Film Noir,* 3rd ed. Woodstock, NY: Overlook Press, 1992.

Sitney, P. Adams. *Visionary Film,* 2nd ed. Oxford: Oxford University Press, 1979.

Sklar, Robert. *Movie-Made America* (revised and updated). New York, Vintage, 1994.

Skloot, Rebecca: *The Immortal Life of Henrietta Lacks.* New York: Random House, 2010.

Slocum, J. David. *Violence and American Cinema.* New York: Routledge, 2001.

Smith, Don G. *The Poe Cinema: A Critical Filmography.* Jefferson, NC: McFarland, 1999.

Smith, Ronald L. *Poe in the Media: Screen, Songs, and Spoken Words Recordings.* New York: Garland, 1990.

Soren, David. *The Rise and Fall of the Horror Film, Revised Edition.* Baltimore: Midnight Marquee Press, 1997.

Spillane, Mickey. *I, the Jury.* New York: Signet, 1947.

Stevenson, Jack. *Addicted: An Illustrated Guide to Drug Cinema.* Creation Books, 2000.

Stokes, Melvyn, and R. Maltby (eds.). *Hollywood Spectatorship.* London: BFI, 2001.

Stroman, Duane. *The Disability Rights Movement: From Deinstitutionalization to Self-Determination.* University Press of America, 2003.

Swartz, Marvin S., Jeffrey W. Swanson, Virginia A. Hiday, Randy Borum, Wagner, H. Ryan, and Barbara J. Burns. "Violence and Severe Mental Illness: The Effects of Substance Abuse and Non-Adherence to Medication." *American Journal of Psychiatry* 155 (February 1998): 226–231.

Thomson, David. *The New Biographical Dictionary of Film.* New York: Knopf, 2004.

Torrey E. F., and R. H. Yolken. "Psychiatric Genocide: Nazi Attempts to Eradicate Schizophrenia." *Schizophrenia Bulletin* 36, no. 1 (September 16, 2009): 1–7.

Tredell, Nicholas. *Cinemas of the Mind.* Cambridge: Icon Books, 2002.

Tyler, Parker. *The Hollywood Hallucination.* New York: Creative Age Press, 1944.

Vernet, Marc. "The Fetish in the Theory and History of Cinema." In *Endless Night,* edited by J. Bergstrom, 88–95. Berkeley: University of California Press, 1999.

Vollmann, Jochen, and Rolf Winau. " Informed Consent in Human Experimentation Before the Nuremberg Code." *British Medical Journal* 313 (December 7, 1996): 1445.

Walker, Janet. *Couching Resistance.* Minneapolis: University of Minnesota Press, 1993.

Walter, G. "Portrayal of ECT in Movies from Australia and New Zealand." *Journal of ECT* 14 (1998): 56–60.

Weinberg, Robert. *Horror of the 20th Century.* Hong Kong: Collectors Press, 2000.

Wilson, Duff. "F.D.A. Is Studying the Risk of Electroshock Devices." *New York Times,* January 23, 2011.

Yanni, Carla. *The Architecture of Madness: Insane Asylums in the United States.* Minneapolis: Minnesota University Press, 207.

Žižek, Slavoj (ed.). *Lacan: The Silent Partners.* London: Verso, 2006.

Internet Sources

http://articles.cnn.com/2007-07-09/health/antidepressants_1_antidepressants-high-blood-pressure-drugs-
    psychotropic-drugs?_s=PM:HEALTH (accesssed online 10-16-11)
http://www.Atkinsononfilm.com
http://www.cnn.com
http://www.imdb.com (Internet Movie Database)
http://www.imdbpro.com (Internet Movie Database Professional)
http://www.jewishfilm.org
http://www.mentalhealth.gov/statistics
http://www.nimh.nih.gov/statistics
http://www.ProPublica.org
http://www.psychflix.com
http://www.ptsd.va.gov/professional/pages/epidemiological-facts-ptsd.asp
http://www.yiddishfilmworld.org
http://www.yivoinstitute.org/index.php?tid=45&aid=193

Index

Page numbers in **bold italics** indicate pages with illustrations.

www.ingramcontent.com/pod-product-compliance
Lightning Source LLC
Chambersburg PA
CBHW080551270326
41929CB00019B/3267